Standard-Bearers of Equality

Standard-Bearers *of* Equality

AMERICA'S FIRST ABOLITION MOVEMENT

PAUL J. POLGAR

Published by the
OMOHUNDRO INSTITUTE OF
EARLY AMERICAN HISTORY AND CULTURE,
Williamsburg, Virginia,
and the
UNIVERSITY OF NORTH CAROLINA PRESS,
Chapel Hill

*The Omohundro Institute of Early American History and Culture (OI)
is sponsored by William & Mary. On November 15, 1996, the OI adopted
the present name in honor of a bequest from Malvern H. Omohundro, Jr.,
and Elizabeth Omohundro.*

Cover illustration: Detail of Seal of the Pennsylvania Society for
Promoting the Abolition of Slavery. Pennsylvania Abolition Society Papers.
Courtesy, Historical Society of Pennsylvania

Library of Congress Cataloging-in-Publication Data
Names: Polgar, Paul J., author. | Omohundro Institute of
Early American History & Culture, publisher.
Title: Standard-bearers of equality : America's first
abolition movement / Paul J. Polgar.
Description: Williamsburg, Virginia : Omohundro Institute of Early
American History and Culture ; Chapel Hill : University of North Carolina
Press, 2019. | Includes bibliographical references and index.
Identifiers: LCCN 2019027186 | ISBN 9781469653938
(cloth : alk. paper) | ISBN 9781469653945 (ebook)
Subjects: LCSH: Pennsylvania Society for Promoting the Abolition
of Slavery—History. | New-York Society for Promoting the Manumission
of Slaves, and Protecting Such of Them as Have Been, or May Be Liberated—
History. | Antislavery movements—Middle Atlantic States—History—18th
century. | Antislavery movements—Middle Atlantic States—History—19th
century. | Free African Americans—Political activity. | African Americans—
Civil rights—History. | United States—Race relations—History.
Classification: LCC E446 .P65 2019 | DDC 305.800973—dc23
LC record available at https://lccn.loc.gov/2019027186

The University of North Carolina Press has been a
member of the Green Press Initiative since 2003.

To

Valerie, Arlene, Josephine,

and my parents

Your love is my foundation

Contents

Illustrations

Standard-Bearers of Equality

Reimagining American Abolitionism

He should be standing, not kneeling. This was the conclusion the Pennsylvania Abolition Society (PAS) had reached in the fall of 1789 as the group reviewed an illustration that might serve as the centerpiece of the certificates of membership for the newly reconstituted organization. They were most likely referring to Josiah Wedgewood's famed depiction of an enslaved man on bended knee pleading, "Am I Not a Man and a Brother," printed in London two years earlier and embraced by abolitionists throughout the Atlantic world (Figure 1). In designing its own emblem, the PAS wanted to make sure that the black man "be represented in a Standing posture." Their decision appeared prescient. Only months later, James Pemberton, the chair of the PAS's Committee of Correspondence, wrote to the London Society for Effecting the Abolition of the Slave Trade that, in revising the state constitution, the Pennsylvania Assembly had voted down an attempt to define citizenship in racially exclusive terms "by a large and very respectable majority." Pemberton celebrated that the "Free Black-Man is to be put on the Footing of a citizen of Pennsylvania" and underscored the momentousness of this "equitable and important decision," sewing together the end of slavery and African American incorporation as part of the same enterprise.[1]

1. Papers of the Pennsylvania Abolition Society (PPAS), Series 1, reel 1, I, 107, reel 11, I, 33, Historical Society of Pennsylvania (HSP), Philadelphia. In February 1788, the British abolitionist printer James Phillips sent Benjamin Franklin (a member of the PAS and president of the society at the time of his death) a package with antislavery ephemera. Included in this package was an impression of Wedgewood's "Am I Not a Man and a Brother" woodcut, which by this time served as the seal for the London Society for Effecting the Abolition of the Slave Trade and which Phillips intended for James Pemberton to receive. Phillips most likely imagined that the PAS would adopt Wedgewood's impression as the society's emblem and spread its likeness throughout the early United States. Yet the PAS did not greet Wedgewood's image with the same zeal as the London society. See J. R. Oldfield, *Transatlantic Abolitionism in the Age of Revolution: An International History of Antislavery, c. 1787–1820* (Cambridge, 2013), 60.

The emblem that the PAS ended up adopting reflects Pemberton's un-bridled optimism. Whereas Wedgewood's original design cast a man weighed down by chains and with hands clasped in pleading, almost des-perately, for deliverance from bondage, the PAS's seal projected a very dif-ferent conception of abolitionism and black freedom. In the PAS's image, the black man stands tall and appears in mid-stride, chest open, arm ex-tended, and one palm facing out, as if greeting freedom with an assured sense of self-possession. Though the traces of bondage remain, unlike in Wedgewood's illustration the manacle in the PAS seal lies broken at the formerly enslaved man's foot, implying that slavery would not continue in-definitely to define either people of African descent or the new nation in which they lived (Figure 2).

The formerly enslaved man in this etching does not stand alone. His gaze is fixed upon a white abolitionist who has taken the black man's left hand and is looking forward, seemingly announcing to the world the ar-rival of a new epoch characterized, not by racial slavery, but black liberty and empowerment. The white activist's presence projects the conviction of abolition societies such as the PAS that they would play a key role in assist-ing enslaved peoples' transition to free persons, even as it indicates that the cause of emancipation would be a joint effort made up of both white

FIGURE 2. Seal of the Pennsylvania Society for Promoting the Abolition of Slavery.
Papers of the Pennsylvania Abolition Society. The seal's heading, "Work and Be
Happy," suggests that the PAS sought to repurpose ideas of black labor that, when
associated with slavery, invoked subjecthood and degradation as instead an outlet
for self-fulfillment and virtue. At the same time, the heading gestures to how
the PAS, and other abolition societies, intended to carefully structure African
American freedom. Courtesy, Historical Society of Pennsylvania

and black actors. Yet the seal also implies a vision of the young Republic
in which people of color are included, their humanity recognized, their belonging confirmed, their rights as members of the new nation self-evident.

The sentiments embodied in the PAS's seal were not mere fantasy, and
neither did the society have to look to an illustration alone to confirm its
brand of antislavery reform. A decade and a half after the PAS created its
trademark, Peter Williams, Jr., a free black minster and abolitionist, communicated to a group of abolition societies that included the PAS a similar
understanding of emancipation and black liberty. Whereas African Americans had once been held as "beasts of burthen" and "reduced" to the "de-
plorable situation" of human bondage, the tide of oppression was now falling away. Instead, Williams was struck that abolition societies were helping
to place "thousands at liberty, and are daily casting off the shackles of numbers more." By "rising above the mean prejudices imbibed against" people
of color, abolition societies had been instrumental in striving to assure that
"equal justice is distributed to the black and the white." These developments indicated that just over the horizon lay a promised land in which

America would eliminate "all distinctions between the inalienable rights of black men, and white," Williams boldly predicted.[2]

The emphasis on African American empowerment and civic membership by abolition societies like the PAS and their free black allies like Williams illuminates much about the values of America's first abolition movement. What this book terms *first movement abolitionism* was composed of an ideological and strategic coalition of black and white activists with three shared ideals for abolishing slavery: a commitment to enforcing northern emancipation statutes and enlarging the elemental rights of people of color through pragmatic, on-the-ground activism; the belief that free blacks were entitled to the rights of American citizenship and could become virtuous members of the body politic; and the expectation that through black uplift and incorporation, and a campaign of public persuasion, white prejudice could be defeated and the arguments of slavery's defenders about the incapacity of people of African descent for freedom proved wrong. Adherents of first movement abolitionism applied a gradual cast to much of their reform—particularly in their agenda of achieving virtuous black citizenship and nullifying white prejudice—but their efforts to enforce and expand emancipation-related laws brought a more immediate form of freedom to people of color than applying to them the label of gradual abolitionists implies. First movement abolitionists had been preceded by individual activists, writers, and religious reformers who pressed for the abolition of slavery and the slave trade—historical actors generally referred to as early abolitionists. Although these individuals provided important precursors for elements of first movement abolitionism, their agitation lacked the same level of systematic and institutionally organized activism of the abolition societies and free black communities that are the primary subjects of this study.[3]

2. *Minutes of the Proceedings of the Eleventh American Convention for Promoting the Abolition of Slavery and Improving the Condition of the African Race . . .* (Philadelphia, 1806), 35–37.

3. Scholarship on early abolitionists continues to grow. See Thomas P. Slaughter, *The Beautiful Soul of John Woolman, Apostle of Abolition* (New York, 2008); Maurice Jackson, *Let This Voice Be Heard: Anthony Benezet, Father of Atlantic Abolitionism* (Philadelphia, 2009); Brycchan Carey, *From Peace to Freedom: Quaker Rhetoric and the Birth of American Antislavery, 1657–1761* (New Haven, Conn., 2012); Geoffrey Plank, *John Woolman's Path to the Peaceable Kingdom: A Quaker in the British Empire* (Philadelphia, 2012); Jackson and Susan Kozel, eds., *Quakers and Their Allies in the Abolitionist Cause, 1754–1808* (London, 2015); Manisha Sinha, *The Slave's Cause: A History of Abolition* (New Haven, Conn., 2016); Marcus Rediker, *The Fearless Benjamin Lay: The Quaker Dwarf Who Became the First Revolutionary Abolitionist* (Boston, 2017); and

The mid-Atlantic region served as the nexus for first movement abolitionism. In Pennsylvania and New York, vibrant free black communities and energetic abolition societies developed a unique partnership that powered the movement's program. From historically obscure people of African descent who brought cases of illegal enslavement to the attention of the abolition societies to a leadership class that sought to foster communities of virtuous black citizens as a weapon to defeat slavery, people of color informed nearly every facet of first movement abolitionism. The abolition societies of the mid-Atlantic—particularly the PAS and New-York Manumission Society (NYMS)—furnished critical organizational and ideological infrastructure. But, without the active participation of people of color, these societies would have had no agenda to execute. Recapturing the contours of America's first abolition movement necessitates restoring the essential part played by blacks in making this movement possible.

The full story of the sweeping challenge first movement abolitionists posed to slavery and black inequality has yet to be told. A generation of scholarship on gradual emancipation has demonstrated the halting and incomplete nature of African American liberation in the late eighteenth and early nineteenth centuries. Between slaveholder resistance to their slaves' liberty and white skepticism about the merits of black freedom, abolitionists faced daunting obstacles to ending slavery in the new nation. Yet it was these very obstacles that generated first movement abolitionists' racially progressive approach to reform. This racially progressive reform program was defined by its commitment to the gradual accumulation of black rights, including liberty, propertyownership, equality under the law, suffrage, and other civil and civic privileges that were housed under the larger

---

Gary B. Nash, *Warner Mifflin: Unflinching Quaker Abolitionist* (Philadelphia, 2017). My choice to avoid the term *early abolitionists* in characterizing the abolition societies and their black allies is not intended to undercut those activists whose work largely predated the abolition societies or the reach and sophistication of their activism. In fact, early abolitionists served as critical exemplars for first movement abolitionism, making the movement possible and giving it shape in multiple ways. For example, those Quaker Meetings that were heavily involved with antislavery activism provided an organizational model that the abolition societies would largely mimic. Additionally, key early abolitionists like Anthony Benezet trailblazed free black educational efforts and helped form Atlantic networks of exchange that the abolition societies would later draw on. Other early abolitionists, like Benjamin Lay and John Woolman, were cited by both abolition societies members and black activists in the early national era as having inspired their joint campaign. The distinction I make between early abolitionists and first movement abolitionists is not aimed at suggesting that these categories were mutually exclusive. Some early abolitionists, such as Warner Mifflin, were also involved in first movement abolitionist activism.

umbrella of citizenship in post-Revolutionary and early national America. By seeking to obtain and enforce antislavery laws, guard and expand the rights of illegally enslaved and free blacks, uproot white prejudice, and overturn racial inequality by making African Americans virtuous citizens of the new Republic, first movement abolitionists met the formidable barriers to emancipation with a cohesive vision of black freedom and equality.[4]

Gradual emancipation brought a prolonged conflict between slaveholders and dealers and the abolition societies and people of color in which first movement abolitionists' fight to end slavery consistently endeavored to extend the rights of enslaved and free blacks alike. Beginning in the 1780s, abolitionists launched a campaign to establish the basic validity of African American freedom. They defended the rights of free blacks and enlarged those of the enslaved by widening the scope of statutory emancipation. That hundreds of people of color looked to the abolition societies to protect or assert their liberty reveals the delicate state of black freedom in the post-Revolutionary and early national mid-Atlantic and the limitations of a gradual emancipation that continued to countenance slavery's legality. But, by enforcing emancipation in late-eighteenth- and early-nineteenth-century New York and Pennsylvania, where organizational abolitionism was strongest, abolition societies and illegally enslaved blacks joined forces to strengthen the rights of people of African descent and weaken those of slaveholders. From the passage of Pennsylvania's 1780 An Act for the Gradual Abolition of Slavery to New York's decision in 1817 to set a date for the total abolition of slavery, first movement abolitionists contributed to a steady stream of statutory antislavery progress.

The nation's first abolition movement also attacked slavery on a broader level, aspiring to break apart American bondage through the enlightenment of black and white Americans together. The abolition societies and their African American partners drew on an optimistic post-Revolutionary milieu of environmentalist social theory, which to them meant the idea that newly independent America could be shaped to meet rational, equi-

4. On the protracted process of gradual emancipation in the late-eighteenth- and early-nineteenth-century North, see Gary B. Nash and Jean R. Soderlund, *Freedom by Degrees: Emancipation in Pennsylvania and Its Aftermath* (New York, 1991); Shane White, *Somewhat More Independent: The End of Slavery in New York City, 1770–1810* (Athens, Ga., 1991); Joanne Pope Melish, *Disowning Slavery: Gradual Emancipation and "Race" in New England, 1780–1860* (Ithaca, N.Y., 1998); Leslie M. Harris, *In The Shadow of Slavery: African Americans in New York City, 1626–1863* (Chicago, 2003); and James J. Gigantino II, *The Ragged Road to Abolition: Slavery and Freedom in New Jersey, 1775–1865* (Philadelphia, 2015).

table, and just principles of societal formation—and, specifically, that they could shear the infant Republic of black inequality and the narrow-minded racial prejudices of the mass of whites that they saw as endemic to American society. As emancipation laws and black education and civic cultivation gradually transformed people of color into republican citizens, first movement abolitionists looked to persuade a prejudiced white public to extend independent America's egalitarian promises to people of African descent. In doing so, they built a reform agenda premised on the eventual overturning of black degradation and the pervasive white prejudice that they believed undergirded both slavery and the extensive disparities between black and white Americans.

The first movement abolitionist reform blueprint, however, came under increasing pressure during the second decade of the nineteenth century. Although they had found sustenance for their activism in northern emancipation, free black community development, and the defensive ideological position of slavery's supporters in the years following American independence, by the 1820s these activists discovered that white prejudice had hardened and that many reformers had come to view black inequality, not as impermanent and alterable, but as indefinite and unchangeable. Nothing embodied this change more fully than the rise of the colonization movement. The idea of colonizing enslaved and free people of color, and proposals aimed at black removal, predated the creation of the United States. But the founding of the American Colonization Society (ACS) in 1816 signaled the dawn of a new era in antislavery agitation, one in which black removal gained a powerful organizational vehicle. Colonizationists viewed white prejudice as unconquerable and therefore the incorporation of free blacks into the American body politic as impossible. According to the ACS and its northern auxiliary societies, the removal of African Americans was the only viable means of combating slavery. This institutional shift in American antislavery was buttressed by larger socioeconomic and political transformations including the expansion of southern slavery, the growing tide of racial prejudice in the North, and the escalating hostility of many whites to the presence of free blacks in the wake of gradual abolition.

At the heart of this book lies a pivotal transition in the strategy and tactics of American antislavery that unfolded from 1780 to 1830 between first movement abolitionism on the one hand and colonization on the other. Whereas first movement abolitionists dedicated their activism to incorporating people of African descent as members of the body politic, colonizationists associated with the ACS considered these efforts a fool's errand that only exacerbated racial tensions and deepened black American inequality. Instead of fighting white prejudice, as the first abolition movement had done, the ACS and its auxiliaries believed this same prejudice had to be accepted, and even respected, as an unavoidable reality of American life. Stark as these ideological differences were, the organizational tent of colonization included those who sincerely searched for a gradual means of ending American bondage. During the 1820s, colonizationists who opposed slavery pulled many reformers into their orbit, marginalizing first movement abolitionism. Thus, when immediate abolitionists emerged in the 1830s, they confronted an antislavery landscape greatly altered from the post-Revolutionary and early national generations. In condemning the ACS and its views on black Americans and white prejudice, immediate abolitionists—most famously, William Lloyd Garrison—highlighted the link many colonizationists made between gradualism and colonization, labeling both reactionary and exclusionist. As a result, the racially progressive origins of American abolitionism that this work recaptures became buried.

The above synopsis relays the rise and fall of America's first abolition movement. But why does the pathbreaking challenge it posed to black bondage and racial inequality remain relatively unheralded? One answer lies in the reigning interpretation of gradual emancipation with which first movement abolitionists are associated. In the last quarter century, a host of historians have shown how the piecemeal orientation of gradual emancipation and the reluctance of white northerners to countenance African American freedom hampered free blacks socially, politically, and economically. Though richly recounting the complexities of gradual abolition, many scholars are now preoccupied with demonstrating the shortcomings of northern emancipation and the prevalence of white prejudice. In turn, they have rendered both gradual emancipation and those activists who advocated for it as inherently conservative. Gradual emancipation in the New England and mid-Atlantic states between 1780 and 1804 is almost universally depicted as a series of compromises that worked against the interest of enslaved people. The laws did not free a single enslaved person, historians are fond of noting, leaving in slavery those born before their passage. For children born to enslaved women after the adoption of gradual emancipation statutes, the long indentures they would serve their mothers' masters—until age eighteen for females in Rhode Island, for example, to as old as twenty-eight for both sexes in Pennsylvania—unequivocally prioritized the interests of slaveholders, giving property rights in people the upper hand over the natural rights of people to liberty. Also deflating the impact of gradual emancipation, widespread white antipathy for free blacks, lukewarm public support for slavery's abolition, and robust racial prejudice quickly shut down the prospects for substantive African American civil inclusion.[5]

The abolition societies that championed gradual emancipation are often presented in a similar vein as the type of black freedom for which they fought. They held fast to the belief that slavery was unjust even as they recognized the rights of slaveholders to property in persons. They argued for the innate equality of all while they doubted the suitability of the very enslaved people whose bondage they protested to live freely in society. They pressed for the end of enslavement but were inspired by elite concerns of social control — seeking to replace chattel bondage with forms of labor that would echo the disciplinary aims of institutional slavery. These societies' programs of reform, though driven by theoretically egalitarian precepts, at best projected a well-intentioned but narrowly elitist paternalism and at worst repressively perpetuated proslavery principles by setting up an "informal servitude" for free blacks who fell under their moral and intellectual guidance. This scholarship's implicit use of immediate emancipation and unconditional black equality as a historical measuring stick has concealed the underlying philosophy that animated first movement abolitionism.[6]

5. Nash and Soderlund, *Freedom by Degrees*, 137–204; White, *Somewhat More Independent*, 24–75; Melish, *Disowning Slavery*, 84–209; John Wood Sweet, *Bodies Politic: Negotiating Race in the American North, 1730–1830* (Baltimore, 2003), 225–267; George William Van Cleve, *A Slaveholders' Union: Slavery, Politics, and the Constitution in the Early American Republic* (Chicago, 2010), 59–101; Gigantino, *The Ragged Road to Abolition*, 64–148; Ira Berlin, *Many Thousands Gone: The First Two Centuries of Slavery in North America* (Cambridge, Mass., 1998), 228–239; Alan Taylor, *American Revolutions: A Continental History, 1750–1804* (New York, 2016), 466–469; Douglas R. Egerton, *Death or Liberty: African Americans and Revolutionary America* (New York, 2009), 93–121; Gary Nash, *Race and Revolution* (Lanham, Md., 1990), 30–35. One of the farthest-reaching interpretations of gradual emancipation in the North is Melish's *Disowning Slavery*. Melish conceives of gradual emancipation as a conservative process whereby whites grafted onto gradually emancipated free persons their racist assumptions of black inferiority and incapacity for citizenship, thereby eliminating the presence of enslaved people but disqualifying African Americans from the sociopolitical arena of early national America. For exceptions to this depiction of gradual emancipation, see David N. Gellman, *Emancipating New York: The Politics of Slavery and Freedom, 1777–1827* (Baton Rouge, La., 2006); Sarah Levine-Gronningsater, "Delivering Freedom: Gradual Emancipation, Black Legal Culture, and the Origins of the Sectional Crisis in New York, 1759–1870" (Ph.D. diss., University of Chicago, 2014); and Sinha, *The Slave's Cause*, 65–96.

6. Robert J. Swan, "John Teasman: African-American Educator and the Emergence of Community in Early Black New York City, 1787–1815," *Journal of the Early Republic*, XII (1992), 332. For a sampling of this interpretation of the abolitionists who lobbied for

Questioning the objectives and minimizing the activism of the abolition societies is in part possible because the magnitude of black participation in America's first abolition movement, and the imperative part people of color played in it, have yet to be fully recognized. Scholars of American antislavery have long described the indispensability of black activists to the formation of antebellum abolitionism and their work with white immediate abolitionists. But black participation in and contributions to organized abolitionism during the era of gradual emancipation has not received the same level of coverage. Although interracial abolitionist alliances in the early Republic are garnering greater scholastic attention, works on African American community growth and protest thought in the late-eighteenth- and early-nineteenth-century North largely isolate the evolution of black abolitionism from the abolition societies. Instead, this study spotlights the close bonds forged between black and white activists—through both a shared grassroots activism and an ideological affinity—to illustrate that first movement abolitionism was biracial in character and co-created by African Americans, rather than an external force imposed on people of color.[7]

---

gradual emancipation, see Melish, *Disowning Slavery*, 50–83; White, *Somewhat More Independent*, 81–88; David Brion Davis, *The Problem of Slavery in the Age of Revolution, 1770–1823* (Ithaca, N.Y., 1975), 304–306; and John L. Rury, "Philanthropy, Self-Help, and Social Control: The New York Manumission Society and Free Blacks, 1785–1810," *Phylon*, XLVI (1985), 231–241. The most influential study of abolitionism in the early American Republic, Richard S. Newman, *The Transformation of American Abolitionism: Fighting Slavery in the Early Republic* (Chapel Hill, N.C., 2002), paints a dichotomous portrait of the history of American antislavery movements by setting an early republican, conservative approach of gradualism in stark contrast to an antebellum democratic strategy of immediatism. Newman argues that what started as a limited effort led by a group of elite Quaker lawyers, who advocated gradual abolition and focused exclusively on the legalistic strategies of petitioning Congress and working through the courts, transformed itself over the course of the nineteenth century into a mass movement. Drawing on women and African Americans, this new movement called for the immediate abolition of slavery and directed its energy outside the strictures of the political and legal world. While identifying important structural changes in American abolitionism, Newman's dualistic framework causes him to leave unexamined key elements of first movement abolitionism, such as the emphasis placed on public persuasion, black education and civil integration, and the joint building of an abolitionist program between African American activists and their white allies.

7. For histories that isolate the development of black abolitionism from the abolition societies, see Newman, *The Transformation of American Abolitionism;* Harris, *In the Shadow of Slavery;* Paul Goodman, *Of One Blood: Abolitionism and the Origins of Racial Equality* (Berkeley, Calif., 1998); Graham Russell Hodges, *Root and Branch: African Americans in New York and East Jersey, 1613–1863* (Chapel Hill, N.C., 1999); and Leslie M. Alexander, *African or American? Black Identity and Political Activism in*

Reinforcing the conservative reading of gradual abolitionism and emancipation is the reigning narrative of the American Revolution's relationship
to antislavery. As it stands, the story is mostly one of unfulfilled promises
and dashed hopes. The American Revolution, with its decrees of natural
rights and universal equality, seemed to open the door to meaningful freedom for the enslaved. Yet this door soon shut. Southerners won political
concessions at formative moments of nation building that foreclosed any
potential to eradicate slavery throughout the young Republic. The simultaneous emergence of universal equality in theory and a race-based application of those rights spawned the theory of race as an inherent, immutable, and natural fact dividing white from black and disqualifying persons
of African descent from the very freedom and equality espoused by the
nation's founders. And the economic imperatives that pushed slavery to
spread south and west meant professions of natural rights would ring hol-
low for the enslaved. All of these factors worked to circumscribe the potential for emancipation and racial equality in the years after American independence.[8]

New York City, 1784–1861 (Urbana, Ill., 2008). Manisha Sinha rightly labels the separation of white and black abolitionism "racialist and inaccurate" and argues for a cross-
racial history of American antislavery (Sinha, *The Slave's Cause*, 2). Nicholas P. Wood
identifies interracial activism in the late eighteenth century as stretching beyond abolition societies to include activist partnerships between Quaker Meetings and people
of color (Wood, "'A Class of Citizens': The Earliest Black Petitioners to Congress and
Their Quaker Allies," *William and Mary Quarterly*, 3d Ser., LXXIV [2017], 109–144).
For evidence of the interlocking visions of free black uplift between the PAS and black
leaders in Philadelphia and their active cooperation on issues of moral and educational
reform in the post-Revolutionary and early national eras, see Gary B. Nash, *Forging
Freedom: The Formation of Philadelphia's Black Community, 1720–1840* (Cambridge,
Mass., 1988); Julie Winch, *Philadelphia's Black Elite: Activism, Accommodation, and
the Struggle for Autonomy, 1787–1848* (Philadelphia, 1988); and Winch, *A Gentleman
of Color: The Life of James Forten* (New York, 2003). For cross-racial abolitionism in
New York in this era, see Levine-Gronningsater, "Delivering Freedom." See also Patrick
Rael, *Black Identity and Black Protest in the Antebellum North* (Chapel Hill, N.C., 2002),
which links the creation of a black protest tradition to the larger ideological framework
of post-Revolutionary American intellectual thought. For the development of black abolitionism, see Richard Newman, Rael, and Philip Lapsansky, eds., *Pamphlets of Protest:
An Anthology of Early African-American Protest Literature, 1790–1860* (New York,
2001); Timothy Patrick McCarthy and John Stauffer, eds., *Prophets of Protest: Reconsidering the History of American Abolitionism* (New York, 2006); and James Oliver Horton
and Lois E. Horton, *In Hope of Liberty: Culture, Community, and Protest among Northern Free Blacks, 1700–1860* (New York, 1997).

8. For the political, constitutional, and federal limitations of antislavery in the post-
Revolutionary era, see Donald L. Robinson, *Slavery in the Structure of American Poli-*

———

tics, 1765–1820 (New York, 1970); Paul Finkelman, *Slavery and the Founders: Race and Liberty in the Age of Jefferson* (Armonk, N.Y., 1996); David Waldstreicher, *Slavery's Constitution: From Revolution to Ratification* (New York, 2009); and Van Cleve, *A Slaveholders' Union.* For a balanced account of the Federal Constitution's relationship to slavery and antislavery, see Sean Wilentz, *No Property in Man: Slavery and Antislavery at the Nation's Founding* (Cambridge, Mass., 2018). For the stance that the American Revolution created ideas of race and racism, see Duncan J. MacLeod, *Slavery, Race, and the American Revolution* (London, 1974); Melish, *Disowning Slavery;* Gordon S. Wood, *Empire of Liberty: A History of the Early Republic, 1789–1815* (New York, 2009); and David R. Roediger, *The Wages of Whiteness: Race and the Making of the American Working Class* (New York, 1991). For the expansion of American slavery, see Adam Rothman, *Slave Country: American Expansion and the Origins of the Deep South* (Cambridge, Mass., 2007); Edward E. Baptist, *The Half Has Never Been Told: Slavery and the Making of American Capitalism* (New York, 2014); Michael Tadman, *Speculators and Slaves: Masters, Traders, and Slaves in the Old South* (Madison, Wis., 1989); and Damian Alan Pargas, *Slavery and Forced Migration in the Antebellum South* (New York, 2015). The interpretation of the American Revolution as a force that hampered abolitionism has also emerged on a larger Atlantic scale. See Seymour Dresher, *Abolition: A History of Slavery and Antislavery* (Cambridge, 2009). Dresher argues that the American Revolution acted to break up an already existing transatlantic antislavery movement and slowed down the momentum of Atlantic abolitionism. For a counterview that instead identifies the American Revolution as having birthed both American and British abolition movements, see Christopher Leslie Brown, *Moral Capital: Foundations of British Abolitionism* (Williamsburg, Va., and Chapel Hill, N.C., 2006). The growing scholarly focus on the Haitian Revolution and its direct, violent, and relatively immediate destruction of chattel bondage at a key site for Atlantic world slavery has likewise made both the American Revolution and the activism of the abolition societies it helped spur appear by contrast staid and compromised. For the Haitian Revolution as a radical event and the embodiment of revolutionary ideals of liberty and equality, see Robin Blackburn, "Haiti, Slavery, and the Age of the Democratic Revolution," *WMQ,* 3d Ser., LXIII (2006), 643–657; Blackburn, *The American Crucible: Slavery, Emancipation, and Human Rights* (London, 2011); and Laurent Dubois, *Avengers of the New World: The Story of the Haitian Revolution* (Cambridge, Mass., 2004). The scholarly diminishing of the American Revolution as a potential agent of abolitionism has perhaps reached its apex with the publication of Robert G. Parkinson, *The Common Cause: Creating Race and Nation in the American Revolution* (Williamsburg, Va., and Chapel Hill, N.C., 2016). Parkinson argues that American Revolutionaries created a "common cause" that bound white Americans together by depicting enslaved blacks and Native Americans as depraved enemies of independence, thus binding nationalism and racism at the heart of America's founding creed. According to Parkinson, therefore, historians are misguided who see the post-Revolutionary and early national periods as telling a "declension story" away from Revolutionary ideals of equality and natural rights that might have been applied to people of African descent. These years did not embody "an opportunity lost ... for it was never there in the first place" (662). For accounts that characterize ideals of equality and equal rights coming out of the Revolution as very much alive and contested from the 1770s through the 1860s, see Richard D. Brown, *Self-Evident Truths: Contesting Equal Rights from the Revolution to the Civil War* (New Haven, Conn., 2017); and Wilentz, *No Property in Man.*

The way historians have perceived the concept of race in late-eighteenth-and early-nineteenth-century America contributes elementally to first movement abolitionism's minimization. Long ago, Barbara Fields helped to reconfigure the way historians understand race in American history. Whereas scholars had given race a "transhistorical, almost metaphysical, status" beyond the realm of rigorous historical inquiry, Fields countered that race represented a social construction, constantly in flux and changing according to the course of other ideologies that inform social experience at a given historical moment. Fields's conceptual breakthrough invigorated studies of slavery and race in the early American Republic. Yet perhaps anticipating the undeniable vitality of black slavery and white racism by the antebellum era, scholars have frequently framed their analyses to explain why abolishing human bondage and inequality in the early Republic was inescapably doomed. A leading answer has been what one historian has called a "racial consensus" (either through a general white racism or abolitionist paternalism) that limited the potential for emancipation and racial equality from the commencement of nationhood.[9]

Assuming a racial consensus has impeded an appreciation of the ways first movement abolitionists challenged both white prejudice and the institution of slavery and its legacies. Accepting a racial consensus during independent America's early years means overlooking a movement joining black and white reformers and tethering slavery's abolition to African American incorporation. I contend that competing ideas of race and their relationship to antislavery reform imbued much of the debate over abolitionism in the early Republic—from first movement abolitionists' belief that human difference was superficial and white prejudice was capable of being altered, to the claims of slavery's defenders that skin color embodied a fixed marker of inherent black inferiority, to colonizationists' allegation that black degradation served as an insuperable barrier to emancipation

9. Barbara J. Fields, "Ideology and Race in American History," in J. Morgan Kousser and James M. McPherson, eds., *Region, Race, and Reconstruction: Essays in Honor of C. Vann Woodward* (New York, 1982), 143–177, esp. 144; James Oakes, "Conflict vs. Racial Consensus in the History of Antislavery Politics," in John Craig Hammond and Matthew Mason, eds., *Contesting Slavery: The Politics of Bondage and Freedom in the New American Nation* (Charlottesville, Va., 2011), 291–303. The assumption of a racial consensus working against abolitionism in the post-Revolutionary and early national eras continues to cast a long shadow over the historical literature. These narratives range from regional accounts of northern emancipation that depict advocates of gradual abolitionism as having helped to forge a racial consensus of black exclusion to broader, transnational syntheses that skip over first movement abolitionism almost entirely. See Melish, *Disowning Slavery*, 50–83; and Drescher, *Abolition*, 115–145.

and African American uplift. Viewing notions of race as multivalent, frequently shifting, and continually challenged is central to the story this book tells. Reevaluating our understanding of race and reform in early America reveals the post-Revolutionary and early American Republic as eras of fervent contestation over the shape and meaning of slavery, African American freedom, and black citizenship.[10]

Approaching the study of antislavery and race in early America within a framework of conflict rather than consensus opens space for reconstructing first movement abolitionism. Historical literature profiling post-Revolutionary and early national abolitionist agitation increasingly acknowledges the close working relationship between white and black reformers, their shared dedication to free black citizenship, and the idealism that undergirded their activism. This book, however, is the first to fully recover America's first abolition movement as a movement in its own right—tracing its origins, restoring the full breadth of its program and agenda, and accounting for its eventual fall and relative historical marginalization.[11]

10. James Alexander Dun, in his account of the Haitian Revolution's impact in early national America, also identifies the post-Revolutionary period as one of a contest over race and rights and portrays the PAS as having a larger vision of black incorporation. Yet for Dun the heady idealism underlying first movement abolitionism wilted soon after the start of the nineteenth century, as the PAS's optimism and universalist Revolutionary vision receded by the mid-1790s and was all but dead by 1804. See Dun, *Dangerous Neighbors: Making the Haitian Revolution in Early America* (Philadelphia, 2016), 25; and Dun, "Philadelphia Not Philanthropolis: The Limits of Pennsylvanian Antislavery in the Era of the Haitian Revolution," *Pennsylvania Magazine of History and Biography*, CXXXV (2011), 73–102.

11. Gellman, *Emancipating New York;* Kirsten Sword, "Remembering Dinah Nevil: Strategic Deceptions in Eighteenth-Century Antislavery," *Journal of American History*, XCVII (2010), 315–343; Sinha, *The Slave's Cause*, 97–129; Wood, "'A Class of Citizens,'" *WMQ*, 3d Ser., LXXIV (2017), 109–144; Dun, "Philadelphia Not Philanthropolis," *PMHB*, CXXXV (2011), 73–102; Paul J. Polgar, "'To Raise Them to an Equal Participation': Early National Abolitionism, Gradual Emancipation, and the Promise of African American Citizenship," *JER*, XXXI (2011), 229–258; Nicholas Perry Wood, "Considerations of Humanity and Expediency: The Slave Trades and African Colonization in the Early National Antislavery Movement" (Ph.D. diss., University of Virginia, 2013); Levine-Gronningsater, "Delivering Freedom." Sinha applies the term "first wave" abolitionists to those who preceded immediate abolitionists, running from as early as sixteenth-century criticisms of the Atlantic slave trade through the end of the 1820s with the rise of interracial immediate agitation of the "second wave" (Sinha, *The Slave's Cause*, 9–191). Though I trace the early roots of the abolitionist protagonists I profile, my own term of first movement abolitionism is more chronologically and demographically compressed, relating specifically to the abolition societies and their black allies from approximately the early 1780s to the late 1820s. These distinctions in terminology aside, *The Slave's Cause* is the most prominent account to acknowledge the core values of first

Recovering America's first abolition movement blazes new pathways to understanding the trajectory of slavery, race, and antislavery reform in the early Republic. Histories written from the vantage point of immediate abolitionists, with their ardent rejection of the ACS, have long tended to discount first movement abolitionism by portraying antislavery reform before the 1830s as having fused colonization with emancipation. *Standard-Bearers of Equality* definitively upends that narrative, showing that the emergence of colonization as a movement represented a departure from an earlier abolitionist organizational tradition. Fleshing out the version of antislavery that came before colonization rose to prominence demands that we reorient the history of American abolitionism, pushing its development much farther back into the American past. Distinguishing first movement abolitionism from colonization shows the persistence of the reform project established by abolition societies like the PAS and NYMS and their black activist allies. Manisha Sinha, in her comprehensive synthesis of American abolition, has argued for "continuity rather than rupture in the abolitionist tradition." This book joins that call, demonstrating that immediate abolitionism's basic tenets—especially its commitments to achieving black integration and quashing white prejudice—were inherited from its first movement predecessors and did not represent a novel break from past strategies.[12]

––––

movement abolitionists that this book is committed to fully uncovering. While scholarship on post-Revolutionary and early national abolitionism has grown in recent years, it still pales in comparison to the historiography of the antebellum, immediate abolitionist movement. For additional coverage of first movement abolitionism, see Davis, *The Problem of Slavery in the Age of Revolution*, 213–342; Newman, *The Transformation of American Abolitionism*, 16–106; Nash and Soderlund, *Freedom by Degrees*, 74–166; Melish, *Disowning Slavery*, 50–83; Gellman, *Emancipating New York*, 56–186; T. Robert Moseley, "A History of the New-York Manumission Society, 1785–1849" (Ph.D. diss., New York University, 1963); Wayne J. Eberly, "The Pennsylvania Abolition Society, 1775–1830" (Ph.D. diss., Pennsylvania State University, 1973); and Robert Duane Sayre, "The Evolution of Early American Abolitionism: The American Convention for Promoting the Abolition of Slavery and Improving the Condition of the African Race, 1794–1837" (Ph.D., diss., Ohio State University, 1987).

12. Sinha, *The Slave's Cause*, 5. McCarthy and Stauffer, *Prophets of Protest*, reflects a bifurcated conception of antislavery activism that has obscured first movement abolitionism and structures many historical narratives, contrasting a "gradualist embrace of colonization" with "an immediatist belief in racial equality" (xxix). Revealing the continuing resilience of this viewpoint, U.S. history textbooks either skip over first movement abolitionism altogether or present the ACS as the first organized American antislavery movement. See Eric Foner, *Give Me Liberty! An American History*, 5th ed. (New York, 2017), 228, 435; Rebecca Edwards et al., *America's History*, I, *To 1877*, 9th ed. (Boston, 2018), 250–251, 280; John M. Murrin et al., *Liberty, Equality, Power: A History*

Stepping forward in time, recognizing the reform program of first movement abolitionism magnifies the relevance of several crucial questions that
would reverberate long after the movement itself fell away, including who
would be defined as citizens in the American Republic, whether white attitudes toward black Americans could be altered, and what societies in
transition from slavery to freedom should look like—all issues that would
reemerge with fresh urgency in the aftermath of the American Civil War.
The period under study did not ultimately live up to the lofty hopes envisaged by the PAS's seal and Williams's buoyant expectations. But the accomplishments of first movement abolitionism and the potential for black

————

of the American People, I, To 1877, 6th ed. (Boston, 2012), 430–431; Jennifer D. Keene,
Saul Cornell, and Edward T. O'Donnell, *Visions of America: A History of the United
States, Combined Volume* (Upper Saddle River, N.J., 2010), 290–291; David H. Goldfield
et al., *The American Journey: A History of the United States*, I, 6th ed. (Upper Saddle
River, N.J., 2010), 344–345; James L. Roark et al., *The American Promise: A History of
the United States*, I, To 1877, 2d ed. (Boston, 2003), 252; H. W. Brands et al., *American
Stories: A History of the United States, Combined Volume*, 2d ed. (Boston, 2009), 330;
and Gary B. Nash et al., *The American People: Creating a Nation and a Society, Combined Volume* (1992; rpt. New York, 2008), 410. Likewise, one of the premier syntheses of American abolitionism ignores the first abolition movement; see James Brewer
Stewart, *Holy Warriors: The Abolitionists and American Slavery*, rev. ed. (New York,
1997).
   A surge in scholarship on the ACS and colonization has complicated the meaning of
the movement. For years viewed as a proslavery device of southern slaveholders eager to
strengthen human bondage, more recent works have ascertained the antislavery bona-
fides of some of colonization's proponents, especially in the northern states. Fewer of
these studies, however, have analyzed the ACS in relation to its organizational precursor
and examined colonization's reform views in relation to first movement abolitionism.
An important exception to the general approach of narrating histories of colonization
and first movement abolitionism separately is Beverly C. Tomek's *Colonization and Its
Discontents: Emancipation, Emigration, and Antislavery in Antebellum Pennsylvania*
(New York, 2011). Yet Tomek argues for continuity between the PAS and the Pennsylvania Colonization Society, whereas this work finds a striking disparity in the reform phi-
losophy of first movement abolitionists and that of colonizationists. On the "benevolent"
or "humanitarian" strain among northern colonizationists and their antislavery values,
see ibid., 93–131; Nicholas Guyatt, "'The Outskirts of Our Happiness': Race and the
Lure of Colonization in the Early Republic," *JAH*, XCV (2009), 986–1011; Guyatt, *Bind
Us Apart: How Enlightened Americans Invented Racial Segregation* (New York, 2016);
Hugh Davis, "Northern Colonizationists and Free Blacks, 1823–1837: A Case Study of
Leonard Bacon," *JER*, XVII (1997), 651–675; Hugh Davis, *Leonard Bacon: New England
Reformer and Antislavery Moderate* (Baton Rouge, La., 1998); Eric Burin, "Rethinking
Northern White Support for the African Colonization Movement: The Pennsylvania
Colonization Society as an Agent of Emancipation," *PMHB*, CXXVII (2003), 197–229;
and George M. Fredrickson, *The Black Image in the White Mind: The Debate on Afro-
American Character and Destiny, 1817–1914* (Middletown, Conn., 1971), 1–42.

civil and civic integration it embodied must have been just as tangibly felt by people of color in post-Revolutionary New York and Pennsylvania as the analogous potential and accomplishments of Radical Reconstruction were by African Americans in post–Civil War Georgia and South Carolina. Likewise, it must have felt every bit as disappointing to black northerners when the path to racial equality appeared blocked in the 1820s as it did for black Southerners when their hopes began to dissolve in the 1870s. Of course, by comparing the post-Revolutionary and early national gradual emancipation North and the post–Civil War and Reconstruction South, I do not intend to place these two periods on an identical historical plane or to argue that they included the same scope in their respective challenges to black inequality. Rather, I seek to encourage recognizing the thematic links that connected these periods and demonstrate that battles over racial equality, color-blind citizenship, and white prejudice did not only emerge systematically in the later nineteenth century but have been present since the American nation's creation. Historians have long considered the five decades from the 1830s through the 1870s as integral to larger narratives of race, rights, and reform in America. It is time they did the same for the years stretching from the 1780s through the 1820s.

In plotting the history of abolitionism in America before 1830, this study stresses the shifting ideological beliefs of reformers and the greater societies in which they operated. Much important scholarship on the origins of anti-slavery throughout the Atlantic world has examined the relationship between capitalism and the rise of movements in opposition to slavery. Other accounts have looked to explain the emergence of organized antislavery and abolitionism from an imperial or Atlantic perspective. Additionally, a burgeoning literature on the politics of slavery in the early American Republic has traced the political development of antislavery. *Standard-Bearers of Equality* highlights the terms of the debates over slavery, race, and abolitionism in the early American Republic rather than the structural or political developments that made this debate possible.[13]

13. I define *ideology* throughout this work as the underlying body of beliefs, values, and societal doctrines that set the terms for the reform efforts of first movement aboli-tionists and colonizationists. I underscore the role of ideology in interpreting organized antislavery under the assumption that we need to gain access to the mindset of reform-ers, distilling the thought that informed their various versions of reform, to effectively understand the meaning of their activism. For some of the major works on the debate over the relationship between antislavery and capitalism, see Eric Williams, *Capitalism and Slavery* (Chapel Hill, N.C., 1944); Seymour Drescher, *Capitalism and Antislavery: British Mobilization in Comparative Perspective* (New York, 1986); Davis, *The Prob-*

For several reasons, this book's geographic focus is on the mid-Atlantic states of New York and Pennsylvania and, to a lesser extent, New Jersey and Delaware. First, the organizational nucleus of first movement abolitionism was located in the mid-Atlantic. With a legacy of Quaker antislavery activism that inspired a wider campaign in the post-Revolutionary era, the region possessed the two most prominent societies of the first abolitionist movement, the PAS and the NYMS. These two organizations were the most active and influential in setting the tone for the broader movement's agenda, and they also led the way in founding a national conglomeration of abolition societies.[14]

The contested character of emancipation in the mid-Atlantic provides a

---

lem of Slavery in the Age of Revolution; Thomas L. Haskell, "Capitalism and the Origins of the Humanitarian Sensibility, Part 1," *American Historical Review,* XC (1985), 339–361; and Haskell, "Capitalism and the Origins of the Humanitarian Sensibility, Part 2," ibid. (1985), 547–566. Two important works on the imperial roots of Atlantic abolitionism include Brown, *Moral Capital;* and Robin Blackburn, *The Overthrow of Colonial Slavery, 1776–1848* (London, 1988). On abolitionism from an Atlantic world perspective, see Blackburn, *American Crucible;* Drescher, *Abolition;* Dun, *Dangerous Neighbors;* Oldfield, *Transatlantic Abolitionism;* and Patrick Rael, *Eighty-Eight Years: The Long Death of Slavery in the United States, 1777–1865* (Athens, Ga., 2015). For the growing historiography of the politics of slavery and antislavery in the early Republic, see Hammond and Mason, eds., *Contesting Slavery;* Matthew Mason, *Slavery and Politics in the Early American Republic* (Chapel Hill, N.C., 2006); Gellman, *Emancipating New York;* John Craig Hammond, *Slavery, Freedom, and Expansion in the Early American West* (Charlottesville, Va., 2007); Robert Pierce Forbes, *The Missouri Compromise and Its Aftermath: Slavery and the Meaning of America* (Chapel Hill, N.C., 2007); Rachel Hope Cleves, *The Reign of Terror in America: Visions of Violence from Anti-Jacobinism to Antislavery* (New York, 2009); Van Cleve, *A Slaveholders' Union;* Suzanne Cooper Guasco, *Confronting Slavery: Edward Coles and the Rise of Antislavery Politics in Nineteenth-Century America* (Dekalb, Ill., 2013); Padraig Riley, *Slavery and the Democratic Conscience: Political Life in Jeffersonian America* (Philadelphia, 2016); Corey M. Brooks, *Liberty Power: Antislavery Third Parties and the Transformation of American Politics* (Chicago, 2016); Wood, "Considerations of Humanity and Expediency"; and Levine-Gronningsater, "Delivering Freedom."

14. Although an argument could be made for placing Delaware in the upper South in a study of slavery and antislavery in the early Republic, I have included the state in the mid-Atlantic region owing to a few important factors. During the post-Revolutionary and early national eras, Delaware's ratio of free blacks to enslaved African Americans was comparable with that of New Jersey, Pennsylvania, and New York. Delaware also had communities of Quaker antislavery reformers and several abolition societies throughout the period under study. Additionally, although Delaware did not legally abolish slavery in the late eighteenth or early nineteenth centuries, its manumission laws and statutes regarding free blacks were more in line with those of its northern neighbors than those of Maryland or Virginia.

second major reason for the presence of organized abolitionism in the region. Emancipation in the mid-Atlantic was a divisive and drawn-out affair, taking several decades to accomplish. This protracted battle over black freedom did much to engender the activist strategy and ideological approach of first movement abolitionists. Even when abolitionists in the mid-Atlantic achieved statutory emancipation, the proximity of the region to southern slave states demanded the attention of the abolition societies and drew others to colonization when the ACS arrived as an alternative in 1816.

Third, the mid-Atlantic states possessed 80 percent of the northern black population in the early Republic and, in the cities of New York and Philadelphia, two of the most organized and vocal free African American communities. The late eighteenth and early nineteenth centuries witnessed the vast expansion of the free black population in the urban centers of Philadelphia and New York, the rapid ascent of African American community and institutional development, and the emergence of an economically successful and politically engaged black leadership group. From this wellspring of African American betterment emerged a vision of abolitionism based on an optimistic belief in black civic progress that was part and parcel of what it meant to be a first movement abolitionist.

In narrating America's first abolition movement, *Standard-Bearers of Equality* emphasizes the optimism of its proponents. Early on in my research, I was struck by the sense of confidence and idealism that first movement abolitionists continually applied to their activism. Where I had expected to find grim nods to racism and chastening acknowledgements of slavery's ubiquity, I instead discovered durable assurances that people of color could become equal citizens and that black bondage would eventually give way to the steady, if incremental, flow of humanity's progress. First movement abolitionists might have been idealistic, but they were not naive. These activists recognized the hurdles to abolishing slavery and routinely acknowledged the social, legal, and economic disparities faced by free blacks. In re-creating the mentality of first movement abolitionists, I have sought to strike a balance between recapturing their optimism and paying heed to the many stumbling blocks they saw standing in the way of their agenda. Ultimately, it is only by tapping into the optimistic ethos of first movement abolitionism that we can clarify the dramatic metamorphosis in organized antislavery brought by the emergence of the American Colonization Society.

Any study that surveys the landscape of American opposition to slavery over a half century encounters thorny definitional choices. Throughout this work, *abolitionists* are defined as those who opposed both human bondage and the racial inequality that they viewed as propping up the institution of slavery. *Abolitionism*, by this definition, consisted of working for the emancipation of enslaved people and the integration of free blacks into society as citizens. This study designates the term *antislavery* more capaciously to refer to anyone who enunciated public opposition to slavery. Key to differentiating between abolitionism and antislavery is to interrogate how their respective agents envisioned the future of free blacks. Thus, Thomas Jefferson's including an emancipation plan in his *Notes on the State of Virginia* that depended on the removal of all those liberated means that he conveyed antislavery but not abolitionist principles. Yet members of the PAS and NYMS and the mid-Atlantic black activists who allied with them, in agitating for statutory emancipation and free black incorporation, engaged in both antislavery and abolitionism. The term *abolitionism* also had specific connotations within the American context that distinguished it from connected movements in the Atlantic world of the late eighteenth and early nineteenth centuries. While connoting emancipation and free black incorporation in the early United States, abolitionism in Britain during this same period referred primarily to abolishing the slave trade. This crucial difference in the meaning of the word *abolitionism* hints at how debates over the place of emancipated blacks within the American Republic formed a focal point of antislavery reform in post-Revolutionary and early national America.[15]

The appellation *colonization* in this work refers to several iterations of the term held by multiple groups and taking shape under a spacious ideological umbrella, including, among others, southern slaveholders who expressed antislavery sentiments and those who did not; northern members of ACS auxiliary societies who wanted to spread emancipation southward but also looked to expatriate northern free blacks; and reformers who believed they were being pragmatic in promoting partial colonization as a solution to slavery in southern states while simultaneously championing

15. For a comparison of the strategies of abolitionists across the Atlantic world in the late eighteenth century, see Oldfield, *Transatlantic Abolitionism,* 68–99. French abolitionists, too, zeroed in on eliminating the slave trade, but as the Haitian Revolution began to unfold they came to focus more on free black rights. As Chapter 4 of this study shows, abolitionists in the United States, Britain, and France shared many of the same goals—including ending the slave trade—exchanged information and tactics, and viewed their total efforts as part of a singular cause. But shared identification and mutual communication did not mean that these activists defined their particular movements in identical ways.

free black northern rights. Free black activists who supported various schemes of black repatriation abroad but who did not tie this support to their advocacy of emancipation are termed *emigrationists*. Chronicling the dynamism of abolitionism and antislavery before 1830 relies on delineating its complexities. And it is to that rich story that this book now turns.[16]

16. I use the terms *black, African American,* and *persons of color / people of color* interchangeably, as they have all been recorded within the timeframe this work covers, though used to varying degrees. For evidence that the term African American was part of the American lexicon as early as 1782, see Jennifer Schuessler, "Use of 'African American' Dates to Nation's Earliest Days," *New York Times,* Apr. 21, 2015, https://www.nytimes.com/2015/04/21/arts/use-of-african-american-dates-to-nations-early-days.html. Though the phrase "people of African descent" does not appear to have been within the recorded vocabulary of the late eighteenth and early nineteenth centuries, it does gesture to the conscious and conspicuous links that black Americans made between themselves and their African heritage.

CHAPTER 1

The Making of a Movement

Progress, Problems, and the Ambiguous Origins
of the Abolitionist Project

What could an illegally enslaved West Indian migrant, the first treasury secretary of the United States, a New York playwright, a Philadelphia physician, a northern free black minister, and a Quaker educator possibly have in common? They all contributed to first movement abolitionism. An admixture of free black community leaders, elite white Americans, Quaker activists, and unfree black laborers would seem to make for a strange set of allies and a disjointed reform movement. Yet each of these groups shared a measured confidence and basic optimism that sustained the program of abolitionism they would jointly create. This mix of historical actors firmly committed themselves to the idea of antislavery progress, or the belief that, through the agency of reformers, the trajectory of post-Revolutionary and early national America would lead toward emancipation, black uplift, and the dissolution of white prejudice.[1]

While first movement abolitionists coalesced around the idea of antislavery progress, the many obstacles they faced informed the shape and scope of their activism. For one, slavery in the mid-Atlantic was based on racial oppression and long-standing white prejudice toward people of color, facts that would continually haunt the efforts of first movement abolitionists. Second, the American Revolution, which influenced and gave broader purchase to opposing slavery, also made abolitionism problematic.

---

1. On the relationship of the concept of progress to ideas of antislavery reform in the early modern Atlantic world, see David Brion Davis, *Slavery and Human Progress* (New Haven, Conn., 1984), 107–168. Davis distinguishes between those who championed the rhetoric of progress to "soothe the individual conscience, neutralize effective action, and thus protect the slave system," and those who turned to "a faith in progress that would provide assurance that individual action could be effective, in gear with the underlying thrust of history, and hence ethically mandatory" (159). Of these two models, first movement abolitionists clearly were of the second stripe.

Slavery's defenders responded to claims of universal liberty and underlying black equality at the heart of first movement abolitionism by counterclaiming that people of African descent remained ineligible to join independent America as responsible free men and women. Questions derived during the Revolutionary era regarding the capacity of African Americans for freedom posed thorny dilemmas for abolition's advocates. Third, the nature and pace of black freedom in the late-eighteenth- and early-nineteenth-century mid-Atlantic left African American liberty tenuous and free black rights contested. Thus, if the idea of antislavery progress informed the ethos of first movement abolitionists, the roadblocks to emancipation galvanized them into action.

THE BEASTS OF THE PEOPLE

Examining the solidification of racial slavery in the colonial mid-Atlantic reveals the entrenched barriers facing first movement abolitionists. Slavery never took root in the colonies north of Maryland to the same extent as it did in the southern colonies. Lacking a staple crop from which to form the large-scale plantation system that came to define the colonial South, the middle colonies did not end up staking their social, economic, and cultural systems on chattel slavery. Still, slavery's presence in the region was undeniable. From the wheat fields of Pennsylvania, New York, New Jersey, and Delaware to the artisan shops of New York City and the bustling port of Philadelphia, enslaved people filled a variety of roles for the labor-hungry white settlers as domestics, mercantile workers, craftsmen, and farm laborers.[2]

Beginning with the English takeover of the mid-Atlantic region from

2. For slavery and the black experience in bondage in the colonial mid-Atlantic, see Edgar J. McManus, *A History of Negro Slavery in New York* (Syracuse, N.Y., 1966); Leslie M. Harris, *In The Shadow of Slavery: African Americans in New York City, 1626–1863* (Chicago, 2003), 11–48; Graham Russell Hodges, *Root and Branch: African Americans in New York and East Jersey, 1613–1863* (Chapel Hill, N.C., 1999), 6–139; David N. Gellman, *Emancipating New York: The Politics of Slavery and Freedom, 1777–1827* (Baton Rouge, La., 2006), 15–25; Henry Scofield Cooley, *A Study of Slavery in New Jersey* (Baltimore, 1896); Marion Thompson Wright, "New Jersey Laws and the Negro," *Journal of Negro History*, XXVIII (1943), 159–171; Gary B. Nash, *Forging Freedom: The Formation of Philadelphia's Black Community, 1720–1840* (Cambridge, Mass., 1988), 8–38; Nash and Jean R. Soderlund, *Freedom by Degrees: Emancipation in Pennsylvania and Its Aftermath* (New York, 1991), 3–41; Edward Raymond Turner, *The Negro in Pennsylvania: Slavery—Servitude—Freedom, 1639–1861* (Washington, D.C., 1911), 1–54; Ira Berlin, *Many Thousands Gone: The First Two Centuries of Slavery in North America* (Cambridge, Mass., 1998), 47–64; and Patience Essah, *A House Divided: Slavery and Emancipation in Delaware, 1638–1865* (Charlottesville, Va., 1996), 9–35.

the Dutch and Swedes in the 1660s, the Restoration monarchy adopted a policy of encouraging the African slave trade and rewarding slaveholders with land. During the first decade of the 1700s, mid-Atlantic colonial officials wrote into law statutes clearly demarcating slavery as a heritable and unalterable condition. A 1702 New York law officially acknowledged the chattel principle of American slavery by deeming enslaved people "the property of Christians." In 1706, the New York Assembly sanctioned slavery as an inherited state following the status of the mother. This same law, along with one issued in East Jersey in 1704, shut the door to Christianity as a means for the enslaved to claim their freedom by decreeing that baptism could not change slave status. In 1700, the Pennsylvania Assembly (whose laws at this time also applied to the colony of Delaware) issued an edict entitled A Supplement to An Act for the Better Regulation of Servants that endorsed black bondage as a lifelong condition, legally distinct from that of indentured servitude.[3]

Mid-Atlantic colonial officials did more than inscribe racial slavery in the record books. From the close of the seventeenth century through the 1740s, the assemblies of the middle colonies enacted a spate of codes that condemned bondspersons to an inferior and unequal status. All four of the middle colonies created special courts for enslaved people accused of crimes. The fate of those subject to these courts was decided, not by a jury, but by a group of justices and prominent freeholders called specifically to mete out an often rough justice to enslaved blacks. Further handicapping the ability of the enslaved to receive a fair trial, none of the middle colonies sanctioned enslaved peoples' testimony unless it was directed at other black bondspersons. The testimony of the enslaved was almost always used

---

3. Charles Z. Lincoln, William H. Johnson, and Ansel Judd Northrup, [eds.], *The Colonial Laws of New York from the Year 1664 to the Revolution* ... , I (Albany, N.Y., 1894), 521, 598; Bernard Bush, comp., *Laws of the Royal Colony of New Jersey*, I, *1703–1745*, New Jersey Archives, 3d Ser., II (Trenton, N.J., 1977), 28–30, esp. 30; George M. Stroud, ed., *A Digest of the Laws of Pennsylvania; from the Year One Thousand Seven Hundred, to the Twenty-Second Day of April, One Thousand Eight Hundred and Forty-Six*, 7th ed. (Philadelphia, 1847), 1064. Slavery was never explicitly codified in Pennsylvania as an inherited status, though the body of slave codes in the colony and the widespread use of enslaved labor indicates that the institution was firmly established there. A Supplement to An Act for the Better Regulation of Servants in This Province and Territories gives indirect evidence of slavery's inherited and racial nature in Pennsylvania as early as 1700. The law extended the service of white indentured servants found guilty of stealing goods but meted out corporal punishment for blacks convicted of identical crimes—assumedly because black laborers, as chattel, had no more years of service to pledge for restitution.

to implicate bondspersons in plots against their masters or the state, and an enslaved person was never permitted to answer the accusations of a free person. The slave courts allowed colonial authorities to expedite the punishment of bondspersons, limit the ability of the enslaved to defend themselves, and inflict upon those found guilty penalties reserved only for persons of African descent.[4]

And those penalties were harsh. Even in a period when corporal punishment for a variety of crimes was standard, condemned enslaved people faced an especially cruel and unusual type of punishment. In Pennsylvania, Delaware, and New York, enslaved men and women found guilty of stealing goods could be whipped as much as the judges and freeholders

4. Aaron Leaming and Jacob Spicer, [eds.], *The Grants, Concessions, and Original Constitutions of the Province of New Jersey: The Acts Passed during the Proprietary Governments, and Other Material Transactions before the Surrender Thereof to Queen Anne*..., 2d ed. (Somerville, N.J., 1881), 357; Bush, comp., *Laws of the Royal Colony of New Jersey*, I, *1703-1745*, 136–140; James Blair Linn, ed., *Charter to William Penn, and Laws of the Province of Pennsylvania, Passed between the Years 1682 and 1700; Preceded by Duke of York's Laws in Force from the Year 1676 to the Year 1682* ..., I, *1680 to 1700* (Harrisburg, Pa., 1879), 297; James T. Mitchell and Henry Flanders et al., comps., *The Statutes at Large of Pennsylvania* ..., 17 vols. (Harrisburg, Pa., 1896–1915), II, 77–79; Lincoln, Johnson, and Northrup, [eds.], *Colonial Laws of New York*, I, 521, 598, 631, 765–766; *Laws of the State of Delaware, from the Fourteenth Day of October, One Thousand Seven Hundred, to the Eighteenth Day of August, One Thousand Seven Hundred and Ninety-Seven*, I (New Castle, Del., 1797), 102. The Dutch were the first European imperial power to use the labor of enslaved people in the middle colonies. If the presence of black slavery hardly made New Netherland unique compared with other North American colonies, its form differed markedly from that which the English would later institute once they had wrested control of the region in the 1660s. Enslaved people possessed the right to own property, had equal rights to trial, and were able to sue whites and testify against them in a court of law. Some of the enslaved in New Netherland also attained a status known as "half-freedom." In this system, bondspersons who pledged to pay an annual fee to the Dutch West India Company in agricultural produce were liberated, thus helping to further erode the distinctions between black and white and slave and free. Slavery was a heritable condition for most New Netherland bondspersons, and equal freedom remained out of reach for the majority of the colony's black population. Yet, the institution's fluidity in New Netherland does stand in contrast to the English colonial conception of black bondage. On slavery, race, and the experiences of persons of African descent in New Netherland, see McManus, *History of Negro Slavery in New York*, 11–22; A. Leon Higginbotham, Jr., *In the Matter of Color: Race and the American Legal Process: The Colonial Period* (New York, 1978), 100–114; Harris, *In the Shadow of Slavery*, 12–26; Susanah Shaw Romney, *New Netherland Connections: Intimate Networks and Atlantic Ties in Seventeenth-Century America* (Williamsburg, Va., and Chapel Hill, N.C., 2014), 191–244; and Andrea C. Mosterman, "Sharing Spaces in a New World Environment: African-Dutch Contributions to North American Culture, 1626–1826" (Ph.D. diss., Boston University, 2012).

who decided the case deemed appropriate, even as equivalent white trans-gressions were limited to a set number of lashes. New York made it law-ful for towns to employ a "common Whipper" for enslaved violators of the law. In addition to being given forty stripes, New Jersey law mandated that enslaved people found guilty of pilfering goods be branded with the let-ter *T* on their left cheek. For other misdemeanors in which free offenders would have received a fine, enslaved persons, because they had no legally recognized possessions, found themselves tied to the whipping post. Penn-sylvania and New Jersey required the castration of bondspersons who at-tempted to rape "or have carnal Knowledge" of white women, whereas Delaware ordered their ears cut off.[5]

But the most brutal punishments were reserved for enslaved people deemed guilty of murdering their masters or conspiring to incite a rebel-lion. In 1694, an enslaved man in New Jersey convicted of murder was to have his hand severed and "burned before thine eyes," after which he was to be hanged and his corpse burned. Fourteen years later, two en-slaved people on Long Island who had killed their master and his family were put to death. One was burned alive while the other was "hung in gib-bets, and placed astride a sharp iron." They were subjected "to all the tor-ment possible for a terror to others." Enslaved people were often called to witness these brutal executions. One formerly enslaved man never forgot the "dreadful screams" of a twenty-year-old bondsperson whom he was forced to watch burn at the stake not long before the American Revolution. The misery of the man being executed was compounded when the flames "kindled but slowly," causing his cries to "be heard at a distance of three miles." The aftermath of slave rebellions in New York in 1712 and 1741 left many enslaved people to be broken on a wheel, hanged, and burned at the stake (the last of these capital punishments was one that bondspersons re-ceived particularly often). If these executions disregarded the humanity of the enslaved, the property rights of slaveholders were not forgotten. Mas-ters of those executed were compensated for their property, symbolizing

5. Mitchell and Flanders et al., comps., *Statutes at Large of Pennsylvania*, II, 79, 299; Lincoln, Johnson, and Northrup, [eds.], *Colonial Laws of New York*, I, 520; *Laws of the State of Delaware*, I, 104; Bush, comp., *Laws of the Royal Colony of New Jersey*, I, *1703–1745*, 28–30. The English crown repealed the punishment of castration for attempted rape by persons of color. The resulting revised penalties passed by the Pennsylvania and New Jersey Assemblies were reduced but still harsh. Pennsylvania law now required the black offender to be branded on the forehead with the letters *R* or *T* and exported out of the colony "never to return ... upon pain of death." See Mitchell and Flanders et al., comps., *Statutes at Large of Pennsylvania*, II, 235.

how the value of the enslaved was measured, not by their personhood, but by their status as chattel objects. In sum, the middle colonies instituted a special system of justice for enslaved persons marked by a level of physical violence and brutality far exceeding that applied to free persons.[6]

Not only did the middle colonies seek to violently repress enslaved defiance, but bondspersons were also subject to a much greater number of legal restrictions than their free counterparts. To mitigate the threat of enslaved blacks running away or meeting to potentially instigate a rebellion, the mid-Atlantic legislatures restricted the free movement of the enslaved. New Jersey, Pennsylvania, and Delaware ordered enslaved persons to stay within ten miles of their masters' homes at all times, unless given special written authorization by their owners. New Jersey and Pennsylvania enlisted the assistance of white inhabitants by handing out a monetary reward to the person who tracked down and then whipped on the spot the enslaved individual found outside the ten-mile boundary. Enslaved people were also forbidden from gathering in groups because of the widespread fear that such meetings could lead to insurrection plans. These laws hampered the lives of the enslaved and discouraged the construction of vibrant enslaved communities. Additional withholdings of the rights of bondspersons to trade goods, carry arms, drink spirits, and stay out past a certain time of night worked to stifle the autonomy of enslaved people and leave them vulnerable to stark penal correction.[7]

Free blacks of the colonial mid-Atlantic likewise found their rights highly circumscribed. In societies where slavery and blackness were nearly

6. Judge John Johnstone, presiding over Monmouth Court of Sessions, Sept. 23, 1694, quoted in Andrew D. Mellick, Jr., *The Story of an Old Farm; or, Life in New Jersey in the Eighteenth Century* (Somerville, N.J., 1889), 225; James Riker, Jr., *The Annals of Newtown, in Queens County, New-York* ... (New York, 1852), 143; *Boston News-Letter,* Feb. 9, 1708, [2], Feb. 23, 1708, [2]; William J. Allinson, *Memoir of Quamino Buccau, a Pious Methodist* (Philadelphia, 1851), 4–5; McManus, *History of Negro Slavery in New York,* 136. For colonial laws that compensated masters for the execution of enslaved people, see Lincoln, Johnson, and Northrup, [eds.], *Colonial Laws of New York,* I, 631; Bush, comp., *Laws of the Royal Colony of New Jersey,* I, *1703-1745,* 136–140; Mitchell and Flanders et al., comps., *Statutes at Large of Pennsylvania,* IV, 59–60; and *Laws of the State of Delaware,* I, 103.

7. Leaming and Spicer, [eds.], *Grants, Concessions, and Original Constitutions,* 340–342; Mitchell and Flanders et al., comps., *Statutes at Large of Pennsylvania,* II, 79, IV, 63; *Laws of the State of Delaware,* I, 104–105, 215; Lincoln, Johnson, and Northrup, [eds.], *Colonial Laws of New York,* I, 519–520, 766–767. Many of these restrictions were often not fully enforced. It was mainly in periods following slave insurrections or suspected conspiracies that the full force of the laws was felt. Despite the restrictions they faced, enslaved people in the mid-Atlantic created families and forged communities.

synonymous terms, colonial lawmakers viewed free persons of color as dangerous aberrations and made a concerted effort to discourage black freedom. Anticipating that free and enslaved blacks would always be in league with one another in illicit activities, free persons of color were barred from trading with bondspersons and entertaining enslaved people in their homes. Stripping a basic right of freedom, a 1704 New Jersey law denied the right of liberated blacks to own property. Masters who manumitted their enslaved laborers were mandated to post bond, often for sums far exceeding the value of any individual enslaved person. A 1712 New York law labeled free blacks "Idle slothful" and a "charge on the place where they are," requiring a two-hundred-pound surety for each enslaved person manumitted. Pennsylvania's Assembly correspondingly identified free persons of color as "idle, slothfull people" who "often prove burdensome to the neighborhood and afford ill examples to other negroes." A law passed in the 1725–1726 session threatened reenslavement for Pennsylvania's persons of color who "loiter and misspend" their time and required the overseers of the poor to bind out for indenture all manumitted blacks under the age of twenty-one and every child of free blacks. The message of these laws was clear. Free people of color were unsuited for liberty and in need of being prevented from injuring the sanctity of white society.[8]

Intended to cow enslaved and free blacks into submission, the slave laws led instead to a cycle of enslaved resistance and still more draconian measures, all of which worked against recognizing the humanity of black people. Many of the slave codes were written in response to, or in anticipation of, slave insurrections. New York City was thrown into a panic in 1712 when some twenty-four enslaved Africans set a building on fire and then hid in the surrounding woods. When a group of whites arrived to stifle the flames, the insurrectionists pounced, killing nine whites and wound-

8. Bush, comp., *Laws of the Royal Colony of New Jersey*, I, *1703–1745*, 28–30, 136–140; Lincoln, Johnson, and Northrup, [eds.], *Colonial Laws of New York*, I, 761; Mitchell and Flanders et al., comps., *Statutes at Large of Pennsylvania*, IV, 61–62. New York outlawed free black property holding in 1712, but the ban was not reinstituted when the colony revised its slave code in 1730 (Lincoln, Johnson, and Northrup, [eds.], *Colonial Laws of New York*, I, 764–765). Pennsylvania also criminalized interracial marriages. The black spouse would be sold into slavery in the county where he or she resided. And blacks who lived with white partners "under pretense of being married" or committed adultery with whites were subject to bound labor for seven years (Mitchell and Flanders et al., comps., *Statutes at Large of Pennsylvania*, IV, 63). For a general discussion of the place of free blacks in the slave societies of colonial North America, see Winthrop D. Jordan, *White over Black: American Attitudes toward the Negro, 1550–1812* (Williamsburg, Va., and Chapel Hill, N.C., 1968), 122–128.

ing seven others. Upon capture, multiple blacks were put to death. An Act for Preventing Suppressing and Punishing the Conspiracy and Insurrection of Negroes and Other Slaves, which set legal precedents for much of the colony's slave laws, soon followed the executions. In 1734, New Jersey whites got word of a supposed plot by enslaved people in the eastern portion of the colony. The enslaved were to slay their masters and then escape to Indian territory, where they would ally themselves with the French. Many of those accused were fortunate enough only to have their ears chopped off.[9]

Most enslaved people neither killed their masters nor plotted to destroy white society through a violent uprising. Yet colonial whites of the mid-Atlantic came to associate blacks, whether enslaved or free, with crime, violence, and barbarous tendencies. These white perceptions of enslaved blacks are elucidated in a printed account of the 1741 New York slave conspiracy. During the winter of 1740–1741, after several city buildings were set ablaze and an enslaved person was seen fleeing one of these fires, New York's authorities uncovered a supposed crime ring implicating lower-class whites and blacks in the conflagrations. The prosecution's evidence was based on the unreliable testimony of a sixteen-year-old white servant. By the time the trials ceased, thirty enslaved people were executed and seventy banished from the colony. Not long after the prosecutions had ended, the presiding judge, Daniel Horsmanden, published a transcript of the trials. In a diatribe directed at one of the condemned bondspersons during the 1741 trials, Horsmanden harangued the soon-to-be-executed enslaved man that "most, of your Complexion" are "worthless, detestable Wretches." Estimating that cruelty and a savage disposition was "in the very Nature and Temper of ye," Horsmanden declared that blacks had clearly "degenerated" so far "below the Dignity of Humane Species, that even the *brute Animals* may upbraid ye." Black people as a whole, he concluded, were the *"the Beasts of the People."*[10]

9. Kenneth Scott, "The Slave Insurrection in New York in 1712," *New-York Historical Society Quarterly*, XLV (1961), 43–74; Lincoln, Johnson, and Northrup, [eds.], *Colonial Laws of New York*, I, 761–767; Cooley, *A Study of Slavery in New Jersey*, 42–43. The colonies of Pennsylvania and Delaware were undoubtedly aware of these and other alleged slave conspiracies. Inhabitants of these colonies must have similarly remained on guard for any signs of suspicious activity by enslaved people. Certainly, the slave codes of these two colonies seem to indicate as much.

10. [Daniel Horsmanden], *A Journal of the Proceedings in the Detection of the Conspiracy Formed by Some White People, in Conjunction with Negro and Other Slaves, for Burning the City of New-York in America, and Murdering the Inhabitants* ... (New York, 1744), 186. On the 1741 conspiracy, see McManus, *History of Negro Slavery in New York,*

This phrase, "the Beasts of the People," is an apt metaphor to describe the way many white colonists must have viewed people of African descent. Although a racism based on biological difference would not emerge until the nineteenth century, colonial whites did not need pseudoscientific theories to prove to them that black people were degraded and naturally fitted for chattel bondage. The way their societies were structured told them as much. The legal and social dynamics of racial slavery in colonial America codified white prejudice and made it visceral. When human bondage came under widespread attack for the first time during the Revolutionary era, the defenders of slavery would turn to the well-established and deeply engrained colonial white American belief that persons of African descent belonged in slavery.[11]

126–139; and Harris, *In the Shadow of Slavery*, 43–36. There is a debate among historians about whether a plot actually existed, but, for this study, the importance of the 1741 conspiracy lies in what it says about the fragile psyche of colonial whites when it came to the potential of enslaved people revolting.

11. White prejudice toward persons of African descent long preceded the creation of racial slavery in the English North American colonies. For the deep roots of anti-black thought in western European society, see James H. Sweet, "The Iberian Roots of American Racist Thought," *William and Mary Quarterly*, 3d Ser., LIV (1997), 143–166; Jordan, *White over Black*, 3–40; and David Brion Davis, *In the Image of God: Religion, Moral Values, and Our Heritage of Slavery* (New Haven, Conn., 2001), 123–136. On the centrality of animalization and dehumanization to racial slavery, see Davis, *The Problem of Slavery in the Age of Emancipation* (New York, 2014), 3–35. I do not mean to imply here that white American colonists viewed blacks literally as beasts. The dominance of single creation theory foreclosed the chance that most whites would have thought of blacks as a different species. As Davis writes, "'Dehumanization' means the eradication not of human *identity* but of those elements of humanity that evoke respect and empathy and convey a sense of dignity" (17). For a critique of dehumanization as a lens through which to view the effects of bondage on the enslaved, see Walter Johnson, "To Remake the World: Slavery, Racial Capitalism, and Justice," *Boston Review*, Feb. 20, 2018, http://bostonreview.net/forum/walter-johnson-to-remake-the-world. Johnson argues that the concept of dehumanization obscures the nature of American slavery, which relied on "the human capacities of enslaved people"—including not only their reproduction and labor but also a host of other human attributes recognized, and depended on, by slaveholders themselves. More problematic to Johnson, dehumanization "suggests an alienation of enslaved people from their humanity," and thus historians who use the term become "locked in an inextricable embrace with the very history of racial abjection" that they seek to push against. Johnson's caveat that scholars should resist concluding that the institution of slavery dehumanized the enslaved is compelling. But the idea of slavery as a dehumanizing institution was a tangible belief held by at least some, and probably many, colonial American whites. And it is white prejudice toward the enslaved and a sense of black "otherness" that is important to acknowledge in order to appreciate what first movement abolitionists were up against when they confronted slavery and racial inequality in the post-Revolutionary years. The lived experience be-

THE PROMISE AND PROBLEM OF ANTISLAVERY
IN THE REVOLUTIONARY ERA

The American Revolution would have an ambivalent but formative influence on the first abolition movement. Although instigated by colonial grievances over British imperial policies, the Revolution politicized chattel slavery and gave the institution a discursive significance it had previously lacked. Revolutionary writers and orators claimed that they were being made into "virtual" slaves by the unrighteous impositions of the British government. When white Americans railed at Britons for keeping them in virtual slavery, they did not speak simply for the sake of political hyperbole. The concept of political slavery was vital to the colonial American rationale for independence from Britain. Revolutionary pamphleteers and newspaper writers attempted to persuade the public that, through the arbitrary power and autocratic coercion of a distant British crown, the individual agency, personal independence, and even bodily autonomy of the American colonists was under serious duress. In order for the colonists to avoid the fate of millions of subjects in tyrannical Europe, these Revolutionaries wrote, they needed to reclaim their natural rights as a free and independent people or become slaves to the British Empire's despotic rule. Repeatedly in the literature of the Revolutionary War era, warnings of imminent enslavement to English oppressors rang through the political discourse.[12]

In the imperial debate between the metropole and British North American colonies, slavery became a kind of political cudgel used to indict the other side as base posers of moral virtue. British imperial writers labeled the American patriots sanctimonious hypocrites who rhapsodized about natural liberty and equality while holding people in chains. The patriots shot back that it was under the fostering guidance of British imperial policy that slavery had taken root in the colonies in the first place, and it was at the hands of English officials that colonial restrictions on the importation of enslaved Africans had been defeated. Slavery had been made "not merely a moral problem, but a political problem." In this changed context from the colonial era, that chattel slavery was the plight of more than half a million people did not escape the attention of some Americans. From Pennsylvania to Massachusetts, politicians, preachers, and propagandists

---

tween white and black colonists, specifically among the lower classes, was not as starkly divided as theories of black inferiority would seem to imply. See Lois Horton, "From Class to Race in Early America: Northern Post-Emancipation Racial Reconstruction," *JER*, XIX (1999), 629–649.

12. Bernard Bailyn, *The Ideological Origins of the American Revolution* (Cambridge, Mass., 1967), 233–234.

drew on the newfound political salience of the institution of slavery in extending the rhetoric of natural rights to the enslaved.[13]

Some of the most powerful antislavery rhetoric in this era came from enslaved people themselves, who repurposed Revolutionary discourse to bring to bear a biting critique of the American Revolutionary cause absent abolition. Between 1773 and 1777, bondspersons in Massachusetts submitted a series of petitions to Governor Thomas Hutchinson and the colonial legislature pressing for emancipation. Seizing on the antislavery potential of the American Revolutionary War era, the enslaved and free blacks of Massachusetts appealed directly to their state's political system to extend the promises of freedom to those imprisoned in bondage. The petitioners cleverly drew on patriot claims of political slavery to expose the hypocrisy of leaving unaddressed chattel slavery. One petition insisted that "every Principle from which Amarica has Acted in the Cours of their unhappy Dificultes with Great Briton Pleads Stronger than A thousand arguments in favours of your petioners." An April 1773 memorial to the members of the Massachusetts House of Representatives brought to the surface the disjuncture between the Revolution's lofty ideals and the reality of American slavery, informing the legislature, "We expect great things from men who have made such a noble stand against the designs of their *fellow-men* to enslave them." American Revolutionaries fighting for white liberty could ill afford to ignore the iniquities of black slavery if they hoped to maintain the rectitude of their bid for independence.[14]

13. Christopher Leslie Brown, *Moral Capital: Foundations of British Abolitionism* (Williamsburg, Va., and Chapel Hill, N.C., 2005), 105–153 (quotation on 114). Those who used Revolutionary ideals and rhetoric to attack slavery in the heat of the American Revolutionary War included a wide cast of characters, such as the patriot lawyer James Otis, the political pamphleteer Thomas Paine, the Congregationalist minister Samuel Hopkins, and groups of enslaved New Englanders. See Otis, *The Rights of the British Colonies Asserted and Proved* (Boston, 1764); Hopkins, *A Dialogue concerning the Slavery of Africans; Shewing It to Be the Duty and Interest of the American Colonies to Emancipate All Their African Slaves; with an Address to the Owners of Such Slaves . . .* (Norwich, Conn., 1776); *Pennsylvania Journal; and the Weekly Advertiser* (Philadelphia), Mar. 8, 1775, [1]; and "Slaves Petition for Freedom during the Revolution, 1773–1779," in Herbert Aptheker, ed., *A Documentary History of the Negro People in the United States*, I, *From Colonial Times through the Civil War* (New York, 1951), 6–12. For an overview of Revolutionary-era antislavery, see Manisha Sinha, *The Slave's Cause: A History of Abolition* (New Haven, Conn., 2016), 34–64.

14. Peter Bestes et al., "For the Representative of the Town of Thompson," Apr. 20, 1773, and "To the Honorable Counsel and House of Representatives for the State of Massachusetts Bay in General Court Assembled, January 13, 1777," in Aptheker, ed., *Documentary History of the Negro People*, I, 7, 10; Sinha, *The Slave's Cause*, 41–44. Sinha

These petitioners linked the battle for American independence with the universality of human freedom and instructed New England legislatures that black bondspersons were born heirs to the same basic rights as their white counterparts. A 1777 petition from a group of free and enslaved blacks to the Massachusetts General Court cited the "Natural and Unaliable Right to that freedom which the Grat Parent of the Unavers hath Bestowed equalley on all menkind" as the premise on which slavery should be abolished and then, alluding to the British charge of American hypocrisy, assured its audience that the abolition of slavery would leave the patriots "no longer chargeable with the inconsistancey of acting themselves the part which they condem and oppose in others." Two years later, nineteen enslaved men in New Hampshire petitioned their state legislature, adeptly merging political despotism with chattel slavery and placing them in opposition with ideals of equality. "Tyranny and slavery are alike detestable to minds conscious of the equal dignity of human nature," the petitioners wrote. Although rebuffed time and again by state authorities, these antislavery petitions helped to make slavery a political issue, prodding the Revolutionary generation to address the quandary of human bondage.[15]

Although the American Revolution undoubtedly gave slavery currency as a topic of political discussion, it is easy to overstate the case for the antislavery nature of the Revolution. The Revolution did not create antislavery in America. There was a long, albeit demographically narrow, record of American antislavery thought far before the first shots were fired at Lexington and Concord. Quaker activists had developed an antislavery discourse stretching back as early as the late seventeenth century, using rhetoric consonant with later Revolutionary-era emphases on natural rights, inherent equality, and fundamental human liberty. The Revolution did not lead inevitably to emancipation policies in the newly independent American states. Of the seven states that would abolish slavery in the late eighteenth and early nineteenth centuries, only Vermont and Pennsylvania would do so during the Revolutionary War. Even though the Revolution might have set in motion a critical examination of slavery, it by no means made most Americans concerned enough to square their professions of liberty with the existence of chattel bondage. As Christopher Brown has written, "Most

---

argues that the enslaved New England petitioners "did not simply appropriate revolutionary ideology but critically engaged it to highlight their plight" (44).

15. "To the Honorable Counsel and House of Representatives," in Aptheker, ed., *Documentary History of the Negro People*, I, 10; John Cooper, "To the Publick," Sept. 20, 1780, in Roger Bruns, ed., *Am I Not a Man and a Brother: The Antislavery Crusade of Revolutionary America, 1688–1788* (New York, 1977), 459.

in Revolutionary America cared much less about the problem of slavery than the few abolitionists active at the time and the many historians who have written about them since." Slavery might have posed a problem to some, but there were several more pressing issues to sort in the wake of independence, such as forging a new nation of several disparate states and maintaining political sovereignty from European imperial threats.[16]

If the Revolution failed to burden the consciences of most Americans with the problem of slavery, neither did Revolutionary thought lead solely down a path hostile to human bondage. In fact, Revolutionary ideology posed formidable obstacles to opponents of chattel slavery. The pillar of property rights embedded in the axioms of American independence provided one important check on antislavery in Revolutionary thought. Just as the rhetoric of the Revolution seemed to proffer a natural right of all men to their freedom, so, too, did slaveowners claim a natural right to property in the form of enslaved people. Mid-Atlantic slaveholders used the mantle of natural rights as a powerful tool to assert absolute control over those they classified as their private, unalienable property. Defenders of slavery

16. Christopher Leslie Brown, "The Problems of Slavery," in Edward G. Gray and Jane Kamensky, eds., *The Oxford Handbook of the American Revolution* (Oxford, 2013), 428. On early Quaker antislavery discourse, see Brycchan Carey, *From Peace to Freedom: Quaker Rhetoric and the Birth of American Antislavery, 1657–1761* (New Haven, Conn., 2012). The War of Independence sidelined antislavery in certain locales. In New Jersey, Quaker reformers used a transatlantic antislavery network built up before the Revolution to pressure the state's assembly into considering a manumission bill. Yet this effort was set aside in large part because the war with Britain raged. See Jonathan D. Sassi, "Anthony Benezet as Intermediary between the Transatlantic and Provincial: New Jersey's Antislavery Campaign on the Eve of the American Revolution," in Marie-Jeanne Rossignol and Bertrand Van Ruymbeke, eds., *The Atlantic World of Anthony Benezet (1713–1784): From French Reformation to North American Quaker Antislavery Activism* (Leiden, 2017), 129–146; and Robert G. Parkinson, *The Common Cause: Creating Race and Nation in the American Revolution* (Williamsburg, Va., and Chapel Hill, N.C., 2016), 471. On the failure of the American Revolution to create a cohesive and sustained movement for abolition in New Jersey, see James J. Gigantino II, *The Ragged Road to Abolition: Slavery and Freedom in New Jersey, 1775–1865* (Philadelphia, 2015), 18–30. For an account that downplays the role of Revolutionary ideology in explaining the adoption of gradual emancipation in Pennsylvania, see Nash and Soderlund, *Freedom by Degrees*, 74–113. In New York and New Jersey, gradual emancipation laws came a quarter of a century after the War for Independence began. David Gellman writes that, in New York, the "Revolutionary War changed everything and nothing for the institution of slavery." On these ambiguities, see Gellman, *Emancipating New York*, 26–42 (quotation on 26). The historiographical term the "problem of slavery" was coined by David Brion Davis, whose writings on slavery, Atlantic world development, and the Revolutionary era have had a seminal influence on virtually every piece of scholarship on American slavery.

in New Jersey grabbed on to property rights as a major component of their case against legislative abolition. One writer exclaimed that "slaves" were "as much their owners property as any thing we possess." Another New Jersey essayist called the principle of property in enslaved people "one of the unalterable particulars of our rights" and proclaimed that it was unconstitutional for this human property to be emancipated "without the concurrence of their possessors." A third New Jersey apologist for slavery thought that it was no "trifling thing" for slaveholders "to be deprived of their *legal property*" and caustically suggested a "perusal of our constitution" by abolitionists. Opposing emancipation in New York, "Justice" asked rhetorically if abolitionists meant to tell slaveholders that "you shall not hold that property [enslaved people] any longer, which by the laws of your country you were before authorized to hold?" The writer asserted that such an act would be "an outrage on justice and liberty" much greater than the practice of holding people in bondage.[17]

Virginian defenders of slavery articulated one of the strongest formulations of the property rights argument. Soon after American independence had been secured, antislavery activists pushed the Virginia Assembly to abolish slavery. In response, several groups of proslavery memorialists submitted countervailing petitions fusing liberty with property rights and making use of Revolutionary ideology to defend slaveholding. Virginia's proslavery memorialists used the legacy of Revolutionary liberty and the meaning of American independence as confidently as antislavery advocates, though for very different ends. Stating that Americans had "risked their Lives and Fortunes" to be "put in the Possession of our Rights of Liberty and Property," the petitioners warned the assembly that antislavery laws of any sort violated "our sacred rights of property." In the judgment of the petitioners, through the trials of war Americans had "seald with our Blood, a Title to the full, free, and absolute Enjoyment of every species of our Property," and yet now abolitionists threatened to destroy everything the Revolution had been fought over. When antislavery activists began advocating for emancipation, the defenders of slavery countered by citing the long-sanctioned practice of holding property in people and by making use of Revolutionary ideology for proslavery purposes.[18]

17. *New-Jersey Gazette* (Trenton), Jan. 10, 1781, [1], Feb. 14, 1781, [1], Apr. 11, 1781, [2]; *Argus, or Greenlead's New Daily Advertiser* (New York), Jan. 23, 1796, [2]. See also *Pennsylvania Journal*, Jan. 31, 1781.

18. Fredrika Teute Schmidt and Barbara Ripel Wilhelm, "Early Proslavery Petitions in Virginia," *WMQ*, 3d Ser., XXX (1973), 138–143. The petitions calling for an abolition bill came at a time of momentum for antislavery activists in the Old Dominion, on the

American Revolutionary ideology was neither antislavery or proslavery. It is probably true that many white Americans cared little for the issue of slavery and ranked the institution's presence low on the priority list of problems facing the infant Republic. To the extent that most white Americans did think about slavery, they probably concluded that claims of the natural rights of all to freedom would have to take a backseat to the natural rights of property that had codified chattel bondage in America for generations. Yet, even if independent America's promises of liberty and equality were intended primarily for free white men, antislavery writers and activists harnessed these universally couched principles and applied them to enslaved persons, arguing that people of African descent came under the Revolutionary covenant. This argument called for a response from slavery's defenders that black Americans were ineligible for freedom based on a line of attack that explicitly racialized the new nation's ideals.

NATURE, RACE, AND THE PROBLEM
OF BLACK FREEDOM

The role of the Revolution in putting race at the center of debates over emancipation framed the agenda of the first abolition movement in pivotal ways. The rhetoric of American independence transformed rights from specific, social, and limited to a sweeping creed, natural, inherent, and universal in scope. The resulting assumption of a fundamental natural right to freedom was a noteworthy development when considering that since the beginning of English colonization of North America the exact opposite belief had held sway. The English did wrestle with the formation of chattel bondage in their colonies, and slavery was contested at points in the early Anglo-Atlantic world. Yet, for the most part, in colonial America little external rationale for slavery was needed because human bondage did not run counter to the dominant line of social thought.

From the initial period of European exploration of the Americas, slavery was couched as a traditionally sanctioned practice. Slavery in colonial America was supported by a series of universal truths. The ancient belief in a dualism between the body and soul of mortals permitted the worldly practice of slavery. According to this doctrine, the best route to freedom for

---

heels of the 1782 manumission act that made it possible for Virginia's slaveholders to voluntarily free their bondspersons. For the successful lobbying efforts of the Quakers to obtain a voluntary manumission law from the Virginia legislature, see Eva Sheppard Wolf, *Race and Liberty in the New Nation: Emancipation in Virginia from the Revolution to Nat Turner's Rebellion* (Baton Rouge, La., 2006), 28–35; and Gary B. Nash, *Warner Mifflin: Unflinching Quaker Abolitionist* (Philadelphia, 2017), 120–124.

the enslaved was in the afterworld, where heavenly reward awaited duti-ful bondspersons. The concept of the ideal Christian servant—in which enslaved people took their place in a hierarchy of human relationships joined by reciprocal obligations and contingent on fealty to social superi-ors—additionally supported slavery. The biblical themes of the sinful slave and the oft-cited allegory of the Curse of Ham also sustained the practice of slavery. Bondspersons continually challenged their servile status, and pockets of opposition to slavery did materialize. But, in a colonial society where hierarchy and subordination informed every facet of human exis-tence, those parties interested in slavery's preservation rarely needed to rationalize a practice taken for granted as a natural fact.[19]

The American Revolution brought an ideological shift toward freedom as natural and bondage as unnatural. This shift did not give antislavery advocates an unmitigated victory, as revealed by the Revolutionary-based arguments of slavery's defenders. Nor did it doom the institution of slavery, a point made obvious by the spread of slavery south and west in the decades following American independence. But this ideological reconfiguration did have profound consequences for the growing debate over American slavery. As David Brion Davis has put it, "given the widespread enthusiasm for lib-erty and equal rights," slavery's defenders were hard-pressed to argue that "the freedom of some Americans depended on the exploitation of others." In a revolution in which abstract principles were, not mere window dress-ing, but seen as essential to the very meaning of American independence, attacking these principles head-on made little sense. Finding nature no

---

19. David Brion Davis, *The Problem of Slavery in Western Culture* (Ithaca, N.Y., 1966). For the ways the English grappled with and contested slavery much earlier than histo-rians had once believed, see Michael Guasco, *Slaves and Englishmen: Human Bond-age in the Early Modern Atlantic World* (Philadelphia, 2014); John Donoghue, "'Out of the Land of Bondage': The English Revolution and the Atlantic Origins of Abolition," *American Historical Review*, CXV (2010), 943–974; and John N. Blanton, "This Species of Property: Slavery and the Properties of Subjecthood in Anglo-American Law and Politics, 1619–1783" (Ph.D. diss., City University of New York, 2016). Jonathan Saffin, a Boston merchant, penned one of the few public defenses of slavery in the colonial era. Replying to the anti-slave-trading pamphlet of Judge Samuel Sewall, Saffin indicted the integrity of enslaved blacks and questioned their humanity in much the same manner as Revolutionary-era defenders of slavery would do. Yet Saffin's arguments relied on the assumption that social inequality and a fixed social hierarchy were natural truths uni-versally desired by all. Later defenders of slavery could not make this same claim—at least not to the same degree—causing late-eighteenth-century apologists for slavery to defame blacks even more than colonial defenders such as Saffin. See Saffin, *A Brief and Candid Answer to a Late Printed Sheet, Entitled, the Selling of Joseph*, in George H. Moore, *Notes on the History of Slavery in Massachusetts* (New York, 1866), 251–256.

longer on the side of human bondage, the most effective rhetorical route for slavery's defenders was to dehumanize the enslaved and argue for their inherent incapacity for freedom. Slavery's opponents would respond that color was only a superficial marker of difference and that black inequality was but a transitory state capable of being overcome. But, regardless of the position taken, debates over slavery, from the incipient stages of American independence, came to concentrate on debates over the nature of black people.[20]

Out of the Revolutionary rights discourse swirling in the early 1770s, antislavery writers and defenders of human bondage engaged in a telling dialectic. Both slavery's opponents and its defenders would stake a claim on "nature," with one side championing the natural rights of man to liberty and the other advancing enslaved Africans' natural suitability for slavery. One of the clearest expressions of this discursive dynamic took place during the Harvard commencement of 1773 when two students, Theodore Parsons and Eliphalet Pearson, debated the issue of slavery. Pearson, representing the antislavery perspective, quickly turned to his side's staple argument. He expressed "painful astonishment, that in this enlightened age and land, where the principles of natural and civil Liberty" as well as "the natural rights of mankind are so generally understood," Americans continued to hold others in chattel slavery. Colonists who claimed "natural equality in defence of their own Liberties" and at the same time overlooked the natural rights of enslaved Africans—though "nature has made no distinction" between them and whites—"flagrantly contradicted" the cause of independence. Extending the rhetoric of Revolutionary rights to enslaved people and calling out the hypocrisy of patriot silence on slavery, Pearson presented a powerful if predictable argument against black bondage.[21]

Parsons, tasked with defending slavery, had a more difficult assignment. He started by acknowledging "that Liberty to all is sweet" but soon added that "all" could not "equally enjoy" it. Parsons had begun his defense of slavery by acknowledging the ideal of liberty but denying such an ideal applied to all people in American society. Nodding at the theory of natural rights but rejecting its universalism, Parsons argued that in order for

20. David Brion Davis, *The Problem of Slavery in the Age of Revolution, 1770–1823* (Ithaca, N.Y., 1975), 303. I follow here Davis's perspicacious observation that "Revolutionary debates over slavery moved irresistibly to the question of race," making the topic of black capacity for freedom a major barrier to abolition (302–303).

21. [Theodore Parsons and Eliphalet Pearson], *A Forensic Dispute on the Legality of Enslaving the Africans, Held at the Public Commencement in Cambridge, New-England, July 21st, 1773, by Two Candidates for the Bachelor's Degree* (Boston, 1773) 4–5.

societies to function "degrees of authority and subordination" were essential, meaning that the liberty of some necessarily hinged on the inequality of others. Here Parsons was situating his defense of slavery in the traditional colonial view of the importance of a hierarchy of human relationships premised on social inequality. Cognizant that this assertion alone would fail to persuade an audience of Revolutionary-era Americans of the necessity of chattel bondage, Parsons extended his argument. Although the "principle of natural equality" was fine in theory, Parsons stated that "slavery *in general*," or the "involuntary subordination of the will of one to that of another," was the governing premise of all human existence. No one would deny that God governed man and that parents must have authority over their children. Both of these relationships were in the best interest of the dependent party. Implying an analogy between the fallibility of man or the helplessness of children and the depravity of chattel bondspersons, Parsons was ready to impugn the character of enslaved Africans.[22]

Anticipating Parsons's next move, Pearson shot back that, although he accepted the limited sense of slavery in general as it applied to the distribution of authority between God and man and parents and children, he utterly rejected this distinction when it came to blacks and whites. No "natural inequality" existed between these groups because "nature seems to have made no such difference," unless something as superficial as "the darkness of a man's skin" or "the quality of their hair" qualified people of African descent for slavery. But Pearson had inadvertently walked into Parsons's trap of racial difference. Nature, Parsons offered, had "made differences … among the human species," meaning that "the notion of *equality*, in the strict sense, had no foundation *in nature*." Now came the clinching argument. Africans, in Parsons's estimation, possessed a "depraved nature" and were saddled with a "brutal stupidity" and "savage barbarity" that left them destitute of those qualities "by which the human species is distinguished from the other parts of the animal creation." Leading lives of "misery" and "wretchedness" in their native land, Africans were done a favor when brought into slavery in the civilized Americas. The natural inequality of Africans, who shared character traits with "a child, an ideot, or a madman," meant that no consent on their part was necessary to justify American slavery, "notwithstanding all the uneasiness attending subordination." Rejecting the application of natural rights ideology to enslaved

22. [Parsons and Pearson], *A Forensic Dispute*, 7–16. Interestingly, Parsons had a personal connection with slavery through his slaveholding minister father who had come under attack by his parishioners for keeping bondspersons. See Larry E. Tise, *Proslavery: A History of the Defense of Slavery in America, 1701–1840* (Athens, Ga., 1987), 30.

blacks, Parsons's defense of slavery ultimately rested on attacking the nature of people of African descent.[23]

A related and highly publicized dialogue between slavery's apologists and chattel bondage's opponents broke out over whether nature or the environment of slavery explained black inequality. In the same year that Pearson and Parsons debated black bondage, Anthony Benezet persuaded the Philadelphia physician Benjamin Rush to pen a pamphlet attacking slavery and the slave trade. The youthfully enthusiastic Rush employed a bevy of arguments against the morality of slavery, from its incompatibility with Christianity to the inhumanity of holding people as chattel. But it was no coincidence that Rush began his pamphlet by defending the "capacities for virtue" of persons of color. Claiming that the accounts of travelers to Africa proved that blacks "are equal to the Europeans" in "ingenuity" and "humanity," Rush blamed slavery for stifling the innate positive qualities of Africans. Slavery, according to Rush, "debased, and rendered torpid" Africans' "moral faculties, as well as those of the understanding," making all the negative attributes attached to enslaved people only the "offspring of slavery" and "an argument to prove that they were not intended for it." This early environmentalist argument in favor of underlying black equality led Rush to conclude that slavery should be gradually abolished and liberated youths, after receiving a religious and literary education, should be given "all the privileges of free-born British subjects."[24]

Slavery's defenders hurried to answer Rush's arguments. Piqued by Rush's depiction of the hard-heartedness of slaveholders and the brutality of slavery, Richard Nisbet, a recent West Indian migrant to Philadelphia, responded with a pamphlet of his own. Nisbet based much of his rationalization for slavery on the alleged inferiority of Africans. He believed it was "probable" that Africans were "a much inferior race of men to the whites, in every respect." African societies appeared "unacquainted with arts, letters, manufactures, and every thing which constitutes civilized life." Nisbet asserted that Africans cared not when separated from one another for

23. [Parsons and Pearson], *A Forensic Dispute*, 21–28.

24. Benjamin Rush, *An Address to the Inhabitants of the British Settlements, on the Slavery of the Negroes in America*, 2d ed. (Philadelphia, 1773), 1–2, 20, 25. Rush qualified his abolitionist recommendation by suggesting that only "young Negroes" be freed and incorporated into society while those enslaved people who had "acquired all the low vices of slavery" or "from age or infirmities are unfit to be set at liberty" remain in bondage "for the good of society" (19–20). In other words, slavery so degraded its victims that some enslaved people were beyond repair, according to Rush—a conclusion that shows the limits of this early expression of antislavery environmentalism.

sale into slavery and attributed this to their supposedly lacking "friend-ship, gratitude," and other humane sentiments. From firsthand experience in the plantations of the West Indies, Nisbet attested that African imports were "stupid" and "lazy" when first arriving at the islands but improved their behavior after being acclimated to life in bondage. Thus, Nisbet be-lieved bondage in the Americas improved Africans and saved them from a "more wretched slavery to their fellow barbarians." Nisbet reversed Rush's argument that slavery damaged Africans and debased their inborn talents. He claimed instead that black persons discovered their humanity only in slavery.[25]

With the defenders of slavery pinning much of their case for human bondage's justness on the natural inferiority of people of African descent, antislavery activists had to come up with a counterargument. The Quaker antislavery writer Anthony Benezet was up to the challenge. In a series of pamphlets highlighted by *A Short Account of That Part of Africa, Inhab-ited by Negroes* and *Some Historical Account of Guinea*, Benezet sought to construct a positive image of African culture and convince the reading pub-lic of the capacity of black persons for virtue. Benezet perused the leading travel narratives by Europeans describing the social and cultural disposi-tions of Africans and selectively excerpted quotations that depicted those of African descent as a noble, virtuous, and intelligent people. Before in-undating his readers with positive descriptions of African societies, Bene-zet instructed the public in *A Short Account* that the travel accounts proved "the *Negroes* are generally sensible, humane and sociable" and that "their Capacity is as good, and as capable of Improvement, as that of the White People." It was the deleterious effects of slavery and "an Idea of a Superi-ority" that made many whites view blacks "as an ignorant and contemptible Part of Mankind." The image of Africans Benezet put forth was of a sober, industrious, and honest people, capable of self-government but corrupted by the slave trade and then denied their essential humanity in slavery.[26]

25. [Richard Nisbet], *Slavery Not Forbidden by Scripture; or, A Defence of the West-India Planters* ... (Philadelphia, 1773), 21–25. The travel writer, Bernard Romans, also painted Africans as naturally made for slavery in his history of East and West Florida. Panning Rush's pamphlet as the product of unthinking fanaticism, Romans assured his readers that the "Treachery, theft, stubbornness, and idleness" he attributed to en-slaved people was "natural to them and not originated by their state of slavery." Romans believed that the "perverse nature of this black race" made Africans a "naturally sub-jected species of mankind." See Romans, *A Concise Natural History of East and West-Florida* ... (New York, 1776), 105–107.

26. Anthony Benezet, *Some Historical Account of Guinea, Its Situation, Produce, and General Disposition of Its Inhabitants; with an Inquiry into the Rise and Progress of*

The exchange between slavery's antagonists and the institution's defenders regarding the nature of Africa and Africans manifests how black capacity for freedom was early established as a primary terrain on which the contest over slavery's abolition would be waged. In this exchange, slavery's defenders had a compelling card to play: republicanism. When they claimed that abolition imperiled the experiment in American republicanism, mid-Atlantic defenders of slavery once again drew on Revolutionary ideology. Pointing to the threat of black freedom and the unfitness of African Americans for citizenship gave the opponents of abolition formidable ideological artillery to combat antislavery. As Americans put in place a republican society dependent on the virtue of the people to govern themselves, slavery's defenders claimed that emancipating a people ill-suited for freedom would ruin American independence by subverting the liberties of the body politic and corrupting the fragile new Republic. In Pennsylvania, one writer warned that it was *"impolitic and dangerous"* to emancipate enslaved blacks and make them "free citizens." Abolition would "injure ourselves and them too," bringing "a new kind of bondage" wherein "theft, murder and rapine" by a people filled with "ignorance" and intent on enacting revenge for being held in slavery would roil the Republic.[27]

Opponents of emancipation in New York and New Jersey also relied heavily on making dire predictions of what black freedom would mean for republican America. A New York essayist contemptuously dismissed

---

the Slave-Trade, Its Nature and Lamentable Effects ... (Philadelphia, 1771), 1–2; [Benezet], *A Short Account of That Part of Africa, Inhabited by the Negroes; with Respect to the Fertility of the Country; the Good Disposition of Many of the Natives, and the Manner by Which the Slave Trade Is Carried on* ... (Philadelphia, 1762), 8, 51. That Benezet constructed these positive images of Africans through excerpting travel accounts beginning in 1762 shows he realized the immense task of overturning white prejudices early on in the debate over slavery. It also indirectly illustrates that whites in colonial America held negative conceptions of Africans long before slavery's apologists started denigrating African culture. For an incisive analysis of the ways Benezet selectively excerpted travel account narratives to combat negative depictions of Africans and African society, see Jonathan D. Sassi, "Africans in the Quaker Image: Anthony Benezet, African Travel Narratives, and Revolutionary-Era Antislavery," *Journal of Early Modern History*, X, nos. 1–2 (2006), 95–130. Sassi argues that Benezet created his depiction of Africans to fit the Quaker model of the virtuous individual. Although Benezet certainly imparted Quaker attributes to Africans in his writings, those attributes were also consonant with the ideals that many Americans in the Revolutionary era found desirable. Benezet's pamphlets caught the attention of slavery's proponents. Several of the defenders of slavery in the late eighteenth century disputed Benezet and his positive renderings of Africans in their pamphlets.

27. *Pennsylvania Journal*, Feb. 21, 1781. An antislavery writer replied to this piece in *Pennsylvania Journal*, Apr. 4, 1781.

any efforts at the emancipation of so many "villains and vagabonds" and dreaded the prospect of *"black republicans"* replete with "vice, roguery, [and] indolence" joining the ranks of civil society. "A Lover of True Justice," writing in the *New-Jersey Gazette,* lectured the public that *"the preserva-tion and interest of civil society ought to be regarded"* before New Jerseyans rushed to abolish slavery. If a people accustomed only to dependence and unfit for freedom were unleashed from slavery, the writer asked ominously, "What kind of a nation" would America become?[28]

Another defender of slavery in New Jersey, "Eliobo," outdid his fellow writers in painting a horrifying portrait of African American emancipation. Eliobo "denied" the "speculative notion" of abolitionists that "the spirits of Negroes can be operated upon by education." Those of African descent were naturally inferior to whites and ready-made for human bondage. By freeing enslaved people and "declar[ing] them intitled to the liberties of freemen," blacks would gain a misguided pride and look to "erect a king-dom and empire of their own." Having "returned to their native wildness and brutality," emancipated blacks would look to the "murder and rapine" of whites, leading the Republic to reverberate with the "shrieks and cries of murdered children and the lamentations of assassinated friends welter-ing in gore." Eliobo portrayed himself as the voice of reason, chiding aboli-tionists for not having "weighed into the consequences" of emancipation.[29]

Delaware's defenders of slavery likewise sounded alarm bells regarding the damage emancipation would do to the fledgling Republic. Stating that "nature has marked the line of distinction" between enslaved blacks and free whites "too strong to be erased," the essays of "Camillus" in the *Dela-ware Gazette* argued that emancipation would embolden the savagery of African Americans and bring "the black cloud of discord and confusion." The result would be "one general scene of rapine, and all the complicated horrors of a most cruel civil war." Camillus implored Americans "as patri-ots, as freemen" to "combat" abolitionism "under every form." Otherwise, "an ignorant an[d] unprincipled race" would "involve your country in mis-

28. *New-York Journal, and Patriotic Register,* Jan. 17, 1791, 19; *New-Jersey Gazette,* Feb. 14, 1781, [1].

29. *New-Jersey Journal* (Chatham), Dec. 27, 1780. See the antislavery response to these essays in the *New-Jersey Gazette,* Mar. 14, 1781, [1], Mar. 21, 1781, [1]; *New-Jersey Journal,* Jan. 10, 1781, [1]; *Loudon's New-York Packet,* Mar. 28, 1785, [2], Mar. 31, 1785, [3]; and *Argus,* Feb. 3, 1796, [2]. See, especially, the biting satirical response to Eliobo by "Eliobo Secundus" in the *New-Jersey Journal,* Jan. 10, 1781. The piece was penned by the Reverend Jacob Green, whose antislavery sermons had earlier been published in the state's newspapers.

rule." "Humanus" seconded these arguments when he wrote that "the person who manumits his negroes, does an essential injury to the neighbourhood where he lives." The writer believed that the "public good," which evidently worked against the freeing of a people in a state "altogether uncivilized," should be consulted before abolition took place. A third opponent of abolition in Delaware thought emancipation would "sever the bands of society, excite the Negroes to rebellion," and leave "government prostrate at the feet of barbarians," ready to wreak havoc.[30]

Although the arguments of these writers were hyperbolic, to a prejudiced American public, who over the course of the colonial era had come to view those of African descent as inferior beings and enemies of the state, they held a potentially potent resonance. Emphasizing the dangers of emancipation and the racial qualifications of American liberty allowed for slavery's defenders to sidestep a head-on battle with the mores of liberty and equality while still waging a vigorous war against them.

QUAKER ROOTS

Any origin story of American abolitionism must acknowledge the Society of Friends. Quakers played a generative role in the first abolition movement. Founded in England during the late 1640s, the Society of Friends was premised on religiously equalitarian ideals. Even though these ecclesiastical tenets seemed to leave no room for slavery in the Quaker sect, many Friends became both slave traders and slaveholders. Despite the hold of chattel bondage on Quakerism, pockets of protest to slaveholding among Friends did surface. But the Quaker Meetings that received

30. *Delaware Gazette* (Wilmington), Sept. 23, 1789, [1], Sept. 26, 1789, [2], Oct. 24, 1789, [1–2], Oct. 31, 1789, [1–2]. "A Plain Citizen" writing in the *Delaware Gazette*, Oct. 28, 1789, [1–2], evidenced how the defenders of slavery created a dichotomy between black slavery and black rule, and black subjugation or black equality, with no inbetween, effectively making emancipation a fatal choice for independent America: "To make them [blacks] good subjects, all the rights of freemen must be restored to them, if they are not, you make them turbulent and factious, if they are, you make them governors and masters." The debate over slavery in the *Delaware Gazette* started in response to a writer who questioned whether slaveholders should be representatives of the people in a free government. The discussion soon turned into a larger debate about emancipation, wherein slavery's defenders turned the ideals of republican self-government in their favor by claiming that black freemen would tear asunder the Republic. For the antislavery retort to these arguments, see the *Delaware Gazette*, Oct. 10 and Oct. 14, 1789, [1–2], and Nov. 7, 1789, [1–2]. Abolitionist writers countered the claims of slavery's defenders based on racial republicanism by arguing for inherent black equality, the universalism of natural rights, the fitness or capacity of African Americans for virtuous freedom, and the threat of slavery to the meaning of the Revolution.

remonstrances from dissenting members against Friends' selling, buying, or holding enslaved people took a slow and cautious approach to these entreaties. Opponents of slavery among the Society of Friends finally broke through in 1758. The Philadelphia Yearly Meeting's decision that year to deny leadership positions to members who bought, sold, or imported enslaved persons and its blanket condemnation of not only the slave trade but also of slaveholding in general set an influential precedent. In 1776, the Philadelphia Yearly Meeting came to the fateful decision to disown any remaining slaveholding Friends. This edict applied to Meetings in Pennsylvania, New Jersey, and Delaware, bringing the ultimate demise of chattel bondage among Quakers there. By 1783, the antislavery committees had reported that nearly all slaveholding Friends had either been disowned or forced to free their human property.[31]

One obstacle to ending slavery among Friends would become a perennial problem for the later, post-Revolutionary abolitionist movement: doubts

31. Beginning in the mid-eighteenth century, Quakers moved to purge slaveholding from the ranks of their society. The most common explanation historians give for the triumph of antislavery among Friends points to the Quakers' withdrawal from colonial politics during the Seven Years' War. When the pacifist axioms of the Friends caused them to stay neutral in the battle for European control of North America, the Quakers turned inward and underwent a critical period of self-searching that led them to return to their founding principles, so at odds with the practice of slavery. As they lost political power in Pennsylvania and were roundly castigated for their refusal to participate in the Seven Years' War, the Quakers remembered their beginnings in England as a persecuted minority sect and might have begun to identify more readily with the sufferings of the enslaved. Freed from the demands of colonial politics, Quakers began to reconnect with their radical sectarian roots, making themselves more open to the activism of reform-minded Friends. On the origins of and reasons for the Quaker reform movement beginning in the 1750s, see Thomas E. Drake, *Quakers and Slavery in America* (New Haven, Conn., 1950); Jean R. Soderlund, *Quakers and Slavery: A Divided Spirit* (Princeton, N.J., 1985); Sydney V. James, *A People among Peoples: Quaker Benevolence in Eighteenth-Century America* (Cambridge, Mass., 1963); Jack D. Marietta, *The Reformation of American Quakerism, 1748–1783* (Philadelphia, 1984); and Davis, *The Problem of Slavery in Western Culture*, 291–332. Another key factor in making Friends more open to antislavery might have been that slaveholders had a much reduced presence in the Society's leadership by the mid-eighteenth century, at least in Pennsylvania. Soderlund found for the Philadelphia Yearly Meeting that the share of slaveholders with leadership positions had shrunk by more than half—from 70 percent between 1681 and 1705 to 34.2 percent between 1731 and 1753 (Soderlund, *Quakers and Slavery*, 34). New York's Quakers moved more slowly than their mid-Atlantic neighbors. The New York Yearly Meeting first advocated the liberation of the enslaved in 1771, but it was not until 1787 that New York Friends were free of slaveholders. For the New York Yearly Meeting's struggle against slaveholding Friends, see James, *A People among People's*, 229–230; and Gellman, *Emancipating New York*, 28–29.

about the suitability of the enslaved for freedom. Fears about the presence of persons of African descent and their comportment can be found in the Quaker leadership's earliest statements on slavery. When enough individual Friends began urging Quaker authorities to address the issue of slavery by the end of the seventeenth century, the Philadelphia Yearly Meeting responded with a warning that Friends be "Careful not to Encourage the bringing in of any more Negroes," while, for those already in bondage, they recommended "Restrain[ing] them from Loose, and Lewd Living ... and from Rambling abroad." Once Quakers shifted from debating the slave trade to slavery, these trepidations about the character of persons of African descent remained. David Ferris, an antislavery member of the Wilmington Monthly Meeting of Delaware, believed that slaveholding Friends were skeptical of the ability of blacks to handle freedom. Ferris was certain that, if given "advantages for improv[e]ments" equal to whites and "the same Education," people of African descent would prove themselves more than capable of liberty. But he lamented that those "accustomed to Slave keeping can hardly believe it should be so." By the last third of the eighteenth century it became clear that antislavery Friends' efforts to end black slavery would have to take on reservations about black freedom.[32]

Partially in response to this obstacle to abolition, several Quaker Meetings urged the religious and educational instruction of formerly enslaved people who had been manumitted by slaveholding Friends. Quakers in New Jersey, Delaware, and Pennsylvania formed committees for the "improvement in the Knowledge of Truth, and the practice of Piety and Virtue" of recently liberated blacks. In 1770, the Philadelphia Monthly Meeting established a school for free black children with the hope of "qualify[ing]" freedpeople "for the proper enjoyment of freedom, and for becoming useful and worthy citizens." This preoccupation with educating the formerly en-

32. Minutes of the Yearly Meeting of the Pennsylvania and New Jersey Society of Friends, 1696, quoted in *The Ancient Testimony of the Religious Society of Friends, Commonly Called Quakers, respecting Some of Their Christian Doctrines and Practices; Revived and Given Forth by the Yearly Meeting, Held in Philadelphia in the Fourth Month, 1843* (Philadelphia, 1843), 8; David Ferris to James Rigby, Apr. 7, 1766, in J. William Frost, ed., *The Quaker Origins of Antislavery* (Norwood, Pa., 1980), 74, 182–186. For an interpretation that highlights fears of the presence of blacks in Pennsylvania as a major driver of Quaker antislavery, see Beverly C. Tomek, *Colonization and Its Discontents: Emancipation, Emigration, and Antislavery in Antebellum Pennsylvania* (New York, 2011), 18–43. For works that stress the radical origins and antiracist nature of Quaker antislavery, see Sinha, *The Slave's Cause*, 12–24; and Marcus Rediker, *The Fearless Benjamin Lay: The Quaker Dwarf Who Became the First Revolutionary Abolitionist* (Boston, 2017).

slaved and proving they were capable of equal freedom would come to form an essential strategy of the abolition societies of post-Revolutionary America, spearheaded by Quakers.[33]

Antislavery Quakers believed they could persuade Friends to dissociate from slavery and recognize the equal humanity of black people by visiting with and persuading individuals to abandon chattel bondage. The itinerant activist John Woolman reflected on his visits to Friends who held enslaved laborers. Born in 1720 to a New Jersey Quaker family, John Woolman trained as a tailor and was on track to live the typical commercial life of a middling Quaker. But, when he was asked one day to draft a bill of sale for a fellow Quaker's enslaved woman, Woolman was troubled by the thought of playing a role in the selling of "one of my fellow-creatures." His conscience pricked, Woolman became an itinerant Quaker reformer tirelessly seeking to persuade slaveholding Friends to liberate their bondspersons. In December 1758, Woolman reported that he had entered some "sharp conflicts" with those slaveholding Quakers "who were grievously entangled by the spirit of this world." On other occasions, Woolman characterized these meetings as bringing out a "true sympathizing tenderness of heart." Following the example set by John Woolman's journeys to the homes of slaveholders, several Quaker Meetings created committees to visit slaveholding Friends and sway them to release their bondspersons. The committees grappled with thorny issues, such as at what age enslaved persons should be freed, how ready persons of color were for freedom, and manumission laws requiring costly bonds for the release of the enslaved. A belief in the efficacy of moral suasion, combined with a commitment to confront slaveholders, would go on to inform the abolitionist organizations Quakers would later initiate.[34]

33. James, *A People among Peoples,* 233–234; *A Brief Sketch of the Schools for Black People and Their Descendants, Established by the Religious Society of Friends in 1770* (Philadelphia, 1867), 3, quoted in Nancy Slocum Hornick, "Anthony Benezet and the Africans' School: Toward a Theory of Full Equality," *Pennsylvania Magazine of History and Biography,* XCIX (1975), 404. The attention of Quakers to the religious and educational development of the formerly enslaved came not only from a desire to counter the prejudices of slaveholders but also from a sense of responsibility within the sect for the welfare of persons of color after they were liberated. See James, *A People among Peoples,* 231–238.

34. *The Journal of John Woolman; with an Introduction by John G. Whittier* (Boston, 1871), 64, 141–142. On Woolman's life and antislavery activism, see Drake, *Quakers and Slavery,* 51–62; and Thomas P. Slaughter, *The Beautiful Soul of John Woolman, Apostle of Abolition* (New York, 2008). On the Quaker committees to visit slaveholders, see James, *A People among Peoples,* 225–226; Arthur Zilversmit, *The First Emancipation: The Abolition of Slavery in the North* (Chicago, 1967), 75–77; and Geoffrey Plank,

Over the course of a century, antislavery Friends developed and refined an antislavery discourse that would help to define the principles of post-Revolutionary and early national organized abolitionism. The Quakers' paramount theological principle, the Inner Light, assumed every person, regardless of gender, race, creed, or other earthly distinctions, possessed an inborn spirit that rendered all souls equal before God. The concept was based on the biblical passage, "That was the true light, which lighteth every man that cometh into the world," communicating a divinely inspired imperative of basic equality and human sameness. One seminal early Quaker antislavery statement came from Germantown Friends. In 1688, Friends of German and Dutch origin who had established the Quaker settlement of Germantown outside Philadelphia introduced a humanitarian argument against slavery that reverberated for generations. Their petition, intended for the Quaker Meetings of Pennsylvania, criticized the racial lines of slavery, determining that it made "no difference" what "descent or colour" enslaved people were, for "tho they are black, we can not conceive there is more liberty to have them slaves, as it is to have other white ones." The Germantown protest pressed Quakers who partook in the enslaving of Africans to ask themselves "if you would be done" in "this manner"—a biblical reference to the Golden Rule that later antislavery writers would repeat.[35]

John Woolman's Path to the Peaceable Kingdom: A Quaker in the British Empire (Philadelphia, 2012), 117–119.

35. Garrey Henderich et al., "This Is to Ye Monthly Meeting Hold at Rigert Warrells," known as the "Germantown Protest," 1688, Quaker and Special Collections, Haverford College Library, Haverford, Pa.; excerpts from the "Germantown Protest" in Katharine Gerbner, "Antislavery in Print: The Germantown Protest, the 'Exhortation,' and the Seventeenth-Century Quaker Debate on Slavery," *Early American Studies*, IX (2011), 559–563. Other antislavery protests and petitions by individual Quakers in this early period reflected similar themes, including those by George Keith and the Christian Quakers John Hepburn and William Southeby. See Keith, *An Exhortation and Caution to Friends concerning Buying or Keeping of Negroes* (New York, 1693); Hepburn, *The American Defence of the Christian Golden Rule; or, An Essay to Prove the Unlawfulness of Making Slaves of Men; by Him Who Loves the Freedom of the Souls and Bodies of All Men* ([New York], 1715); Kenneth L. Carroll, "William Southeby, Early Quaker Antislavery Writer," *PMHB*, LXXXIX (1965), 416–427; and Nicholas P. Wood and Jean R. Soderlund, "'To Friends and All Whom It May Concerne': William Southeby's Rediscovered 1696 Antislavery Protest," *PMHB*, CXLI (2017), 177–198. Perhaps the most influential of early Quaker antislavery figures was Benjamin Lay, whose radical strain of abolitionist activism is chronicled in Rediker, *The Fearless Benjamin Lay*. Brycchan Carey traces what he calls "a coherent discourse of antislavery" in Quaker texts between the late seventeenth and mid-eighteenth centuries. Although historians traditionally begin their analyses of Quaker antislavery discourse in the 1750s, Carey instead argues for the

The Germantown protest presaged enduring Quaker antislavery literary themes. But, when a later generation of Quaker activists constructed
antislavery arguments, they did not look solely within their own religious
sect for inspiration. Melding Quaker theology with enlightenment thought
and Revolutionary ideology, activist Friends of the late eighteenth century created an antislavery medley based on restoring enslaved blacks to
their natural freedom and providing persons of African descent with the
rights of free persons that would go on to infuse the post-Revolutionary
abolition movement. Quaker mores and enlightenment and Revolutionary ideals shared much in common. The Quakers' sense of the Inner Light
gelled with the enlightenment conception of the inner moral sense. Quaker
doctrine described the Inner Light as capable of "illuminating" the individual's "understanding and assisting him to distinguish good from evil."
The Scottish enlightenment belief in the inner moral sense similarly held
that all people had "a general approbation of benevolence" waiting to be
tapped. The enlightenment's rejection of custom as serving to perpetuate irrational, unjust institutions and societal practices meshed with the
Quakers' long-standing distrust of both religious and social customs as
impure agents of worldly corruption. Quaker antislavery writers often presented slavery as an oppressive custom to which people must apply their
Inner Light and moral sense. Fortified by these currents of thought, antislavery Friends sought to persuade Quakers, and then American society, to
abandon slavery while convincing them that emancipated blacks could be
made into responsible free persons.[36]

Enlightenment and Revolutionary rhetoric of natural rights had a profound influence on Quaker perceptions of slavery. In one of their first pro-
nouncements against human bondage, the New York Yearly Meeting exclaimed in 1769 that enslaved blacks were "rational creatures" and had

---

relevance of an earlier history of Quaker antislavery thought, linking several generations of writing hostile to slavery among activist Friends (Carey, *From Peace to Freedom*).

36. [Anthony Benezet], *A Short Account of the People Called Quakers; Their Rise,
Religious Principles, and Settlement in America; Mostly Collected from Different Authors, for the Information of All Serious Inquirers, Particularly Foreigners* (Philadelphia, 1780), 11. For the congruence between the Inner Light and inner moral sense and
Quaker theology and enlightenment thought generally, see Ned C. Landsman, *From
Colonials to Provincials: American Thought and Culture, 1680–1760* (Ithaca, N.Y., 1997),
71–77. Following Caroline Winterer's lead, I do not capitalize the term *enlightenment*,
which avoids presenting enlightenment thought and expression as part of a unitary
movement and subsequently helps to allow for interpreting first movement abolitionism as a form of enlightenment in America. See Winterer, *American Enlightenments:
Pursuing Happiness in the Age of Reason* (New Haven, Conn., 2016).

been "by Nature born free." Five years later, the Philadelphia Yearly Meeting issued a formal statement saying that slavery was "evidently contrary to our Christian Principles ... and the common Rights of Mankind." The Philadelphia Meeting then wrote to neighboring Meetings that "restoring" the enslaved to their "natural and just Right to Liberty" should be on the agenda of all Quakers. Across the Atlantic, the London Yearly Meeting similarly declaimed against slavery for suspending the "natural rights of mankind" and relegating persons of color to "oppressive and unnatural bondage." Whereas nature had previously represented the sinful state of fallen man, by the 1760s and 1770s Quaker antislavery writers started to depict nature positively and natural liberty as a Godly ordained state to which enslaved people must be restored.[37]

Anthony Benezet, a foremost figure in the Friends' antislavery movement, embodies the interaction between Quaker sectarian values and enlightenment and Revolutionary principles. Arriving in Philadelphia in 1731, the eighteen-year-old Benezet was soon drawn to the Quakerism of Pennsylvania. Born in France to Huguenot parents, Benezet chose not to follow his father and two of his siblings when they converted to the Moravian faith, pledging himself instead to the Society of Friends. After an extended foray in the family mercantile business, Benezet left the life of worldly gain behind. Pledging himself to the philanthropic spirit sweeping Quakerism, Benezet became a schoolmaster and educator as well as the most prolific antislavery pamphleteer of the eighteenth century. In relying on biblical principles like the Golden Rule and arguing that slavery violated God's love for the entirety of humankind, Benezet grounded his antislavery writings in Quaker interpretations of Christian morality.[38]

37. James, *A People among Peoples*, 222; New England Yearly Meeting Minutes, 1774, and London Yearly Meeting Minutes, 1760 and 1772, in Frost, ed., *The Quaker Origins of Antislavery*, 174, 240–241. My depiction of the changed beliefs of the Society of Friends in their understanding of the nature of humanity and the important influence of natural rights ideology over Quaker antislavery comes from James, *A People among Peoples*, 222–225. The blending of enlightenment and Revolutionary rhetorical ideals with Quaker mores is particularly evident in the petitions antislavery Friends submitted to state and national governments in the 1780s and 1790s—an unsurprising fact considering that these petitions aimed to speak to a non-Quaker audience. For illustrative examples, see Nash, *Warner Mifflin*, 122, 128, 136, 146.

38. Maurice Jackson, *Let This Voice Be Heard: Anthony Benezet, Father of Atlantic Abolitionism* (Philadelphia, 2009), 2–9. For an analysis of Quaker antislavery texts that presents the humanitarian arguments of Friends hostile to human bondage as concerned with the sin and moral guilt of slaveholders and traders rather than the rights of enslaved blacks, see Margaret Abruzzo, *Polemical Pain: Slavery, Cruelty, and the Rise*

Benezet, however, also positioned his arguments in the realm of enlightenment thought, citing or excerpting a panoply of enlightenment thinkers in his antislavery publications. As early as 1766, Benezet realized the powerful boost proto-Revolutionary rhetoric gave to antislavery advocates when he published *A Caution and Warning to Great Britain and Her Colonies.* Benezet alerted those on both sides in the imperial political struggle that "at a time when the general rights and liberties of mankind" were "subjects of universal consideration" it behooved the "Advocates of Liberty" to admit that only "tyrant custom" rationalized leaving blacks in their present state of bondage.[39]

Other Quaker antislavery activists leaped at the opportune moment provided by the Revolution to stretch the relevance of their writings beyond the Society of Friends. David Cooper, a New Jersey Quaker, wrote two anonymous pamphlets using Revolutionary rhetoric to call on Americans to live up to their lofty ideals. Cooper cited John Locke's definition of the law of nature as prohibiting the "absolute arbitrary power" of one man over another. He insisted that "Every man has a property in his own person." Cooper excerpted the Declaration of Independence and several of the state constitutions. He asserted that the high-minded proclamations of liberty and equality in these cherished documents applied with the same force to enslaved Africans. Already influenced by enlightenment thought

----

of Humanitarianism (Baltimore, 2011), 16–49. Quaker antislavery writers were especially bothered by what they saw as the inherently sinful actions required of individuals involved in slave trading and slaveholding. But many of the humanitarian themes that their texts touched on were concerned with the rights and condition of people of African descent.

39. To prove that the desire for freedom was natural and universal among all people, Benezet looked to the father of Scottish moral philosophy, Francis Hutcheson. To show that no man could rightfully claim ownership over another, he turned to the enlightened jurist George Wallace. To substantiate slavery's detrimental effects on civil society, he quoted the famed French philosophe Montesquieu. And to demonstrate that slavery had unreasonably prejudiced white Americans toward enslaved blacks, Benezet relied on the enlightenment literary figure Abbé Raynal. See Anthony Benezet, *A Caution and a Warning to Great Britain and Her Colonies; in A Short Representation of the Calamitous State of the Enslaved Negroes in the British Dominions ...* (Philadelphia, 1766), 3, 22–26; [Benezet], *A Short Account of That Part of Africa,* 22–26; and Benezet, *Short Observations on Slavery, Introductory to Some Extracts from the Writing of the Abbe Raynal, on That Important Subject* ([Philadelphia, circa 1783]), 8–12. For additional analyses of the influence enlightenment thought and natural rights theory had on Benezet's antislavery writing, see David L. Crosby, "Anthony Benezet's Transformation of Anti-Slavery Rhetoric," *Slavery and Abolition,* XXIII, no. 3 (2002), 39–58; Roger A. Bruns, "Anthony Benezet and the Natural Rights of the Negro," *PMHB,* XCVI (1972), 104–113; and Jackson, *Let This Voice Be Heard,* 57–61.

and Revolutionary ideas, Quaker antislavery activism had now been seamlessly inserted into the discourse of mainstream America.[40]

The near century-long struggle of reformist Quakers to rid their sect of
slaveholding highlights the long-standing presence of Quaker antislavery
in the mid-Atlantic, even as it foreshadows themes that would eventually compose key elements of the first abolition movement in the United
States. Blazing a long and bumpy, but ultimately successful, road to intra-
Quaker emancipation primed antislavery Quakers to maintain a patient
and steady optimism about the viability of eventually abolishing slavery
outside their sect. This faith that the battle against human bondage could
be won imbued the abolition societies that Friends would play a central
role in founding.

THE ABOLITION SOCIETIES AND THE
ETHIC OF IMPROVEMENT

The 1770s opened a path to a larger antislavery movement outside the
Society of Friends that had not previously existed. To translate the growing, if minority, view of human bondage as a problematic institution, the
opponents of American slavery founded abolition societies. The two most
influential of the abolition societies of the post-Revolutionary and early
national eras were the Pennsylvania Abolition Society (PAS) and the New-
York Manumission Society (NYMS). The PAS began life in 1775 as the Society for the Relief of Free Negroes Unlawfully Held in Bondage. Inspired
by the case of Dinah Nevil, who, along with her children, was held illegally
in slavery, ten men (seven of whom were Quakers) met at Philadelphia's
Sun Tavern and started an organization to aid individuals illicitly enslaved.
Although forced to disband during the war years, the society met and reconstituted itself at the urging of Anthony Benezet in 1784.[41]

40. [David Cooper], *A Mite Cast into the Treasury; or, Observations on Slave-Keeping*
(Philadelphia, 1772), iii, 19, 23; Cooper, *A Serious Address to the Rulers of America, on
the Inconsistency of Their Conduct respecting Slavery: Forming a Contrast between the
Encroachments of England on American Liberty, and, American Injustice in Tolerating
Slavery* (Trenton, N.J., 1783), 5–20.

41. Wayne J. Eberly, "The Pennsylvania Abolition Society, 1775–1830" (Ph.D. diss.,
Pennsylvania State University, 1973), 22–27; Nash and Soderlund, *Freedom by Degrees*,
114–118. Dinah Nevil's suit for her freedom and that of her four children, guided by
local Quakers, was unsuccessful. But Thomas Harrison, a founding member of the PAS,
bought and set at liberty Nevil and her two surviving children following the Revolutionary War. For what is known about Nevil and the importance of her case to the founding of the PAS, see Kirsten Sword, "Remembering Dinah Nevil: Strategic Deceptions in
Eighteenth-Century Antislavery," *Journal of American History*, XCVII (2010), 315–343.

During the Confederation period, the PAS pursued a bevy of initiatives. The society aided blacks who had already gained their freedom with educational and economic assistance, provided legal representation to individual bondspersons who had fled to Pennsylvania from the bordering slave states of Maryland and Virginia, lodged legal challenges on behalf of formerly enslaved people kidnapped into bondage, and pressured the Pennsylvania legislature to enforce the state's 1780 Act for the Gradual Abolition of Slavery. The PAS reorganized again in 1787 as the Pennsylvania Society for Promoting the Abolition of Slavery, and the Relief of Free Negroes, Unlawfully Held in Bondage. A combination of a growing membership and the creation of a new national government with potentially broad powers over slavery encouraged the PAS to broaden its activism. The society now sought to directly influence public opinion by publishing antislavery literature and establishing a presence in the social and political spheres of early national America. When the PAS added the cultivation of black freedom to its agenda in 1789, it put "Improving the Condition of Free Blacks" at the end of the society's name, rechristening itself for the final time. Beginning as a relief organization for the illegally enslaved, the PAS had enlarged its aims to abolishing slavery beyond Pennsylvania's borders and buttressing black liberty by uplifting free persons of color.[42]

Not far behind the PAS in organizational scope was the NYMS. On January 25, 1785, a group of New York's leading merchants, bankers, judges, and lawyers (many of them Quakers) gathered in the home of innkeeper John Simmons to found the New-York Society for Promoting the Manumission of Slaves, and Protecting Such of Them as Have Been, or May Be Liberated. The ostensible motivation for the society's formation came from the "Violent Attempts lately made to seize, and export for Sale, several free negroes." The NYMS, like its sister organization the PAS, would expend much of its energies working with black New Yorkers to defend African American liberty and enforce antislavery laws. From its inception, however, the NYMS

42. Eberly, "The Pennsylvania Abolition Society," 22–31; Nash and Soderlund, *Freedom by Degrees*, 114–124. In "Remembering Dinah Nevil," *JAH*, XCVII (2010), 315–343, Kirsten Sword argues that, when the PAS reorganized itself in 1787, it erased its earlier history as an agent of black liberty that combined the efforts of white and black activists. In taking on a broader national agenda, she argues, the PAS reinvented itself as a national entity with politically elite white male members. It is true that Quaker leaders of PAS strategically sought to broaden the appeal of the organization to the public at large and looked to gain powerful allies to advance their antislavery agenda. Yet the records of the PAS do not reveal any disjunction between the pre- and post-1787 years, other than that the society was expanding its agenda, not moving away from aiding wrongfully enslaved blacks or ceasing to work with African Americans to realize emancipation.

had additional goals. In a preamble to its administrative rules and regulations, the society announced its intentions to not only set the state's bondspersons free but also to "enable them to share, equally with us, in that civil and religious Liberty with which an indulgent Providence has blessed these States; and to which these, our Brethren are by nature, as much entitled as ourselves." The NYMS's founders believed that the rights and liberties attendant with freedom should not be defined along the lines of race.[43]

Although the NYMS's name seemed to signal that its members favored the manumission of enslaved people rather than the abolition of slavery, it was a misnomer. Immediately after forming, the NYMS petitioned the state legislature for a gradual abolition act and continued to push for an emancipation law until finding success in 1799. The NYMS diligently lobbied for gradual abolition and pressed for legislation that would prohibit the exportation of the enslaved outside the state, limit the rights of slaveholders, and expand the purview of antislavery laws to grant liberty to as many enslaved people as possible. Like the PAS, the NYMS also paid heed to the condition of free blacks. In 1787, the NYMS established the African Free School, which provided education for hundreds of free black New Yorkers. The NYMS believed the African Free School would display to the public that persons of color were as capable of learned and righteous freedom as their white brethren.[44]

Together the PAS and the NYMS made up the organizational marrow of first movement abolitionism, but these two societies did not stand alone.

43. New-York Manumission Society (NYMS) Records, 1785–1849, VI, 3–4, New-York Historical Society; Davis, *The Problem of Slavery in the Age of Revolution*, 239–240. It has been estimated that twelve of the first eighteen members present at the founding of the NYMS were Quakers. See T. Robert Moseley, "A History of the New-York Manumission Society, 1785–1849" (Ph.D. diss., New York University, 1963), 85.

44. Moseley, "A History of the New-York Manumission Society," 20–21; Gellman, *Emancipating New York*, 56–57. The NYMS admitted slaveholding members. Quaker leaders of the NYMS, hoping to attract a socially and politically prominent membership, might have been willing to overlook slaveholding in their society—especially if these members indicated that they would gradually free their enslaved laborers. Nevertheless, allowing for slaveholders in the NYMS caused internal disagreement. In 1809, the NYMS banned slaveholders from the society (Moseley, "A History of the New-York Manumission Society," 23–24). That the NYMS permitted slaveholding among their members should not detract from their activism or raise questions regarding the goals of the society. As Chapters 2 and 3 of this book make clear, the NYMS unequivocally worked for slavery's abolition. For an interpretation of the NYMS that uses the admittance of slaveholders to openly question whether the society advocated for the abolition of slavery, see Shane White, *Somewhat More Independent: The End of Slavery in New York City, 1770–1810* (Athens, Ga., 1991), 81–86.

The post-Revolutionary years generated a groundswell of antislavery organizational activity sprinkled throughout the New England, mid-Atlantic, and upper southern states. By 1793, abolition societies existed in Rhode Island, Connecticut, Delaware, Maryland, Virginia, western parts of Pennsylvania, and New Jersey. The activities and goals of these societies differed according to the various local antislavery exigencies facing state activists. In Rhode Island, long the northern capital of the transatlantic slave trade, antislavery forces focused on eliminating the slave trade after helping to enact a gradual emancipation act in the state in 1784. In western Pennsylvania, the Washington County Abolition Society, located in the southwest corner of the state, concentrated on assisting formerly enslaved people whose tenuous hold on freedom was threatened by slave catchers eager to reenslave them. In 1790, the Virginia Quaker Robert Pleasants formed an abolition society headquartered in Richmond and urged nonslaveholding Virginians to join him in transferring private manumission efforts into public policy. The PAS and NYMS helped found abolition societies in New Jersey and Delaware. Although lacking the clout of their Pennsylvanian and New York analogues, the New Jersey and Delaware abolition societies advocated emancipation in their respective states and guarded and enlarged the rights of enslaved and free blacks.[45]

Looking to expand their activities beyond the local level, the PAS and NYMS attempted to take their abolitionist formula of black uplift to a national stage. In March 1793, the NYMS dispatched a circular letter to its sister groups, stretching from Connecticut to Virginia, requesting that they send delegates to a national convention of the abolition societies. With the

45. For the Rhode Island Abolition Society, see John Wood Sweet, *Bodies Politic: Negotiating Race in the American North, 1730–1830* (Baltimore, 2003), 251–263; and Charles Rappleye, *Sons of Providence: The Brown Brothers, the Slave Trade, and the American Revolution* (New York, 2006), 305–309. On the Maryland Abolition Society, see Anita Aidt Guy, "The Maryland Abolition Society and the Promotion of the Ideals of the New Nation," *Maryland Historical Magazine*, LXXXIV (1989), 342–349. For the New Jersey Abolition Society, see Gigantino, *The Ragged Road to Abolition*, 77–82. On the Virginia Abolition Society, see Wolf, *Race and Liberty in the New Nation*, 9–10. On the Connecticut Abolition Society, see Peter P. Hinks, "'It Is at the Extremest Risque If We Still Hold Fast to the Accursed Thing': Connecticut's Abolition Bill of 1794, the New Divinity, and Antislavery in the Late Eighteenth Century Atlantic World," paper presented at the conference "Yale, New Haven, and American Slavery," Yale University, Sept. 27, 2002. For the Delaware abolition societies, see Gordon E. Finnie, "The Antislavery Movement in the Upper South before 1840," *Journal of Southern History*, XXXV (1969), 320–322; and Monte A. Calvert, "The Abolition Society of Delaware, 1801–1807," *Delaware History*, X (1963), 295–320.

intent of forming a more united antislavery front that could coordinate a spectrum of activities, from petitioning the federal Congress for antislavery and slave trade legislation to coordinating resources for the protection of free blacks from kidnapping, the NYMS urged the societies to come together in promoting the "great cause of their oppressed Fellow Creatures the African race." When society delegates met in Philadelphia in January 1794, they inaugurated the first American Convention for Promoting the Abolition of Slavery and Improving the Condition of the African Race, a body that would continue to convene sporadically until 1837. Between 1794 and 1806, the Convention met annually, except for 1799 and 1802. It was during this twelve-year period that the body also enjoyed its greatest influence, pressing the New York and New Jersey legislatures to enact gradual emancipation laws, successfully lobbying Congress to ban the participation of Americans in the foreign slave trade, and gaining the attention of free black audiences receptive to its program of social and economic uplift.[46]

Membership in the abolition societies was dominated by Quakers. To conclude that these organizations were simply bastions of Quaker sectarian activism, however, would be to overlook the currency of antislavery in the early national period and to misread the ideological framework within which the abolition societies operated. Antislavery Friends initiated the establishment of both the NYMS and PAS. Quakers also were often the most involved members of the abolition societies. Friends made up at least 75 percent of the most active members of the PAS and at least half of those most active in the NYMS. Yet the PAS and the NYMS also enlisted members of the political vanguard. Having already brought politically weighty Americans like Benjamin Rush and Tench Coxe into the organizational fold, when the PAS reorganized for a second time in 1787 it named Benjamin Franklin as its president. In the NYMS, such political luminaries as Alexander Hamilton, Noah Webster, and Egbert Benson along with three of the state's first four governors—George Clinton, John Jay, and Daniel Tompkins—all were either present at the NYMS's founding or manned high-ranking positions in the society. The inclusion of such national dignitaries partially represents an attempt by the Quakers, who were socially and politically marginal-

46. For a comprehensive treatment of the American Convention, see Robert Duane Sayre, "The Evolution of Early American Abolitionism: The American Convention for Promoting the Abolition of Slavery and Improving the Condition of the African Race, 1794–1837" (Ph.D. diss., Ohio State University, 1987). The Convention took on an exclusively mid-Atlantic, regional composition from 1803 until 1817, when upper southern abolition societies reemerged, driving the controversial issue of colonization onto the American Convention's agenda.

ized by their neutrality during the Revolutionary War, to give their societies popular credence. But the choice of these luminaries to accept membership in the societies, and the fact that some of them served as more than mere figureheads, reflects that by the early national period antislavery in the mid-Atlantic had moved far beyond the religious fringes.[47]

The cachet of antislavery among reform-minded figures in the early national mid-Atlantic aside, the abolition societies did not constitute anything like a mass movement. The membership rolls of the PAS and NYMS numbered in the hundreds. Soon after the founding of the NYMS, the society had gained more than two hundred supporters. The PAS enjoyed its highest enrollment numbers between the late 1780s and mid-1790s, with between sixty and ninety persons annually elected to society membership. Between 1775 and 1840, roughly twelve hundred people were elected members of the PAS. The NYMS and PAS membership numbers, however, are not an accurate indicator of involvement in these societies. Those elected for membership in the PAS did not always join the society and, even when they did, could remain inactive participants. The number of NYMS members who regularly attended the society's quarterly meetings was no more than about twenty. If judging participation in the NYMS and PAS by the immersion of individuals in various committees (where the activism of the societies was carried out), the count of active members shrinks even further. Therefore, a small contingent of highly committed activists animated the abolition societies.[48]

The motivating spirit and activist strategy of the abolition societies blended Quaker benevolence and enlightenment values. These two influences are exemplified in the reformism of Anthony Benezet and Benjamin

47. Davis, *The Problem of Slavery in the Age of Revolution*, 216–217. For John Jay's and Alexander Hamilton's involvement in the early years of the NYMS, see Moseley, "A History of the New-York Manumission Society," 37–38. Hamilton served the NYMS in several capacities during the initial years of the society's existence. He was a member of at least four committees and served as a legal counselor. Jay was pivotal in helping to provide political clout to the NYMS, connecting the society to the state government through his governorship in the late 1790s. Daniel Tompkins would go on to be instrumental in the passage of a law mandating the total abolition of slavery by 1827 while serving as governor of New York in 1817. The PAS's efforts in 1787 to broaden the organization brought prominent non-Quaker members like Franklin (who was mostly a figurehead) and other politically prominent and wealthy individuals, but their participation did not last very long (Nash and Soderlund, *Freedom by Degrees*, 130–131). Two exceptions to this pattern were Tench Coxe and, especially, Benjamin Rush, both of whom were members of the PAS before 1787.

48. Eberly, "The Pennsylvania Abolition Society, 1775–1830," 49–52; Gellman, *Emancipating New York*, 56; Moseley, "A History of the New-York Manumission Society," 52.

Rush. Benezet's benevolence knew few bounds. He not only opposed slavery but argued against war, advocated for the fair treatment of Native Americans, and pushed for a more progressive system of education that substituted moral suasion for corporal punishment. Perhaps stemming from his family's experience as a persecuted religious minority, Benezet possessed a peculiarly sensitive disposition that made him acutely aware of the agony of others. He refused to eat meat, believing that one living creature should not depend on the suffering of another. No suffering touched Benezet more than that of Philadelphia's blacks. His house was located not far from the city's slave-trading markets, and the brutality and inhumanity of chattel bondage left an indelible mark on the Quaker reformer. Benezet devoted himself to befriending the black community. He learned of their grievances, assisted them whenever possible, and championed their rights. Though he did not live to partake in much of the PAS's activism, Benezet's compassion for the concerns of enslaved and free blacks would be carried on by the most committed members of the abolition societies, many of whom were also Quakers.[49]

Benjamin Rush's fervor for reforming American society matched that of his friend Benezet (see Figure 3). Born near Philadelphia in 1746, Rush received medical training in Scotland before returning to the City of Brotherly Love, where he established a medical practice and eventually became the most prominent physician in America. When the Revolution arrived, Rush served in the Continental Congress and acted as a surgeon in the Continental army. These experiences instilled in Rush a patriotic zeal for the future of newly independent America. The Revolution, in Rush's eyes, had broken with the ancient iniquities of Europe and opened the way for reformers to create a new society based on principles of republican equality. Influenced by the enlightenment's commitment to social progress and the perfectibility of human nature, post-Revolutionary reformers confidently went about trying to remake society. Rush was at the head of this movement. First brought to the fight against slavery by Benezet, Rush joined the PAS in 1784 and later served as president of a national convention of abolition societies. Flush with an optimism born of the reform spirit of his

49. Jackson, *Let This Voice Be Heard*, 18–19. For a sampling of some of Benezet's non-antislavery reformist publications, see Anthony Benezet, *Thoughts on the Nature of War, and Its Repugnancy to the Christian Life* ... (Philadelphia, 1766); [Benezet], *The Mighty Destroyer Displayed, in Some Account of the Dreadful Havoc Made by the Mistaken Use as Well as Abuse of Distilled Spirituous Liquors* (Philadelphia, 1774); and Benezet, *The Pennsylvania Spelling Book; or, Youth's Friendly Instructor and Monitor* ... (Philadelphia, 1779).

FIGURE 3. *Dr. Benjamin Rush.* By Charles Willson Peale, 1783–1836.
Philadelphia. Oil paint on canvas. Gift of Mrs. Julia B. Henry, 1959.160.
Courtesy, Winterthur Museum

age, Rush foresaw "some great revolution in behalf of our oppressed Negro brethren" that would lead ultimately to the abolition of slavery.[50]

50. Carl Binger, *Revolutionary Doctor: Benjamin Rush, 1746–1813* (New York, 1966); Gordon S. Wood, *Empire of Liberty: A History of the Early Republic, 1789–1815* (Oxford, 2009), 469–479; Rush to William Peterkin, Nov. 27, 1784, in L. H. Butterfield, "Further Letters of Benjamin Rush," *PMHB*, LXXVIII (1954), 26; Benjamin Rush to Gran-

The optimistic outlook of reformers like Rush gestures to a greater ethic of reform. The emergence of organized abolition in the final decades of the eighteenth century was part of a larger body of social movements that blossomed following American independence. An amalgam of Christianity-based philanthropic impulses and enlightenment ideals of the ability of humans to improve and reform their societies touched off the initiation of a dizzying array of movements and aid societies. From providing poor relief, to making prisons rehabilitative rather than punitive, to standardizing education, to improving the efficiency of agriculture, to aiding orphans and widows, to the resuscitation of drowning victims, the urge to reform newly independent America spread far and wide. Two currents of thought connected these efforts. First, a republican America without monarchy required an enlightened populace for which the degradation of social ills like poverty, slavery, and ignorance would have to be relieved. Second, a faith in the idea that the new United States was already improving and capable of being further improved underlay all early national reform movements. This commitment to and faith in improvement married well with the perspective of reformers, most of whom enjoyed a great deal of social authority and economic status that had only increased with American independence. These lawyers, medical professionals, merchants, ministers, professors, and bankers projected "a broad, optimistic outlook of progressive changes" onto post-Revolutionary America that told them they could remake their societies in what they saw as enlightened ways.[51]

-----

ville Sharp, Oct. 29, 1773 (quotation), in John A. Woods, ed., "The Correspondence of Benjamin Rush and Granville Sharp, 1773–1809," *Journal of American Studies*, I (1967), 3, 13. Rush involved himself in a host of post-Revolutionary-era reform movements, including temperance, female education, penal reform, the cessation of both corporal and capital punishment, and ending the practice of dueling, among others.

51. Amanda B. Moniz, *From Empire to Humanity: The American Revolution and the Origins of Humanitarianism* (New York, 2016), 85. For an overview of the influences and impulses that informed late-eighteenth- and early-nineteenth-century American reform, see Moniz, *From Empire to Humanity*; Steven Mintz, *Moralists and Modernizers: America's Pre-Civil War Reformers* (Baltimore, 1995); and Wood, *Empire of Liberty*, 469–507. On poverty and poor relief in the early Republic, see Billy G. Smith, ed., *Down and Out in Early America* (University Park, Pa., 2004); John K. Alexander, *Render Them Submissive: Responses to Poverty in Philadelphia, 1760–1800* (Amherst, Mass., 1980); and Seth Rockman, *Welfare Reform in the Early Republic: A Brief History with Documents* (Long Grove, Ill., 2003). For prison reform, see Michael Meranze, *Laboratories of Virtue: Punishment, Revolution, and Authority in Philadelphia, 1760–1835* (Williamsburg, Va., and Chapel Hill, N.C., 1996); Mark E. Kann, *Punishment, Prisons, and Patriarchy: Liberty and Power in the Early American Republic* (New York, 2005); and Jen Manion, *Liberty's Prisoners: Carceral Culture in Early America* (Philadelphia,

These trends in post-Revolutionary social reform are evident in the viewpoints of abolition society members. For example, the Friendly Club of New York City, a literary association that included ministers, merchants, elected officials, and writers, contributed seven members to the NYMS. Premised on the elitism of intellectual exchange, the Friendly Club aspired to spread, through social activism, the ideals of human improvement and societal betterment that participants discussed during sessions of learned conversation. William Dunlap, a respected playwright as well as a member of the Friendly Club and the NYMS, saw the theatrical performances he penned not primarily as a mode of entertainment but also as a vehicle for the moral and civic improvement of the American public. Dunlap believed he was espying an era in which "the mind of man is expanding to receive the whole light of truth, and enjoy the whole beauty of benevolence." It was a small step for Dunlap then to imagine that men like him could enlighten the minds of formerly enslaved people and those who opposed emancipation, resulting in the white public recognizing the error of its prejudices against black freedom.[52]

Other abolition society members illustrate how organized antislavery in early national America was enmeshed within a broader culture of reform. Thomas Eddy, heavily involved with the NYMS in its first years, engaged with several philanthropic causes. His economic status secured by the fortune he had made as a financier, Eddy turned to bettering the society

---

2015). For educational reform, see Carl F. Kaestle, *Pillars of the Republic: Common Schools and American Society, 1780–1860* (New York, 1983). On the movement to resuscitate drowning victims, see Amanda Bowie Moniz, "Saving the Lives of Strangers: Humane Societies and the Cosmopolitan Provision of Charitable Aid," *Journal of the Early Republic*, XXIX (2009), 607–640. For the centrality of the concept of improvement to informing the worldview of late-eighteenth-century reformers, see Moniz, *From Empire to Humanity*.

52. [William Dunlap] to Mssrs. Swords, "Remarks on the Love of Country," Nov. 13, 1797, in *New-York Magazine; or, Literary Repository*, VIIII (November 1797), 583, quoted in Catherine O'Donnell Kaplan, *Men of Letters in the Early Republic: Cultivating Forms of Citizenship* (Williamsburg, Va., and Chapel Hill, N.C., 2008), 49. Friendly Society members who joined the NYMS include the Presbyterian minister Samuel Miller, the merchant brothers William and George Woolsey, the writer and physician Elihu Smith, attorneys William Johnson and Thomas Mumford, and William Dunlap. For the life and views of William Dunlap, see Dorothy C. Barck, ed., *Diary of William Dunlap (1766–1839): The Memoirs of a Dramatist, Theatrical Manager, Painter, Critic, Novelist, and Historian*, 3 vols. (New York, 1930). For the activities and philosophies of the Friendly Club, see Bryan Waterman, *Republic of Intellect: The Friendly Club of New York City and the Making of American Literature* (Baltimore, 2007); and Kaplan, *Men of Letters in the Early Republic*.

that surrounded him. He was instrumental in financing the construction of
the New York Public Hospital, founded a charitable bank for the working
poor, promoted free schools for the underprivileged, and worked to reform
New York's penal laws in order to turn prisons from houses of punishment
into incubators for transforming criminals into carriers of morality, religion, and virtue. Eddy's exuberant participation in reform was tinged with
a patrician sensibility that told him lower classes needed rescuing from
the depraved influences that allegedly undergirded their poverty. And to
go along with Eddy's faith in social progress was an aristocratic fear that,
were men like him not to inculcate virtuous habits in the subjects of their
reform, groups like recently emancipated blacks might dislodge the order
and stability of the Republic.[53]

During the 1790s, many of the delegates to the American Convention of
Abolition Societies personified the elitist influences on early national organized abolitionism. The first president of the American Convention, Joseph
Bloomfield, was a Revolutionary War major and New Jersey attorney general who would go on to serve as governor of the state. He was joined at
the 1794 Convention by William Rodgers, a chaplain in the Continental
army and professor of oratory and the English language at the University
of Pennsylvania, Joseph Warner, the founding director of the Bank of Delaware, and Uriah Tracy, a member of the House of Representatives, among
other prominent Americans. The second Convention likewise consisted of
a roll call of preeminent men. Caspar Wistar was a physician, anatomist,
and professor at the University of Pennsylvania. Benjamin Say, a practic-
ing doctor and member of the College of Physicians of Philadelphia, represented his state in Congress and belonged to the Pennsylvania Humane
Society and Prison Society. His fellow delegate, the wealthy Quaker merchant Samuel Coates, served as the president of the Board of Managers
of the Pennsylvania Hospital. These three Pennsylvanians were perhaps

53. On Thomas Eddy, see Samuel L. Knapp, *The Life of Thomas Eddy; Comprising
an Extensive Correspondence with Many of the Most Distinguished Philosophers and
Philanthropists of This and Other Countries* (New York, 1834). For the ideas and assumptions that drove Eddy's participation in the social movements that garnered much
of his attention, prison reform and poor relief, see M. J. Heale, "Humanitarianism in
the Early Republic: The Moral Reformers of New York, 1776–1825," *Journal of American Studies*, II (1968), 161–175; and Christopher Adamson, "Evangelical Quakerism and
the Early American Penitentiary Revisited: The Contributions of Thomas Eddy, Roberts
Vaux, John Griscom, Stephen Grellet, Elisha Bates, and Isaac Hopper," *Quaker History*,
XC, no. 2 (Fall 2001), 35–58. For the condescending, controlling, and elitist overtones of
poor relief in early America, see Alexander, *Render Them Submissive*.

eclipsed in stature by Richard Bassett, who served as a delegate to the Constitutional Convention, a U.S. senator, and the governor of Delaware.

Scholars have noted the elite standing of many abolition society members as a means of couching their activism as conservative. Indeed, the paternalistic tendencies of the abolition societies owe a great deal to the class background of its more affluent members. But another way to think about the way class influenced the reformism of the abolition societies is to recognize how the position of men like Rodgers, Wistar, and Bloomfield must have emboldened these reformers to believe that they could remake the new nation in provocative ways. The commitment to overturning human bondage and incorporating the formerly enslaved as citizens united abolition society members, from patrician elites to pious Quakers.[54]

BURGEONING BLACK LEADERS

Elite white reformers were not the only contributors to first movement abolitionism who entered the opening years of the new Republic with an optimistic vantage point. Although many people of color in New York City and Philadelphia found their freedom curbed by severe socioeconomic constraints, for a not inconsiderable number of African Americans in the urban mid-Atlantic freedom was followed by economic progress and personal empowerment. A handful of exceptional free African Americans emerging out of a budding black middle class would propagate an abolitionist philosophy based on turning formerly enslaved people into virtuous citizens. These free black community leaders would found independent churches, mutual relief societies, and reform and educational organizations as they waged a concerted antislavery campaign. Identifying with the values they believed propelled the new nation of which they considered themselves full members, it was this group of newly empowered black leaders who would cling so tenaciously to American Revolutionary ideals in choosing the mores of republican ideology as a path to total emancipation and black betterment.

By 1816, about 20 percent of Philadelphia's free blacks had established themselves in proprietary, professional, or artisanal employment, and 11 percent ran their own businesses. Skilled African American workers ran

54. On the link between the elite orientation and outlook of many abolition society members and their allegedly conservative reform strategy and agenda, see Davis, *The Problem of Slavery in the Age of Revolution*, 239–242; and Richard S. Newman, *The Transformation of American Abolitionism: Fighting Slavery in the Early Republic* (Chapel Hill, N.C., 2002), 39–59.

the gamut from carpenters, cabinetmakers, shoemakers, tailors, silver-smiths, hatters, jewelers, butchers, and bakers, while proprietary professions included carting, food catering, hairdressing, and shopkeeping. Some industrious free blacks saved money and bought real estate, an act that brought them from being claimed as property in slavery to owning property in freedom. As many as one in three of New York City's free black male heads of household were artisans, a profession lionized in the early national era as the bulwark of an independent citizenry. In New York and Philadelphia, many African Americans earned their livelihood as mariners. All of these economically self-sufficient free blacks reached a degree of autonomy unimaginable in slavery.[55]

The greatest measure of African American socioeconomic progress in this period is the number of free blacks who established independent households. The American body politic was supposed to be built on the backs of independent male freeholders. Many free black men from among the burgeoning population of heads of household must have met this criterion for inclusion in the young Republic. In New York City, a substantial number of African American males, 946, were counted as heads of household in the 1810 census. The proportion of free black male heads of household expanded almost twofold between 1800 and 1810 as former bondspersons gained their freedom and established independent lives. Philadelphia's total number of free black men heading their own homes went from 369 in 1800 to 1,188 in 1820. From this group, an emerging middle class of African Americans would spearhead the black abolitionist drive and, along with the abolition societies, attempt to raise the mass of people of color to higher levels of economic success and republican virtue.[56]

55. Nash, *Forging Freedom*, 148–153; White, *Somewhat More Independent*, 158–161. As White notes, free black skilled workers in New York City greatly outnumbered those in Philadelphia because of the widespread use of the enslaved as artisans in New York City's labor force in the years leading up to emancipation.

56. I compiled the number of free black male heads of households in New York City from the genealogical reference book by Alice Eichholz and James M. Rose, *Free Black Heads of Households in the New York State Federal Census, 1790–1830* (Detroit, Mich., 1981). This collection lists alphabetically all free black heads of households recorded in the New York State census from 1790 through 1830. To derive the total, I picked out the males according to their given names. Before the census of 1820, New York state census takers did not record the sex of the state's free black persons, listing them under the category "other free persons." The Philadelphia numbers come from Tom W. Smith, "The Dawn of the Urban Industrial Age: The Social Structure of Philadelphia, 1790–1830" (Ph.D. diss., University of Chicago, 1980), 178. Black women headed between 10 percent and 20 percent of the total number of free black households in Philadelphia and New York City from 1790 through 1820.

The post-Revolutionary era brought with it the meteoric rise of a set of accomplished free black individuals. Their stories manifest the sense of progress and optimism felt by African American community leaders in Philadelphia and New York. One of these leaders was Richard Allen. Born into slavery in Philadelphia in 1760, Allen as a child was sold south to Delaware. Soon after converting to Methodism as a teenager, Allen was on the road to freedom, his owner offering him the chance to buy his freedom through a series of payments. Gaining his liberty in 1783, Allen began his new life as an itinerant preacher. He traveled the mid-Atlantic region, preaching the gospel, making converts, and encouraging his audiences to live sober, industrious, and moral lives. One of the most extraordinary elements of Allen's early career is the number of positive interracial experiences he had while serving as a peripatetic missionary. There was the influential apostle Benjamin Abbott, whom Allen referred to as "a friend and father." There was the "kind and affectionate" Jonathan Bunn of Bennington, New Jersey, from whom Allen would later buy the land on which he built the first independent Methodist black church in America. Then there was Bishop Francis Asbury, who noticed Allen's talents and served as the young black preacher's spiritual mentor. Even though white Methodists had moved away from their antislavery stance and biracial beginnings by the early 1800s, Allen's understanding of black uplift and abolitionist reform came first from his belief that white people could be convinced of the humanity of persons of color. After all, Allen himself was living proof of such an assumption.[57]

57. Richard Allen, *The Life, Experience, and Gospel Labors of the Rt. Rev. Richard Allen* ... (Philadelphia, 1880), 6–7, 9–12 (quotations on 9); Richard S. Newman, *Freedom's Prophet: Bishop Richard Allen, the AME Church, and the Black Founding Fathers* (New York, 2008), 42–43. Newman's biography is the most complete secondary account of Allen's life available. It is not clear whether Allen was born in Philadelphia or Kent County, Delaware, as the man who first held him in slavery, Benjamin Chew, had residences in both locations. In his autobiography, Allen states only that he was born "a slave to Benjamin Chew, of Philadelphia" (Allen, *Life, Experience, and Gospel Labors*, 5). The evangelical brand of Christianity taking shape in the 1780s resonated deeply with Allen and other black Americans. Promoting spiritual access to all and using emotive appeals and forms of worship, Methodism, to which Allen and a growing number of black Americans would claim allegiance, was particularly effective in garnering black converts. For the explosive growth of black Christianity in the late eighteenth and early nineteenth centuries and the unique stamp African Americans put on American evangelicalism, see Silvia R. Frey and Betty Wood, *Come Shouting to Zion: African American Protestantism in the American South and British Caribbean to 1830* (Chapel Hill, N.C., 1998), 118–208; and Nathan O. Hatch, *The Democratization of American Christianity* (New Haven, Conn., 1989), 102–118.

Allen settled down in Philadelphia, where he founded a chimney sweeping business, purchased property, and gathered a growing body of black Methodists. It was also in Philadelphia where Allen met another African American on the rise, Absalom Jones. Fourteen years Allen's senior, Jones was born enslaved in Sussex, Delaware, in 1746. In 1762, Jones was separated from his mother, five brothers, and a sister when his master, Benjamin Wynkoop, sold his entire family and took the eighteen-year-old Absalom to the city of Philadelphia. Eight years after arriving in Philadelphia, Jones married an enslaved woman and talked her owner into letting him buy her freedom. Taking on extra work whenever he could, Jones also raised money from local Quakers and was able to purchase his wife's liberty. By 1778, still enslaved, Jones bought a house and, aware that it could be seized "as the property of my master," pressed Wynkoop for his freedom. At last, in 1784, his master granted Jones his request. Through hard work and disciplined saving, Jones had gone from a subjugated, enslaved orphan to a respectable, propertyowning freeman in a little more than two decades. His life embodied the perfect model of what "industry, frugality, and economy"—central republican virtues—could yield to Philadelphia's growing free black population. Jones would team up with Richard Allen in religious, reform, and antislavery projects, always carrying his acquaintance with the power of republican principles close at hand.[58]

While Allen and Jones entered the world enslaved, James Forten was born free in Philadelphia in 1766. Forten's grandfather had managed to obtain his liberty at a time when being free and black was an anomaly. Forten's father, Thomas, became a sailmaker, and he made enough money to support a family of four. Hoping to improve further the status of the next generation of Fortens, James's parents registered their son in the African School run by the Society of Friends. Here, until the age of nine, Forten learned reading, writing, bookkeeping, and mathematics. By 1775, his father dead and the family struggling economically, Forten had to abandon school and get a job as a storekeeper's assistant. A year after leaving his studies, Forten took part in an event that would cement his identification as an American citizen for the rest of his life. On July 8, 1776, the

58. "Sketch of the Rev. Absalom Jones," in W[illia]m Douglass, *Annals of the First African Church, in the United States of America, Now Styled the African Episcopal Church of St. Thomas, Philadelphia* ... (Philadelphia, 1862), 118–122. Douglass, a black historian and minister of Philadelphia's St. Thomas African Church, published a short autobiographical account of Jones penned sometime before his death in 1818. See also Nash, *Forging Freedom*, 67–68.

newly minted Declaration of Independence was presented to the public for the first time, and Forten made sure he was there to hear its ideals pronounced. In 1785, James Forten apprenticed himself to his father's former boss, the sailmaker Robert Bridges. Thirteen years later, Bridges retired and made the momentous decision to hand over his sailmaking business to Forten. Forten's sailmaking loft thrived. He hired apprentices and journeymen, bought real estate, and became a creditor. But wealth did not make Forten complacent. He remained determined to extend to all black Americans the ideals of freedom and equality that had inspired him since his earliest days.[59]

New York City had its share of distinguished free blacks as well. One of the most illustrious was Peter Williams, Jr. (Figure 4). Williams's father—a former enslaved tobacconist and one of the wealthiest African Americans in New York—was, according to his son, a fervent supporter of the American Revolution. Williams Jr. was weaned on his father's identity as a patriotic citizen. Born in the midst of war in 1780, Williams Jr. later recalled his father instilling in him "an ardent love for the American government" that "made me feel ... that it was my greatest glory to be an American." Lacking an education, the elder Williams made sure to provide his son with one. He enrolled Williams Jr. in the New-York Manumission Society's African Free School. Williams Jr. attended the Trinity Episcopal Church and eventually was ordained the first black Episcopal minister in New York City. Pairing his growing knowledge with a commitment to abolitionism and black uplift, Williams Jr. believed that making African Americans "intelligent, useful and virtuous members of the community" would lead to a time when all blacks would have "abundant reason to rejoice in the glorious Declaration of American Independence." In the early national era, he helped to found black reform organizations, delivered antislavery speeches, and wrote editorials on behalf of New York's African Americans in the city's press. Joining Williams Jr. in the free black leadership vanguard were Wil-

59. Julie Winch, *A Gentleman of Color: The Life of James Forten* (Oxford, 2003), 11, 24–25, 31, 52, 63–76; *Liberator* (Boston), Mar. 11, 1842, 39. Winch's magisterial biography of Forten fleshes out his identification as an American citizen and Forten's complex but steady allegiance to the country of his birth. Forten signed on to fight for the cause of independence as a member of the privateer *Royal Louis* in 1780. After his ship was captured by the English, Forten became a captive of war. Following seven months of captivity, he made his way back to Philadelphia. On the culture of activism and protest developed by Allen, Jones, Forten, and others of Philadelphia's leading free blacks of the early Republic, see Winch, *Philadelphia's Black Elite: Activism, Accommodation, and the Struggle for Autonomy, 1787-1848* (Philadelphia, 1988).

REV. PETER WILLIAMS,
First Colored Protestant Episcopal Priest in the United
States. (See page 46.)

FIGURE 4. *Rev. Peter Williams [Jr.].* From Daniel Alexander Payne, *Recollections of Seventy Years,* introduction by Rev. F. J. Grimke, comp. Sarah C. Bierce Scarborough, ed. Rev. C. S. Smith (Nashville, Tenn., 1888). Courtesy, New York Public Library

liam Hamilton, a house carpenter and orator, Henry Sipkins, the son of the founder of New York's second black Methodist Church, William Miller, a Methodist reverend, the educator John Teasman, and political activist Joseph Sidney, among others.[60]

60. [Peter] Williams, [Jr.], "To the Citizens of New York," July 14, 1834, *African Repository,* X (1834), 186–188, in Carter G. Woodson, ed., *The Mind of the Negro: As Reflected in Letters Written during the Crisis, 1800–1860* (Washington, D.C., 1926), 630–631; Graham Hodges, "Peter Williams Jr.," in Henry Louis Gates, Jr., and Evelyn Brooks-Higginbotham, eds., *African American National Biography,* VIII (New York,

Patriotic, respectable, successful, confident, and optimistic about what was to come—all of these qualities describe the mentality of the men who began setting up communities of color in the American Republic during the late eighteenth and early nineteenth centuries. From their respective transformations from obscurity to republican respectability, the likes of Forten, Allen, Jones, and Williams Jr. drew faith that their fellow free persons of color could achieve a similar level of virtuous liberty. Indeed, the abolitionist agenda of free black leaders in early national New York City and Philadelphia would be dedicated to the belief that their newly liberated brethren needed to become virtuous citizens to complete the abolition of slavery.

A TENUOUS BUT MEANINGFUL FREEDOM

African Americans of the late-eighteenth-century and early-nineteenth-century mid-Atlantic encountered both discernible progress and imposing hurdles to gaining and maintaining their freedom. It is in the space between the permeable barriers of slavery and freedom created by gradual emancipation that otherwise obscure people of color emerge in the historical record as agents of first movement abolitionism. The Revolutionary and early national eras brought sweeping changes to the status of enslaved and free blacks in the mid-Atlantic region. State legislatures passed gradual emancipation acts and liberalized manumission standards, while new laws recognized the rights of free African Americans and in some cases enslaved people as well. It all began with Pennsylvania's 1780 abolition law. This law annulled the 1725 slave codes, but it did more than that. The first section of the bill denounced racial prejudice in a way that would have been unthinkable only a generation earlier. By throwing off "those narrow prejudices and partialities we had imbibed," the state legislature consid-

---

2008), 341. When the American Revolution arrived in New York, Williams's master, a loyalist, fled to New Jersey. It was here that Williams, "a decided advocate for American independence," in the words of his son, demonstrated his dedication to American sovereignty. After helping a patriot parson to safety from British capture, Williams was confronted by a royal officer who commanded the abettor to reveal where he had taken the parson. To the British soldier, who initially threatened Williams with death by drawing his sword and then tempted him with money, Williams stoically replied, "I cannot tell." On the lives and religious culture of Peter Williams, Jr., and his father, see Kyle T. Bulthuis, "Peter Williams Sr.," ibid., 342–343; and Kyle Bulthuis, *Four Steeples over the City Streets: Religion and Society in New York's Early Republic Congregations* (New York, 2014). On the lives of Henry Sipkins and John Teasman, see *Colored American* (New York), Nov. 17 and 24, 1838, for a eulogy of Sipkins; and Robert J. Swan, "John Teasman: African-American Educator and the Emergence of Community in Early Black New York City, 1787–1815," *JER*, XII (1992), 331–356, for what little is known about Teasman's educational career.

ered it "a peculiar blessing granted to us" to end "the sorrows of those who have lived in undeserved bondage." Among the act's clauses, white and black, enslaved or free were now to be tried "in like manner" before the same courts of law.[61]

Antislavery sentiment evident in Pennsylvania echoed throughout the mid-Atlantic states. The New Jersey legislature insisted that it was "desirous of extending the Blessings of Liberty." In 1788, that body enacted legislation giving blacks equal justice before the law and, in anticipation of the abolition of slavery, requiring that all masters teach enslaved people under the age of twenty-one how to read. New York's Gradual Abolition Act of 1799 included no mention of the civic exclusion of African Americans, causing one free black to conclude that the state had "made the same provision for the security of our rights as for the rights of others." For those still in bondage, New York granted the right to marry and own and transfer property in 1809. Even in Delaware, where the state's former tobacco economy and its proximity to the upper South made difficult the adoption of an abolition bill, the state legislature lifted bond requirements for private manumissions and passed laws prohibiting the sale of enslaved people out of state. Measures apparently at odds with the long-term survival of slavery and racial inequality proliferated, and enslaved and free blacks, from New York to Delaware, undoubtedly took notice.[62]

If the legal arc of the post-Revolutionary mid-Atlantic, when compared to the colonial era, appeared to be leaning toward increased black rights, many shortcomings circumscribed this progress. The 1780 Pennsylvania Act for the Gradual Abolition of Slavery contained numerous loopholes that empowered slaveholders to sell their enslaved laborers out of state and otherwise skirt the intent of the law. Statutory emancipation in New York was blocked for nearly a decade and a half, in part owing to the efforts of abolition's opponents to insert racially divisive measures into the act. When gradual emancipation finally did come to New York in 1799, slaveholders maintained a host of advantages—from the right to imprison enslaved people not accused of crimes to the ability of Saint Domingue migrants to maintain their bondspersons despite a French decree giving them freedom. In states throughout the mid-Atlantic, penalties set for those who violated

61. An Act for the Gradual Abolition of Slavery, Nov. 2, 1779, in Bruns, ed., *Am I Not a Man and a Brother*, 446, 448–449.

62. *Acts of the Eleventh General Assembly of the State of New-Jersey; at a Session Begun at Trenton on the 24th Day of October, 1786, and Continued by Adjournments ...* (Trenton, N.J., 1786), 368; *New-York Evening Post*, Aug. 20, 1814, [3]; McManus, *A History of Negro Slavery in New York*, 178; Essah, *A House Divided*, 40–41.

emancipation-related legislation were enforced sporadically at best and did
little to stop slaveholders from acting for their pecuniary advantage, often
in contradiction to the interests of those whose labor they claimed. On the
national level, the Fugitive Slave Act of 1793 struck a blow against the cause
of abolitionism. While justified as a means of reinforcing the right of slaveholders to recover those who fled their enslavement—a promise implied by
the Federal Constitution—the act brought people back into bondage and
reified the growing practice of free black kidnapping.[63]

Though their liberty was fragile, the free black population experienced
explosive growth in the early national mid-Atlantic (see Table 1). The aggregate number of free persons more than doubled between 1790 and 1800,
going from just under 18,000 in 1790 to almost 38,000 in 1810. The free
black population nearly doubled in the next decade, reaching a total of
68,804. By 1820, three-fourths of mid-Atlantic blacks were free, whereas
only thirty years earlier 6 in 10 blacks had been held in chattel bondage.
However gradual or compromised this liberty might have been, the position of a majority of African Americans in the mid-Atlantic states had
shifted from slavery to freedom in a relatively short period of time.[64]

Nowhere was this demographic change more evident than in New York
City and Philadelphia (see Table 2). On the eve of the American Revolution,

63. Chapter 2 of this work surveys the many ways mid-Atlantic slaveholders resisted
the passage of statutory emancipation and, once enacted, exploited the shortcomings
and loopholes of emancipation statutes to maintain their prerogatives and curb the
scope of northern abolition. The NYMS was aware of the 1794 proclamation of the
French assembly freeing all enslaved people in its colonial possessions. But the continuing whirlwind of events in Saint Domingue and the unsettled nature of the decree's
implementation in France's Caribbean colonies made it unclear to the NYMS the exact
status of persons of color brought into the state from these locations. For a notorious
case involving a Saint Domingue slaveholding refugee who sought to transport her enslaved laborers outside state boundaries after migrating to New York, see Martha S.
Jones, "Time, Space, and Jurisdiction in Atlantic World Slavery: The Volunbrun Household in Gradual Emancipation New York," Law and History Review, XXIX (2011), 1031–
1060. The PAS beat back an attempt by Saint Dominguan slaveholders to gain exemption from the law prohibiting incoming Pennsylvania residents from holding in bondage
enslaved people for longer than six months upon entering the state (Gary B. Nash, "Re-
verberations of Haiti in the American North: Black Saint Dominguans in Philadelphia,"
Pennsylvania History, LXV [1998], 54). On the Fugitive Slave Act, see Paul Finkelman,
Slavery and the Founders: Race and Liberty in the Age of Jefferson (Armonk, N.Y., 1996),
80–104; and Carol Wilson, Freedom at Risk: The Kidnapping of Free Blacks in America,
1780–1865 (Lexington, Ky., 1994), 40–66.

64. In the upper South, the only other region with comparable numbers of free blacks
in the early national era, no more than 37 percent of African Americans in Maryland and
less than 9 percent of African Americans in Virginia were free in this period.

TABLE 1. *Black Population in the Mid-Atlantic, Free and Enslaved, 1790–1820*

	New York		New Jersey		Pennsylvania		Delaware	
Year	Free	Enslaved	Free	Enslaved	Free	Enslaved	Free	Enslaved
1790	4,682	21,193	2,762	11,423	6,531	3,707	3,899	8,887
1800	10,374	20,613	4,402	12,422	14,564	1,796	8,286	6,153
1810	25,333	15,017	7,843	10,851	22,492	795	13,136	4,117
1820	29,279	10,088	12,460	7,557	30,202	211	12,968	4,509

Source: Census data derived from the University of Virginia Historical Census Browser, from the University of Virginia, Geospatial and Statistical Data Center, accessed Sept. 24, 2010, http://fisher.lib.virginia.edu/collections/stats/histcensus/index.html (site discontinued).

only 300 free African Americans inhabited these two cities. By 1810, that number stood at 18,651. This increase was especially pronounced during the early national era. Whereas 8 in 10 blacks in New York and Philadelphia were enslaved in 1790, 9 in 10 African Americans were free by 1810. Between 1800 and 1810 alone, the free black population of New York increased by 132 percent, going from 3,499 to 8,137. Philadelphia's biggest growth in its free black inhabitants took place in 1790–1800, when the population more than tripled. By 1820, the City of Brotherly Love had the largest number of free blacks in the urban North, with a total of 11,884. This growth rate is particularly notable when compared to other northern cities. For instance, in 1800–1820, Boston's free black population grew by only 552, bringing the total to 1,726 persons.[65]

Free African Americans flocked to New York City and Philadelphia during the post-Revolutionary years for several reasons. Both of these cities' growth as bustling ports with sprawling urban centers offered ample employment and cultural opportunities for free blacks when compared to outlying areas. Much of the free black in-migration to New York and Pennsylvania came from outside its borders, especially from upper southern slave states like Maryland, Virginia, and North Carolina. The growth of the free black population in New York City far outpaced the rate of emancipation among enslaved people in the state. In Pennsylvania, where slaveholding had never been as widespread as in New York, Philadelphia was a magnet

65. Gary B. Nash, "Forging Freedom: The Emancipation Experience in the Northern Seaport Cities, 1775–1820," in Ira Berlin and Ronald Hoffman, *Slavery and Freedom in the Age of the American Revolution* (Charlottesville, Va., 1983), 5.

TABLE 2. *Black Population in New York City and Philadelphia,*
Free and Enslaved, 1790–1820

| Year | New York City | | Philadelphia | |
	Free	Enslaved	Free	Enslaved
1790	1,119	2,373	2,099	373
1800	3,499	2,868	6,795	85
1810	8,137	1,686	10,514	8
1820	10,368	518	11,884	7

Source: Census data derived from the University of Virginia Historical Census Browser, from the University of Virginia, Geospatial and Statistical Data Center, accessed Sept. 24, 2010, http://fisher.lib.virginia.edu/collections/stats/histcensus/index.html (site discontinued).

for upper southern newly freed blacks and fugitives from slavery thanks to its reputation as a beacon of liberty for the nation's African Americans. Urban areas imparted a type of anonymity and autonomy sorely lacking for African Americans living in rural communities. Marine and merchant work, which attracted many free black men, flourished in the transatlantic commercial economies of post-Revolutionary New York City and Philadelphia and provided another strong pull. Once free blacks began establishing churches, schools, and other community institutions, word of these two cities as incubators for free black community development spread far and wide. All of these factors resulted in heavy African American migration into New York City and Philadelphia, where, throughout the early national era, more than a quarter of the mid-Atlantic's free blacks resided.[66]

As African Americans transitioned from slavery to freedom, they looked to position their liberty on sound financial footing. Limited to work as domestics and unskilled laborers, many struggled to meet this goal. Part of the problem was the gradual nature of northern emancipation. More than 30 percent of New York City's free blacks in 1810 lived in white households in the affluent city wards as domestic servants. For this assemblage

66. For an overview of free black community development in post-Revolutionary and early national New York City and Philadelphia, see Nash, *Forging Freedom,* 100–172; White, *Somewhat More Independent,* 150–184; Harris, *In the Shadow of Slavery,* 72–95; and Hodges, *Root and Branch,* 187–227. Black migration from Saint Domingue was also rather sizable in this period. As they fled their war-torn island, French masters took enslaved people with them to American seaports. Many of these slaveholders and their bondspersons settled in New York City and Philadelphia.

of domestics, freedom did not add up to independence. Others lacked skills denied them in bondage and were forced to find work that was both low-paying and transitory. These free persons toiled as bootblacks, sweepers, chimney sweeps, gravediggers, and loaders of ships, among an assortment of undesirable occupations. Consequently, even though they were no longer enslaved, a numerical majority of freedpeople, grouped at the bottom of New York City's and Philadelphia's economy, found themselves marginalized both socially and economically.[67]

A tenuous freedom marked the everyday lives of persons of color in the early national mid-Atlantic. To be black did not necessarily mean to be free, and to be free meant maintaining an acute sense that the battle to end slavery had just begun. Unlike in New England, where by 1810 only 418 blacks were enslaved, the mid-Atlantic states contained the largest proportion of both enslaved and free blacks in the North, ranging from 90 to 99 percent of the North's enslaved population and 60 to 75 percent of its free black populace from 1790 to 1820. A great number of free blacks in early national Philadelphia and New York City were not free from servitude. Instead, they worked as indentured servants, a form of labor that not only curtailed their liberties but made them vulnerable to illegal enslavement. Because slavery remained a legal institution in both New York and Pennsylvania, black servants lived under the constant threat of being fraudulently claimed as bondspersons, sold out of state as chattel, or having their liberty otherwise stolen from them. The deficiencies of northern emancipation aroused the activism of white and black abolitionists, but they also speak to the important limitations of an unalloyed sense of antislavery progress in this period.[68]

67. White, *Somewhat More Independent*, 156–157; Nash, *Forging Freedom*, 144–146. Despite their marginalization, nonelite free blacks in New York City and Philadelphia developed a rich culture of self-expression. For example, see White, *Somewhat More Independent*, 185–206.

68. While indentured blacks and other marginalized free persons of color were particularly vulnerable to illegal enslavement, the specter of being falsely claimed a slave did not elude more prominent free blacks of the urban mid-Atlantic. Richard Allen, one of Philadelphia's most distinguished men of color, was temporarily imprisoned when a Maryland man wrongly identified Allen as a fugitive from slavery. Allen was quickly released from confinement and brought a successful suit against his accuser. Yet that even one of the foremost free persons of color in the entire mid-Atlantic could find himself on the precipice of wrongful enslavement gestures to the fragility of African American freedom in the early national North. See Carol Wilson, "Active Vigilance Is the Price of Liberty: Black Self-Defense against Fugitive Slave Recapture and Kidnapping of Free Blacks," in John R. McKivigan and Stanley Harrold, eds., *Antislavery Violence: Sectional, Racial, and Cultural Conflict in Antebellum America* (Knoxville, Tenn., 1999), 108–127.

Learning of laws passed by mid-Atlantic legislatures that curtailed the legality of chattel slavery, persons of color sought to secure their freedom. By teaming up with white activists of the PAS and NYMS, hundreds of persons of color made their mark in the annals of first movement abolitionism. Examples of the antislavery activism of persons of color in the urban mid-Atlantic abound. In the winter of 1794, a twenty-year-old West Indian man named Rodie appeared before the PAS informing members of the society that he, along with four others who had been brought from Hispaniola around eight months prior, were about to be shipped back into slavery (Pennsylvania law disallowed the holding of enslaved people who had been brought into the state after November 1, 1780, and were resident therein for at least six consecutive months). When the PAS quickly brought the case before a judge, Rodie and his four compatriots were declared free. A year later, Mauro Meet informed the NYMS that he had been sold by his New Jersey owner to a man in New York in violation of a 1785 state law banning the importation of enslaved people for sale. After an attempted kidnapping, Meet attained his freedom with the aid of the NYMS's legal counsel.[69]

Other persons of color ensured the integrity of a freedom they had already established. When the manumitted bondsman Moses Browne learned that the new husband of his former Maryland mistress planned to travel to Philadelphia and kidnap him into slavery, he sought the counsel of the PAS. The society's acting committee drew up a certificate verifying the free status of Browne in order "to Protect him" from the prospect of reenslavement. In 1785, an enslaved woman named Grace traveled to Philadelphia and told the PAS of a "Verbal Declaration" from her former owner, Ann Crackett. Made one year earlier in the presence of multiple witnesses, the declaration, part of Crackett's will, stated that Grace would no longer be considered a slave after her master's death with the stipulation that the executors of Crackett's estate bind out Grace for a seven-year indenture to the person of Grace's choice. Her erstwhile master now dead, the executors of Crackett's estate were claiming Grace's "Services," endangering her path to liberty. Grace turned to the PAS to help guard the agreement she had made with Crackett, written proof of which the society noted was in its possession.[70]

The efforts of Rodie, Mauro, Moses, and Grace to enforce emancipation and uphold their tenuous liberty make them, and the many other per-

69. Papers of the Pennsylvania Abolition Society (PPAS), Series 1, reel 4, II, 286, 288, Historical Society of Pennsylvania (HSP), Philadelphia; NYMS Records, VII, 50, 58–60, 64, 67, 71, 74, 79–80, 216, NYHS.

70. PPAS, Series 1, reel 4, I, 54, 110, 112, 116, 124, HSP. Thomas Harrison of the PAS bought out the remainder of Grace's indenture and presumably freed her.

sons of color on the margins of freedom who also partook in antislavery activism, abolitionists just as much as the white reformers whose aid they sought. Though facing formidable social and economic constraints, those persons of color who reached out to the NYMS and PAS yielded newfound power as deliberate agents in emancipation. That they often found their grievances remedied must have given blacks of the urban mid-Atlantic a hopefulness about the efficacy of the first abolition movement of which they were a vital part.[71]

By the time the Constitution's ratification brought cheers from the backers of a federal republic, the PAS and NYMS, along with their black abolitionist allies, similarly looked to the future of their cause with hope. Slavery in America no longer went unquestioned. People of color in the urban mid-Atlantic seized upon antislavery laws, at times tipping the scales of power against those who claimed their labor. A number of formerly enslaved free people of color in Philadelphia and New York gained an agency inconceivable before the Revolutionary era. Antislavery Quakers, once maligned even within their own sect, now founded abolition societies that attracted some of America's most prominent statesmen and reformers. A confidence that their activism was already making great strides, together with the hope that the progression of American society would continue in the direction of antislavery, served as a powerful unifying force linking otherwise disparate individuals in a cohesive abolitionist movement.

But the emergence of abolitionism in America neither guaranteed black freedom nor ensured that white Americans could be disarmed of the racial prejudices that had for nearly two centuries undergirded chattel slavery. The late-eighteenth-century debates over abolition show that proponents of slavery had mighty weapons to wield against their antislavery foes. Slavery's defenders used Revolutionary ideology, in the form of property rights arguments and assertions that black people were incapable of civic membership, to put the onus back on abolitionists. Moreover, the liminal space between slavery and freedom occupied by many people of color in the post-Revolutionary North led to continual infringements upon black rights and threatened the integrity of African American liberty. First movement abolitionists' responses to these crucial challenges would go on to dictate their program of reform.

71. The combined efforts of persons of color and the PAS and NYMS to enforce and expand antislavery laws in the mid-Atlantic is the topic of the second chapter of this book.

CHAPTER 2

The "Just Right of Freedom"

Enforcing and Expanding Gradual Emancipation

In the summer of 1800, Lewis Martin De Moor set foot in Manhattan as an enslaved man—brought from the southern Caribbean island of Curaçao. Six months after disembarking in the expanding commercial city, De Moor found himself subject once again to involuntary transportation. De Moor's master sold him in late January 1801 to a man from Philadelphia who planned on promptly leaving New York. But this time De Moor was able to take control of his fate. Capitalizing on state laws that banned both the importation and exportation of enslaved people for sale, De Moor conveyed his situation to the NYMS, which interceded on his behalf. First ensuring that "measures were taken to keep" him "out the hands of his Master's reach," the manumission society then went to confront De Moor's new owner, intending to inform him that he was in violation of the law and that the man he thought was his enslaved property was, in fact, free. But, realizing that "something more than friendly" was intended by the manumission's society's visit, De Moor's master skipped town. The society's standing committee gave De Moor a "Certificate of protection" to safeguard his newly acquired liberty. De Moor's case is one of hundreds taken on by the New-York Manumission Society (NYMS) and Pennsylvania Abolition Society (PAS) in the post-Revolutionary and early national periods. These societies appointed committees that enforced laws curbing institutional slavery and acted as agents for blacks seeking redress from illegal enslavement and other attempts to curtail their freedom.[1]

De Moor's story provokes more questions than it provides answers. What brought him into contact with the NYMS? By what means had he become aware of the law banning the importation of enslaved people for sale? The standing committee records are even more silent on De Moor's

---

1. New-York Manumission Society (NYMS) Records, 1785–1849, VII, 181, New-York Historical Society (NYHS).

life after he gained liberty. Was the NYMS's certificate of freedom enough to secure him in his new condition? Did he remain in New York as a free man? Was he reenslaved? These records simply do not tell. Instead of narrating comprehensive stories, the minutes of the NYMS standing committee and PAS acting committee provide fleeting glimpses of recurring moments when people of color like De Moor, otherwise obscure in the historical record, teamed up with abolition society members as fellow activists in a joint cause (see Figure 5).[2]

Yet, although these glimpses are brief and the stories they unveil incomplete, they are also invaluable for what they do disclose. By privileging the perspectives of those like De Moor and the abolition societies that worked to gain freedom for him and hundreds of others similarly situated, we are able to peer into the inner workings of first movement abolitionism. Reconstructing the individual cases recorded in the minutes of the acting and standing committees displays a pitched contest pitting slaveholders and dealers on the one side and black northerners and the abolition societies on the other. Out of this contest arose a campaign dedicated at its core to the conviction that persons of African descent had rights worthy of respect. At the very heart of first movement abolitionism, from a street-level view of this activism, enforcing emancipation fueled a cause premised on the progressive gains of black northerners as rights-bearing individuals.[3]

2. The overviews of the many cases like De Moor's profiled in this chapter are derived exclusively from minutes of the PAS's acting committee and the NYMS's standing committee. Written for the internal reference of the societies and sketching the proceedings of the committees' meetings, these records are by their very nature incomplete. They afford only partial snapshots of how these cases unfolded and how the committees handled them. The standing and acting committees' records give especially fragmentary evidence of the lives, backgrounds, and perspectives of those people of color who appear in its pages. Yet, acknowledging these limitations, I have tried to reconstruct as full a narrative as the records allow.

3. I am not the first historian to examine the caseload of the PAS and NYMS. Some of the works that have showcased individual stories from these sources include David N. Gellman, *Emancipating New York: The Politics of Slavery and Freedom, 1777–1827* (Baton Rouge, La., 2006), 162–165; Gary B. Nash and Jean R. Soderlund, *Freedom by Degrees: Emancipation in Pennsylvania and Its Aftermath* (New York, 1991), 119–124; Manisha Sinha, *The Slave's Cause: A History of Abolition* (New Haven, Conn., 2016), 188–120; and Richard S. Newman, *The Transformation of American Abolitionism: Fighting Slavery in the Early Republic* (Chapel Hill, N.C., 2002), 60–85. Much of the coverage in these accounts is anecdotal. My approach to these same sources is at once quantitative, in that I present generalized conclusions based on statistical data, and qualitative, in that I aim to push us to rethink how we conceive of first movement abolitionism in light of this material. Analogous bodies to the acting and standing committees, including those belonging to abolition societies in Rhode Island and Delaware,

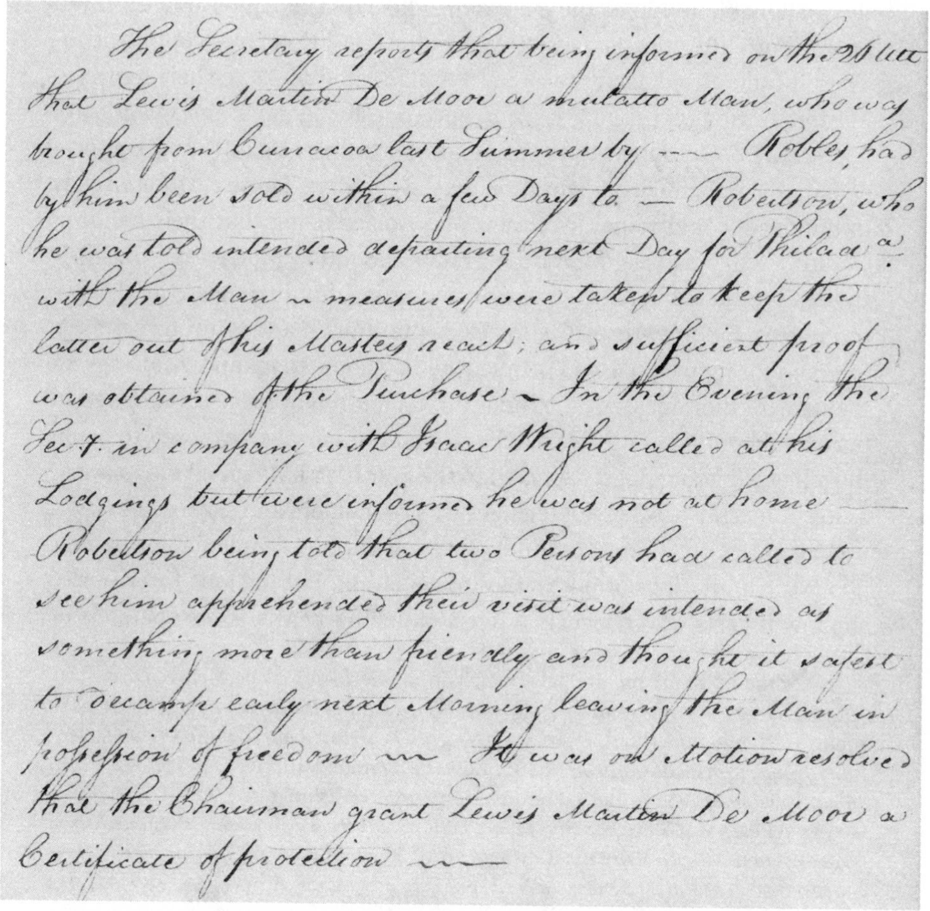

The Secretary reports that being informed on the 26 ult
that Lewis Martin De Moor a mulatto Man, who was
brought from Curacoa last Summer by —— Robles, had
by him been sold within a few Days to — Robertson, who
he was told intended departing next Day for Philada.
with the Man ~ measures were taken to keep the
latter out of his Masters reach; and sufficient proof
was obtained of the Purchase ~ In the Evening the
Secy. in company with Isaac Wright called at his
Lodgings but were informed he was not at home —
Robertson being told that two Persons had called to
see him apprehended their visit was intended as
something more than friendly and thought it safest
to decamp early next Morning leaving the Man in
possession of freedom ~ It was on Motion resolved
that the Chairman grant Lewis Martin De Moor a
Certificate of protection ~

FIGURE 5. Minutes, May 18, 1791–Feb. 18, 1807, New-York Manumission Society Records, 1785–1849, VII, 181. Courtesy, New-York Historical Society

On the one hand, De Moor's appearance in the minutes of the NYMS's standing committee exhibits the circumscribed nature of northern emancipation. De Moor arrived in New York one year after abolition became state law. He would have remained enslaved, however, if not sold by his master. Nowhere in the post-Revolutionary North did slavery die a fast death. Several northern state legislatures enacted gradual abolition acts that balanced the claims of slaveowners to their property rights in persons against

partook in activism similar to that of the NYMS and PAS. See John Wood Sweet, *Bodies Politic: Negotiating Race in the American North, 1730–1830* (Baltimore, 2003), 251–264; and Monte A. Calvert, "The Abolition Society of Delaware, 1801–1807," *Delaware History*, X (1963), 295–320.

the inalienable rights of the enslaved to liberty. The children of enslaved people born after the passage of the gradual abolition laws would be considered indentured servants and were mandated to serve their mothers' masters until ages ranging from twenty-one for females and twenty-five for males in New Jersey to twenty-eight for both sexes in Pennsylvania— essentially providing compensation for slaveholders. Those persons already in bondage would remain so, their only solace being that their children would one day be free. Moreover, gradual abolition blurred the lines between slave and free. Slavery's continuing legality juxtaposed with laws promoting the growth of free black communities added up to a fragile freedom for many. Enslaved people who had come to manumission agreements with their masters, the indentured children of those condemned to perpetual bondage, and free blacks all found themselves exposed to being illegally held in bondage, exported to the South, or kidnapped into slavery, among an array of other subterfuges by slaveholders and slave dealers.[4]

This dire depiction of gradual abolition captures undeniable realities about the limitations of northern emancipation. But the long interpretive shadow it casts also conceals other compelling truths. Those persons of

4. For the literature on gradual emancipation, see Joanne Pope Melish, *Disowning Slavery: Gradual Emancipation and "Race" in New England, 1780–1860* (Ithaca, N.Y., 1998); Nash and Soderlund, *Freedom by Degrees*, 99–204; Newman, *The Transformation of American Abolitionism*, 60–85; Edward Raymond Turner, *The Negro in Pennsylvania: Slavery—Servitude—Freedom, 1639–1861* (Washington, D.C., 1911), 64–109; George William Van Cleve, *A Slaveholders' Union: Slavery, Politics, and the Constitution in the Early American Republic* (Chicago, 2010), 59–93; Shane White, *Somewhat More Independent: The End of Slavery in New York City, 1770–1810* (Athens, Ga., 1991), 24–55; Edgar J. McManus, *A History of Negro Slavery in New York* (Syracuse, N.Y., 1966), 161–179; Gellman, *Emancipating New York*, 153–186; Leslie M. Harris, *In The Shadow of Slavery: African Americans in New York City, 1626–1863* (Chicago, 2003), 48–133; T. Robert Moseley, "A History of the New-York Manumission Society, 1785–1849" (Ph.D. diss., New York University, 1963), 97–169; James J. Gigantino II, *The Ragged Road to Abolition: Slavery and Freedom in New Jersey, 1775–1865* (Philadelphia, 2015), 64–148; George Fishman, "The Struggle for Freedom and Equality: African Americans in New Jersey, 1624–1849/50" (Ph.D. diss., Temple University, 1990), 221–321; Graham Russell Hodges, *Root and Branch: African Americans in New York and East Jersey, 1613–1863* (Chapel Hill, N.C., 1999), 162–186; Simeon F. Moss, "The Persistence of Slavery and Involuntary Servitude in a Free State (1685–1866)," *Journal of Negro History*, XXXV (1950), 298–310; Marion Thompson Wright, "New Jersey Laws and the Negro," ibid., XXVIII (1943), 171–189; and Gary K. Wolinetz, "New Jersey Slavery and the Law," *Rutgers Law Review*, L (1998), 2237–2257. For an account that, like the one in this chapter, couches the northern emancipation process as a contest featuring the defenders of slavery against northern blacks and the abolition societies, see Sinha, *A Slave's Cause*, 96. For the still standard overview of northern emancipation, see Arthur Zilversmit, *The First Emancipation: The Abolition of Slavery in the North* (Chicago, 1967).

color like De Moor who were able to communicate their stories of illegal enslavement to the PAS and NYMS in the post-Revolutionary era were overwhelmingly successful in winning their liberty. There are a combined 520 cases logged in the minutes of the acting and standing committees during the first decade for which records survive (1784–1794 for the PAS and 1791–1801 for the NYMS). The PAS oversaw 299 of these cases, while 221 belonged to the NYMS. Of the 313 cases reported resolved (or concluded), an aggregate of 329 blacks were freed with the assistance of the acting and standing committees. The total number of persons of color freed by the committees during this ten-year period almost certainly represents an undercount. More noteworthy, however, the success rate of extant cases. Of the cases reported resolved by the committees, 84 percent ended in freedom gained or protected for the black applicant. Of the cases concluded by the PAS's acting committee, 9 in 10 ended in victory, while the NYMS's standing committee oversaw a 73 percent rate of success. Thus, for some persons of color, the era of gradual emancipation ushered in not only hope for the future but also empowerment in the present.[5]

5. The 520 cases recorded almost certainly represent an undercount of the actual number of cases handled by the NYMS and PAS in these years. For example, there is direct evidence that the standing committee oversaw cases that it did not record in the meeting minutes because they were resolved by abolition society members outside the regularly scheduled committee sessions. See NYMS Records, VII, 269–270, NYHS. Indirect evidence also exists that cases that were not reported concluded were, in fact, resolved. See Papers of the Pennsylvania Abolition Society (PPAS), Series 1, reel 4, I, 10, 27, II, 110, 294, Historical Society of Pennsylvania (HSP), Philadelphia; and NYMS Records, VII, 91, 99, 169, 172, NYHS. Additionally, both the standing and acting committees remained active for more than half a century, so the research I have done for the initial ten years of the committee records covers only a portion of these rich archives. When including cases unresolved, or those not reported concluded in the committee minutes, the success rate does dip considerably—52 percent for the PAS and 41 percent for the NYMS. Yet counting all unresolved cases as failures would be a mistake. Many of these unresolved cases went to court, and, when considering that the percentage of court cases that were reported resolved were won by the committees at a whopping 96 percent, including those unresolved cases that went to court and applying this same 96 percent figure would move the success rate of all cases to 67 percent. This number still assumes the bulk of unresolved cases failed and would most certainly be raised if we could access their outcomes. Neither the standing committee nor acting committee had any rationale for hiding failed cases considering that their records remained for the internal use of abolition societies and not for public consumption. Many of the cases that appear in the committee minutes were recorded because they were legally intricate or required further investigative work and evidence gathering, therefore necessitating the aid of the entire committee rather than individual members alone. These stand in contrast to what must have been the many cases that were not noted in the minutes owing to the relative ease with which they could be favorably dispatched.

Approaching the gradual emancipation era via the records of the acting and standing committees of the PAS and NYMS opens revealing vistas on first movement abolitionism. First movement abolitionists used a host of laws to liberate hundreds of persons of color. With enslaved and free blacks often serving as guides, the NYMS and PAS persuaded state legislatures to pass an evolving set of statutes limiting the rights of slaveholders while enlarging those of blacks. These facts emboldened people of African descent in the mid-Atlantic and endowed America's first abolition movement with a sense of tangible progress that nourished its broader reform program, which included plans to make citizens of the formerly enslaved and overturn white prejudice. Probing these records also showcases an implicit compact that powered the activism of first movement abolitionists. The efforts to enforce abolition laws crossed racial lines and joined black with white actors. Blacks held illegally in bondage and the abolition societies worked together to enforce emancipation and expand the liberties of persons of color. These biracial activist partnerships nurtured deep and lasting ties between black communities and the abolition societies in New York and Philadelphia. Finally, the minutes of the acting and standing committees evince that, in their many acts defending the sanctity of black freedom, first movement abolitionists staked a claim for persons of color as incorporated members of the localities and states in which they resided. Enforcing emancipation necessarily entailed asserting the fundamental rights of citizenship for liberated blacks living in the mid-Atlantic region.

AN ENDURING PARTNERSHIP

The alliance of people of color in the mid-Atlantic looking to secure or maintain their freedom and the acting and standing committees forms a constitutive element of first movement abolitionism. Capturing the dynamics of this relationship illustrates why blacks in New York and Pennsylvania reached out to the PAS and NYMS throughout the early republican period. It all started with the actions of people of color. As the African American population mushroomed in the postwar years, so, too, did black community development. In the late eighteenth century, African Americans in the mid-Atlantic founded three independent black churches headed by pastors such as Richard Allen and Absalom Jones, who had direct contact with members of the PAS and NYMS. During these same years, blacks in Philadelphia and New York started mutual relief societies that gave monetary support to and looked to improve the condition of its members. One of these groups, the Free African Society, joined the PAS in visiting the homes of black Philadelphians to gather basic information on the community at large. More informal venues could also serve as channels of communication. Taverns and dance halls brought together urban people of color to socialize and exchange news, which would have surely included recounting some of the same riveting and harrowing experiences that appear in the acting and standing committee records. It is easy to imagine word quickly spreading through these mediums that those looking to establish freedom or in danger of losing their liberty had a valuable resource in the abolition societies. Nor is it hard to envision enslaved and free black migrants quickly assimilating into these channels of communication. Persons of color make up the great majority of informants in acting and standing committee cases, showing that those in need of aid knew of the committees without a concerned white citizen or corresponding member of the abolition societies serving as an intermediary.[6]

There is little doubt that the abolition societies were well known to blacks throughout Philadelphia and New York. And there must have been no doubt to people of color in these cities that the NYMS and PAS, obvious in the very names of the organizations, promoted black freedom from slavery. The abolition societies made frequent, direct contact with black New Yorkers and Philadelphians. The NYMS's African Free School sent society members for visits to the homes of prospective pupils, and the society surveyed people of color to identify those black children who had not been registered as indentured servants after the passage of the 1799 abolition act. The agenda of the PAS's Committee for Improving the Condition of Free Blacks depended on fostering a working relationship with black Philadelphians, as the committee gave socioeconomic advice to free black families and helped people of color find employment. Moreover, members of the standing and acting committees need not have stepped far outside their houses to take the pulse of black life and cultivate contacts among black residents. New York and Philadelphia of the late eighteenth and early

6. The three churches were the St. Thomas African Methodist Church, founded in 1794 and pastored by Absalom Jones; the Bethel African Methodist Episcopal Church, also founded in 1794 by Richard Allen; and the African Methodist Episcopal Zion Church, founded in 1796 by a group of free black New Yorkers, including the former NYMS African Free School pupil Peter Williams, Jr. For the Free African Society's work with the PAS, see PPAS, Series 1, reel 6, 14–17, HSP. I have identified informants in 184 of the acting and standing committee cases examined. Of those informants, 72 percent were persons of color. The reputation of the acting and standing committees as resources for enslaved and free blacks stretched far beyond the mid-Atlantic region, reaching into the lower South and Caribbean. See PPAS, Series 1, reel 4, II, 91, HSP; NYMS Records, VII, 172, 174, NYHS; and Newman, *The Transformation of American Abolitionism*, 68.

nineteenth centuries consisted of concentrated populations. The segregation of these cites by both class and race did not predominate in the 1790s.
In this post-Revolutionary urban landscape, elite merchants, middling
artisans, free laborers, indentured servants, and the enslaved remained
familiar with one another's environs (see Figure 6).[7]

When blacks in New York and Philadelphia decided to look for aid in
waging their freedom bids, they had powerful allies ready to help. The
PAS's acting committee lay at the center of the organization's activism.
Appropriately named, the acting committee was constantly in motion. Its
members fanned out across the city of Philadelphia learning of cases of illegal enslavement, responding to black calls for aid, and confronting slaveholders who flouted the new abolition laws. Made up of a rotating cast of
three to five members, the committee met weekly to discuss and assign new
and ongoing cases and transcribe the minutes of its proceedings.

Quakers dominated the acting committee. The acting committee's most
active member, Thomas Harrison, was a Quaker tailor who, like the enslaved he aided, had experienced his fair share of tribulation. Yet his own
suffering over the death of seven of his nine children seemed only to in-
spire Harrison to mitigate the suffering of others. Characterized as "a lively,
bustling man," Harrison led the way in gathering accounts from individual
persons of color, providing bonds to release from detention those accused
of being enslaved, and seeking to persuade white New Yorkers to acknowledge black freedom. But not all acting committee members identified as
Friends. One noteworthy non-Quaker, Antiguan-born Charles Crawford,
wrote poetry and published a pamphlet dismissing racial distinctions, stating instead that people of color were "in every respect similar" to whites.[8]

7. For the visits of African Free School trustees to the homes of people of color, see
Harris, *In the Shadow of Slavery*, 65. For the overtures of the NYMS to black New Yorkers in response to the problem of unregistered servant children who were in danger of
being claimed as slaves, see NYMS Records, IX, 193, NYHS. Members of the NYMS
"attended Several meetings of Coloured people" regarding this topic. On the founding
and goals of the Committee for Improving the Condition of the Free Blacks, see *Plan
for Improving the Condition of Free Negroes* (Philadelphia, 1789). On the lack of firmly
established residential segregation in late-eighteenth-century Philadelphia and New
York, see White, *Somewhat More Independent*, 171–179; and Gary B. Nash, *Forging Freedom: The Formation of Philadelphia's Black Community, 1720–1840* (Cambridge, Mass.,
1988), 164. Although black households were evenly distributed throughout Philadelphia
in the 1790s, by 1820 75 percent of Philadelphia's black homes were located in the southern section of the city. See ibid., 167.

8. Nash and Soderlund, *Freedom by Degrees*, 123–124; Charles Crawford, *Observations upon Negro-Slavery*, 2d ed. (Philadelphia, 1790), 13. On Crawford, see Lewis

For more complex cases that went to court, the acting committee relied on a cohort of prominent legal counselors including Miers Fisher, William Lewis, Jonathan Dickinson Sergeant, and William Rawle. Fisher, Rawle, and Lewis were Quakers by birth and prominent Pennsylvanian lawyers. Fisher trained under the future state supreme court justice, Benjamin Chew. During the Revolutionary War, he was among a group of Quakers temporarily exiled to Winchester, Virginia, for refusing to take up arms against the British. After the war, he served as the director of the National Bank and briefly as a member of the state House of Representatives. Rawle, whose Quaker roots traced back to the mid-seventeenth century, founded a successful law office in 1783 and was appointed U.S. district attorney for Pennsylvania under the Washington administration. He belonged to other reform movements of the period and would go on to be elected the president of the PAS. Lewis earned his lawyerly reputation providing legal representation for conscientious objecting Friends accused of treason during the Revolution, perhaps applying this morally driven legal work to cases of illegally enslaved blacks. The well-born Sergeant joined early the patriot protest of British imperial policies. He was a member of the Continental Congress and helped to draft the New Jersey Constitution. After moving to Philadelphia, he was chosen attorney general of Pennsylvania and served in that capacity from 1770 to 1780. Quaker identification with persecution and, in the case of Sergeant, fervent allegiance to Revolutionary ideology, may help explain why these men offered their services to the PAS. More socially and economically elite than members of the acting committee, these distinguished counselors nonetheless shared a similar commitment to enforcing and expanding the state's abolition policies.[9]

Leary, "Charles Crawford: A Forgotten Poet of Early Philadelphia," *Pennsylvania Magazine of History and Biography*, LXXXIII (1959), 293–306.

9. On Miers Fisher, see Henry Simpson, *The Lives of Eminent Philadelphians, Now Deceased; Collected from Original and Authentic Sources* (Philadelphia, 1859), 359–361. On Rawle, see T. I. Wharton, *A Memoir of William Rawle, LL. D.: President of the Historical Society, etc.* ([Philadelphia, 1840]). On Lewis, see Esther Ann McFarland and Mickey Herr, *William Lewis, Esquire: Enlightened Statesman, Profound Lawyer, and Useful Citizen* (Darby, Pa., 2012). On Sergeant, see *Biographical Directory of the United States Congress, 1774–2005* ... (Washington, D.C., 2005), 1888–1889. In attempting to account for the motivation of the standing committee members, and those of the PAS as a whole when the society reorganized in 1784, Gary Nash and Jean Soderlund point to the middling economic status of a majority of the active members at this time, including artisans, shopkeepers, and manufacturers. Singling out master artisans as particularly active in the PAS during this period, Nash and Soderlund suggest that this group's antislavery motivations might have stemmed from their view of chattel bondage as a

This Plan OF THE City OF Philadelphia and its Environs, shewing the improved Parts is Dedicated to the MAYOR, ALDERMEN and CITIZENS thereof, By their most obedient Servant, John Hills, Surveyor and Draughtsman.

May 30. 1796.

Sir, I have the pleasure of presenting to You the thanks of the Corporation, especially to Their resolution of this day for the Elegant Plan of the City of Philadelphia which You have Inscribed to them, and with which their Chamber is decorated.

I am, Sir,
Philad.ª Sep.ʳ 5.ᵗ 1796.   Your most humble Servant,
M.ʳ Ja.ˢ Hills.   Matth Clarkson, Mayor

REFERENCE

N.º 1. Christ Church	N.º 24. Jews Synagogue
2. S.ᵗ Peters — Protestant Episcopal Churches	25. Pennsylvania — Hospital
3. S.ᵗ Pauls —	26. Pennsylvania — Hospital
4. S.ᵗ Thomas — for the Africans	27. Christ Church
5. S.ᵗ Michaels — German Lutheran	28. Friends Alms House
6. Zion Church —	29. University of Pennsylvania
7. German Reformed Church	30. German Lutheran Free School
8. The Old Roman Chapel — Roman Catholic	31. Library with the Loganian Library
9. S.ᵗ Marys — Roman Catholic	32. Carpenters
10. Holy Trinity — German	33. Philosophical Halls
11. First Presbyterian	34. Surgeons
12. Second D.º — Church	35. United States
13. Third D.º —	36. North America Banks
14. Friends Meeting house	37. Pennsylvania
15. Pine Street Friends M.ᵗ and School house	38. State House
16. Keys Alley Friends Meeting	39. City Hall
17. Fourth Street Friends M.ᵗ and School house	40. County Court house (Section of Congress)
18. Free Friends Meeting house	41. House of Employment & Alms house
19. Sardine Meeting house	42. New Theatre
20. Moravian Church	43. Circus
21. Baptist Church	44. Goal for Indians
22. Methodist Episcopal Meeting	45. Goal for Felons
23. Quakers Meeting	46. Market
24. Universalits Meeting	47. Fish house
	48. Burying Ground

In Southwark
N.º 1. Swede Church
2. Methodist Meeting house
3. Old Theatre

In the Northern Liberties
N.º 1. Presbyterian Church
2. School house
3. Market

N.B. The Line from Federal Street Public Landing to Cedar Street was fixed by the Port Wardens as the Boundary of the Wharfs, April 2.ᵈ 1788. The Line from Pine Street Public Landing to Spruce Wharf, was fixed by the Port Wardens, March 21.ˢᵗ 1796.
The Streets and Roads that are dotted thus .... are to be opened according to Law.
Brick Yards & Kilns.

PART OF THE N

RIVER

SCHUYLKILL

PART OF PASSYUNK

PART OF MOYA

FIGURE 6.
This Plan of the City of Philadelphia and Its Environs.... By John Hills and John Cooke. 1797. Throughout the 1790s, Philadelphia's landscape was characterized by a thick collection of residential housing and commercial establishments running north to south and bounded by the streets immediately surrounding the Delaware River. Courtesy, Library of Congress

Similar to the PAS's acting committee, the NYMS's standing committee was inundated with freedom claims from people of color. Consisting
of five to seven members serving temporary terms, the standing committee met biweekly to monthly. In its meetings, the standing committee not
only received testimony from black applicants; its members also shared
their stories of patrolling the city's waterfronts looking for kidnappings
and ships clandestinely outfitted for illegal slave exportations, showdowns
with prickly slaveholders, and encounters with black New Yorkers in need
of the committee's protection.

Like its counterpart in Philadelphia, Quakers played a pivotal part in
the NYMS's standing committee. Friends Lawrence Embree and Willet
Seaman are particularly ubiquitous in the committee's minutes during
the 1790s. The Long Island merchant Seaman, a founding member of the
NYMS, served on the standing committee for nearly a decade. Seaman
took on the largest number of cases of any member during his time on the
committee, his energy and commitment unwavering despite his turning
sixty in 1797. Embree, a fellow NYMS founder, practiced law but found
himself on the wrong side of the law in 1789. That year, Embree was indicted for being among a group of men who prevented a local constable
from putting a fugitive from slavery on a ship due to transport her back into
bondage, demonstrating the depth of his commitment to black freedom.[10]

Friends were central to the standing committee. But, as with the PAS
acting committee, notable non-Quakers played important roles. William
Walton Woolsey came from a family of wealthy merchants and married the
sister of Yale's president, Timothy Dwight. Yet Woolsey's wealth and status
did not keep him from aiding those far less connected. He served frequently

---

threat to the work of free craftspeople like themselves. Although this could have been a
factor in explaining the commitment of some acting committee members, it is possible
that identification with or empathy for the sufferings of enslaved people and the fragile freedom of people of color—whether from the persecution of Quakers, a belief that
Revolutionary ideals extended to all people, or more personal experiences that are forever lost to the historical record—undergirded the work of the acting committee and its
counselors. See Nash and Soderlund, *Freedom by Degrees*, 117–119.

10. Willet Seaman's son, Valentine, who studied under Benjamin Rush and became a
physician, was also a member of the NYMS. Much of the surviving traces of Willet Seaman's life are probably owing to Valentine, who is largely credited with the adoption of
smallpox inoculation in New York. See *The Memorial History of the City of New York:
From Its First Settlement to the Year 1892, Volume IV*, ed. James Grant Wilson (New
York, 1893), 398–399. On Embree's involvement in preventing the return of the enslaved
woman Molly to bondage, see Hodges, *Root and Branch*, 166. The charges against Embree were subsequently dropped.

as chairman of the committee and often hosted the standing committee in his home. Woolsey was joined on the committee by William Dunlap, both men members of the New York literary society the Friendly Club, which counted NYMS members Elihu Smith and Samuel Miller among their number. Assisting the committee as a counselor, the young attorney Peter Munro Jay might have been inspired by his distinguished uncle John Jay, the inaugural president of the NYMS. Thus, the standing committee was no monolithic bastion for Quaker activism, even as Friends outnumbered all other discernible groups extant in the committee's records.[11]

Though blacks had a valuable resource in the acting and standing committees, could not persons of color in the era of gradual emancipation simply have asserted their own freedom? Why did they need the PAS and NYMS? The loss of the hereditary component of slavery made slaveholders more receptive to striking individual agreements with their bondspersons in which the enslaved would work for a set number of years in exchange for their release from bondage, while others simply bought their freedom outright. A great many slaveholders, however, held tight to their property claims, sold their bondspersons, and attempted to game the abolition laws. Blacks accused of being legally enslaved and thrown in jail could hardly afford the monetary resources it took to be released. To have recourse for being illegally detained in slavery, whether imprisoned or not, often meant taking out writs of habeas corpus or replevin (the latter of which provided for the release of personal property—that is, an enslaved person—wrongfully detained). Both of these legal maneuvers required money and legal knowledge out of the reach of most enslaved and free blacks. Approximately 40 percent of acting and standing committee cases went to trial, where the able legal counselors of the PAS and NYMS made particularly potent surrogates for black litigants and more than evened the score against their antagonists.[12]

11. On William Woolsey, see Bryan Waterman, *Republic of Intellect: The Friendly Club of New York City and the Making of American Literature* (Baltimore, 2007). Woolsey's brother, George, was also a member of the standing committee, though a more infrequent one. For both Peter Munro Jay and the larger Jay family's participation in the antislavery movement, see David N. Gellman, *Liberty's Chains: The Jay Family, Slavery, and Emancipation, 1685–1912* (Ithaca, N.Y., forthcoming).

12. The PAS and NYMS took legal action in 36.4 percent of the cases recorded in the acting and standing committees' minutes. More often, the committees found that confronting slaveholders proved sufficient to win black liberty. Six of every ten blacks freed with aid from the acting and standing committees secured their liberty without any legal action taken.

Even in those cases that did not go to court, the interposition of the committees paid dividends for the enslaved. It was easy for slaveholders and dealers, accustomed to regarding black persons as chattel, to disregard the claims of persons of color. When one or more members of the abolition societies stepped in to these disputes, it became much harder to avert the abolition laws. Not surprisingly, the "meetings" and "visits" that the committees held with slaveholders on behalf of enslaved applicants were often tempestuous. In 1796, two members of the standing committee told Luke Van Orden that Jane, the woman he had purchased, was free owing to the law prohibiting the importation of enslaved people for sale; Van Orden replied in "abusive terms" that he would not acknowledge Jane's freedom. But, as soon as the standing committee's head counselor threatened a suit against him, Van Order gave up his claim to Jane and released her.[13]

Although it is impossible to recapture the exact details of the relationship between black applicants and the members of the standing and acting committees, certain themes are discernible. In accordance with the broader dictates of post-Revolutionary-era reform movements, the acting and standing committees must have viewed those persons of color who sought their assistance as vulnerable victims, oppressed by the unjust institution of human bondage and clients of the abolition societies' benevolent patronage.

Yet focusing on the paternalistic aspects of this relationship distracts from the ways the acting and standing committees buttressed black agency and respected black autonomy. Of course, in the largest sense, enslaved applicants used the committees as a vehicle to achieve their freedom, a most empowering experience. At times, though, black applicants did not wait for the committees to declare them free but rather liberated themselves in an even more direct fashion. John Phillips approached the standing committee in 1796 to relate that he had been brought into New York and illegally sold to John Lamb. Before the standing committee closed the case, Phillips left his master, assured that both the law and the NYMS backed his actions. A Danish West Indian, James St. Peter, went before the acting committee in August 1792 to protect himself from his soon-to-be-former master. St. Peter had come to Philadelphia with his owner from Saint Croix fourteen months earlier—he was apparently aware that he was thus free according to the Pennsylvania law disallowing migrants to the state from holding enslaved people for longer than six months—and asked "to be Assisted in Case he Should be deprived of his Liberty by Imprisonment

13. NYMS Records, VII, 79, NYHS.

or Otherways." Three weeks later, the acting committee reported that St. Peter had "Proposed to his Master his Right of Freedom and has Since Left his Service." With the PAS ready to protect him, St. Peter must have relished delivering the news of his freedom to his unsuspecting master.[14]

The committees consistently rebuffed any arrangements that impinged on the ability of newly liberated people to determine their own futures. Thomas and Mary applied to the acting committee in the winter of 1799. Their master, Samuel Young, had taken them from New Orleans to Philadelphia and resided with them in the city for just over six months, making them eligible for freedom. To corroborate their story, Thomas and Mary told the acting committee that Young had purchased a carriage when he first arrived in Philadelphia. After contacting the store and gathering evidence, the acting committee informed Young that Thomas and Mary were no longer his property. Thomas and Mary had left the service of Young, but the spurned slaveholder pleaded with the acting committee to help him work out a compromise. "Being clearly informed" that Thomas and Mary were "very unwilling" to serve Young in any capacity, the committee succinctly stated that "the Liberty of the Blacks will be defended." Slaveholders grasped at alternative arrangements that would permit them continued control over the people whose labor they had owned. The abolition societies refused to cooperate.[15]

Blacks who turned to the committees to generate or protect their liberty and the committees that responded to these initiatives developed an enduring partnership. Applicants like Thomas and Mary made resolute decisions to wrest control of their lives from those who claimed them. In turn, the abolition societies held steadfastly to the unassailable worthiness of black liberty. They treated persons of color as fellow human beings with corresponding rights that post-Revolutionary white Americans had to acknowledge. This duo's efforts at enforcing and bolstering northern emancipation gave first movement abolitionism its lifeblood.

FREE MEN AND FREE WOMEN

People of color in Pennsylvania and the PAS's acting committee would undertake a long battle to secure and extend black rights. But first they needed laws to work from. On March 1, 1780, the Pennsylvania Assembly passed An Act for the Gradual Abolition of Slavery. The centerpiece of the act, and the element that gets most remembered, set slavery on the road

14. Ibid., 59, 66, 75; PPAS, Series 1, reel 4, II, 231, 234, HSP.
15. PPAS, Series 1, reel 4, 47–48, HSP.

to gradual extinction. The assembly declared that the children of enslaved mothers born following the bill's enactment would no longer be designated slaves, but indentured servants. The offspring of the enslaved would be in- dentured to the owners of their maternal parents until the age of twenty- eight. If one were to stop here, the act would appear to have left untouched the status of thousands of enslaved persons—those alive when the act was passed—and delayed its effects for a later, yet unborn, generation, who would retain an unfree label until well into adulthood.[16]

This assessment of the Pennsylvania abolition act overlooks the more immediate applicability of the law to the activism of first movement abo- litionists. Two sections of the act regarding the registration of all enslaved blacks in the state would become mechanisms for emancipation by people of color and the acting committee. Pennsylvanians who held enslaved people were required to register them with the clerk of their respective county and had to provide the enslaved person's name, age, and sex and the master's name, occupation, and place of residence by November 1, 1780. If slaveholders failed to register their bondspersons, they would lose their claim to these people. After November 1, 1780, only those registered would be considered enslaved. Here the assembly anticipated that many slaveholders would seek to thwart the law by simply ignoring it. Thus, the bill included a means to ensure that the emancipation process maintained its integrity. The act did exempt some slaveholders from the registration clause. Sojourners in Pennsylvania were immune from the abolition law as long as they did not sell their enslaved laborers or keep them in the state for more than six months. If this section of the law was meant to accom-

16. In 1778, the Executive Council (a body that replaced the role of the governor in Revolutionary-era Pennsylvania) under the leadership of the radical whig George Bryan, urged the assembly to take up the issue of abolition. A previous version of the abolition bill, drafted by the Pennsylvania Assembly in 1779 but not voted on, would have freed the children of enslaved women born after the act's passage at ages eighteen for females and twenty-one for males. In a concession to slaveholders, the 1780 act ex- tended the age in which both sexes of the offspring of the enslaved would have to serve their indentures to twenty-eight. But a ban on intermarriage and a clause threatening "idle" free blacks with bound labor, included in the 1779 bill, were stricken from the 1780 act. See *Pennsylvania Packet or the General Advertiser* (Philadelphia), Mar. 4, 1779, [1], and Mar. 30, 1780, [2]. The Revolution's politicization of slavery formed a central ratio- nale for abolition in Pennsylvania. The Executive Council accompanied its 1778 direc- tive to the legislature on abolition with a note that passing an emancipation law would eliminate the "opprobrium of America" and send a message to "all Europe, who are astonished to see a people eager for Liberty holding Negroes in Bondage." See James T. Mitchell and Henry Flanders et al., comps., *The Statutes at Large of Pennsylvania ...*, 17 vols. (Harrisburg, Pa., 1896–1915), X, 67.

modate slaveholders, the enslaved, in tandem with their white abolitionist allies, would turn it into a tool of liberation.[17]

The law gave other hints that many individuals would do their best to continue the institution of bondage in Pennsylvania. Expecting that slaveholders would try to get around the abolition act by bringing into Pennsylvania blacks whom they had bound "to serve for long and unreasonable terms," the assembly forbade any indenture or apprenticeship of more than seven years unless the servant or apprentice was under the age of twenty-eight, in which case the indenture would be legally recognized only until the servant reached the age of twenty-eight. The intention of this stipulation was to ban the further importation of enslaved people into the state. Legislative opponents of emancipation published a list of objections to the abolition act. Among their complaints was that the law pushed people of color toward "confronting" those who claimed their labor. On this point, emancipation's opponents could not have been more prophetic. The PAS and those persons of color who sought their aid would bring an array of just such confrontations.[18]

17. The 1780 act allowed congressmen and foreign counsels and ministers to retain enslaved people in Pennsylvania indefinitely, perhaps because Philadelphia did not want to risk its role as the political capital of Revolutionary America. Yet it was not clear whether this exemption applied to other federal officials. One of these officials, the first president of the United States, decided not to take any chances. George Washington routinely sent his enslaved laborers temporarily outside the state to avoid their remaining in Pennsylvania for six consecutive months, even as this expedient directly violated a 1788 amendment to the 1780 abolition act outlawing that very practice. For Washington's handling of the enslaved men and women he brought with him to Philadelphia, see Erica Armstrong Dunbar, *Never Caught: The Washingtons' Relentless Pursuit of Their Runaway Slave, Ona Judge* (New York, 2017). The efforts of the acting committee to enforce the six-months clause drew the ire of Washington, who complained to the financier Robert Morris that the PAS "tampered with and seduced" the enslaved to flee their masters. Washington caustically labeled the acting committee's activism productive of "oppression" to slaveholders rather than "humanity" to the enslaved. See Washington to Robert Morris, Apr. 12, 1786, in J. C. Fitzpatrick, ed., *The Writings of George Washington*, XXVIII (Washington, D.C., 1939), 408.

18. Mitchell and Flanders et al., comps., *Statutes at Large*, X, 72; *Pennsylvania Packet*, Mar. 25, 1780, [3]. Opponents of abolition also used the uncertain and chaotic social atmosphere created by the ongoing war with Britain as a reason for voting against gradual emancipation in 1780. The Pennsylvania gradual abolition act passed the assembly by a vote of 34–21. The vote tally demonstrates that abolitionism in Pennsylvania lacked consensus. A larger percentage of German Lutherans than Presbyterian assemblymen voted in opposition to emancipation. But, among the legislators, no religious sect was wholly united in favor of or against the bill. Far more telling was whether a given legislator was directly invested in slavery, as slaveholding representatives voted in opposition to the bill at almost double the rate of nonslaveholders, previewing the

With previously unimaginable paths toward a release from bondage now open, blacks in Pennsylvania exploited their opportunities. The registration clause proved especially helpful. Cases related to the registration clause dominated the acting committee's minutes, constituting nearly half of the committee's caseload. It thus became clear not long after the abolition act's passage that the failure of many Pennsylvanians to register their human property would bring a more immediate version of black freedom than gradual emancipation seemed to allow. Whereas before the 1780 act black persons had been assumed to be enslaved unless proven otherwise, the registration clause inverted this long-standing principle by laying out that "no man or woman of any nation or colour, *except the Negroes or Mulattoes who shall be registered* ... shall, at any time hereafter, be deemed, adjudged or holden, within the territories of this commonwealth, as slaves or servants for life, but as free men and free women." In other words, the bedrock dichotomy upon which chattel bondage rested—that between free and white and enslaved and black—had been significantly weakened.[19]

Black individuals and the PAS transformed the liberating potential implicit in the registration clause from inert words into pulsating reality. Sometimes slaveholders put up little resistance. In 1784, for example, the acting committee heard an enslaved man named Osman tell his story. Osman was the property of Daniel Cox from Trenton, New Jersey, who had moved with Osman to Pennsylvania in 1777, a perfectly legal act. But, according to Osman, Cox had neglected to register him as his slave in accordance with the 1780 abolition law. Now Cox had left Philadelphia and put Osman in the care of John Redman. Osman saw his chance to leave the service of his master for good. Losing any viable claim to a man he had considered his property, Cox had to accept that Osman was his slave no more. The same year as Osman claimed his freedom, Caesar approached the acting committee to recount that during the Revolutionary War he had been traveling on the *Lord North* from Charleston to London. The ship had been overtaken on the high seas, most likely by privateers, and soon Caesar found himself in Philadelphia, where he was held in slavery by Lucius Mallet. Before 1780, Cesar's freedom claim would have been based on his word

---

extralegal resistance of slaveholders to the 1780 law to come. See Nash and Soderlund, *Freedom by Degrees*, 105–108, for a detailed breakdown of the legislative vote on the abolition bill.

19. Thomas D. Morris, *Free Men All: Personal Liberty Laws of the North, 1780–1861* (Baltimore, 1974), 6 (emphasis added). From 1784 to 1794, the PAS's acting committee took up 143 cases concerning the registration law, or 48 percent of its total number of 299.

versus that of Mallet, and he would undoubtedly have remained enslaved. But now Caesar had both the law and an eager set of abolitionists on his side. When apprised of Caesar's illicit enslavement, Mallet "Admitted him to his Right of Freedom." The acting committee reported that Caesar was now "Employing himself as a Free Man." In approximately 25 percent of those cases handled by the acting committee that resulted in freedom for the applicant, slaveholders cut their losses and admitted defeat.[20]

Almost two-thirds of registration cases taken up by the acting committee involved sojourning masters whose enslaved laborers had resided in Pennsylvania past the six-month period permitted by law. The abundance of these case types hints at the existence of extensive networks of communication among Philadelphia's black residents. Enslaved migrants had to learn of laws favoring their freedom before they could apply them. And here a knowledgeable population of persons of color aware of the PAS's acting committee made gradual abolition much more impactful than it would have otherwise been. In one particularly remarkable case, a sixteen-year-old native of Virginia, Jack, alerted the acting committee that he had been sold twice in New Jersey and then carried to Philadelphia where Barnibus McShean purchased him in 1782. Cognizant that the registration clause of the abolition act made him free, Jack asked the acting committee for aid. The acting committee subsequently arranged to have Jack legally removed from McShean's possession, but before it could do so McShean transported Jack to Charleston, South Carolina, for sale. Deeply disturbed by Jack's fate, the committee determined, "for Example, as well as the Restoration of the lad to his Right of Freedom," to take legal action against McShean. Perhaps convinced of the acting committee's earnestness in seeing the case through, McShean met with the PAS and agreed to have Jack returned from slavery in South Carolina in exchange for dropping the charges against him. Unlike the many northern blacks kidnapped into bondage during this time, Jack made it back from slavery in the lower South, his liberty won.[21]

20. PPAS, Series 1, reel 4, I, 16, 24, 12, 54, HSP. From 1784 to 1794, there are thirty-eight instances, or 26 percent of the acting committee cases, in which freedom for the applicant was achieved by slaveholders' acknowledging the liberty of those whose labor they had claimed without putting up any resistance.

21. PPAS, Series 1, reel 4, I, 45, 47, 65, 67–68, 73, 79–80, HSP. Of the 143 registration clause cases the acting committee undertook from 1784 to 1794, eighty-eight were based on the six-month exemption stipulation of the 1780 act. On the extensiveness of kidnapping in the North, see Carol Wilson, *Freedom at Risk: The Kidnapping of Free Blacks in America, 1780–1865* (Lexington, Ky., 1994).

Not all enslaved people whose masters had violated the registration clause could get their stories to the PAS. The acting committee thus made frequent visits to city prisons looking for these individuals. In 1787, the PAS's acting committee learned of the case of the enslaved man Charles. Charles had arrived in Philadelphia with his Maryland master in 1780, just as the abolition law went into effect. Charles lived in the city for two years—long past the six-month residential grace period granted to out-of-state slaveholders—before being returned to Maryland. Following his bankrupt master's death, Charles was to be sold at auction to John Dove, but he escaped to Philadelphia before being arrested in response to an advertisement calling for his recapture. Visiting the jailhouse and learning of Charles's plight, the acting committee served a writ for the black man's freedom on the basis of his residence in Philadelphia for more than six months and had Charles released from prison.[22]

Enslaved applicants and the acting committee not only enforced emancipation; they also used their experiences to exploit ambiguities in the law and broaden the rights of persons of color in Pennsylvania. Section 13 of the 1780 abolition act capped the length of indentures for persons of color in the state at seven years or until the age of twenty-eight. Most likely intended to stamp out slaveholder attempts to skirt the ban on the importation of enslaved people by binding blacks for unduly long terms, the law was geared toward giving the same indentured status to black minors brought to the state by slaveholders as the children of the enslaved born in Pennsylvania who were scheduled to be freed gradually. But, by the 1790s, this section of the abolition act was routinely used as a justification for indenturing black laborers of all statuses until the age of twenty-eight. When overseeing the making of indentures for those it helped free from illegal slavery, the acting committee hewed strictly to binding blacks no longer than whites, or until the ages of twenty-one for males and eighteen for females. In 1784, Thomas Harrison argued that a recently manumitted nineteen-year-old, though indentured until twenty-eight, could not "be Legally Holden" past twenty-one. Two years later, after obtaining the freedom of the fourteen-year-old Dafney, the acting committee noted that it had ensured the indenture made out on her behalf specified that she was to serve four years and "no longer."[23]

22. PPAS, Series 1, reel 4, I, 92, 129, HSP.

23. Ibid., 19, 152. For instances of persons of color who were not the children of enslaved women scheduled for gradual emancipation being indentured by their former owners until the age of twenty-eight rather than twenty-one, see ibid., 187, II, 48, 256–257, 259, 261.

But the PAS discovered that their color-blind interpretation of indenturing was not the predominant one. So, when a suitable case presented itself, the acting committee sought to solidify their reasoning in law. In 1794, the acting committee brought forth a suit on behalf of Robert. Once the enslaved property of William Tharpe of Maryland, Robert had been freed with the help of the standing committee ten years earlier but had entered an indenture with his former master until the age of twenty-eight. By 1794, Robert had reached the age of twenty-one and, following the acting committee's understanding of the legal limits of free black indenture terms, left the service of Tharpe only to be jailed by his former owner. In the trial, *Respublica v. Goaler of Philadelphia County*, the Pennsylvania Supreme Court ruled that, because Robert had not been registered, he was a free man and therefore Tharpe had no right to his labor past the age of twenty-one. The court had ratified the acting committee's stance that free blacks had the same rights as whites with respect to indenture.[24]

The acting committee sought additional ways to attain identical status for white and black indentures. In one particularly complex and drawn-out case, Enoch and Peter Elliot in their wills had directed that a group of enslaved men and women be freed once reaching the age of thirty. Many of those scheduled to be manumitted had birthed children after the deaths of Enoch and Peter. These children were subsequently registered as slaves by one of the inheritors of the Elliot estate, Christopher. Altogether, five children were being held by Christopher Elliot, while four others had been sold by him within the state of Pennsylvania. The PAS's legal counsel concluded that, as soon as the elder Elliots had died, the condition of those enslaved people they had ordered to be freed at thirty had been altered from lifetime slavery to temporary servitude. Therefore, "the children born of the Testators Female Negroes are and were Born Absolutely Free For there is no Difference or Distinction between Temporary Servants—Whether White or Black—on Account of the length of time they have to serve." These children, born to servant, not enslaved, parents, had to be "Treated as children

24. Ibid., I, 10, 294; Paul Finkelman, *An Imperfect Union: Slavery, Federalism, and Comity* (Chapel Hill, N.C., 1981), 56; Robert J. Steinfeld, *The Invention of Free Labor: The Employment Relation in English and American Law and Culture, 1350–1870* (Chapel Hill, N.C., 1991), 40. For an earlier case in which the PAS interpreted the 1780 act as paving the way for equal indenture rights for white and black laborers, see PPAS, Series 1, reel 4, I, 50, 78, 82, HSP. In the decision of *Commonwealth v. Hambright* of 1818, the Pennsylvania courts did very belatedly clarify that indentures to twenty-eight were permissible for enslaved blacks brought into the state who were indentured to their former masters or others. The state supreme court explained that in these cases those enslaved would ultimately get "the most valuable of all considerations, *freedom*."

borne of Free Parents are usually Treated." Following this advice, the acting
committee confronted Elliot and tracked down the other holders of these
illicitly enslaved children. Without legal action, the acting committee obtained the freedom of the children, six of whom were indentured with the
consent of their parents until the ages of eighteen or twenty-one. Here the
standing committee counselors looked to interpret the scope of statutory
abolition as liberally as possible. Just as important, they judged that skin
color could not qualify rights that belonged to all free people.[25]

Though the acting committee obtained the freedom of the children held
and sold as slaves by Christopher Elliot without contention, slaveholders
often did not accept black liberty without a fight. More common than renouncing their rights to what they saw as their rightless chattel, slaveholders resisted the efforts of the acting committee to enforce emancipation. Slaveholder intransigence made evident to black Pennsylvanians
and the PAS that the 1780 abolition act possessed serious shortcomings.
With chattel bondage on the way to extinction in Pennsylvania and persons of color seizing on the chances the law offered for a more immediate
freedom, many slaveholders sought to export their enslaved laborers out
of the state.

Several of the cases persons of color brought to the acting committee
exhibited to the PAS the alarming practice of exporting enslaved people
from the state. When the acting committee learned of the case of Dafney, a thirty-five-year-old enslaved woman brought into Pennsylvania
from South Carolina and kept in the state for ten months, they arranged
a meeting with the man who claimed her body, John Mitchell. But by the
time the committee spoke with Mitchell he had already sent Dafney south
to Charleston. Dafney, Mitchell truculently intoned, was his slave, and he
"would Retain hir as Sutch as Long as he Could." Sometimes slaveholder
defiance took stealthier form. The PAS responded to the entreaty of Tom, a
nineteen-year-old enslaved man who had come to Philadelphia from Saint
Croix with Miles Sweeney and had been in the city for six months. Though
a newcomer to Philadelphia, Tom knew to turn to the acting committee for
help when Sweeney prepared to take him back to the West Indies. When
interviewed, Sweeney assured the committee that he was not holding Tom
as his slave and planned on staying in Philadelphia "for some time" as he
recovered from an illness. The acting committee made a grievous error by

25. PPAS, Series 1, reel 4, I, 12, 17, 23, 31, 49–50, 53, 63, 77, 155, 157, 161–164, 169, II,
2, 34, 36, HSP.

taking Sweeney at his word. Soon after their visit, the committee learned that Tom had been sent to Saint Croix.[26]

The acting committee had mixed success in preventing the removal of enslaved people from Pennsylvania. A Philadelphian slaveholder planned to have his three bondspersons sent out of the state when one of them got word to the PAS. The acting committee discovered that none of those held as slaves had been registered or indentured, and they had the three blacks removed from their now former master's possession. Yet the acting committee did not always learn of such cases in time. Jude had been promised freedom upon reaching her eighteenth birthday, but she was hired out to a James Patton who then took her to Dominica, "where tis to be feared She Will Remain a Slave." For years, the acting committee attempted unsuccessfully to have Jude sent back to Philadelphia where she could gain free status.[27]

Without laws explicitly prohibiting the removal or sale of enslaved people out of state, the acting committee had to come up with alternative means of protecting blacks. In 1785, the committee discovered that an enslaved man named Sambo, who had been placed in jail for alleged "Offences given his master and family," was in danger of being shipped to "Carolina" and forever separated from his wife and children. Powerless to stop Sambo's master, Thomas Harrison instead purchased Sambo and freed him. Yet buying bondspersons hardly constituted a workable policy to counter the removal of enslaved and servant blacks from Pennsylvania.[28]

Through firsthand experience with enslaved and indentured persons of color, the acting committee had identified loopholes in the 1780 act that benefited slaveholders. The PAS subsequently drafted a memorial asking state legislators to amend the gradual abolition law to answer the call of "humanity and justice to the oppressed part of the human Species." The legislature formed a committee to examine the petitioners' supplication. In March 1788, the committee filed a report. It began by acknowledging that the 1780 act was "not sufficiently calculated" to meet the emancipatory spirit of the original legislation. Citing "the mischiefs and subtle evasions, which artful and unprincipled men are too apt to embrace," the com-

26. Ibid., II, 29–30, 32, 129–131, 134.

27. Ibid., I, 17–18, 20, 124. For the ongoing efforts of the acting committee to procure Jude's return to Philadelphia, see ibid., 184, 190, II, 2, 3, 25, 36–37, 44, 48, 74, 116, 119.

28. Ibid., II, 34. That there was no clause preventing the removal of enslaved people out of state might have been a purposeful privilege implicitly granted to slaveholders. For just such a speculation, see Van Cleve, *A Slaveholders' Union*, 80.

mittee agreed with the petitioners that the time had come to amend the law.[29]

In their report, the committee revealed the several ways slaveholders worked surreptitiously to scorn the intent of the 1780 act. Although the law gave gradual freedom to the children of enslaved people born after March 1, 1780, it did not ban their being exported into slavery in "neighbouring states or foreign countries" with the purpose of depriving these persons of the "liberty to which they would be entitled here." The 1780 law also did not prohibit pregnant enslaved women from being forced to leave the state while they gave birth so that their offspring could be legally deemed slaves, allowing their owners to continue to reap the hereditary benefits of chattel bondage. Furthermore, the law did not stop slaveholders from selling enslaved people out of the state of Pennsylvania, forcing the separation of wives from husbands and parents from children. Even stipulations specifically laid out in the law were being subverted. The committee noted that the six-month exemption for slaveholding nonresidents had been violated by those who sent enslaved people out of Pennsylvania immediately before the end of this half-year period and then quickly brought them back into the state. Finally, no penalties or punishments existed for *"men-stealers"* who kidnapped free blacks and took them from Pennsylvania and into slavery.[30]

To remedy these defects in the law, the committee recommended a host of amendments. The assembly assented to these suggestions, passing them into law on March 29, 1788, three weeks after the report was first submitted. Dubbed An Act to Explain and Amend an Act, Entitled, An Act for the Gradual Abolition of Slavery, the legislation is better viewed as Pennsylvania's second abolition law. According to the 1788 act, no enslaved or servant black individual of the state (except those belonging to persons legitimately entitled to the six-month exemption) could be legally "removed" from Pennsylvania to deny freedom to children of enslaved mothers, to have enslaved women give birth to their children in slave states, or to bypass the six-month exemption without the express consent of the person being taken out of the state. This consent had to be given by him or her in

29. PPAS, Series 1, reel 1, I, 26–29 (quotation on 27), HSP; *Constitution and Act of Incorporation of the Pennsylvania Society, for Promoting the Abolition of Slavery and the Relief of Free Negroes, Unlawfully Held in Bondage; and for Improving the Condition of the African Race; to Which Are Added, the Acts of the General Assembly of Pennsylvania for the Gradual Abolition of Slavery, and the Acts of the Congress of the United States, respecting Slaves and the Slave Trade* (Philadelphia, 1800), 33.

30. *Constitution and Act of Incorporation of the Pennsylvania Society,* 35–36.

front of two justices of the peace or, if under twenty-one, through the testimony of a parent. If permission was granted, the justices had to make an
official record of it, including the name, age, status, and place of residence
of the enslaved or servant individual, and provide the person being removed with a copy. Anyone who sold or took an unfree person of color out
of the state in violation of the law "whereby such slave or servant would lose
those benefits and privileges, which by the laws of this state are secured to
him or her," would be subject to a fine of seventy-five pounds. The penalty
of seventy-five pounds for illegally removing bondspersons from the state
amounted to as much as double the cost of an enslaved person in post-
Revolutionary Pennsylvania, indicating the serious intent of the legislature to guard against the exportation of enslaved and servant blacks from
the state without their consent. In closing the original emancipation law's
loopholes, the Pennsylvania legislature decided that to abolish slavery it
needed to expand the rights of black people.[31]

This expansion of rights also protected enslaved families. No one claiming the service of an enslaved or servant person of color would be permitted, as of June 1, 1788, to separate families by more than ten miles without the express consent of those being separated. Evidence of permission
for the separation had to be given in court according to the same proce-
dure as enslaved or servant blacks being taken from the state. Violators of
this clause would be fined fifty pounds. The 1788 law also solidified the ban
on the importation of enslaved people. The six-month exemption for non-
state resident slaveholders would no longer be considered sufficient cover
by inhabitants or residents of Pennsylvania to evade the registration clause
of the 1780 act. The assembly held that each enslaved individual brought
into Pennsylvania by state inhabitants and residents or persons "intending
to inhabit or reside therein" would be considered "immediately . . . free."
Lastly, the 1788 act dictated that kidnappers of free blacks or enslaved and
servant residents of Pennsylvania were subject to a fine of one hundred
pounds and would be sentenced to "hard labour" for a term of between six
months and a year.[32]

---

31. Ibid., sec. II, 38–39; Van Cleve, *A Slaveholders' Union*, 81–82. The 1788 act also required that slaveholders register the indentured children of enslaved mothers by April 1,
1789, or else, within six months of the birth of these children, they would be considered
free.

32. *Constitution and Act of Incorporation of the Pennsylvania Society*, sec. I, 37, sec.
VII, 42–43, sec. VIII, 43. The act also imposed the extraordinarily high penalty of one
thousand pounds for anyone participating in the slave trade from Pennsylvania ports,
effectively banning the practice in the state. George William Van Cleve uses the large

The acting committee and black applicants for its aid wasted little time implementing the 1788 amendments. In June 1788, an enslaved woman named Phillis escaped her owner, a tavernkeeper of Philadelphia named Henry Young, who was moving to New Orleans. Perhaps in part spurred by the amendments to the 1780 abolition act passed only weeks before, Phillis realized that turning to the acting committee gave her the best chance to save her daughter, Dinah, whom Young planned on dragging to slavery in the lower South. Phillis met with the acting committee and implored its members to intervene. The acting committee quickly ascertained that neither Phillis nor her daughter had been registered as slaves and, learning that Young was about to leave for New Orleans, hurried as a group, along with Phillis, to Young's house. Young replied that the abolition laws would not stop him from taking his property southward, at which time the acting committee, who probably had informed legal authorities, saw to it that Young was taken into custody. The force of the law now clear, Young relented and turned over Dinah to her mother.[33]

Black Pennsylvanians and the acting committee likewise sought to use the 1788 amendments to obtain freedom for those enslaved people who had already been removed from the state. In August 1788, the committee responded to the case of a sixteen-year-old enslaved boy, Will, who had been sent out of Pennsylvania by his master without the consent of Will or his mother, who most likely informed the acting committee of the case. Will's master, Thomas Harper, "Confessed" that he had sent Will to Jamaica and, informed that his actions were now illegal, "Made some Appolagy." Apprised of the law, he "assured" the acting committee that he would "Order his [Will's] return," and acting committee members continued to make visits to Harper, reminding him that Pennsylvania law now required his cooperation. Just one month later, the acting committee heard that an enslaved woman named Mary had been sold by Michael Cainer of Philadelphia to Alexander Work of Roane County, North Carolina. "Desirous of supporting the Law" passed that spring, the acting committee impressed

---

disparity between the fines for taking part in the slave trade and those for illegally exporting enslaved and indentured blacks or kidnapping free people of color as evidence of the public's ambivalence in protecting the rights of Pennsylvanian African Americans. See Van Cleve, *A Slaveholders' Union*, 81–82. Valuations using pounds and dollars as monetary units were used interchangeably in late-eighteenth-century America. For the case of Pennsylvania, see Ronald W. Michener and Robert E. Wright, "State 'Currencies' and the Transition to the U.S. Dollar: Clarifying Some Confusions," *American Economic Review*, XCV (2005), 682–703.

33. PPAS, Series 1, reel 4, I, 159–160, 167, HSP.

upon Cainer his duty to "Restore" Mary to "Hir Right as a Pennsylvanian" and warned that unless he complied a suit would soon be lodged against him. When Cainer made only a partial attempt to find Mary, the acting committee sued him, and lengthy legal proceedings leading to trial followed.[34]

As the activism of the acting committee and the applicants that gave it its case load show, the quest to effect abolition in Pennsylvania was a protracted struggle in which the elemental rights of black freedom and belonging took center stage. Throughout the late eighteenth century, knowledge of laws that provided them freedom spread among blacks in greater Philadelphia, and word traveled that the PAS offered recourse to the multipronged infringements of slaveholders. As a result, hundreds of black individuals reached out to the acting committee. From enforcing the registration clause, to preventing the removal of persons of color from Pennsylvania, the acting committee responded by advocating for the rights and privileges of myriad black individuals.

UNDER GREAT DISADVANTAGE IN
ASSERTING THEIR RIGHTS

While the PAS and black Pennsylvanians enforced statutory abolition, the NYMS, founded in the same year as the legislative defeat of a New York emancipation bill in 1785, turned to alternative laws to limit slaveholder rights and enlarge those of the enslaved. The New York state legislature agreed to make it illegal to buy or sell enslaved people imported into the state after June 1, 1785. This law would serve as a launching pad for a long campaign to obtain an emancipation act. But, like their counterparts in Philadelphia, black New Yorkers and the NYMS made use of, and helped garner, a spate of laws beyond gradual emancipation statutes to liberate persons of color and augment the rights of enslaved and free blacks in the state.[35]

The NYMS began its petitioning efforts by urging a ban on the exportation of enslaved people, agitating for the enactment of basic protections for black New Yorkers. The NYMS's preoccupation with this issue was as old as the society itself. The NYMS communicated in the preamble to its constitution that blacks were "under great disadvantage in asserting their

34. Ibid., 171–173. For the lengthy legal process surrounding the Cainer case, see ibid., 175, 179, 182–183, 185–186, II, 93, 95, 216, 218.

35. *Laws of the State of New York: Passed at the Sessions of the Legislature ...*, 5 vols. (Albany, N.Y., 1886–1887), II, 120–122.

Rights." Drawing on personal knowledge of the plight of black New Yorkers, the founders of the NYMS referenced the "Violent Attempts lately
made, to seize, and export for sale" free blacks as a primary reason for
forming the organization. In late-eighteenth-century New York, kidnappers apprehended free blacks, claimed them as chattel, and then, according
to the legal practice of taking enslaved people out of state, sold freepersons
into perpetual bondage. Although the standing committee minutes do not
begin until 1791, as will become evident in the paragraphs that follow, the
appeals of black New Yorkers for aid informed the NYMS's activist agenda.
In February 1786, finding that the exportation of enslaved and free blacks
"is still Continued," the NYMS drafted a memorial to the state legislature.
Alluding to the "frequent and very affecting Instances" of families being
torn apart, the petition instructed the legislature that there were many
"manumitted Slaves and other Freemen whose Colour exposed them to
such Outrages [exportation]; being Kidnapped and carried to Market in
distant Parts." It was exactly these outrages that the NYMS sought to tamp
down.[36]

Within two years of the NYMS's petition, in 1788, the New York legislature decreed that anyone who purchased an enslaved person or served
as an agent for a buyer "with intent to remove, export or carry such slave
from this state" would be fined one hundred pounds, half of the sum going
to the person bringing the suit and the other half to the state. The enslaved person being illegally removed from New York would be "declared
... free." The state government also chose to reissue the 1785 moratorium
on the purchase or sale of enslaved people imported, implementing the
same one-hundred-pound fine for violators and a declaration of freedom
for the enslaved individuals who had been illegally brought into New York.
In essence, the state's market in the selling and trading of enslaved people
had been frozen while the issue of slavery itself remained unresolved.[37]

The laws against slave importation and exportation would allow many

36. NYMS Records, VI, 4, 35, 41, NYHS. Reports of a kidnapping ring and editorials in support of a law against the exportation of enslaved and free persons of color
appeared in New York newspapers only one month after the NYMS submitted its 1786
petition, suggesting the manumission society sought public support for its memorial.
See *New-York Packet,* Mar. 13, 1786, [3]; and *Independent Journal; or, the General Advertiser,* Mar. 15, 1786, [2]. Around the same time, the *New-York Packet* also published a
notice warning African Americans "to be upon their guard, lest they should meet with
some kidnappers, and share the fate many have heretofore done." See *New-York Packet,*
Mar. 16, 1786, [3].

37. Zilversmit, *The First Emancipation,* 151; *Laws relative to Slaves and the Slave-
Trade* (New York, 1806), 3–5.

enslaved New Yorkers to turn to the NYMS's standing committee to gain freedom. Several of the illegal importation cases demonstrate a bustling market in enslaved people that endured throughout the 1790s. Yet black New Yorkers turned the act of being sold as property, one of the quintessential elements of chattel bondage, on its head by using the purchase of their bodies as a device of liberation. Sylvia, for example, told the standing committee in 1797 that she had been brought from Connecticut in 1787 and sold a total of seven times in western New York over a ten-year period. Sylvia's most recent master had now sent her to New York City for yet another sale. Unlike the several other times she was sold, Sylvia now gained the opportunity to alter her state. Standing committee members made frequent trips to the city's docks scanning for illegally enslaved and kidnapped free blacks on the brink of being transported from New York. Perhaps it was on one of these occasions that Sylvia had the chance to communicate her story, in this case to standing committee member William Woolsey. Learning of her predicament, and knowing that the law against the importation of enslaved people for sale made Sylvia free, the standing committee pressed the agent empowered to sell Sylvia, and he released her. The committee then wrote a letter to Sylvia's master informing him that she was no longer his chattel, and Sylvia walked away "in possession of her liberty."[38]

Other persons of color brought their cases of illegal importation directly to the standing committee. In 1792, the standing committee took on the case of Harry Henry. Contrary to the ban on the importation of enslaved people for sale, Henry was brought as a slave to New York from New Jersey in 1792 and sold five times before being hired out as a coachman. Henry appeared before the committee to give its members details on the dates of his several sales and the names of the many individuals who had held him as a bondsman. The standing committee urged Henry to prepare his testimony and gather witnesses to build his case, which he would go on to win. Seven years later, Getty Simmons, born enslaved on Staten Island, appeared before the standing committee and related that she had been sold several times before ending up with a master who took her to New Jersey and then, after a year, returned to New York and sold Simmons. Two members of the standing committee confronted Simmons's current owner, apprising him that his purchase of the woman was illegal. The man admitted that Simmons's assertions were true and, without litigation, gave up his claims to her labor. Three-fourths of the standing committee's cases regarding laws limiting slaveholder rights were based on the illegal importation of en-

38. NYMS Records, VII, 94–95, NYHS.

slaved people for sale, primarily because it was far easier for bondspersons
sold in New York than those exported from the state for sale to relay their
narratives to the NYMS.[39]

Oftentimes slaveholders did not give up as easily as Getty Simmons's
erstwhile master, displaying the same contested process over black freedom in early national New York as in Pennsylvania. The predicament of an
illegally held woman, Dinah, and her two children is a case in point. Dinah's
children were willed to a New York man who manumitted them, but they
were being claimed as slaves by Thomas Skinner in September 1797. When
the standing committee paid Skinner a visit, he admitted that the children
had a right to freedom and yet refused to release them. After the NYMS
informed Skinner that they would press charges against him, the standing
committee learned that Skinner planned to abscond with the children to
South Carolina, where no one would interfere with his illegally obtained
property. The NYMS hastened to bring its suit forward, and Skinner, under
the immediate threat of a lawsuit he knew he could not win, renounced
his fraudulent claim to Dinah's children. Persons of color and the standing committee stood tall to audacious slaveholder actions. Lucy Merritt
turned to the standing committee for relief in the fall of 1796. She had been
brought into New York by William Cutting and sold twice, ending up in the
hands of John Watkins. Noncompliant at first, Watkins recognized Merritt's freedom when the NYMS filed charges against him. But soon after,
Watkins imprisoned Merritt and insisted that she was his lawful property.
When the standing committee recommenced the suit, the state supreme
court ruled in favor of Merritt, and Watkins's duplicity cost him forty dollars in damages awarded to a woman he had once held as property.[40]

The passage of New York's gradual abolition law did not lessen the activism of the standing committee and persons of color. In fact, it intensified
it. An Act for the Gradual Abolition of Slavery gave freedom gradually to
the children of enslaved women born after July 4, 1799. Males would serve
their mothers' masters as indentured servants until the age of twenty-eight,
and females, until twenty-five. As with Pennsylvania's abolition law, the act
required slaveholders to register the indentured children of their bondspersons. Whereas in Pennsylvania slaveholders were given six months to
report to the clerk, in New York they had nine months to do so. In a more
crucial way, New York's registration clause was weaker than Pennsylvania's. New York's slaveholders were asked to register only the children of

39. Ibid., VII, 73, 79–80, 109, 131.
40. Ibid., 54, 56, 58, 66, 69, 75, 99, 173, 178, 182–183, 185, 187.

enslaved women and not those they held in slavery—closing off a route to freedom used by enslaved persons of Pennsylvania. The New York act also inflicted a much lighter penalty on slaveholders who neglected to register the emancipated offspring of their enslaved laborers. Rather than declaring these unregistered servants free, the New York act imposed relatively paltry fines of five dollars for the first offense and one dollar for every month thereafter in which the servant went unregistered.

New York's abolition law addressed the gradual phasing out of slavery but did even less than Pennsylvania's 1780 law to confront the problem of enforcement. The NYMS therefore had little time to celebrate the new legislation. Within a year of the gradual abolition act's passage, the NYMS reported that the practice of exporting enslaved people had increased greatly. Now that the legislature had put human bondage on the road to extinction, it made more economic sense than ever for New York slaveholders to sell enslaved laborers out of state. Slaveholders and persons interested in acquiring bonded labor were also buying enslaved people outside New York and claiming them as legal property when returning to the state.[41]

The NYMS's intelligence on these issues came from the standing committee's experiences responding to the efforts of slaveholders and dealers to rob black New Yorkers of their freedom. In the spring of 1800, for example, the standing committee had been dealing with multiple cases in which persons of color were being shipped from New York to Norfolk and Savannah and then on to the West Indies to be sold as slaves. The standing committee described their dramatic interventions in some of these cases. In one instance, three members of the committee, acting on intelligence they received from an unnamed source, boarded a vessel and heard a sailor cry out that the ship's crew had "been discovered." Members of the committee then warned the ship's captain that his and his crew's actions were "contrary to the Law" and called for their cooperation. The captain responded by ordering two of his subordinates to open a hidden trap door in the boat's hold, whereupon four people of color, ranging from ages ten to thirty-five, emerged. Despite success in this case, the standing committee openly admitted to having stopped only a portion of these exportations and kidnappings. The NYMS resolved that something had to be done to combat these threats to abolition's effectiveness.[42]

41. Ibid., IX, 40, 50–51.
42. Ibid., VI, 158–162. The standing committee determined to sue the men responsible for the kidnapping of the four blacks whom they stopped from being transported from New York for the maximum penalty allowed by the law at the time, one hundred pounds.

In 1800, the NYMS petitioned the state legislature to strengthen the restraints on the importation and exportation of enslaved people. "Influenced by a regard to the rights of men," the NYMS called attention to "a Subject so highly interesting to the welfare of Society and the safety of individuals." The rights of enslaved, indentured, and free blacks had been "sacrificed to the rapacious views" of "unprincipled men" determined "to elude the benign intention" of New York's laws through exporting and selling or bringing into the state persons of color unlawfully. The New York legislature responded favorably to the NYMS's requests and, in 1801, bolstered the laws against the importation and exportation of bondspersons. Violators would now be fined $250, and ship captains who received illicitly enslaved people for exportation would be subject to the same penalty as the agent or seller of the enslaved individual. To discourage the state's internal market in enslaved people, the legislature ruled that only those migrants who intended to "reside permanently" in New York could bring with them enslaved laborers.[43]

As long as slavery remained a legal institution in New York, new laws boosting the rights of persons of color were necessary. In 1804, the NYMS petitioned the municipal government of New York to prohibit slaveholders from confining enslaved people not accused of crimes in the infamous New York City prison, Bridewell. As with nearly all of the NYMS's initiatives, this effort stemmed from visceral narratives provided by persons of African descent. The society's standing committee informed the full society in December 1804 of a case in which a black man had been placed in Bridewell until arrangements could be made for his transportation to Richmond, Virginia, where, it was claimed, his owner resided. Members of the committee spoke with the man who "asserted his Freedom" and told his visitors that he had resided in New York for four years. Because the imprisoned man's accuser could not gather enough evidence to prove his slave status, he had detained him in Bridewell and left him "without the hope of Liberty." Troubled by this strategy of exportation by slaveholders and kidnappers, in 1805 the NYMS persuaded the Corporation of New York City to prohibit the holding of enslaved people in Bridewell who had "not been criminally accused." Despite their success on the Bridewell confinement problem, the NYMS could not persuade the state legislature to overturn the law permitting slaveholders to export from the state enslaved people convicted of certain crimes, one of their few failed initiatives. When its

43. Ibid., IX, 50–51; *Laws relative to Slaves and the Slave Trade*, 8, 11, 13.

legal strategy came up short, the NYMS formed a committee to visit New York judges and try to "dissuade them from using their discretionary power of Transportation," looking to strip the removal power of slaveholders.[44]

Continuing to lobby for African American rights, the NYMS initiated a raft of laws favorable to blacks, free and enslaved, passed by the state legislature between 1807 and 1817. In 1807, the legislature decided that slaveholders planning to move from the state with those whom they held in slavery had to have resided for at least a decade in New York and needed to produce two witnesses to attest to their claims. Black servants could not now be removed from New York without those who claimed their labor giving monetary security for their return. One year later, New York enacted its first anti-kidnapping law, with violators facing imprisonment of up to fourteen years for the first offense and life in jail for the second.[45]

The standing committee's ongoing attempts to stop kidnapping inspired the NYMS to press the legislature for these legal changes. In 1804, a boy was spotted being chased and overtaken by a man in the streets of New York who then brought him aboard a ship. The NYMS issued a writ to prevent the boy's exportation and the ship from disembarking. When members of the standing committee boarded the vessel, they discovered two other boys being forcibly held against their will. The ship's captain clearly intended to carry the three boys into slavery and would have done so without the interference of the NYMS. By 1810, the legislature had banned the importation of enslaved people by permanent residents of the state in all cases and explained that it would judge free all blacks brought into the state as slaves after nine months of their masters' residence.[46]

44. NYMS Records, IX, 244, 270–271, NYHS. The NYMS began lobbying against the holding of blacks accused of crimes in Bridewell prison beginning in 1801. See ibid., 63. For a petition requesting the legislature to prohibit the exportation out of state of enslaved people convicted of certain crimes, see ibid., 230, 244, 268–269.

45. *Laws of the State of New York, Passed at the Thirtieth Session of the Legislature, Begun and Held at the City of Albany, January 27th, 1807* ([Albany, N.Y., 1807]), 92–93; *Laws of the State of New-York Passed at the Thirty-First Session of the Legislature: Begun and Held at the City of Albany, the Twenty-Sixth Day of January, 1808* (Albany, N.Y., 1808), 108–109.

46. NYMS Records, VII, 266–267, NYHS; *Public Laws of the State of New-York, Passed at the Thirty-Third Session of the Legislature, Begun and Held at the City of Albany the Thirtieth Day of January, 1810* (Albany, N.Y., 1810), 45–46; Moseley, "A History of the New-York Manumission Society," 120. The NYMS waged petition campaigns urging the enactment of many of the laws restricting slaveholding rights. See NYMS Records, IX, 165, 182, 205, NYHS. Cognizant that slaveholders would continue to circumvent the ban on the importation of enslaved people by indenturing out-of-state

After multiple petition attempts by the NYMS for the total abolition of slavery, on March 31, 1817, at the behest of the state's governor and NYMS member Daniel Tompkins, the legislature passed the inconspicuously titled An Act relative to Slaves and Servants. It decreed that all enslaved people born before July 4, 1799, would be made free by July 4, 1827, allotting gradual freedom to those bondspersons untouched by the original emancipation act. Enslaved persons born between July 4, 1799, and July 4, 1817, would be considered free but had to serve as indentured servants under provisions of the 1799 act, and those born after the passage of the 1817 act would remain servants until the age of twenty-one.[47]

While bringing a staggered rather than immediate end to slavery, the 1817 act consummated thirty years of antislavery agitation by the NYMS and black New Yorkers. The standing committee and its counsel constituted pivotal players in this activism. But the poignant experiences of persons of color and their stories of illegal enslavement and kidnapping gave the committee its caseload and pushed the NYMS to work toward extending the reach of laws that could protect and foster black freedom. Although many people of color suffered illicit bondage and kidnapping without relief from the NYMS, those whose narratives did make it to members of the standing committee often found that the society's assistance could make a profound difference in their lives. Long before New York became a free state, the standing committee and black New Yorkers endeavored fervently to gain and guard black liberty.

THE SEEDS OF CITIZENSHIP

In the struggle for emancipation, persons of color and the committees carved out rights that acted as the foundation for the wider first movement abolitionist commitment to free black citizenship. The records of the standing and acting committees divulge how this commitment hinged on an elemental assertion of rights establishing that persons of color belonged to the larger free community of autonomous individuals making up the

---

bondspersons, the 1810 act stated that all indentures, bonds of service, and contracts made with anyone who was enslaved in another state before coming to New York were considered void and the person so bound was to be "declared free."

47. *Laws of the State of New York, Passed at the Fortieth Session of the Legislature, Begun and Held at the City of Albany, the Fifth Day of November, 1816* (Albany, N.Y., 1817), 136–144. The NYMS petitioned the state legislature for total abolition in 1811 and 1816. See NYMS Records, IX, 283–284, NYHS; and *Minutes of the Proceedings of the Fifteenth American Convention for Promoting the Abolition of Slavery, and Improving the Condition of the African Race* ... (Philadelphia, 1817), 5–6.

THE "JUST RIGHT OF FREEDOM"

body politic in places like Pennsylvania and New York. If, as an authoritative account of citizenship in early America puts it, "Americans came to see that citizenship must begin with an act of individual choice" and one of "volitional allegiance," then each time a person of color contacted the committees, fought for their right to remain in New York or Pennsylvania, and used the legal system to ensure their freedom they were exercising their choice to declare themselves citizens of the young Republic. In this sense, enslaved people, free persons of color, and the abolition societies derived their basic understanding of black citizenship from the very act of enforcing and expanding gradual emancipation laws. In a period in which American ideas of citizenship were just beginning to be worked out, both the standing and acting committees and blacks who sought their aid were making an unequivocal statement that people of color held an underlying claim on civil membership in the new nation.[48]

The most indispensable right of citizenship was freedom from bondage. As the records of the acting and standing committees of the PAS and NYMS illustrate, by expanding statutory emancipation and protecting free blacks from kidnapping and wrongful enslavement, the abolition societies and people of color fought for the fundamental rights of blacks. An 1801 statement by the New Jersey Abolition Society captured this aspect of black citizenship when it explained that slavery represented "the most palpable violation of those boasted equal rights by withholding from several thousand human beings their just and natural claim to Liberty." For

48. The literature on citizenship in the post-Revolutionary and early national eras is vast. For a representative cross-section of works, see Douglas Bradburn, *The Citizenship Revolution: Politics and the Creation of the American Union, 1774–1804* (Charlottesville, Va., 2009); Seth Cotlar, *Tom Paine's America: The Rise and Fall of Transatlantic Radicalism in the Early Republic* (Charlottesville, Va., 2011); Rosemarie Zagarri, *Revolutionary Backlash: Women and Politics in the Early American Republic* (Philadelphia, 2007); Nathan Pearl-Rosenthal, *Citizen Sailors: Becoming American in the Age of Revolution* (Cambridge, Mass., 2015); Alexander Keyssar, *The Right to Vote: The Contested History of Democracy in the United States*, rev. ed. (New York, 2009); and Rogers M. Smith, *Civic Ideals: Conflicting Visions of Citizenship in U.S. History* (New Haven, Conn., 1997). On volitional citizenship, see James H. Kettner, *The Development of American Citizenship, 1608–1870* (Chapel Hill, N.C., 1978), 208–209 (quotations). Interpretations of citizenship in post-Revolutionary and early national America focus mainly on politics and political rights. Chapter 3 of this manuscript does reveal that the abolition societies supported black political rights. But my use of the term *citizenship* in this chapter stems from a more basic and less formal understanding of *civil / civic* belonging in this period. For an alternative to the political emphasis on citizenship in the early Republic, see Catherine O'Donnell Kaplan, *Men of Letters in the Early Republic: Cultivating Forums of Citizenship* (Williamsburg, Va., and Chapel Hill, N.C., 2008).

the many people of color serving indentures, the transition to full independence would take time. But the vital revolutionary rights of human autonomy and self-ownership remained the end goal.[49]

A primary right of liberty in the early American Republic was access to legal mechanisms of justice in pursuit of personal freedom. Each time illegally enslaved people were released from the confinement of the persons who claimed their bodies through writs of habeas corpus, brought before a judge, and freed from bondage by a court of law, they obtained the building blocks of membership in civil society. The abolition societies also helped black litigants attain another essential right of free people: the fruits of one's labor. In 1796, Joe alerted the NYMS that he had been carried into New York as a slave from Nova Scotia and sold to George Warner just after the passage of the law prohibiting the importation of enslaved people for sale in 1785. A skilled sailmaker, Joe had worked "very profitably" for Warner for almost eleven years. The standing committee, in direct consultation with Joe, demanded Warner pay Joe $500 in restitution for lost wages or face a suit. Warner turned down the offer. When the NYMS prosecuted Warner, the state supreme court awarded Joe $460, hardly enough to fully recover the wages he had lost but a sizable sum to begin life as a free person.[50]

The acting and standing committees also fought to uphold the integrity of black families, a right commonly denied enslaved persons but taken for granted in post-Revolutionary America as a key ingredient for fostering a republican citizenry. For instance, in 1794 the standing committee got wind that Caesar Lee's son Daniel, freeborn and under no indenture, was being "kept" from his father by Thomas Wills of Mendham, New Jersey. The NYMS wrote to a lawyer in Newark who saw to it that the boy was liberated. Sometimes relatives of illegally enslaved people of color turned to the abolition societies once their own efforts at regaining family members hit a dead end. In 1796, Richard Lawrence reported to his fellow standing committee members the case of eighteen-year-old George Burt. A free black who had traveled to New York with his relatives, Burt was sold into slavery to a resident of Wall Street who then sold him to John Hutson. Burt's grandmother came to the city to face down her grandson's putative owner, but to no avail. When she informed Lawrence of the case and the standing committee filed a suit, Hutson changed his mind and gave up Burt. The abolition societies were sensitive to the distresses of people of

49. *Minutes of the Proceedings of the Seventh Convention of Delegates from the Abolition Societies Established in Different Parts of the United States* ... (Philadelphia, 1801), 15.
50. NYMS Records, VII, 71, 87–88, 99, NYHS.

color in cases involving black families. In 1786, Susannah, whose freedom
the acting committee had previously established, was about to be taken
against her will to New Jersey by her former owner, "to the great Grief of
her Husband," when the PAS got a writ of habeas corpus and the Pennsylvania Supreme Court declared Susannah free. A year later, Lucy noti-
fied the acting committee that the woman who had once owned her, Mary
Bears, was planning on selling her two-year-old daughter to a slave trader
who intended to take her from the state. The full acting committee visited
Bears and had her vow that she would not sell Lucy's daughter. The committee made note that they would monitor the case to ensure that Bears
kept her promise.[51]

One of the most central expressions of the first abolition movement's
commitment to black citizenship lay in preventing the removal and kidnapping of enslaved and free persons of color. Here the acting and standing committees exhibited a crucial component of their conception of black
rights. If the goal of the abolition societies had been simply to eliminate
slavery from state borders, there would have been no need to stop the removal of persons of color from the mid-Atlantic region. Yet the committees
staunchly opposed such actions whenever they learned of enslaved and free
blacks being forced out of New York and Pennsylvania.

More than one in four acting committee cases revolved around preventing the removal of enslaved and servant people of color from Pennsylvania or attempting to bring back those who had been taken from the state.
One of these cases involved a woman named Mary, who, at some point in
the late 1780s, was hired by her Maryland master to an employer in Pennsylvania and kept in the state for more than six months, thus liberating
her. While subsequently laboring as a free woman in Lancaster, Pennsylvania, Mary was apprehended in August 1790 by a set of Maryland men
most likely connected to her former master and "forcibly dragged" back
into slavery just over the state line in Cecil County. The acting committee
responded by reaching out to correspondents in Maryland to gather evidence in order to bring an indictment against the guilty parties. In explaining their rationale behind pursuing the case, the acting committee proclaimed that they wanted Mary "Restored to hir just right of Freedom and
Brought again to Pennsylvania." It is unclear whether the acting committee
succeeded in having Mary returned to Pennsylvania, but the language the
PAS used in cases like these is instructive (see Figure 7). The acting committee proclaimed repeatedly that persons of color had a "right to remain"

51. Ibid., 33, 52, 54, 57, 60–62; PPAS, Series 1, reel 4, I, 12, 70, 101, 103, HSP.

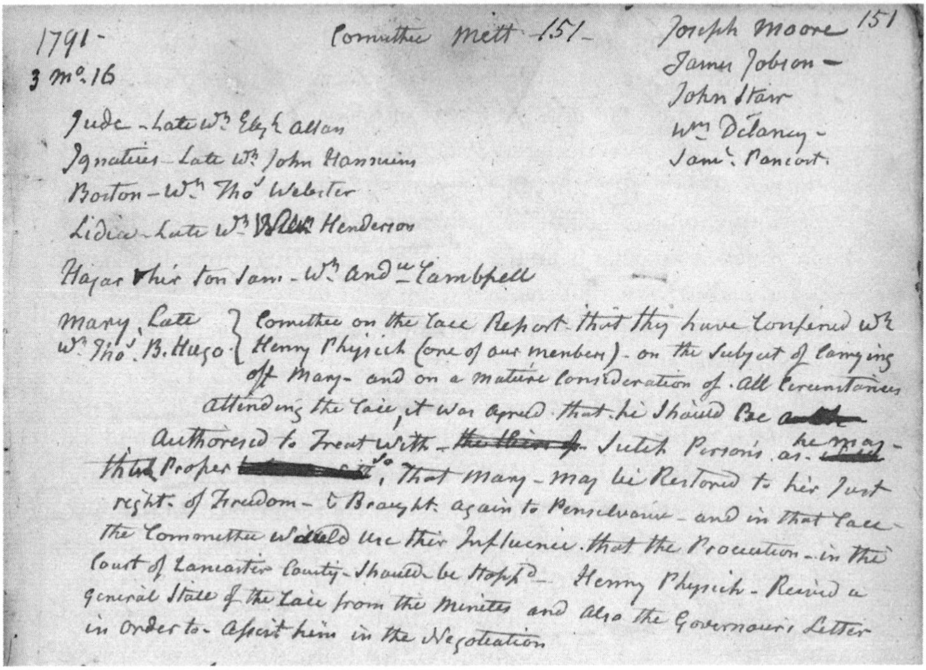
1791-
3 mo. 16
Committee mett 151-
Joseph Moore 151
James Jobson -
John Stair
Wm. Delaney -
Saml. Pancoast

Jude - Late Wt. Elizh Allan
Ignatius - Late Wt. John Hannum
Borton - Wt. Thos Webster
Lidia - Late Wt. Henderson

Hagar & her son Sam - Wt. Andw. Cambpell

Mary, Late Wt. Thos. B. Hugo } Committee on the Case Report that they have Conferred wh Henry Physick (one of our members) - on the Subject of Carrying off Mary - and on a mature Consideration of All Circumstances attending the Case, it was agreed that he Should Be Authorised to Treat with Such Persons as he may think Proper so, That Mary - may be Restored to her Just right of Freedom - & Brought again to Pensylvania - and in that Case the Committee would use their Influence that the Procecution - in the Court of Lancaster County - Should be stopt - Henry Physick - Received a general State of the Case from the Minutes and also the Governour's Letter in Order to assist him in the Negotiation

FIGURE 7. Acting Committee Minutes of the Pennsylvania Abolition Society, Mar. 16, 1791, Papers of the Pennsylvania Abolition Society. Courtesy, Historical Society of Pennsylvania

in Pennsylvania that trumped the right of slaveholders and dealers to dispose of black people as they saw fit.[52]

In at least one recorded instance, the acting committee joined forces directly with a prominent member of free black Philadelphia to safeguard the liberty of African American Pennsylvanians in opposition to those who sought to reenslave them. Betty Anderson had moved with her owner, William Morton, to Pennsylvania in 1788. Looking to ensure the perpetuation of his slave holdings, Morton sent a pregnant Anderson to Baltimore, where he assumed she would give birth to an enslaved rather than free per-

52. PPAS, Series 1, reel 4, II, 131, 151, HSP. The acting committee wrote to the governor of Pennsylvania, Thomas Mifflin, about Mary. Mifflin advised the committee to have the state attorney general pursue an indictment of the suspected guilty parties. The acting committee wanted the men responsible for Mary's kidnapping severely punished to "afford an example to deter similar outrages in the future." Nearly a year after the acting committee first determined to pursue the case of Mary's reenslavement, they were still gathering evidence and identifying witnesses (169). For two examples of PAS cases in which the acting committee used the language "right to remain," see ibid., I, 78.

son. But, according to both the registration clause of the 1780 abolition act and the 1788 amendment that forbade removing enslaved laborers from Pennsylvania without their consent, Betty and her child had gained their freedom. Soon after assuming her liberty, Betty moved to Philadelphia, where she and her son Harry were suddenly seized by Morton in July 1790 and taken from the city. Moving quickly, the acting committee plotted a plan and enlisted the free black minister Richard Allen, along with a member of the PAS, to chase down Morton. The two men caught up with Morton in Lancaster, where they obtained a writ of habeas corpus. Anderson and her son were declared free by a judge and returned to Philadelphia, their liberty now secured in law.[53]

The acting committee responded just as decisively when it received information pertaining to the removal of enslaved people for sale outside Pennsylvania's borders. In one notable case, the committee directed its ire at a member of the PAS. In the late summer of 1786, Tench Coxe, the secretary of the PAS, acting on behalf of an unnamed slaveholder, played a key part in having Peggy and her daughter Mariah shipped from Philadelphia to Saint Croix, where they were to be sold. Coxe was no ordinary member of the PAS. A prominent politician and economist, Coxe would soon serve as assistant treasury secretary to Alexander Hamilton. But Coxe's elevated status did nothing to shelter him from the denunciation of the acting committee, which penned an address that they had delivered to Coxe for his consideration. The address lamented that Coxe's actions, "public and notorious," had "wound[ed] an institution" faced "with many formidable enemies." The acting committee then lectured Coxe that people of color "are or ought to be born free and alike entitled to all the blessing of Religious and civil Liberty" and that the "African descendants" were "our common brethren in the scale of human creation." Coxe took the acting committee's censure seriously. He appeared before the committee and expressed regret for his actions, pledging to have both mother and daughter returned to Philadelphia. By January 1788, Coxe had made good on his word.[54]

53. Ibid., II, 99.
54. Ibid., 119, 131, 138. Coxe arranged to have Peggy and Mariah sold to Thomas Harrison of the acting committee, with the expectation that the two women would then serve as indentured servants before gaining their complete freedom. Coxe wrote a letter to the acting committee explaining his actions and expressing his responsibility and regret. See ibid., I, 136–137. Upon resolution of the case, the acting committee "Sincerely Rejoice[d] that a Painfull Consideration of a Continued Slavery" of Peggy and Mariah had been averted. With "the Principles of our Society Vindicated," the acting commit-

Like the PAS's acting committee, the NYMS's standing committee, in its several documented cases involving the kidnapping of free blacks and the illegal carrying of enslaved people out of state for sale, made a bold statement that persons of color had a right to inhabit New York soil. By 1800, clandestine slave-trading outfits kidnapping and exporting New York City blacks for sale had become endemic, leading to the removal of many hundreds of people of color from the state. Learning of one of these illicit operations, members of the standing committee boarded a ship and informed the captain and crew that their actions were "contrary to Law, and that it would be most advisable" that they cooperate. The captain then ordered a small hatch door unlocked, whereupon four black New Yorkers emerged, their relief, one would imagine, visceral. Six years earlier, a black youth had been illegally sold as a slave in New York before his new master attempted to ship him to Savannah for sale. But the boy escaped and ended up in the care of Lawrence Embree, who worked to secure the child's freedom.[55]

As far as the abolition societies were concerned, the emancipation laws assumed that persons of African descent would remain within their states of residence, where they would gain their liberty and be incorporated into the American Republic. Beyond helping to establish black freedom, the abolition societies, often directly responding to those who sought their aid, fought to gain for persons of African descent rights that any citizen of the new Republic would expect to receive—such as the right to the recourse of habeas corpus, the right to a legally permissible labor contract, the right to maintain families, and the right to remain a free member of society. Fighting for black citizenship thus formed a mandatory component of the first movement abolitionist battle against slavery.

---

tee forgave Coxe (ibid., 138). Soon after resolving this case, the PAS petitioned the state legislature to close loopholes in Pennsylvania's abolition law, including the removal of servants and enslaved people from the state for sale. Ironically, then, the actions of one of the PAS's own members might have played a part in galvanizing the society to strengthen the 1780 act. Though he apologized, Coxe's wayward behavior was perhaps a preview of his later apostasy of abolitionism in the early nineteenth century, when he condemned black citizenship and embraced emerging racist theories of black inferiority. See Gary Nash, "Race and Citizenship in the Early Republic," and Richard Newman, "The Pennsylvania Abolition Society and the Struggle for Racial Justice," in Newman and James Mueller, eds., *Antislavery and Abolition in Philadelphia: Emancipation and the Long Struggle for Racial Justice in the City of Brotherly Love* (Baton Rouge, La., 2011), 90–117, 118–146.

55. NYMS Records, VI, 31–32, VII, 159, NYHS.

IDENTIFYING LIMITS

Even as the acting and standing committees and black applicants for their aid enjoyed many victories, this activism had limitations. The conversion to absolute freedom for those blacks who used the committees did not always happen immediately. Just about 28 percent of persons of color freed through the interference of the acting and standing committees are recorded as entering indentureships with their former owners or new employers, worked out by the PAS and NYMS. The indenture system in the mid-Atlantic transitioned during the late eighteenth and early nineteenth centuries away from white laborers and toward black ones. This development can be read to have created a dichotomy between free white wage labor and indentured black bonded labor that widened the narrowing chasm in status between free whites and formerly enslaved blacks. In this reading, the gradual emancipation process and, by implication, the abolition societies, helped to maintain black inequality in a new guise. Yet both the acting and standing committees often secured contracts that mandated schooling, and they looked to place people of color in indentures that would prove conducive to gaining skills that would foster eventual independence. Moreover, the decision to indenture did not always come from committee members. Black parents, when they decided that they could not adequately provide for their children, asked the committees to help bind their children. Economic desperation often dictated this decision, but it may also gesture to the hopes that some black parents held for their children to raise their socioeconomic status through the indenture system.[56]

56. Works highlighting indentured servitude in the mid-Atlantic during the early Republic as shutting off socioeconomic opportunities for people of color and perpetuating black inequality include Melish, *Disowning Slavery;* Nash and Soderlund, *Freedom by Degrees;* Harris, *In the Shadow of Slavery;* Sharon V. Salinger, *"To Serve Well and Faithfully": Labor and Indentured Servants in Pennsylvania, 1682–1800* (New York, 1987); and Gigantino, *The Ragged Road to Abolition.* Although this scholarship captures well the formidable obstacles facing free black and newly emancipated men and women in the mid-Atlantic during this period, indentured servitude was not slavery, and both the committees and persons of color would have found equating the two curious. When making indentures on behalf of their clients, the acting committee always adhered to contracts binding black laborers for the same amount of years as their white counterparts, as discussed earlier in this chapter. For indentures overseen by the PAS and NYMS that mandated schooling, see PPAS, Series 1, reel 4, I, 74, II, 257, 280, HSP. For evidence of the acting and standing committees' seeking indentures for blacks who came under their care that would introduce them to artisanal or agricultural occupations rather than household labor, see ibid., I, 55, 79–80. When the parents of those freed through the agency of the committees opted against indenturing their children,

For all their confrontation with those who illicitly claimed the labor of persons of color, the committees often chose compromise with slaveholders, even if it resulted in those liberated being indentured to their former owners. For example, the acting committee learned in 1785 that a seventeen-year-old black man, Lewis, had been sold into the state as a slave and registered as a bondsperson by Ephraim Blane after the passage of the 1780 abolition law making such an act illegal. To pass off the enslavement of Lewis as licit, Blane had changed Lewis's name to Jack—the real Jack having been legally registered but since sold from the state. Instead of ensuring that Lewis be delivered from a clearly duplicitous Blane, the acting committee mediated an agreement by which Lewis would serve his late owner as an indentured servant for four years. The committee reported that the agreement had the "Consent of all Parties," and perhaps the new leverage he had on Blane, along with his status as a temporary servant, sufficed to satisfy Lewis. Still, the safest choice would have been to cut ties with Blane altogether.[57]

In addition to a penchant for accommodation, limited monetary resources hamstrung the acting and standing committees and foreclosed a larger assault on slavery in New York and Pennsylvania. Part of the committees' tendency toward compromise with those who illegally claimed the labor of blacks probably resulted from the abolition societies' relatively meager financial assets. The committees ran a costly risk in each suit they brought against slaveholding defendants. In 1791, for instance, the acting committee was ordered to pay fifty-six pounds in damages in a suit it had launched against Jonas Philips for the freedom of Bill. Other times, committee members found themselves the subjects of legal action by exasperated slaveholders. The indefatigable Willett Seaman had at least two suits brought against him by slaveholders whose bondspersons the Quaker activist had worked to free; the standing committee agreed to indemnify Seaman for the costs he incurred in defending himself.[58]

the abolition societies deferred to this decision. See ibid., 21, 30. Although the percentage of blacks freed by the acting and standing committees who are recorded as entering indenture agreements is less than one-third, this number refers to those indentures that are explicitly noted in the committees' minutes. The aggregate count of persons of color freed through the aegis of these committees who became servants to white employers is almost certainly higher, based on the large number of blacks indentured in early national Philadelphia and New York and keeping in mind that numerous people of color had economic resources too meager to begin a life completely unfettered from bound labor of any kind.

57. PPAS, Series 1, reel 4, II, 35–36, 51.
58. Ibid., 141; NYMS Records, VII, 63, 73, NYHS.

Another check on the activism of the standing and acting committees was their apparent hesitance to consistently prosecute violators of emancipation-related laws. This approach may be partially explained as a product of the committees' successes: if they could come to an agreement that resulted in eventual freedom for the enslaved applicant, the committees had met their primary goal of black freedom. But a dearth of manpower mattered too. The NYMS and PAS oversaw several cases at any given time, with only a handful of acting and standing committee members willing to dedicate themselves to the often grinding and always uncompensated work required of this activism. These explanatory factors aside, it is reasonable to assume that bringing charges against all lawbreakers would have worked more effectively to deter such abuses in the first place.

A more damaging shortcoming than failing to punish law-breaking slaveholders is evidence of the committees' ineffectiveness in upholding the liberty of free blacks. The NYMS oversaw far more cases based on the illegal importation of enslaved people for sale than the anti-exportation law. Yet violations of the anti-exportation law were not rare; the kidnapping of free blacks and the exporting of enslaved New Yorkers for sale out of state constituted a pervasive problem in the gradual emancipation era. On more than one occasion, the standing committee wrote to the full NYMS bemoaning their failure to stop numerous instances of kidnapping "for want of the ability to come at the facts before the violators of humanity have made their escape." Even though the standing committee shielded many free blacks from illegal exportation and kidnapping, there were undoubtedly many more enslaved people taken out of New York for sale.[59]

The abolition societies' deference to existing laws further hemmed in its activism. The acting and standing committees accepted the legality of slavery and opted to work within the legal and legislative sphere rather than reject it outright. Although the idea of holding people as property repelled many committee members, as official bodies they offered little help

59. NYMS Records, X, 302–303, NYHS. One scholar has provocatively argued that the sale of enslaved people out of New York state became so commonplace in the years following the passage of statutory gradual emancipation that as many as double the number of bondspersons were sold to out-of-state locales than received their liberty through the 1799 emancipation act. Although this speculation is almost certainly an overstatement, and does not include manumissions or take into account the use of laws beyond gradual emancipation itself that limited the rights of slaveholders and brought immediate freedom to the enslaved, it does point to the serious issue of exportation for sale faced by enslaved black New Yorkers and the NYMS's standing committee. See Claudia Dale Goldin, "The Economics of Emancipation," *Journal of Economic History*, XXXIII (1973), 70.

to those seeking their services if a legal right to freedom could not be established. In 1794, the standing committee learned that a black man "from some circumstances" was "Supposed entitled to his freedom." Held as a slave, the unnamed person of color remained claimed by the brothers of his deceased owner. The brothers had already attempted to export the enslaved man out of state, most likely for sale. With insufficient proof of his right to freedom, the standing committee left this man who needed their help to an ominous fate. The PAS similarly dropped cases from its rolls when they lacked legal standing. In 1792, the acting committee looked to aid John Jackson, who had left the service of his master and insisted he was free and not a slave. Five months later, the man claiming ownership of Jackson put him in prison, labeling Jackson a runaway bondsman. Once provided with testimony that Jackson was indeed the legal property of his purported owner, the acting committee dispassionately concluded it "most prudent to decline a further interference in the case." Jackson would remain enslaved.[60]

Cases like Jackson's demonstrate that the PAS and NYMS ultimately grounded their activism on fastidious, legally bound facts rather than blunt, extralegal action. The acting and standing committees accepted the legal principle that recognized slavery. But they sought consistently to enforce and broaden laws that expanded the rights of people of color. Legal-based activism, from this perspective, was far from a limited form of abolitionism, driven by staid activists. Instead, it was a dynamic strategy linking the standing and acting committees with the many people of color who gave its members their agenda.[61]

The redefinition of slavery in the mid-Atlantic as a limited but still legal institution created permeable barriers between bondage and freedom that offered both promise and peril to enslaved and free blacks in post-Revolutionary Pennsylvania and New York. Emancipation's gradual nature

60. NYMS Records, VII, 24, 29, NYHS; PPAS, Series 1, reel 4, II, 232–233, HSP.
61. The acting and standing committees generally avoided interfering in cases where they could find no legal right to freedom for those who sought their aid. Yet some individual members, acting outside the official business of the committees, did protect people who had escaped slavery through extralegal means and other bondspersons without a legal basis for freedom. For a detailed narrative of one such committee member's activism, see L. Maria Child, *Isaac T. Hopper: A True Life* (Boston, 1853). Richard Newman casts the decision of the PAS to work within the laws as a "cautious legal strategy" that fits with his larger interpretation of the PAS as a deferential and conservative organization; see Newman, *The Transformation of American Abolitionism*, 84.

left unaffected the daily lives of a great number of enslaved people and made free black life treacherous. Yet, instead of remaining bitterly disappointed in a form of emancipation that was supposed to have kept them enslaved, the many blacks in New York and Pennsylvania whose journeys to freedom have been recounted in this chapter tapped the abolition societies to make slavery's gradual elimination immediately meaningful. And, with their white partners in the NYMS and PAS, they transformed themselves in the eyes of the law from rightless chattel to free citizens.

The minutes of the standing and acting committees reveal that this transformation was highly contested. Paradoxically, appreciating the first abolition movement's steadfast commitment to establishing the civil liberties of persons of color is only possible by recognizing the defiance with which the enemies of emancipation sought to deny the dignity of black freedom. That emancipation did not arrive in one fell swoop demanded that illegally enslaved blacks and the committees they turned to for assistance work together to enforce existing laws, expand the reach of statutory antislavery, and affirm previously unrecognized rights for people of African descent. Discernable progress in achieving these aims buoyed persons of color and the PAS and NYMS. Whereas colonial-era laws worked to support enslavement and black inequality, post-Revolutionary and early national laws made possible both freedom from bondage and membership in society. Despite ongoing struggles to realize the complete abolition of slavery, the trajectory of the late-eighteenth-century mid-Atlantic seemed to be moving toward an increased recognition of black rights.

But the caseload of the acting and standing committees points to imposing obstacles in the way of emancipation and black progress that had been evident from the initial debates over slavery in the Revolutionary era. Slaveholders viewed the activities of the committees as a threat to what they interpreted as their just rights of property in people, people whose status as possessions helped establish slaveholding wealth and power. Property rights—key in mandating a gradual rather than immediate abolition—ensured the continued legality of slavery and ensnared in bondage numerous people of color who had a legal claim to freedom. What is more, those who openly defied the abolition laws reflected a broader white public at best ambivalent and at worst hostile to the idea of black freedom. The abolition societies and their free black allies would look to solve this dilemma by cultivating communities of virtuous citizens among the newly emancipated.

CHAPTER 3

Republicans of Color

*Societal Environmentalism and
the Quest for Black Citizenship*

Less than two years after the official end of the Revolutionary War brought what American patriots considered freedom from British political enslavement, a bid to abolish chattel slavery in New York fizzled out because of a deeply vexed question: What would black liberty look like? In January 1785, the New York Senate took up a bill for the gradual abolition of slavery. The bill proposed that the children of enslaved women born after the legislation's passage would receive freedom in their twenties—males at the age of twenty-five and females at the age of twenty-two. With little debate, the senate approved the bill. Meanwhile, the New York Assembly, responding to an abolitionist petition from Quaker memorialists, had assigned a committee to consider the request. The committee came back with a report approving of the petitioners' aims, and by a three-to-one margin assembly members voted to consider the abolition issue as a whole. The passage of a gradual emancipation bill seemed imminent.[1]

Yet, by preying on doubts about the suitability of people of color for citizenship, slavery's defenders in the legislature found a winning formula for derailing emancipation. In the assembly, proslavery forces offered three amendments setting out a sphere of civic inferiority for liberated blacks. One of these amendments banned blacks from holding elected office and prohibited persons of African descent from serving as jurors or witnesses in cases involving whites. Another made interracial marriages illegal. And a third stipulated that free blacks would be stripped of all voting rights. The assembly adopted all of these provisions and sent the amended bill, now exceedingly altered from the senate's version, to the senate for con-

1. David N. Gellman, *Emancipating New York: The Politics of Slavery and Freedom, 1777–1827* (Baton Rouge, La., 2006), 48; Leslie M. Harris, *In the Shadow of Slavery: African Americans in New York City, 1626–1863* (Chicago, 2003), 56–57.

sideration. The senate demanded that the assembly eliminate all three of these additional clauses. The assembly then voted narrowly to remove the ban on black officeholding and unequal judicial rights but refused to overturn the other two amendments. Unmoved by the lower house's intransigence, the senate requested that the assembly abandon the remaining two amendments. This time the assembly consented to lift the ban on interracial unions but refused to budge on black disfranchisement. Faced with the prospect of losing the battle for an emancipation law altogether, the senate grudgingly accepted the assembly's decision and forwarded the bill to the Council of Revision for approval. But the Council of Revision, a body with the power to veto all laws passed by the state legislature, declined the opportunity to adopt a gradual abolition act that so clearly compromised black citizenship. Unable to hash out their differences, the senate and assembly chose not to enact an abolition law. New York's first attempt at gradual abolition had collapsed over the issue of free black membership in the body politic.[2]

From its inception, the New-York Manumission Society (NYMS), inaugurated as New York's legislature debated the 1785 abolition bill, found itself faced with the potent accusation that black Americans, so long degraded by the institution of slavery, could never be made into responsible free persons. The NYMS was not alone. Even as they struggled to enact gradual emancipation laws, enforce antislavery statutes, and guard the rights and liberties of persons of color, the abolition societies of the mid-Atlantic determined that, without raising the civil status of free blacks, African American freedom would never be complete. The genesis of the reform project implemented to accomplish this racially inclusive version of antislavery stemmed from a central dilemma bequeathed to abolitionists by the American Revolution. The same natural rights Revolutionary ideology that aided the first abolition movement also presented enslaved people as the very antithesis of the independent, virtuous citizenry necessary to uphold representative government and maintain the American experiment in republicanism, making emancipation problematic.[3]

2. Arthur Zilversmit, *The First Emancipation: The Abolition of Slavery in the North* (Chicago, 1967), 148–149; Gellman, *Emancipating New York*, 49–50; Harris, *In the Shadow of Slavery*, 58–59.

3. For the negative conception of enslaved people embedded in Revolutionary ideology, see François Furstenberg, "Beyond Freedom and Slavery: Autonomy, Virtue, and Resistance in Early American Political Discourse," *Journal of American History*, LXXXIX (2003), 1295–1330; and Joanne Pope Melish, *Disowning Slavery: Gradual Emancipation and "Race" in New England, 1780–1860* (Ithaca, N.Y., 1998).

Out of their quest to solve this paradox, abolition society members and their African American collaborators constructed a reform agenda of societal environmentalism. Based on free black socioeconomic uplift and the application of the early Republic's educational mores to persons of color, societal environmentalism aimed to inculcate republican virtue in formerly enslaved people. Black education and citizenship would help to defeat white prejudice and convince the public that African Americans were worthy of emancipation. Through these reformist initiatives, first movement abolitionists sought to prove the capacity of people of color for freedom by integrating black Americans into the American Republic and making them virtuous and independent citizens, fully capable of productively exercising their liberty within greater white society.

Doubts about formerly enslaved peoples' competency for freedom and fears that emancipation threatened the Republic—promoted by slavery's defenders—constituted serious challenges for first movement abolitionists. The quandary of black freedom cut to the very core of the early American Republic's identity. American independence overthrew millennia of monarchical practices and ushered in the ideology of republicanism. Monarchy was based on the idea that people were weak and sinful, lacking self-restraint, unfit to govern, and thus in need of being controlled from above. The societal stratification that reinforced these postulates justified a political order based on dependencies, inequalities, and an assortment of titles, rituals, and ceremonies that helped reinforce the hierarchies considered essential to conserve the stability of the state. The ideology of republicanism, however, turned these assumptions on their head. The ability of the people for self-government and the concept of popular sovereignty, rather than the helplessness of the people and sovereignty in the hands of a monarch, informed the creation of American republicanism. But, if monarchy and the submission of the people at large to a single sovereign power were no longer the standards of society and politics, a great deal more would be demanded of the people.[4]

4. Gordon S. Wood, *The Creation of the American Republic, 1776–1787* (Williamsburg, Va., and Chapel Hill, N.C., 1969); Wood, *The Radicalism of the American Revolution* (New York, 1991). The historiographical concept of republicanism in America has had a long and controversial life. Beginning with Bernard Bailyn, *The Ideological Origins of the American Revolution* (Cambridge, Mass., 1967), and bookended by Wood's *Radicalism of the American Revolution*, it has generated much debate among scholars, especially over whether liberal or republican ideas directed the founding of the American Republic. Historians now generally agree that Revolutionaries used both of these ideologies. For a sampling of this debate, see Robert E. Shalhope, "Republicanism and Early American Historiography," *William and Mary Quarterly*, 3d Ser., XXXIX

American Revolutionary thought warned that virtue and independence would have to replace the depravity and dependence of the body politic if the fragile experiment in American republicanism were to survive. Only a virtuous, knowledgeable, and independent citizenry could withstand the onslaught of corruption, greed, and moral decrepitude that republicanism's purveyors apprehended as inevitable. The problem for those opposed to chattel bondage was that, even as slavery violated the principles of republican theory, enslaved people were seen as degraded, ignorant, and dependent—the exact opposite of every quality needed in the people of the new nation. When Revolutionary writers inveighed against the English imperial government for trying to enslave American colonists, they highlighted this ideological conundrum. First movement abolitionists' attempt to bridge the chasm between the Revolution's antislavery potential and its derogatory understanding of enslaved people would guide their program of reform, which held that people of color had to be made into knowledgeable and virtuous citizens for emancipation to win out.[5]

(1982), 334–356; Joyce Appleby, ed., "Republicanism in the History and Historiography of the United States," special issue of the *American Quarterly*, XXXVII (1985), esp. 461–598; Isaac Kramnick, "'The Great National Discussion': The Discourse of Politics in 1787," *WMQ*, 3d Ser., XLV (1988), 3–32; James T. Kloppenberg, "The Virtues of Liberalism: Christianity, Republicanism, and Ethics in Early American Political Discourse," *JAH*, LXXIV (1987), 9–33; and Alan Gibson, "Ancients, Moderns, and Americans: The Republicanism-Liberalism Debate Revisited," *History of Political Thought*, XXI (2000), 261–307. Although prematurely announcing that republicanism had lost its relevance in the field, Daniel T. Rodgers provides a useful overview of this complex but important ideology. See Rodgers, "Republicanism: The Career of a Concept," *JAH*, LXXIX (1992), 11–38. Wood has received much criticism for claiming that the American Revolution was a radical event. Although Wood casts a one-dimensional and overly progressive transition from republicanism to democracy in the early Republic, American independence did radically alter the theoretical role of the people and marked a significant departure from the colonial past. For the debate between Wood and his critics, see "Forum: How Revolutionary Was the Revolution? A Discussion of Gordon S. Wood's *The Radicalism of the American Revolution*," *WMQ*, 3d Ser., LI (1994), 677–716.

5. Leslie Harris similarly points to the role of republican ideology in disposing white Americans to view formerly enslaved people as lacking the virtue necessary for republican citizenship. Harris uses this framework to argue that free black men were dogged by whites' preconceived notions of their dependency after gaining freedom in early national New York. I use the paradoxical implications of republican thought for the formerly enslaved as an ideological tent within which white antislavery reformers and free blacks tried to overcome the roadblock to slavery's abolition and African American equality engrafted in republican theory. See Harris, *In The Shadow of Slavery*, 97–99. In his article "Beyond Freedom and Slavery," *JAH*, LXXXIX (2003), 1295–1330, François Furstenberg argues that white American Revolutionaries had a nuanced view of freedom that stressed the active role individuals must play in resisting tyranny, equating freedom with

ACKNOWLEDGING A NEGATIVE ENVIRONMENT
AND CREATING A POSITIVE ONE

In confronting the predicament that the republican paradox posed to their reform efforts, first movement abolitionists embraced environmentalism as the lodestar of their activism. They used environmental theory to argue for the underlying sameness present in each human being, irrespective of physical and cultural differences. Tracing the history of environmentalist thought demonstrates the novelty of this use. By the late eighteenth century, environmentalism already had a lengthy career as an explanatory device for assessing the great variety in human appearance and culture. Ancient Greek philosophers first hypothesized that climate dictated both the physiological and behavioral elements of human societies by acting directly on the humors, or the four bodily fluids of black bile, yellow bile, phlegm, and blood. Different climates, these philosophers posited, brought out different combinations of the various humors. In turn, the humors, in their interaction with climate, could determine the character of individuals and the larger civilization of which they were a part. Not all environments were created equal. From the start, environmental theory ascribed a hierarchy of cultural predispositions with temperate and cold climates producing persons with mental and physical superiority to those who lived in hot climates.[6]

For centuries, little about environmentalism changed. Christian theological writers had adopted the ancient Greeks' theories and fully accepted the connection between the humors and climate, seeing no conflict between God's original creation of Adam and Eve and the several variations in humanity that environment had subsequently produced. The age of exploration and colonization in the sixteenth and seventeenth centuries,

---

autonomy and fusing agency with virtue, liberal-republican, and protestant ideologies. Deciding that enslaved people failed to meet these ideological standards, the Revolutionary generation among whites came to view black bondspersons as deserving of their slavery, Furstenberg concludes. Although overreaching in his conclusion that "by choosing to submit" to slavery "slaves had proved themselves unworthy of freedom" (1316) (there is in fact less documentary evidence that the white public thought persons of color consented to their bondage than there are sources showing that white Americans believed slavery fettered people who naturally wanted liberty), Furstenberg's thesis nonetheless helps to highlight the ideological barriers that first movement abolitionists faced in demonstrating that black Americans could become virtuous citizens of the Republic.

6. Clarence J. Glacken, *Traces on the Rhodian Shore: Nature and Culture in Western Thought from Ancient Times to the End of the Eighteenth Century* (Berkley, Calif., 1967), 80–82.

however, took Europeans out of their relative isolation and into contact with an assortment of new peoples and cultures whose differences needed explaining. Eighteenth-century philosophers' usage of environmentalism, when coupled with the rise of enlightenment thought and its emphasis on empiricism, sensationalism, and the study of human nature, greatly expanded the explanatory power of the concept. Crucial to this expansion of environmentalism's importance was John Locke's rejection of innate ideas. If everyone came into the world as a tabula rasa, dependent on sensation and reflection for character formation, then environment took on the god-like role of determining human identity. Other enlightenment writers, such as Montesquieu, while reiterating the effect of climate on personality traits (writing from the perspective of a European, Montesquieu saw cold climates as the most conducive to positive attributes) linked environmentalism with state formation, judging that monarchal, despotic, or republican governments were a product of the area's environment. In short, by the time America declared independence from Britain, environmentalism had become ensconced as a natural science of humanity.[7]

Some influential eighteenth-century philosophers doubted that climate and other environmental factors could explain human diversity. The Scottish enlightenment figure Henry Home, Lord Kames, who had famously advanced that human societies pass through different stages of civilization, posited that the only explanation for the broad spectrum of social formation lay in polygenesis. By the close of the 1700s, the English physician Charles White claimed to have found empirical support for theories of innate human differences in his widely read *Account of the Regular Gradation in Man*. Positioning polygenesis within a comparative study of human anatomy, White measured human skulls and skeletons in constructing a hierarchy of the human form. Not surprisingly, Europeans stood at the top of his rankings, both aesthetically and in intellectual prowess. Blacks on the other hand, White concluded, were "nearer to the brute creation," their skulls, limbs, and sensory strengths placing them closer to apes than to humans in the scale of being. White noted that his book should not be interpreted as a justification for the "pernicious practice of enslaving mankind," but, in the American context, where ideas of black inferiority

7. Ibid., 254–257; Winthrop D. Jordan, *White over Black: American Attitudes toward the Negro, 1550–1812* (Williamsburg, Va., and Chapel Hill, N.C., 1968), 287. On environmentalism and race construction in the early American Republic, see ibid., parts 3–5; and Bruce Dain, *A Hideous Monster of the Mind: American Race Theory in the Early Republic* (Cambridge, Mass., 2002), 40–148.

and proslavery arguments were interrelated, his racially essentialist conclusions said otherwise.[8]

Samuel Stanhope Smith, a Presbyterian minister and president of the College of New Jersey, answered both Kames and White in *An Essay on the Causes of the Variety of Complexion and Figure in the Human Species*, published originally in 1787 and then revised in 1810. No antislavery activist, Smith nevertheless rejected the "arbitrary hypothesis that men are originally sprung from different stocks, and are therefore divided by nature into different species." While he asserted the original sameness of the human constitution, Smith, meeting White on his own ground, claimed that the skulls, facial features, and limbs of blacks exposed to white American civilization were beginning to approximate those of "the fair native of Europe." Smith tied these physical changes directly to his vision of black liberty. He concluded that, were enslaved people "perfectly free, enjoyed property, and were admitted to a liberal participation of the society, rank and privileges of their masters, they would change their African peculiarities much faster," implying that black Americans would begin to express their fundamental equality when they started looking like Europeans. Smith did briefly argue that the environment of slavery and its tendency to stunt the social and intellectual growth of bondspersons explained African American inequality. But Smith's relatively succinct foray into explaining the unequal societal conditions of persons of African descent made up a minor element in his environmentalist formula for disproving African American inferiority, affixed as it was to the bodies of people of color. Environmentalism as African American improvement for Smith hinged on a black metamorphosis into whiteness.[9]

8. Henry Home, Lord Kaims, *Six Sketches on the History of Man; Containing, the Progress of Men as Individuals* ... (Philadelphia, 1776); Jordan, *White over Black*, 499–502; Charles White, *An Account of the Regular Gradation in Man, and in Different Animals and Vegetables* ... (London, 1799), [iii], 42. White identified himself as an opponent of the slave trade and professed that he only wanted to "investigate a proposition in natural history" (137). In denying any connection between his findings of natural black inferiority and arguments in favor of racial slavery, White wrote that "laws ought not to allow greater freedom to a *Shakespear* or a *Milton*, a *Locke* or a *Newton*, than to men of inferior capacities" (137–138). Here, White took Thomas Jefferson, whose *Notes on the State of Virginia* ... (Paris, 1782) he liberally quoted, as a model.

9. Samuel Stanhope Smith, *An Essay on the Causes of the Variety of Complexion and Figure in the Human Species: To Which Are Added Strictures on Lord Kaim's Discourse, on the Original Diversity of Mankind* (Philadelphia, [1787]), 1, 92–93; Smith, *An Essay on the Causes of the Variety of Complexion and Figure in the Human Species; to Which Are Added, Animadversions on Certain Remarks Made on the First Edition of This Essay, by Mr. Charles White* ..., 2d ed. (New Brunswick, N.J., 1810), 252, 255. Dain

Spotlighting Smith's writings displays the difficulty activists faced in using environmentalism to create a sustainable abolitionist program. Smith pushed back against claims of the inferiority of Africans and their descendants, so pivotal to slavery's supporters. But as long as environmentalists focused on the bodies of African Americans, they were bound to highlight human difference instead of collapsing it—thus inadvertently conceding important ground to the defenders of slavery. Even though first movement abolitionists agreed with the basic premise of environmentalists like Smith that humans were products of their surroundings, they possessed an entirely separate understanding of environmentalism. Their formulation was disarmingly simple, helping to mask its great divergence from customary ideas of environmental theory. Both the natural rights ideology of the American Revolution and the biblical decree that God had made "of one blood all the nations ... of the earth" meant that all people were created equal, according to abolitionists. The problem was that the environment of slavery had held down the innate faculties of black persons for virtuous freedom at the same time as it corrupted the white public mind into thinking that African Americans were innately inferior. In this model of societal environmentalism, it was not the physical features of blacks that

---

interprets Smith as not believing that blacks had to literally become whitened to attain an equal social condition with white Americans. See Dain, *A Hideous Monster of the Mind*, 47–48. Although Smith did deny the necessity of African American whitening, he also focused on the supposed physiological adaptation of certain privileged blacks to the features of their white betters as proof that African Americans were improving—thus implying black capacity for freedom was contingent on physical transformation. In the 1810 edition of his essay, Smith wrote that more black American males were displaying "foreheads as open, full, and finely arched as the whites," while these men's noses, even if "not yet so much raised as that of the whites," were "far from being so much depressed as that of the natives of Africa" (Smith, *Essay on the Causes of the Variety of Complexion and Figure in the Human Species* [1810], 255–256 [quotations on 256]). Smith's discussion of the damaging effects of slavery on the social and intellectual standing of black Americans came in his countering Thomas Jefferson's suppositions of black inferiority in *Notes on the State of Virginia* (265–276). For background on the life and larger views of Smith, see *Sermons of Samuel Stanhope Smith, D. D., Late President of Princeton College, New Jersey; to Which Is Prefixed, a Brief Memoir of His Life and Writings*, 2 vols. (Philadelphia, 1821). For an American attack on Samuel Smith's environmentalism, see [Charles Caldwell], "An Essay on the Causes of the Variety of Complexion and Figure in the Human Species, etc. etc.," *American Review of History, and General Repository of Literature and State Papers*, II, no. 1 (July 1811), 128–166. Caldwell argued that natural environments could not substantively modify racial groups and, in a later published essay, instead pinned racial differences to polygenesis. See Jordan, *White over Black*, 533–534. Caldwell codified and extended his arguments further in 1830; see Caldwell, *Thoughts on the Original Unity of the Human Race* (New York, 1830).

needed to change; it was the society that had permitted slavery to take root in the first place.[10]

The only time abolitionists fixated on physical appearance was to mock the faulty idea that superficial difference could justify slavery. Samuel Miller, a member of the NYMS, stated that, if color and complexion were to distinguish enslaved from free people, Americans could enslave those Europeans with darker hues than their own. Even some white southerners may be rightfully enslaved according to this type of logic. "How many shades," Miller asked, "must we descend ... before mercy is to vanish with them?" Another antislavery orator rejected the entire hierarchy of the human form as a flimsy pretext for enslavement based on the arbitrary determinate of cultural relativism. The "beauty of [a] complexion is a mere matter of taste," totally inadequate in dictating "the rights of human nature." The "darkness of a skin, the flatness of a nose, or the wideness of a mouth," this speaker proclaimed, were "only deformities or beauties as the undulating tribunal of taste shall determine." Thus, where Samuel Stanhope Smith had fallen into a dead-end discourse with the advocates of polygenesis, abolitionists called out the misguided social conventions that gave physical differences relevance.[11]

10. Bruce Dain alludes to this type of environmentalism but ascribes it solely to black, not white, antislavery activists of the early Republic. See Dain, *A Hideous Monster of the Mind*, 52. My emphasis is on the interracial nature of societal environmentalism and the ways it helped cement a coalition of white and black abolitionists. As Smith's *Essay on the Causes of the Variety of Complexion and Figure in the Human Species* indicates, the common philosophical enemies that united adherents of environmentalism were theories of inherent and unalterable racially based black inequality. The proverbial passages on black inferiority in Jefferson's *Notes on the State of Virginia* were widely rejected by a diverse array of figures, including Samuel Smith and the radical black abolitionist David Walker. Black writers and abolitionists were especially critical of Jefferson's views on race. See Dain, *A Hideous Monster of the Mind*, 51–53, 139–142; and Manisha Sinha, *The Slave's Cause: A History of Abolition* (New Haven, Conn., 2016), 144–146, 153.

11. Samuel Miller, *A Discourse, Delivered April 12, 1797, at the Request of and before the New-York Society for Promoting the Manumission of Slaves, and Protecting Such of Them as Have Been or May Be Liberated* (New York, 1797), 13; William Pinkney, *Speech of William Pinkney, Esq. in the House of Delegates of Maryland, at Their Session in November, 1789* (Philadelphia, 1790), 16. Antislavery arguments ridiculing ideas of physical appearance as a justification for slavery appeared in the American context as early as the 1750s and 1760s from writers as diverse as the Quaker mystic John Woolman to the Boston patriot James Otis. See Woolman, *Some Considerations on the Keeping of Negroes: Recommended to the Professors of Christianity of Every Denomination* (Philadelphia, 1754); and Otis, *The Rights of the British Colonies Asserted and Proved* (Boston, 1764), 29. Winthrop Jordan notes that antislavery writers met the racialized justification for black bondage with dismissive mockery, but they soon realized that they

More commonly, first movement abolitionists used what may be labeled a negative environmentalist position to critique the effects of slavery on African Americans. In large part, this tactic was a defensive response to slavery's proponents, who never lost an opportunity to point out black inequality and deem people of color ill-suited for freedom. The defenders of slavery pilloried the character of black Americans whenever emancipation was debated. For example, in February 1781, a Pennsylvania writer, opposing the extension of statutory emancipation to other newly independent states, warned about the prospect of giving black people liberated from slavery, "with all their ignorance and prejudices, the previleges *[sic]* of free citizens." A nation with "a large number of free Negroes" whose "national disposition, poor education," and "venality" would lead toward "theft, murder, [and] rapine" could only bring "a new and woeful slavery" to Revolutionary America. Nearly a decade later, as the first federal Con-

---

faced a "color problem" that although "at first perceived as a logical absurdity was gradually recognized to be the rock upon which slavery was founded." As this chapter reveals, the first abolition movement sought to get around the problem of color by proving that, although people of African descent may look different from their white counterparts, they were capable of the same virtuous freedom as Euro-Americans. See Jordan, *White over Black*, 278–279. Benjamin Rush's theory of blackness as leprosy provides a notable exception to the general pattern of first movement abolitionists' usage of environmentalism as a tool of antislavery. In a paper delivered before the American Philosophical Society in 1792, Rush hypothesized that black skin color was attributable to the disease of leprosy, which he claimed people of color had contracted in Africa through their diet and allegedly savage habits. See Rush, "Observations Intended to Favour a Supposition That the Black Color (as It Is Called) of the Negroes Is Derived from the Leprosy," American Philosophical Society, *Transactions*, IV (1799), 289–297. Not unlike Samuel Smith, Rush in his essay connected black American progress to the whitening of persons of color, though it remains unclear whether he believed wholesale black metamorphosis into whiteness was a necessary component of black uplift. Regardless, Rush played a key early role in helping to implement the first movement abolitionist program of societal environmentalism. More telling than Rush's bizarre environmentalist theory is the complete silence it received from the PAS and American Convention, of which Rush was a member. That the abolition societies chose not to so much as consider the merit of Rush's theory signals the centrality of societal environmentalism to organized antislavery in this period. For an interpretation of Rush's environmentalism that takes his theory of blackness as leprosy as indicative of a larger antislavery commitment to a white, racialized Republic, see Eric Herschtal, "Antislavery Science in the Early Republic: The Case of Dr. Benjamin Rush," *Early American Studies*, XV (2017), 274–307. Herschtal links the idea that formerly enslaved people should adopt republican values (societal environmentalism) with what he calls Rush's "antislavery science"; the latter augured that black Americans, as they became free and adopted virtuous habits, would turn white. Yet an examination of the records of the abolition societies shows that this same link did not manifest itself in the words and actions of nearly all first movement abolitionists.

gress debated the national government's jurisdiction over slavery and the slave trade, the Georgian congressman James Jackson turned to black poverty to protect African American bondage. According to Jackson, there was a "great distinction between [the] subjects of liberty." Holding up the example of Maryland, where the ongoing manumission of thousands of enslaved people had resulted in a growing free black population, Jackson claimed that those liberated had resorted to stealing rather than working, become "common pickpockets," and only harmed the greater societies into which they were freed. "The sound of liberty" when applied to slavery, Jackson ominously warned, "has this consequence." At both the state and federal levels, proslavery writers and politicians exploited the reality of racial inequality to help stymie abolitionist efforts.[12]

Finding themselves having to answer accusations of the inferior condition of African Americans, abolitionists identified the environment of slavery as the prime culprit. The Pennsylvania Abolition Society (PAS) labeled slavery "an atrocious debasement of human nature" and blamed the institution of bondage for "fetter[ing]" the "intellectual faculties" of African Americans while "impair[ing] the social affections" of bondage's victims. The NYMS believed the "degraded state" that slavery imposed on blacks left many "destitute of those advantages, which enable the commonality amongst the whites, to seek with success a maintenance for themselves and families." Antislavery orators similarly stressed the centrality of environment to black inequality. Elihu Smith of the NYMS insisted that African Americans, like all people, were "creatures of education, of example, of circumstances." "Make them outcasts ... shut from them the

---

12. *Pennsylvania Journal*, Feb. 21, 1781; Charlene Bangs Bickford, Kenneth R. Bowling, and Helen E. Veit, eds., *Documentary History of the First Federal Congress of the United States of America, March 4, 1789–March 3, 1791*, X, *Debates in the House of Representatives, First Session: April–May 1789* (Baltimore, 1992), 635. The first sustained congressional debates over slavery took place during a six-week period in the spring of 1790 and were in response to antislavery petitions from mid-Atlantic Quaker groups and the Pennsylvania Abolition Society. For an overview of these debates, see Howard A. Ohline, "Slavery, Economics, and Congressional Politics, 1790," *Journal of Southern History*, XVI (1980), 335–360; William C. diGiacomantonio, "'For the Gratification of a Volunteering Society': Antislavery and Pressure Group Politics in the First Federal Congress," *Journal of the Early Republic*, XV (1995), 169–197; and Richard S. Newman, "Prelude to the Gag Rule: Southern Reaction to Antislavery Petitions in the First Federal Congress," *JER*, XVI (1996), 571–599. James Jackson made the remarks quoted in this paragraph in an earlier, more short-lived debate over the slave trade during the initial session of the first federal Congress—though several lower southern congressmen, including Jackson himself, offered similar arguments during the longer 1790 debate of Congress's second session.

fair book and salutary light of knowledge, degrade them into brutes, and trample them in the dust," Smith intoned, and only "Madmen" would expect blacks to perform equally with whites. Abolition society members, like Smith, pinned black inequality on the circumstances of slavery, not the inner character of people of color.[13]

By explaining black inequality as the circumstantial product of the debilitating environment of slavery, first movement abolitionists found themselves in a tenuous position, at times sounding rhetorical notes similar to those of the very proslavery partisans they attempted to refute. The PAS's 1789 *Address to the Public* is a case in point. The address depicted the average enslaved person as "the unhappy man who has long been treated as a brute animal" and in turn "too frequently sinks beneath the common standard of the human species." Acclimated to life "like a mere machine," an enslaved person's "reflection is suspended; he has not the power of choice; and reason and conscience, have but little influence over his conduct." When Benjamin Rush confronted accusations that enslaved people tended toward "Idleness, Treachery, Theft, and the like," he accounted for these attributes as the "genuine offspring of slavery," thereby implicitly accepting the charges of slavery's proponents that persons of African descent did indeed possess these unsavory qualities. First movement abolitionists committed themselves to the belief that the negative environment of slavery could be overcome. But highlighting the deleterious effects of human bondage on the individual also lent support to the contentions of slavery's defenders that persons of African descent, in their condition as bondspersons, were far from ideal candidates for liberty.[14]

13. *An Address to the Public, from the Pennsylvania Society for Promoting the Abolition of Slavery, and the Relief of Free Negroes, Unlawfully Held in Bondage* (Philadelphia, 1789), [1]; *New-York Daily Advertiser*, Jan. 22, 1790, [3]; E. H. Smith, *A Discourse, Delivered April 11, 1798, at the Request of and before the New-York Society for Promoting the Manumission of Slaves, and Protecting Such of Them as Have Been or May Be Liberated* (New York, 1798), 28.

14. *Address to the Public, from the Pennsylvania Society for Promoting the Abolition of Slavery*, [1]; Rush, *An Address to the Inhabitants of the British Settlements, on the Slavery of the Negroes in America*, 2d ed. (Philadelphia, 1773), 2. Neither Rush nor the PAS were alone in accentuating the poisonous environment of slavery on persons of African descent. Other abolitionists likewise adopted this rhetorical strategy. In 1794, George Buchanan, drawing on the writing of Montesquieu, told the Maryland Abolition Society that slavery "assimilates a man to a beast" and "clogs the mind, perverts the moral faculty, and reduces the conduct of man to the standard of brutes"; see Buchanan, *An Oration upon the Moral and Political Evil of Slavery: Delivered at a Public Meeting of the Maryland Society for Promoting the Abolition of Slavery, and the Relief of Free Negroes, and Others Unlawfully Held in Bondage; Baltimore, July 4th, 1791* (Balti-

Aware of the limitations of emphasizing the negative environment of slavery as a reform strategy, the abolition societies of early national America pursued a grander vision of African American uplift. To turn back the deleterious effects of slavery, the societal environment of black Americans would have to change for the better. The first step required in this revolutionary reconstruction of black life was the development of African American education and socioeconomic uplift. As with much of post-Revolutionary abolitionism, the PAS and the NYMS took the organizational lead. The NYMS established the African Free School in 1787, constituting the first large-scale, organized effort at black education in the new United States. During its first two decades, the school enrolled between one hundred and two hundred students annually, registering a total of eight hundred pupils by 1822 (see Figure 8). The PAS instituted a series of schools for free blacks beginning in 1793 and endorsed the establishment of independently founded African American schools run exclusively by free blacks. The Delaware Abolition Society launched a day school for African Americans by 1801 and continually expanded the school throughout the decade. In 1810, it founded the African School Society, allowing the abolition society to offer education for free blacks until the school was incorporated by the state in 1824. Meanwhile, educational initiatives took only temporary and incomplete root in New Jersey.[15]

-----

more, 1793), 11. For examples of first movement abolitionists' acknowledging black improvement despite the stifling atmosphere of slavery, see Miller, *A Discourse, Delivered April 12, 1797*, 34; Smith, *A Discourse, Delivered April 11, 1798*, 28–29; and Buchanan, *Oration upon the Moral and Political Evil of Slavery*, 10–11. On the concept of degradation and its limitations as a tool of antislavery in this era, see Nicholas Guyatt, *Bind Us Apart: How Enlightened Americans Invented Racial Segregation* (New York, 2016), 31–38.

15. By the early 1830s, the New-York African Free School had expanded its enrollment to more than one thousand pupils in several schoolhouses. Although even the most thoroughgoing attempts to promote education reached only a fraction of the black population in the urban mid-Atlantic, the schools nonetheless demonstrate the importance abolitionists attached to African American education as a lever of antislavery reform. On the educational efforts of the abolition societies, see Robert Duane Sayre, "The Evolution of Early American Abolitionism: The American Convention for Promoting the Abolition of Slavery and Improving the Condition of the African Race, 1794–1837" (Ph.D. diss., Ohio State University, 1987), 166–178. These efforts owed much to the activism of Anthony Benezet. Benezet provided evening classes for free black youths in his home beginning in 1750, and his successful experiment in black education (his pupils included future leaders of Philadelphia's African American community) influenced the Philadelphia Meeting to open a school for free blacks in 1770. Benezet remained intimately involved with the school's operations until his death in 1784. When the abolition societies turned to free black education to prove wrong the defenders of slavery, they

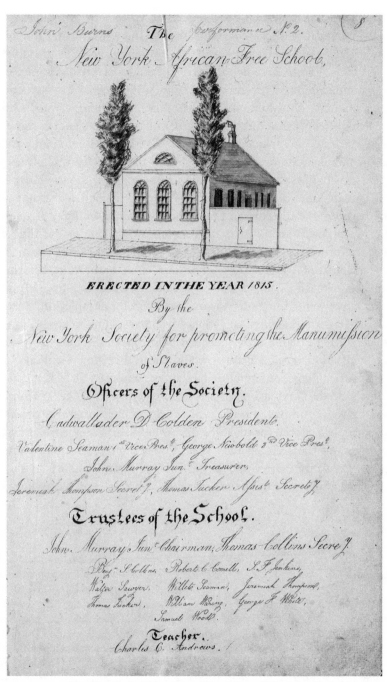

FIGURE 8. *The New York African Free School.* From "The New York African Free School ...," IV, 8, New-York African Free School Records, 1817–1832. Courtesy, New-York Historical Society

The schools established by the antislavery societies implemented a holistic curriculum of classical education intended to nurture the minds of its students and prepare them for the burdens of civic membership. In the NYMS's African Free School, areas of study included reading, writing, grammar, mathematics, and geography, all of which were conventional educational fare for the era. At the end of each academic year, the African Free School held what it referred to as examination day. Meant to showcase the scholarly accomplishments of the school's students for donors, parents, and the public, examination day was geared toward celebrating the intellectual growth of graduating pupils and authenticating to the white public that African Americans were worthy of civic inclusion. In a widely published synopsis of the African Free School's examination day of 1796, an observer (probably an NYMS member) of the event commended the "great spirit and propriety" of the students and professed that "the most prejudiced advocate of African slavery, if present, could have felt his favorite argument weakened." The excellent performance of the students had shown that "the powers of the mind do not depend on the complexion." Instead, "with equal encouragement and equal advantages, the African is capable of the same intellectual improvement as the European." Not only a means of civic inculcation, black education would affirm the equal potential of persons of African descent, unbound by slavery's chains.[16]

Scanning the surviving records of student work from the African Free School gives a glimpse into the type of educational programs the abolition societies adopted for its students. Some examples of student assignments include transcribing an excerpt from Joseph Addison's *Liberty and Slavery Contrasted,* drawing a picture of Benjamin Franklin, "cyphering to the rule of three" (a universally taught math rule), and writing original

had Benezet's legacy to shine the way. See Nancy Slocum Hornick, "Anthony Benezet and the Africans' School: Toward a Theory of Full Equality," *Pennsylvania Magazine of History and Biography,* XCIX (1975), 399–421; and Maurice Jackson, *Let This Voice Be Heard: Anthony Benezet, Father of Atlantic Abolitionism* (Philadelphia, 2009), 22–24.

16. New-York Manumission Society (NYMS) Records, 1785–1849, IX, 28, 101–103, New-York Historical Society (NYHS); *Argus; Greenleaf's New Daily Advertiser* (New York), Nov. 16, 1796, [3]; and *Herald* (New York), Nov. 16, 1796, [3]. Reprinted in *Argus; Greenleaf's New York Journal,* Nov. 18, 1796; and *Register of the Times* (New York), Nov. 18, 1796, [3]. For a description of examination day and annotated examples of student pieces from the African Free School, see David W. Blight et al., *"Hope Is the First Great Blessing": Leaves from the African Free School Presentation Book, 1812–1826* (New York, 2008). See also *Commercial Advertiser* (New York), Apr. 20, 1819, [2], for additional evidence of the NYMS's attempts to use examination day as a vehicle for persuading the public of black talent and virtue.

poems. Other surviving work from the African Free School also suggests that the NYMS might have looked to prepare its graduates for eventual entry into the middling and upper merchant classes of which much of the society's membership was composed. One student demonstrated the stock trading principle called fellowship, in which individual investors gauged their economic profits or losses in a joint-stock company. This was a rule that all merchants of the early Republic would have needed to know as a prerequisite for success in the mercantile profession.[17]

In their monthly visits to the African Free School, the trustees of the school frequently remarked on the unmistakable progress of the pupils. While punctuated by the occasional lament for better attendance or more rigid adherence to the school's rules, for the most part the reports the trustees logged with the NYMS teemed with encouraging news. Not long after the school's founding, the trustees announced that the "improvement" of the "Scholars" had already met their "best expectations." Within a year of this report, the trustees were "happy to find that the progress of the scholars continued to answer their most sanguine expectations" and looked forward to "the most pleasing prospect of the great advantages" that the school would give to the cause of abolitionism. The trustees viewed the school's success as helping to dislodge the prejudiced idea "of their [black people's] incapacity for improvement." The July 1804 Free School report effused, in what had by now become a familiar refrain, that the students "are in a State of Improvement perhaps equal to any School of White Children."[18]

If the African Free School stood as the chief means of reconstructing the environment of New York's people of color, free black Philadelphians and the PAS cast an even wider net in seeking African American uplift. In 1787, Richard Allen and Absalom Jones were among those who founded the Free African Society (FAS), a nondenominational organization that brought together many of Philadelphia's most prominent free blacks (see Figure 9). While the FAS's members pledged to provide economic aid to one another in times of distress, its goals included improving the state of both those who belonged to the organization and larger black Philadel-

17. New-York African Free School Records, 1817–1832, IV, 10, 12, 13–14, 25, NYHS. As *Hope Is the First Great Blessing* reveals, the African Free School served an ambiguous role for black youth. It could act as both an empowering venue for free black knowledge acquisition and self-expression and a constricting medium in which school administrators—through, for example, authoring valedictory speeches that students would then deliver—ventriloquized their pupils' voices.

18. NYMS Records, VI, 123, 127, IX, 104, 124, NYHS.

FIGURE 9. *Absalom Jones*. By Raphaelle Peale (1774–1825). 1810.
Oil on paper mounted to board. Gift of Absalom Jones School, 1971. This
portrait of Absalom Jones embodied many of the values black abolitionists sought
to project among their communities, including piety, learning, and sobriety.
Courtesy, Delaware Art Museum and Bridgeman Images

phia. The FAS's Articles of Association implied that only chaste and virtuous individuals could join and included a clause stating that members who "prove[d] disorderly" would be ejected from the society. The FAS's intolerance for wayward behavior eliminated from its rolls members who could prove unreliable in contributing funds. But a statement two years after the FAS's first meeting showed that the organization's strictures also aspired to influence the behavior of free blacks. In a letter to a sister organization in Rhode Island, the FAS condemned the "superfluity of naughtiness, especially gaming and feasting" that it believed people of color were "particularly guilty of." This behavior, the FAS feared, "enables our enemies to declare that we are not fit for freedom." To counter these accusations, the FAS encouraged free blacks to engage in more sober and virtuous practices.[19]

The PAS concurred with the viewpoint of the FAS and lent organizational support to black uplift. In 1789, the PAS formed the Committee for Improving the Condition of the Free Blacks (CICFB) and issued a broadside appeal to the public to help raise funds for its operation. The new committee was divided into four subdepartments. The committee of Inspection would look to "superintend the morals, general conduct, and ordinary situation of the Free Negroes" and "afford them instruction and advice." The committee of Education was tasked with starting up schools for free blacks that would supply the level of learning necessary for membership in the body politic. Just as the above two committees complimented each other, the committee of Guardians and committee of Employ would work in tandem. The committee of Guardians would oversee the binding out of black indentures, placing, whenever possible, African American youth in labor situations where they could "learn some trade or other business of subsistence" while ensuring that employers did not abuse the terms of the indenture. The committee of Employ sought employment for all free blacks who were looking for work and also hoped to offer to those blacks who "indicate proper talents" jobs in the "various trades." Over the next ten years,

19. Free African Society, "Articles," May 17, 1787, and "Brethren" of the Free African Society to Prince Hall, "Reply," circa 1780–1790, in W[illia]m Douglass, *Annals of the First African Church, in the United States of America, Now Styled the African Episcopal Church of St. Thomas, Philadelphia* ... (Philadelphia, 1862), 15–16, 31–32. Though it began as a nondenominational organization, by 1789 the FAS had come to affiliate itself, in all but name, with the Society of Friends. This connection, in turn, prompted the staunchly Methodist Richard Allen to leave the FAS. For background on the FAS and its activities, see Julie Winch, *Philadelphia's Black Elite: Activism, Accommodation, and the Struggle for Autonomy, 1787–1848* (Philadelphia, 1988), 5–7; Gary B. Nash, *Forging Freedom: The Formation of Philadelphia's Black Community, 1720–1840* (Cambridge, Mass., 1988), 98–99; and Douglass, *Annals of the First African Church,* 15–47.

the CICFB dedicated itself to raising the social, economic, and educational standing of black Pennsylvanians.[20]

One of the CICFB's first actions involved reaching out to black Philadelphians for support. The committee of Inspection discussed the new agency with African American community leaders before holding a public meeting for the black community at large. Indicating that they felt "well Satisfied" with the PAS's plan for black improvement, the members of the FAS even appointed their own committee to assist the CICFB in gathering data on the condition of free blacks. The committee of Inspection next set out to make a comprehensive census of Philadelphia's free African Americans, recording everything from head of household to religious affiliation. This initial recording was followed by periodic visits that took note of the habits of living, moral decorum, educational pursuits, and employment status of the city's free persons of color. Like the African Free School trustees, the committee of Inspection was overwhelmingly positive about what they found. In 1793, the committee reported that they had "with pleasure observed" that most families lived "reputably." They saw a "considerable Improvement" in the "Sobriety and Industry" of free blacks. After another visit to free black families, the committee again sounded an upbeat note. While some blacks were "idle and disorderly," a "much greater number live comfortably and reputably," many proving themselves "very worthy Citizens." Although the committee of Inspection's consultations with people of color were freighted with paternalistic advice on how best to conduct themselves in freedom, its reports illustrate the PAS's belief that many African Americans lived as virtuous citizens of the Republic.[21]

As the committee of Inspection monitored the social state of freedpersons, the Guardian, Employment, and Education committees kept busy trying to improve the economic and educational status of African Americans. The Guardian and Employment committees received a steady supply of applicants. Free black job seekers, parents wishing to indenture their children, and the children of enslaved persons now made indentured servants by the state's gradual abolition act all needed employment. Whenever possible, these committees sought to find employment situations favorable for free black elevation. In the winter of 1796, the committee of Guardians reported that it had won work contracts for a third of its recent applicants

20. *Plan for Improving the Condition of Free Negroes* (Philadelphia, 1789); Gary B. Nash and Jean R. Soderlund, *Freedom By Degrees: Emancipation in Pennsylvania and Its Aftermath* (New York, 1991), 128–129.

21. Papers of the Pennsylvania Abolition Society (PPAS), Series 1, reel 6, 14–17, 59–60, 112, Historical Society of Pennsylvania (HSP), Philadelphia.

in which African Americans would receive an education and learn a trade. In one instance, the committee oversaw the indenture of Toby Barclay for a seven-year term to the hatter Benjamin Scull. Barclay would learn the trade of hatmaking, and Scull was required to teach Barclay to read and write. Another manumitted person of color, Yaws, the committee indentured to a house carpenter, with the same educational benefits as Barclay. In 1794, the committee indentured a person of color to the free black minister Absalom Jones "to learn the Trade of Nailing," showing that the PAS believed free black leaders could improve the standing of their brethren. To guard the integrity of indentured blacks' work status, the PAS also granted permission for the CICFB to provide African Americans with certificates of indenture, sending a warning to potential kidnappers or unscrupulous employers that the abolitionist organization would not tolerate any breach of contract. Before the PAS initiated a school of its own, the committee of Education helped to fund two night schools for black youths. By 1793, the PAS had opened the doors to its first school and during the next decade and a half started several more institutions of learning for free blacks, receiving funds from black churches, among other sources. None of these schools matched the reach of the NYMS's famed African Free School, but they do show the PAS's dedication to black education.[22]

First movement abolitionists intended the educational and economic uplift of black Americans to help persons of African descent raise their status in freedom. This focus on improving the status of free blacks was central to defining what it meant to be an abolitionist in the late eighteenth and early nineteenth centuries. A negative environmentalist strategy that identified slavery as the cause of black inequality could never alone counter the damning charge of African American incapacity for freedom. Black socioeconomic and educational improvement could, however, counter the arguments of slavery's defenders and thus provided a means toward the goal of ending slavery. Just as important, free black uplift constituted an end in itself, making freedom from slavery meaningful.

22. PPAS, Series 1, reel 6, 79, 117, HSP; PPAS, Series 4, Manumissions, Indentures, and Other Legal Papers, Section 2, Indentures for various slaves manumitted in Jamaica by David Barclay of England, unnumbered pages, HSP. For an overview of the committee of Education and its initiatives, see Wayne J. Eberly, "The Pennsylvania Abolition Society, 1775–1830" (Ph.D. diss., Pennsylvania State University, 1973), 136–154. For a statement that the CICFB was looking for indentures that included blacks' learning a trade, see PPAS, Series 1, reel 6, 149, HSP. The CICFB was dissolved in 1803, but the PAS continued to carry out much of the committee's work long after the CICFB disbanded. Eberly, "The Pennsylvania Abolition Society," 129–179, gives a detailed summary of the CICFB's history and activism.

CONSTRUCTING REPUBLICAN CITIZENS

Free black activists and the abolition societies unequivocally conjoined the destruction of slavery and African American citizenship as the same project of reform. To the bedrock contention of slavery's defenders that formerly enslaved people were unsuited for freedom and posed a dire threat to the American body politic, first movement abolitionists responded by cultivating a community of republicans of color. The virtuous conduct, moral behavior, civic engagement, and religious and educational attainments of republicans of color would affirm the ability of blacks to exercise their freedom responsibly and pave the way for the total abolition of slavery in America. When free black community leaders such as Richard Allen, Absalom Jones, and James Forten in Philadelphia and Peter Williams, Jr., Henry Sipkins, and Joseph Sidney in New York set out to persuade the white public of the capacity of blacks for republican virtue, they did so from a profound sense of their own rise to republican respectability. These leading free black men were co-creators with the abolition societies of the first movement abolitionist reform strategy of societal environmentalism and black citizenship. Analogous to the pivotal part played by many people of color in the activism of the standing and acting committees, African American community leaders of the urban mid-Atlantic served as crucial partners of the abolition societies in developing black republican citizenship as a mechanism of emancipation. The white-led PAS and NYMS shared a belief in black civil incorporation and worked with free black activists and institutions. This cross-racial abolitionist alliance hinged on an unswerving commitment to post-Revolutionary republican values and black civic inclusion as central to abolitionist agitation.

Of course, that first movement abolitionists aimed to make republican citizens of persons of color does not mean that free blacks were full citizens in the post-Revolutionary and early national periods. In several states of the union, at any given time during the early Republic, free blacks possessed some of the rights of republican citizenship but were either explicitly or implicitly denied others. Yet, in states where the abolition societies were most active, namely Pennsylvania and New York, free blacks had many of the rights of citizens and were often referred to as citizens, at least through the early nineteenth century. More pertinent than attempting to determine to what degree free blacks were full or partial citizens is to acknowledge that citizenship in the early national period consisted of an ambiguous category whose contours were being sketched out. That citizenship's definition was still in the process of delineation in this era worked to the advantage of free blacks and their abolitionist allies, who believed African Americans had the opportunity to enter the body politic bearing the rights of citizens.[23]

First movement abolitionists conceived of black citizenship at two levels. The first level, elemental citizenship, consisted of freedom and the attendant principal rights of free persons, including but not limited to redress from unlawful detainment, the right to uphold families, and the ability to retain liberty from the threat of enslavement. As Chapter 2 has shown, the commitment of the first abolition movement to elemental citizenship emerged from the enforcement and expansion of statutory antislavery by the abolition societies and black northerners in the mid-Atlantic states. Elemental citizenship conceived of persons of color as incorporated members of the body politic with rights that the new nation must recognize.

If the rights of elemental citizenship acted to uphold the integrity of black freedom, the second level of first movement abolitionist ideas of black citizenship—republican citizenship—laid out what African American freedom should look like. In constructing a road map for a black republican citizenry, abolitionists took the societal orthodoxy of post-Revolutionary American citizenship as their guide. The ability to own property stood front and center. The abolition societies and their black allies held that the adoption of a sober, industrious, and virtuous life, buttressed by an effective education, would bring moral and monetary success to free blacks. Propertyownership, a staple component of early national citizenship discourse, reflected proper civic practices. The abolition societies recognized black freeholders and lauded these African Americans. In 1801, the PAS noted that a good portion of Philadelphia's free persons of color possessed "houses and other valuable property" and connected this fact with their virtuous behavior. The NYMS likewise believed that the "increase of the number of free-holders among black New Yorkers is an evidence of the progress of industry, sobriety, and economy, and strengthens the hope, that they will gradually emerge from their degraded condition." Property-

23. Douglas Bradburn calls the halfway status many people of color experienced "between slave and unfettered citizen" the "denization" of the free black population and rightly concludes that black citizenship "was never truly national" (Bradburn, *The Citizenship Revolution: Politics and the Creation of the American Union, 1774–1804* [Charlottesville, Va., 2009], 238). In fact, citizenship became a more concretized status at the very same time as people of color, and women, were increasingly being explicitly denied its privileges through processes such as disfranchisement in the early decades of the nineteenth century.

ownership and republican citizenship went hand in hand for black Americans, according to the abolition societies.[24]

With property rights came political rights. In a polity where voting represented the highest act of virtuous self-determination, first movement abolitionists yoked black suffrage to the larger meaning of republican America. The PAS's James Pemberton commended the Pennsylvania legislature for upholding black suffrage rights in the state's 1790 constitution, calling the decision consonant with "Liberty and just Government." When the voting rights of northern blacks came under increasing attack in the early nineteenth century, NYMS member and American Convention delegate Peter Jay defended the franchise of propertied free blacks against efforts to enact racial restrictions in New York's electoral politics. Jay depicted the voting rights of black New Yorkers as essential to the nature of American independence and nationhood, arguing that racial restrictions of suffrage would "violate all those principles upon which our free institutions are founded" and "contradict all the professions which we so profusely make, concerning the natural equality of all men." As late as 1837, the PAS, to combat efforts to strip black Pennsylvanians of the vote, put together a comprehensive assessment of the state of African Americans in Philadelphia. The report condemned black disfranchisement as "injurious to the interest of our colored population, and so derogatory to the character of our state." For first movement abolitionists, suffrage was a constitutive right of black citizenship indelibly bound up in the identity of republican America.[25]

Many black northerners actively participated in politics, fashioning themselves model republicans in the process. In New York, free black politics flourished. Many black New Yorkers supported the Federalists. In 1809,

24. PPAS, Series 1, reel 1, II, 1800–1824, 25, HSP; *Minutes of the Proceedings of the Eighth Convention of Delegates from the Abolition Societies Established in Different Parts of the United States* ... (Philadelphia, 1803), 7.

25. PPAS, Series 1, reel 11, I, 34, HSP; Nathaniel H. Carter, William L. Stone, and Marcus T. C. Gould, eds., *Reports of the Proceedings and Debates of the Covention of 1821* ..., in David N. Gellman and David Quigley, eds., *Jim Crow New York: A Documentary History of Race and Citizenship, 1777–1877* (New York, 2003), 142; *The Present State and Condition of the Free People of Color, of the City of Philadelphia and Adjoining Districts, as Exhibited by the Report of a Committee of the Pennsylvania Society for Promoting the Abolition of Slavery, etc.* .... (Philadelphia, 1838), 22. Peter Jay spoke up in support of black voting rights at New York's 1821 Constitutional Convention. The convention did not insert the word "white" in its requirements for voting. But it did disenfranchise the overwhelming majority of African Americans in the state of New York by imposing a $250 freehold standard on black voters. See Carter, Stone, and Gould, eds., *Reports*, in Gellman and Quigley, eds., *Jim Crow New York*, 111–114, 138–142.

Joseph Sidney, a leading black Federalist, announced that emancipation "has broken down that wall of separation, which formerly distinguished our rights and duties, from those of the white inhabitants." This "assimi- lated" state of black rights, according to Sidney, carried with it the "indis- pensable *duty*" of suffrage. Noting wryly that the "great idol of democracy" Thomas Jefferson and his fellow Virginian Republicans were the same people who held "our African brethren" in slavery, Sidney argued that the choice for black electors among the Republicans and Federalists was one between "your enemies and your friends" and between "slavery and free- dom." Partisan politics, for some free black leaders, related directly to the rights and liberties of persons of color.[26]

Other black New Yorkers cast their lot with the Jeffersonian Repub- licans. In their resolutions supporting Republican candidates, African American electors drew on the rhetorical idioms of the party's figurehead, Thomas Jefferson. An 1813 meeting of the "Citizens of Colour" pronounced that "Republican principles are favorable to the equal rights of mankind, and to the preservation of Life, Liberty and Property." The following spring, another meeting of black Republicans declared "that all men are by na- ture created equal." On whichever side of the partisan aisle they stood, free black electors devoted themselves to ending slavery and contributing to racial equality.[27]

While New York City's black activists partook of party politics, Philadel- phia's African American abolitionists turned to the political right of peti- tioning. With the federal capital located in Philadelphia, free black activists sent three antislavery petitions to the House of Representatives between 1797 and 1800. The 1799 petition of Absalom Jones and more than seventy people of color noted the "benefits granted to us in the enjoyment of our natural right to liberty, and the protection of our persons and property" but urged Congress to keep in mind "the condition of our afflicted brethren."

26. Joseph Sidney, *An Oration, Commemorative of the Abolition of the Slave Trade in the United States; Delivered before the Wilberforce Philanthropic Association in the City of New-York, on the Second of January, 1809* (New York, 1809), 8–9, 14. For free black New York Federalist electoral meetings, see *Spirit of '76*, Apr. 25, 1809, [3], reprinted in *New-York Herald*, Apr. 30, 1808, [1], and *Commercial Advertiser*, Nov. 9, 1813, [3]. See also *Evening Post* (New York), Nov. 8, 1813, [3], and *Commercial Advertiser*, Nov. 12, 1813, both reprinted in *Evening Post*, Nov. 11, 1813, [3].

27. *Mercantile Advertiser* (New York), Nov. 10, 1813, [2]; *Columbian* (New York), Apr. 26, 1814, [3]. For additional published reports of free black republican political meetings, see *Columbian*, Apr. 26, 1813, [3], Apr. 25, 1814, [2], Apr. 26, 1814, [3], Nov. 12, 1814, [3], Apr. 11, 1816, [3], Apr. 16, 1816, [2], Apr. 24, 1816, [2], Apr. 18, 1816, [3]; *National Advocate* (New York), Apr. 22, 1816, [2].

Insisting that all African Americans were the "objects of your representation ... in common with ourselves and every other class of citizens"—as set out in the preamble to the Federal Constitution, "We, the people"—Jones and the petition's cosigners requested that Congress do everything in its power to "prepare the way for the oppressed to go free." They called for the federal government to crack down on the kidnapping and reenslavement of northern free blacks in the South, enforce restrictions on American involvement in the foreign slave trade, and review the constitutionality of the Fugitive Slave Act of 1793. The House of Representatives voted to assign a committee to consider the petitioners' protestations to the Fugitive Slave Act, indirectly endorsing the right of free blacks to a vital right of republican citizens: the right to petition government. The Congressional committee greeted the petition positively. Though its report was not presented to Congress, the committee judged that free blacks were "entitled to freedom and Protection" and that the federal government maintained "a Duty to revise" the Fugitive Slave act.[28]

Black Philadelphians also petitioned their state legislature in opposition to a series of proposed anti-free black laws during the early nineteenth cen-

28. Absalom Jones et al., "To the President, Senate, and House of Representatives: The Petition of the People of Colour, Free Men, within the City and Suburbs of Philadelphia," Dec. 30, 1799, in John Parrish, *Remarks on the Slavery of the Black People; Addressed to the Citizens of the United States, Particularly to Those Who Are in Legislative or Executive Stations in the General or State Governments; and Also to Such Individuals as Hold Them in Bondage* (Philadelphia, 1806), 49–50; "Report of the Committee to Whom Was Referred the Petition of Absalom Jones and Others respecting the Fugitive Law etc.," quoted in Nicholas P. Wood, "'A Class of Citizens': The Earliest Black Petitioners to Congress and Their Quaker Allies," *WMQ*, 3d Ser., LXXIV (2017), 138–139. In 1797, Absalom Jones, writing for four free black migrants who had been manumitted in North Carolina but were subject to kidnapping following that state's passage of laws that encouraged the reenslavement of newly emancipated African Americans, submitted an antislavery petition against the Fugitive Slave Act of 1793. See *The Debates and Proceedings in the Congress of the United States ... Fourth Congress—Second Session; Comprising the Period from December 5, 1796, to March 3, 1797, Inclusive ...* (Washington, D.C., 1849), 2015–2018. The petition was presented to the House of Representatives by a former member of the PAS, Nicholas Waln. Both the 1797 and 1799 petitions were most likely coauthored and lobbied for by white antislavery Quaker activists, especially those affiliated with the Pennsylvania Monthly Meeting, whose work with Jones was emblematic of interracial activist cooperation between free blacks in Philadelphia and the Society of Friends in the 1790s. See Wood, "'A Class of Citizens,'" *WMQ*, 3d Ser., LXXIV (2017), 109–144. Absalom Jones gathered black signatures for a third petition effort and submitted an antislavery memorial to the Congress in 1800 directly imploring president elect Jefferson to work toward abolishing slavery and ending the slave trade. See Nash, *Forging Freedom*, 188.

tury. Fearing that "the prejudices, which they [the petitioners] deplore, will be increased and perpetuated against persons of their colour" by one such bill, an 1806 petition told the Pennsylvania Assembly that by voting down the legislation it would "evince an attachment to individual freedom, and the principles of the Constitution." By grounding their antislavery crusade on irrefutable evidence that African Americans were knowledgeable and engaged citizens, free black activists furthered the construction of a community of republicans of color.[29]

Although the ability to hold property and exercise political rights represented key components of republican citizenship, the duties incumbent upon individual black citizens is what would make the enjoyment of these rights possible, according to first movement abolitionists. American republicanism emphasized not only the liberties but also the duties of members of the body politic. Black abolitionists tapped into American republicanism's preoccupation with a virtuous citizenry and invoked it as the proving ground for African American freedom. Free black community leaders and antislavery activists in New York City and Philadelphia used public gatherings to disseminate among their black brethren republican values. Henry Sipkins called for "an upright and steady deportment" among the emancipated, while Peter Williams, Jr., counseled free persons to show "a strict obedience and respect to the laws of the land." To ensure black civil cultivation, Henry Johnson, a black freeholder of New York City, warned his "fellow-citizens" to be vigilant against immoral and depraved behavior, insisting that there were no "greater advocates" for African American freedom than free blacks themselves. Richard Allen wanted persons of color to adopt the entreaty of George Washington's farewell address to "love your country—to obey its laws." Absalom Jones advocated both republican simplicity and austerity, calling for African Americans to be "sober minded ... temperate in our meats and drinks, frugal in our apparel and in the furniture of our houses" and "industrious in our occupations," so as to "fur-

29. *Poulson's American Daily Advertiser* (Philadelphia), Feb. 17, 1806, [3]. Free African American Philadelphians submitted at least two additional petitions to the state legislature opposing antiblack laws in the early national period. See *Journal of the Seventeenth House of Representatives of the Commonwealth of Pennsylvania; Commenced at Lancaster, on Tuesday, the Second Day of December, in the Year of Our Lord, One Thousand Eight Hundred and Six, and of the Commonwealth the Thirty-First* (Lancaster, Pa., 1806 [1807]), 591, 652; and *Journal of the Twenty-third House of Representatives of the Commonwealth of Pennsylvania; Commenced at Harrisburg, Tuesday, the First of December, in the Year of Our Lord, One Thousand Eight Hundred and Twelve, and of the Commonwealth the Thirty Seventh* (Lancaster, Pa., 1812 [1813]), 588.

nish no cause of regret" among white Americans about the merits of black freedom.[30]

An unwavering commitment to American republicanism drove New York City's and Philadelphia's free black abolitionists. African American abolitionists of the early national urban mid-Atlantic looked to the ideals of the Republic in which they lived for their brethren's deliverance from bondage. They believed that the American Revolution's promises of freedom and equality were embedded in republicanism, forming the basis of the new nation's identity and its governing creed. In a speech observing the abolition of the international slave trade in 1808, Peter Williams, Jr., called the Revolution that "illustrious moment" when a "temple sacred to liberty" was erected according to the precepts that "all men are created equal." For Williams it was in the wake of American independence that the "angel of humanity" successfully sought to enter the "bleeding African" into the civil fold by claiming the "inherent rights of man" for people of all colors. Five years later, in another celebration of the slave trade's abolition by New York City's blacks, George Lawrence, a member of the free black self-help organization the New York African Society for Mutual Relief, pointed out to his audience that the American nation had been "founded on the principles of liberty and equality." Lawrence was "confident" that "the land in which we live," operating in accordance with these principles, "gives us the opportunity rapidly to advance the prosperity of liberty." Williams and Lawrence saw no distinction between the ideals of American independence and the interests of persons of color.[31]

30. Henry Sipkins, *Oration on the Abolition of the Slave Trade; Delivered in the African Church, in the City of New-York, January 2, 1809* (New York, 1809), 17; Peter Williams, Jr., *An Oration on the Abolition of the Slave Trade; Delivered in the African Church, in the City of New-York, January 1, 1808* (New York, 1808), 26; Henry Johnson, *An Oration on the Abolition of the Slave Trade, by Henry Johnson; with an Introductory Address, by Adam Carman; Delivered in the African Church in New-York, January 1, 1810* (New York, 1810), 13–14; *Philadelphia Gazette and Universal Daily Advertiser,* Dec. 31, 1799, [2]; Absalom Jones, *A Thanksgiving Sermon, Preached January 1, 1808, in St. Thomas's, or the African Episcopal, Church, Philadelphia; on Account of the Abolition of the African Slave Trade, on That Day, by the Congress of the United States* (Philadelphia, 1808), 17.

31. Williams, *Oration on the Abolition of the Slave Trade,* 20–21; George Lawrence, *An Oration on the Abolition of the Slave Trade, Delivered on the First Day of January, 1813, in the African Methodist Episcopal Church* (New York, 1813), 11. My portrayal of black abolitionists' wholeheartedly embracing American republicanism follows my rendering of the post-Revolutionary and early national eras as offering empowerment and hope for many free blacks in the urban mid-Atlantic. In this depiction, I depart from two notable interpretations of early black abolitionist print culture. Joanna Brooks identi-

The mid-Atlantic's black abolitionists viewed the creation of the United States and the spread of African American emancipation and racial uplift to be a result of simultaneous forces indelibly linked by the principles of freedom and equality. John Teasman, selected in 1811 to deliver the keynote speech on the two-year anniversary of the New York African Society for Mutual Relief's state charter, depicted the African Society's incorporation as indicative of a larger trend by New York state toward the admission of black liberty and citizenship. The state government had "arose, decreed, and stretched forth its arm for the destruction of slavery in itself." Then, following the passage of a gradual emancipation law, it "took you [free blacks] into social citizenship, gave you a charter, placed you on a level with other civil societies of the state, and rendered you a body politic," announced Teasman. Richard Allen, in his eulogy of George Washington (whom Americans saw as the embodiment of virtuous republicanism), exclaimed that the nation's first president was a "sympathising friend and tender father" to America's blacks and one who "thought we had a right to liberty." Allen marked Washington's death as an event in which Philadelphia's people of color "participate in common with the feelings of a grateful people" and pressed his congregation to "shew to the world that you hold dear the name of George Washington." What better way to broadcast black republicanism than to show the white public how African Americans revered a progenitor of American virtue?[32]

----

fies a black print counterpublic that defined black identity "oppositional[ly]" from mainstream post-Revolutionary and early national ideological currents and was "structured by black criticisms of white political and economic dominance." Relatedly, Manisha Sinha argues that black abolitionists developed a radical "counternarrative to the history of revolutionary republicanism in the United States that highlighted slavery rather than freedom and independence as its central legacy." See Brooks, "The Early American Public Sphere and the Emergence of a Black Print Counterpublic," *WMQ*, 3d Ser., LXII (2005), 68, 80, 68; and Sinha, "To 'Cast Just Obliquy' on Oppressors: Black Radicalism in the Age of Revolution," ibid., LXIV (2007), 150. Brooks and Sinha map important characteristics of black abolitionist print culture. Yet their interpretations overemphasize the exclusionary nature of American republicanism and the public sphere while underemphasizing the shared goals and values of black and white abolitionists. For an interpretation that meshes with my own, see Patrick Rael, *Black Identity and Black Protest in the Antebellum North* (Chapel Hill, N.C., 2002), 5. Rael writes that free black northern activists in the pre–Civil War North "crafted challenges to racial inequality that appealed to cherished American values rather than stepped outside the bounds of the American ideological landscape."

32. John Teasman, *An Address Delivered in the African Episcopal Church, on the 25th March 1811, before the New York African Society for Mutual Relief; Being the First Anniversary of Its Incorporation* (New York, 1811), 6; *Philadelphia Gazette*, Dec. 31, 1799, [2].

To assure the progressive march of emancipation, black abolition-ists sculpted a community of republicans of color. The abolition societies played a major role in fostering this community. Like their black activist counterparts, abolition societies coupled the fight to end slavery with vir-tuous black citizenship when they came together as a national body for the first time in 1794 as the American Convention of Abolition Societies. Dele-gates to the inaugural meeting of the American Convention acknowledged the deep reservoir of white American prejudice and skepticism about the ability of African Americans to handle freedom without endangering greater society. The delegates identified black education, specifically in the "principles of virtue and religion," "common literature," and the "useful me-chanical arts," as a primary agent of African American liberation. Educa-tion would "prepare them [formerly enslaved people] for becoming good citizens of the United States" and "gradually tend to the emancipation of slaves" by demonstrating the capacity of African Americans for freedom.[33]

In the estimation of the American Convention, education, an umbrella term that referred to moral conduct, religious practices, and daily habits, would undergird the edifice of republican citizenship for persons of African descent. Calling black education our "noblest and most arduous task," the 1795 American Convention made the case for its importance to their fellow abolitionists: "When we have broken his chains, and restored the African to the enjoyment of his rights, the great work of justice and benevolence is not accomplished—The new born citizen must receive that instruction, and those powerful impressions of moral and religious truth, which will render him capable and desirous of fulfilling the various duties he owes to himself and to his country."[34]

33. *Minutes of the Proceedings of a Convention of Delegates from the Abolition Soci-eties Established in Different Parts of the United States* ... (Philadelphia, 1794), 8, 15, 20–21. Delegates to the first American Convention included representatives of the Con-necticut, New York, New Jersey, Pennsylvania, Delaware, Wilmington (Del.), Maryland, and Chestertown (Md.) abolition societies. The American Convention, consistently dominated by the PAS and NYMS, became regionalized a decade after its first meet-ing—shrinking into a coalition of mid-Atlantic societies by 1803. Nevertheless, the Con-vention's proceedings provide a window into the philosophical underpinnings of first movement abolitionism, predicated on societal environmentalism and black citizenship.

34. *Minutes of the Proceedings of the Second Convention of Delegates from the Aboli-tion Societies Established in Different Parts of the United States* ... (Philadelphia, 1795), 29–30. Quakers had always been at the vanguard of African American education, insti-tuting schools for blacks before the American Revolution. For an analysis that associ-ates the educational programs of the abolition societies exclusively with the Society of Friends, see Jordan, *White over Black*, 356–361. In contrast, I contend that the educa-

The American Convention did not merely aim its pleas for the education of African Americans at the constituent abolition societies. It spent more time communicating to African American communities the absolute necessity of black education and moral living as a strategy for successfully abolishing slavery. Between 1796 and 1805, the American Convention issued four addresses to free blacks, instructing them on how to best behave as republican citizens. The messages put forth in these addresses encapsulate the abolition societies' comprehensive understanding of black education.[35]

Full of paternalistic dogmas on how to live virtuously, the American Convention's addresses to African Americans also dovetailed with the advice of free black mid-Atlantic leaders. In their earliest address, penned at the 1796 Convention, the delegates listed guidelines for people of color to live by. Not surprisingly, the address began by citing the "important duty of public worship," which would help form the moral bedrock of a life of propriety and "proper conduct." Next, they encouraged free blacks to gain a general competency in "reading, writing, and the first principles of arithmetic," which would give them access to the foundational elements of human knowledge. Paralleling the early national values of republican austerity, the address also urged African Americans to be "simple in your dress and furniture" while remaining "frugal in your family expenses." Furthermore, free black parents should teach their children "useful trades" to permit them to "acquire habits of industry." Should African Americans adopt these values, the address promised them that "virtue" and success would follow. Warnings against the follies of "frolicking," "amusements which lead to expense and idleness," and the "use of spirituous liquors" rounded out the advice. It was advice that readers of the paragon-setter of late-

---

tional initiatives of these antislavery groups were not merely an expression of Quaker religious doctrine; they were part of the larger Revolutionary and early national standards of educational cultivation and individual reform that pervaded American society in this period.

35. See *Minutes of the Proceedings of the Third Convention of Delegates from the Abolition Societies Established in Different Parts of the United States* ... (Philadelphia, 1796), 12–15; *Minutes of the Proceedings of the Fourth Convention of Delegates from the Abolition Societies in Different Parts of the United States* ... (Philadelphia, 1797), 16–18; *Minutes of the Proceedings of the Ninth American Convention for Promoting the Abolition of Slavery and Improving the Condition of the African Race* ... (Philadelphia, 1804), 30–32; and *Minutes of the Proceedings of the Tenth American Convention for Promoting the Abolition of Slavery and Improving the Condition of the African Race* ... (Philadelphia, 1805), 36–39.

eighteenth-century republican citizenship, Benjamin Franklin, would have found highly familiar.[36]

Subsequent statements to free blacks echoed much of the same advice dispensed in the 1796 address. The 1804 address asked people of color to "be industrious, diligent in your business, frugal in your expences" while "striv[ing] to acquire that knowledge" of reading and always maintaining "industry and sobriety" in action and thought. The 1805 American Convention acknowledged free black civic growth. "You have found that industry and oeconomy have procured for you, independence; that temperance has greatly promoted, if not absolutely secured to you, health; and that the cultivation of the faculties of the mind, has enlarged the capacity for discharging your various duties, and for enjoying the numerous benefits you have received." In the eyes of the Convention's delegates, the continuing adoption of such virtuous behavior would overcome the "devastations" of slavery inflicted upon bondspersons by the iniquitous institution of bondage. As if to underscore the gravity of its address to free blacks, the delegates had three thousand copies printed and prodded the abolition societies to distribute them among African American communities. The societies answered the Convention's request by holding public gatherings where the addresses were read and discussed with people of color. The number of copies printed of the addresses to free blacks regularly outpaced the printings of the American Convention's minutes, further underscoring the imperative of black education and moral uplift for the delegates.[37]

Virtuous black republican citizenship would prove to Americans everywhere that emancipation could be a safe and secure process. The 1796 address to persons of color closed by asking the nation's blacks to reflect: "It is by your good conduct alone, that you can refute the objections which have been made against you as rational and moral creatures, and remove many of the difficulties, which have occurred in the general emancipation of such of your brethren as are yet in bondage." The 1804 Convention reminded free blacks that "by your worthy conduct, you may destroy the prejudices which some persons entertain against you." First movement abolitionists insisted that virtuous republican citizenship by free blacks would eradicate

<hr/>

36. *Minutes of the Proceedings of the Third Convention of the Delegates from the Abolition Societies* (1796), 13–15.

37. *Minutes of the Proceedings of the Ninth American Convention for Promoting the Abolition of Slavery* (1804), 10, 31; *Minutes of the Proceedings of the Tenth American Convention for Promoting the Abolition of Slavery* (1805), 36–39. For PAS and NYMS reports of reading addresses to free blacks, see NYMS Records, IX, 2, NYHS; and PPAS, Series 1, reel 1, I, 304, HSP.

the prejudices of white Americans, prejudices that so threatened the abolition of slavery.[38]

The American Convention had reason to believe its reform program was working. In 1804, New Jersey passed a gradual emancipation act, becoming the sixth state to abolish slavery and giving a terminal sentence to human bondage throughout the mid-Atlantic and New England regions. And, within some of these states, first movement abolitionists could feel as though they had subdued white prejudice as a political tool of slavery's defenders. New York provided a particularly encouraging example. The racialized restrictions on citizenship that slavery's defenders had dredged up to defeat abolition in 1785 were notably absent from the 1799 act. No suffrage restrictions, bans against black officeholding or jury participation, or injunctions on interracial marriage marred New York's abolition law. If the indentured children of the enslaved faced a long road to full freedom, New York tacitly acknowledged equal citizenship for free blacks. As the activism of the acting and standing committees of the NYMS and PAS show, gradual emancipation statutes proved inadequate in multiple ways. But the abolition societies in their campaign to defeat white prejudice felt justified in continuing to help cultivate virtuous black free persons to fight slavery.[39]

Black education would furnish particularly significant ammunition in this fight. Time and again the delegates to the American Convention labeled African American education as the engine of abolitionism. Black education would "do away [with] the reproach" of those Americans opposed to emancipation by "confound[ing] the enemies of truth" and "evincing that the unhappy sons of Africa, in spite of the degrading influence of slavery, are in no wise inferior to the more fortunate inhabitants of Europe and America," thus furthering abolition. Arguing that an effective program of education would permit people of color to comport themselves as "becomes men, escaped from bondage," the 1804 address told the abolition societies that

38. *Minutes of the Proceedings of the Third Convention of Delegates from the Abolition Societies* (1796), 15; *Minutes of the Proceedings of the Ninth American Convention for Promoting the Abolition of Slavery* (1804), 30–32 (quotation on 31).

39. David Gellman argues that, between the 1785 defeat of legislative abolition in New York and the 1799 emancipation act, antislavery and proslavery writers took to the print sphere to imagine the prospect of black freedom and citizenship through an array of literary forms depicting an African American voice in both positive and negative renderings. Gellman attributes the resulting discourse over the prospect of black citizenship as a contributing factor to the passage of the 1799 act and likewise notes the absence of racially restrictive clauses that had been present in the 1785 abolition bill. See Gellman, *Emancipating New York*, 102–129.

it was the "conduct" of free blacks on which "the liberation of their brethren" would "depend." Expressing similar sentiments, and speaking with the public close in mind, the 1805 American Convention's address to the abolition societies reminded antislavery activists that the "enjoyment of liberty, may be of but little use" were not the newly emancipated "qualified by suitable instruction to conduct with propriety in the various stations allotted to them in civil society." The American Convention expressly connected black education and a successful fight against slaveholding.[40]

The American Convention's educational program of free black moral, religious, and behavioral development emanated from larger early national standards for enduring republican citizenship. Pamphlets and speeches that supported education during the Revolutionary and early national periods show that the Convention's advice to free blacks was a product of commensurable expectations for white Americans, and not specifically tailored for persons of color. Josiah Clark opened his 1794 publication on the education of youth by stating that education was the "the natural means of preserving religion and virtue in the world." Putting forth his outline for a proposed system of public schooling in the state of Pennsylvania, Benjamin Rush singled out "industry and oeconomy" sustained by the inculcation of "republican duties" and "republican principles" as working to "qualify" those emerging from the school system "for becoming good citizens of the republic." In 1785, Enos Hitchcock gave an address in a Providence, Rhode Island, Congregational church arguing that education would "cultivate" the "minds" of pupils, "direct their manners, and 'train them up in the way they should go.'" In Hitchcock's estimation, a system of education centered on

40. *Minutes of the Proceedings of the Second Convention of Delegates from the Abolition Societies* (1795), 30; *Minutes of the Proceedings of the Ninth American Convention for Promoting the Abolition of Slavery* (1804), 17; *Minutes of the Proceedings of the Tenth American Convention for Promoting the Abolition of Slavery* (1805), 7. At the 1798 Convention, the delegates claimed that "too much cannot be said about the necessity of a constant attention to the subject of education" and during the previous year's meeting insisted that, in spite of the amount of ink already spilled in justifying the need for African American education, its role "cannot be too forcibly impressed." See *Minutes of the Proceedings of the Fifth Convention of Delegates from the Abolition Societies Established in Different Parts of the United States . . .* (Philadelphia, 1798), 17; *Minutes of the Proceedings of the Fourth Convention of Delegates from the Abolition Societies* (1797), 23. For additional examples of the Convention's emphasis on the importance of formerly enslaved people's education, see *Minutes of the Proceedings of a Convention of Delegates from the Abolition Societies* (1794), 20; *Minutes of the Proceedings of the Seventh Convention of Delegates from the Abolition Societies Established in Different Parts of the United States . . .* (Philadelphia, 1801), 43; and *Minutes of the Proceedings of the Eighth Convention of Delegates from the Abolition Societies* (1803), 31.

"moral duty, and christian faith" for all Americans was especially important to the fledgling Republic because in "republican States" society's "existence depends on the wisdom and virtue of the people at large." The Convention agreed and included black Americans in its definition of the Republic's people.[41]

The statements of city governments and public officials in the early Republic also sound strikingly similar to the American Convention's addresses to free blacks. A 1789 printing of "Recommendations to the Schoolmasters" by the public education committee of Boston instructed teachers to "address their pupils on moral and religious subjects; endeavouring to impress their minds with a sense of the being and providence of God." The committee alerted the instructors to guard against their students' taking up "the prevailing vices, such as sabbath-breaking, profane cursing and swearing, gaming, idleness" and other immoral behavior. In 1785, the governor of Massachusetts, James Bowdoin, issued a proclamation promoting the benefits of public education. Providing "the rising Generation" with "good Instruction, and disseminating among them the Principles of Wisdom and right Conduct, so that they may become good and useful Citizens" would be key for "the Preservation of the Rights and Liberties of the People." Bowdoin thought "Industry and Frugality, Temperance, Sobriety and decency of Manners" needed to supersede "Gaming, Idleness, Drunkenness, and every other Species of Vice" in a society based on self-government. The abolition societies concurred with these notions of education and the moral development of a virtuous citizenry and viewed their adoption by people of color as the best way to realize emancipation. Once black Americans exhibited these virtuous behaviors, they would show that formerly enslaved people posed no threat to the young Republic and take their place as republican citizens of the new nation.[42]

Delivered in 1797, the speech of the NYMS member and delegate to

41. Josiah Clark, *The Parent's Monitor; or, An Address to Parents and Teachers, concerning the Education of Youth in Several Particulars* (Boston, [1794]), [5]; Benjamin Rush, *A Plan for the Establishment of Public Schools and the Diffusion of Knowledge in Pennsylvania; to Which Are Added Thoughts upon the Mode of Education, Proper in a Republic; Addressed to the Legislature and Citizens of the State* (Philadelphia, 1786), 22–24 (quotations on 22, 24); Enos Hitchcock, *A Discourse on Education, Delivered at the Meeting-House on the West Side of the River, in Providence, November 16, 1785* (Providence, R.I., [1786]), 9–10, 12.

42. *Recommendations to the Schoolmasters, by the Committee Appointed to Carry into Execution the System of Public Education, Adopted by the Town of Boston, the 15th of October 1789* (Boston, 1789); James Bowdoin, *A Proclamation, for the Encouragement of Piety, Virtue, Education, and Manners, and for the Suppression of Vice* (Boston, 1785).

the American Convention Samuel Miller personifies the interplay in the first movement abolitionist strategy between societal environmentalism and claims of republican citizenship for African Americans. A Presbyterian minister, social reformer, and strong supporter of the French Revolution, Miller viewed slavery as incompatible with American liberty. He attacked the pretensions of white prejudice that he believed underlay the institution of bondage. Skin color was not the only means used to rationalize bondage for those of African descent. Many white Americans also asserted that black people were mentally inferior and deficient in *"intellectual capacity."* According to Miller, this claim was disingenuously grounded. Considering that enslaved blacks were cut off from the same society that permitted white citizens to cultivate their intellects, any negative judgment with regard to black potential was wholly unfair. Besides, the African Free School had already demonstrated that, once freed and provided with educational opportunities, blacks performed equal to whites in scholarly and moral endeavors.[43]

As Miller saw it, there was only one solution to the evil of slavery and the injustice of black inequality: gradually abolish slavery and incorporate the formerly enslaved into the body politic. The "INTELLECTUAL AND MORAL CULTIVATION of slaves" must accompany slavery's abolition so freedpersons could "be prepared to exercise the rights, and discharge the duties of citizens, when liberty shall be given them." Both Miller and his antislavery cohorts might have started from the position that enslaved people were inferior in condition, but the key was that this inferiority was a transitory, environmental condition that could be transcended by proper instruction rather than a permanent state of degradation. "Say not that they [enslaved people] are unfit for the rank of citizens ... Make them freemen; and they will soon be found to have the manners, the character, and the virtues of freemen," Miller concluded. Turning the formerly enslaved into citizens would disarm chattel bondage's proponents of a primary weapon in their proslavery arsenal.[44]

That reformers like Miller eschewed making civic distinctions along the lines of race did not mean they opposed all checks on equal citizenship. The abolition societies belonged to a group of several reform organiza-

43. Miller, *A Discourse, Delivered April 12, 1797,* 12–14.

44. Ibid., 31–32. The text of Miller's speech was turned into a pamphlet and published by the NYMS for public consumption in the same year that it was delivered. Miller's address was also circulated among the delegates to the 1798 American Convention and read aloud to the entire assembly during that year's meeting. See *Minutes of the Proceedings of the Fifth Convention of Delegates from the Abolition Societies* (1798), 13.

tions influenced by the concerns of affluent men who hoped to maintain civic order in a society revolutionized by American independence. These groups administered what they saw as benevolent philanthropy on behalf of the "public good." The educated, well-born, and highly connected leading men of society would extend their beneficent patronage to the lower sorts in exchange for deference from the recipients of their good will. The abolition societies, therefore, while applauding free black property holders and working with black community leaders and educators, undoubtedly viewed African Americans as the clients of their patronage.[45]

Early national reformers did not seek to level their societies. Social hierarchy remained a critical component of the worldview of many of these men. Though Elias Boudinot was not a member of one of the abolition societies, his words epitomize important assumptions of social hierarchy that delegates to the American Convention most likely shared. The antislavery sympathizer Boudinot, during his term as president of the Continental Congress, told the Society of the Cincinnati that, although "the rational equality and rights of men" defined the Revolution, the differing talents, abilities, and opportunities of Americans would always create "a pre-eminency and superiority one over another." Thus, Boudinot believed it "essential to good government and necessary for the welfare of every community, that there should be distinctions among members of the same society." In other words, the natural equality of all could not result in the equal social standing of all without tearing the fabric of newly independent America. As scholars have long noted, the very fact that many reformers of the post-Revolutionary and early national eras hailed from the upper echelons of American society probably made them more likely to embrace a raceless version of republican citizenship when compared to their free white contemporaries of lesser means. If men like Boudinot could imagine black citizens, picturing the absolute equality of all men, white or black, conjured an unnatural and socially destructive scene. A categorically egalitarian version of American citizenship was not in harmony with the objectives of early national philanthropic movements of which the abolition societies were a part.[46]

45. For an overview of the early national worldview that imbued this type of reform, see M. J. Heale, "Humanitarianism in the Early Republic: The Moral Reformers of New York, 1776–1825," *Journal of American Studies*, II (1968), 161–175; and Alan Taylor, *William Cooper's Town: Power and Persuasion on the Frontier of the Early American Republic* (New York, 1995).

46. Elias Boudinot, "Oration before the Society of the Cincinnati in the State of New Jersey," July 4, 1793, in J. J. Boudinot, ed., *The Life, Public Services, Addresses, and Let-*

Notwithstanding its limitations, the first abolition movement's program of black citizenship was sincere. If class rather than race determined one's position in the spectrum of citizenship, the abolition societies regarded free blacks as citizens entitled to the same rights and privileges as whites with similar socioeconomic status. Perhaps the best indication of first movement abolitionists' commitment to African American citizenship was that black leaders in the urban mid-Atlantic forged and broadcast the concept of republicans of color. People of color did not passively receive first movement abolitionist ideals of black citizenship. Instead, they actively shaped these ideals in cities like New York and Philadelphia. Free black activists and the abolition societies pictured a raceless version of citizenship rooted in making formerly enslaved people republicans of color, a vision of black belonging that would stand in stark contrast to later antislavery reformers' ideas of African American exclusion.

A SHARED STRUGGLE

Reflecting their mutual embrace of the philosophy of first movement abolitionism, black and white reformers joined forces. In April 1790, five delegates of the PAS met with FAS leaders, familiarizing its members with the efforts of the PAS to improve the condition of free blacks. The PAS emissaries asked the FAS to help them collect information on the state of black Philadelphians, a request with which the FAS eagerly complied. Further advancing this objective, two decades later Philadelphia's free black activists founded the "Society for Suppressing Vice and Immorality." Members of the society planned to visit the homes of free persons and, through "persuasive measures," hoped to "produce [a] reformation of manners" among the newly emancipated. When the "Society of Free People of Colour, for Education of Children of African Descent" started up a school for free blacks with the purpose of making them "useful members of society," they invited the superintendents of the PAS to measure the "progress of the pupils" and give curricular advice.[47]

---

ters of Elias Boudinot, LL.D., President of the Continental Congress, 2 vols. (Boston, 1896), II, 361–363, quoted in Robert Pierce Forbes, "'The Cause of This Blackness': The Early American Republic and the Construction of Race," American Nineteenth Century History, XIII, no. 1 (June 2012), 83. For the standard interpretation of the connections between elite standing and openness to black rights in the realm of early national politics, see Paul Finkelman, "The Problem of Slavery in the Age of Federalism," in Doron Ben-Atar and Barbara B. Oberg, eds., Federalists Reconsidered (Charlottesville, Va., 1998), 154.

47. "Proposition from Old Abolition Society," and "Petition," in Douglass, Annals of

The PAS and free black Philadelphians matched organizational efforts to uplift persons of color with complimentary rhetoric denouncing attempts to roll back the rights of black Pennsylvanians. In opposition to a series of antiblack bills that found their way before the Pennsylvania state legislature from 1805 to 1813, white and black activists submitted petitions remonstrating against the proposals and used congruous language in their appeals. A group of "Free People of Colour, resident in the city of Philadelphia and its neighbourhood," informed the Pennsylvania legislature in 1806 that according to the state constitution "all freemen are placed upon the same equal footing." Since "no difference is made between a white man, a mulatto, or a black freeman" and "all enjoy the same rights and privileges," the Pennsylvania government must not racialize citizenship. In 1813, the PAS announced that the state's free blacks were entitled to "equal rights and common protection" of the state constitution and condemned any attempt "to mark for exception" the access of people of color to the "great and benevolent Maxim" that "'all Men are born equally free and independent and that have certain inherent and indefeasible rights.'" The PAS also cited black republican respectability as a reason to uphold equal rights for persons of color, stating that "a large portion" of free blacks in Pennsylvania were "entitled to the reputation of respectable industrious and useful Members of Society." Both the PAS and black activists zealously guarded the republican rights of free African Americans.[48]

New York City's black activists, and the larger communities to which these reformers belonged, also worked with white abolitionists. In 1796, the NYMS welcomed a group of free blacks who asked for the society's "advice and assistance" in forming "an association" that would root out "every species of vice among the people of their own description, by information, advice, and above all by an example of virtuous conduct." The NYMS approved of the "worthy design" of these free black reformers and offered their assistance. Noting that many New York slaveholders were purposely neglecting to register the indentured offspring of their bondspersons who were scheduled to be gradually emancipated, in 1808 the NYMS appointed a committee to canvas local blacks for the names of the many hundreds of unregistered black children. The committee "attended several meetings of Coloured People on the subject" and soon reported that their exchanges

the First African Church, 39, 113 (quotations); Poulson's American Daily Advertiser, Aug. 7, 1804, [2], Sept. 18, 1804, [3], and Oct. 20, 1804, [4].
    48. Poulson's American Daily Advertiser, Feb. 17, 1806, [3]; PPAS, Series 1, reel 1, II, 182–184, HSP.

with black New Yorkers had brought to light the unregistered names of many who were slotted to receive their gradual freedom. The NYMS and black New Yorkers together sought to secure emancipation and propagate the principles of republican citizenship among free African Americans in the city.[49]

Free black New Yorkers publicly recognized this activist partnership. The NYMS helped to gain a state charter for the New York African Society for Mutual Relief in 1810, causing the society's vice president to remind its members that, in the "great work of extending your liberties, the manumission powers were very active." At the second annual celebration of the abolition of the Atlantic slave trade, a committee of free blacks planned to donate part of the proceeds from their jubilee to the NYMS. Peter Williams, Jr., thanked the American Convention of Abolition Societies in 1806 for helping to "rescue" black Americans from the "evil consequences" of slavery and having "inculcated by precept and example, the lessons of morality, industry and economy" in the persons of the formerly enslaved. And at least one black antislavery oration was printed by a member of the NYMS, who then placed advertisements promoting the publication in New York City newspapers. Although abolitionism in this period was not interracial in its organizational composition, the recipe for antislavery reform bridged the boundaries of race and permeated the rhetoric and actions of both white and black reformers. It is true that there were no black members in the abolition societies. But to judge the first abolition movement solely by the racial makeup of its respective organizations overlooks a considerable degree of congruity between the ideology and actions of white and black activists.[50]

49. NYMS Records, VII, 60, IX, 188–189, 193, NYHS.

50. Teasman, *Address Delivered in the African Episcopal Church*, 6; Sidney, *Oration, Commemorative of the Abolition of the Slave Trade*, 18. For Samuel Wood's printing of Peter Williams's 1808 oration, see *New-York Commercial Advertiser*, Dec. 28, 1808, [3]; and *New-York Gazette and General Advertiser*, Jan. 26, 1808, [4]. The advertisement ran for three months; see *Minutes of the Proceedings of the Eleventh American Convention for Promoting the Abolition of Slavery and Improving the Condition of the African Race* ... (Philadelphia, 1806), 35–37. In his article on John Teasman, Robert J. Swan argues for a rift opening up between Teasman and New York's free blacks on the one side and the New-York Manumission Society on the other following the NYMS's decision to remove Teasman from his post as principal of the African Free School in 1810. But, in a speech given a year after his firing, Teasman had only positive things to say about the NYMS and its members. See Swan, "John Teasman: African-American Educator and the Emergence of Community in Early Black New York City, 1787–1815," *JER*, XII (1992), 348–349; and Teasman, *Address Delivered in the African Episcopal Church*, 6–7. For a documented instance when New York's free black activists and white abolitionists had a

The foremost factor pointed to by scholars as having divided white from black reformers in early America is the abolition societies' paternalism. If abolition society members encouraged blacks to take on universal standards for republican citizenship, they also frequently displayed a paternalistic condescension in their interactions with African Americans. An address by the trustees of the African Free School to the parents of enrolled children exemplifies the condescending tendencies of the abolition societies. Full of supercilious assumptions about the inability of free black parents to raise virtuous children without direction, the address listed meticulous instructions for proper childrearing in areas such as providing a good "Example" to black youth, "Speaking the Truth," the importance of "Cleanliness," and how to effectively give "Commands to Children." The trustees' detailed directives spoke to the NYMS's inference that black parents were themselves in need of paternal oversight.[51]

Abolition society oversight of free blacks went beyond giving advice. The NYMS required the parents of African Free School students to register with the society. Inspectors then went into the houses of free blacks and insisted that these families remain sober, industrious, and orderly, refraining from fiddling, dancing, or hosting any vivacious form of entertainment. Families that failed to meet these strictures were threatened with the loss of the society's patronage. The PAS mirrored this approach. Its committee of Inspection routinely entered the homes of Philadelphia's free blacks and admonished those whom they judged to be falling short of virtuous conduct. In an 1805 pep talk, the American Convention asked its constituent abolition societies whether they were willing to "leave" people of color "friendless and abandoned" or "continue our parental care over them." Abolition society members saw themselves as playing the role of parents for a group of people who many of these activists believed needed consistent monitoring to meet their inherent potential for republican citizenship.[52]

How can one square the commitment of first movement abolitionists to underlying black equality with this paternalism? Abolition society pater-

---

tactical disagreement regarding the manner in which African Americans celebrated the abolition of the slave trade, see Minutes of the New-York Manumission Society, 1810, IX, 10, NYHS; and John J. Zuille, comp., *Historical Sketch of the New York African Society for Mutual Relief* ... ([New York, 1892]), 7.

51. *An Address to the Parents and Guardians of the Children Belonging to the New-York African Free-School, by the Trustees of the Institution* (New York, 1818).

52. NYMS Records, VI, 99–100, NYHS; PPAS, Series 1, reel 6, 27, 181, 237, HSP; *Minutes of the Proceedings of the Tenth American Convention for Promoting the Abolition of Slavery* (1805), 33.

nalism stemmed from the same philosophy of societal environmentalism that fueled the entire movement. If people were products of their social environment and most blacks had been relegated to the degrading state of bondage, then it necessarily followed that the environment in which formerly enslaved people subsisted had to be closely monitored should both emancipation and free black citizenship win the day. To African Americans, this practice could be as constricting as the larger first abolition movement was empowering. The paternalism of the abolition societies, at times overbearing, can be interpreted as threatening the autonomy of free blacks and exerting social control by attempting to mold African American community development. But an overemphasis on paternalism and its objectionable elements should not come at the cost of distorting societal environmentalism and overlooking the ties between first movement abolitionism and free black incorporation.[53]

53. For the scholarly stress on paternalism and social control as the foremost characteristics of first movement abolitionists and their societies, see Swan, "John Teasman," *JER*, XII (1992), 331–356; John L. Rury, "Philanthropy, Self-Help, and Social Control: The New York Manumission Society and Free Blacks, 1785–1810," *Phylon*, XLVI (1985), 231–241; Melish, *Disowning Slavery*, 50–83; Shane White, *Somewhat More Independent: The End of Slavery in New York City, 1770–1810* (Athens, Ga., 1991), 81–88; and David Brion Davis, *The Problem of Slavery in the Age of Revolution, 1770–1823* (Ithaca, N.Y., 1975), 241–242. If social control was the primary impetus behind the reform enterprises of the abolition societies, why agitate to abolish slavery—the most effective means of social control imaginable—at all? For its part, the PAS, in a statement submitted to the 1804 American Convention, reported that "prospects" of black equality "encourage ... the continuance of our labours on their behalf" and motivate "our endeavours to diffuse among them the important benefits of school education" (*Minutes of the Proceedings of the Ninth American Convention for Promoting the Abolition of Slavery* [1804], 11). For an evenhanded assessment of the PAS's paternalistic reform tendencies, see Eberly, "The Pennsylvania Abolition Society," 176–179. Timothy J. Lockley distinguishes between social control and the motivation of reformers, the former term connoting intentions of controlling underprivileged groups in the interest of broader society and the latter seeking to "give individuals the skills they needed to support themselves and their families—to foster eventual self-reliance." Many abolition society members undoubtedly fit both of these descriptions, but Lockley's emphasis on the impulse of reformers to focus on bringing the clients of their patronage long-term autonomy captures well the end goal of first movement abolitionist paternalism. See Lockley, "'To Train Them to Habits of Industry and Usefulness': Molding the Poor Children of Antebellum Savannah," in Ruth Wallis Herndon and John E. Murray, eds., *Children Bound to Labor: The Pauper Apprentice System in Early America* (Ithaca, N.Y., 2009), 133–134. For a critique of the overuse of the concept of "social control" when examining the intentions and actions of antebellum reformers, see Lawrence Frederick Kohl, "The Concept of Social Control and the History of Jacksonian America," *JER*, V (1985), 21–34.

Moreover, paternalist dictums did not solely spring from the abolition societies. Free black leaders who shared the reform agenda of the NYMS and PAS explicated a comparable set of paternalistic prescriptions. Absalom Jones instructed an audience of people of color gathered to recognize the ending of the international slave trade in 1808 that they should be "sober minded, humble, peaceable ... frugal ... and industrious." Richard Allen repeatedly used his pulpit to advance rigorous moral and behavioral standards for both his parishioners and black Philadelphians unaffiliated with his church to pursue. Allen warned congregants of his African Methodist Episcopal Church of being "slaves to Sin" and rebuked those who would display "the tendency of dishonesty and lust, of drunkenness and stealing," demanding that they instead remain pious and chaste. He used the sensational murder of a white woman by two Philadelphia blacks to issue a jeremiad beseeching free persons of color to "never more attend a frolic," give up drunkenness, swearing, and whoremongering, and correct their intemperate behavior by attending church regularly. Jones and Allen presented their paternalistic admonitions as a means for African Americans to raise their status and achieve virtuous citizenship. Yet the counsel of free black leaders could sound as exacting and severe as the advice of the abolition societies.[54]

The free black leadership's concern with regulating black behavior was reflected in the mutual aid societies founded by people of color in Philadelphia and New York. The FAS admitted only persons of color who lived "an orderly and sober life," while the New York African Society for Mutual Relief, "stimulated by the desire of improving our condition," refused to countenance anyone who was "fond of spending his time in brothels, in gambling, or in tippling," social expectations in line with the guidance of the abolition societies. Although these societies wanted to improve the quality of life for the wider community of African Americans, they promoted unity, camaraderie, and a sense of belonging for those blacks who met the republican-based values of its leaders. Part of this exclusiveness was owing to the monetary imperatives necessary for keeping up a reliable communal fund. But it also resulted from the strict and narrow behavioral guidelines to which all members had to adhere.[55]

54. Jones, *A Thanksgiving Sermon*, 17; Richard Allen, *Confession of John Joyce, Alias Davis, Who Was Executed on Monday, the 14th of March, 1808; for the Murder of Mrs. Sarah Cross; with an Address to the Public, and People of Colour* ... (Philadelphia, 1808), 5–6.

55. "Preamble of the Free African Society," in Douglass, *Annals of the First African Church*, 15; *The Constitution of the New-York African Society, for Mutual Relief* (New

In their social and economic backgrounds, abolition society members and free black leaders of the urban mid-Atlantic did not share much in common. They cohered, however, around the urgent need to sculpt republicans of color out of newly freed people. Williams elucidated the first movement abolitionist conception of biracial reform when, in explaining his reluctance to get too involved in the American Antislavery Society of the 1830s, he stated that, as far as he was concerned, while white abolitionists "were laboring to restore us to our rights" African American reformers needed to "labor to qualify our people for the enjoyment of those rights." This rendition of biracial activism is key to understanding the devotion of black and white reformers to the first abolition movement. Having prominent black allies signaled to the abolition societies the viability of making virtuous citizens of formerly enslaved people and gave them a channel to communities of color. And having white allies helped convince black abolitionists that people of African descent had a path to incorporation as respected, and respectable, American citizens.[56]

The incorporation of persons of color into the new United States as republican citizens formed an integral component of first movement abolitionism. No mere matter of abstract rights, the ideal of black citizenship was intimately connected with the goal of abolishing slavery. Answering doubts about the capacity of people of color for freedom, the abolition societies and African American abolitionists of the mid-Atlantic sought to prove that liberated blacks could be just as virtuous and honorable as free whites in the young Republic. Societal environmentalism was a co-created reform strategy, linking the abolition societies and black abolitionists in a shared effort to push back against forces that might derail emancipation.

The cross-racial alliance of those activists who promoted societal environmentalism did not exempt this reform strategy from pitfalls. First movement abolitionists assumed that the negative environment of slavery debased people of color and, if left uncultivated, made them less than ideal candidates for membership in the body politic. The abolition societies maintained a circumscribed conception of what black freedom should look like, at times stifling individual expression and narrowing the autono-

York, 1808) 3, 7. The mutual aid societies were the bastion of a relatively small but highly influential set of free blacks who excluded from membership many persons of color.

56. Williams, "To the Citizens of New York," July 14, 1834, in Carter G. Woodson, ed., *The Mind of the Negro: As Reflected in Letters Written during the Crisis, 1800–1860* (Washington, D.C., 1926), 633.

mous decision-making power of those blacks who came under their purview. The attendant ideology of republicans of color also had limitations.
There are few signs of class antagonism among free blacks in either early
national Philadelphia or New York City. Nevertheless, the continual in-
fusions of manumitted blacks and fugitives from slavery into the urban
mid-Atlantic might have contributed to a clash between black community leaders and the many African Americans stuck on the bottom rung of
the socioeconomic ladder. Removed economically, and perhaps culturally,
from the leadership class, impoverished people of color were overburdened
with trying to scrape out a living. They might have declined, or simply not
had the time, to devote themselves to the austere demands of republican
cultivation that the likes of Richard Allen, Absalom Jones, and Peter Williams, Jr., championed so enthusiastically.[57]

For all their shortcomings, the advocates of societal environmentalism
never wavered in their belief that persons of color could achieve republican citizenship. Presuming that slavery rather than race explained black
inequality gave first movement abolitionists persistent faith that what they
deemed a positive environment outside chattel bondage could transform
formerly enslaved people into virtuous citizens. Yet showcasing free black
respectability as republican citizens was only half the battle. Hanging over
the agenda of the abolition societies and their free black allies lurked the
specter of white prejudice. As a Maryland correspondent wrote to the PAS
in 1789, "It is difficult to conquer hereditary prejudices—to silence fears for
the public Safety—to excite Compassion for those on whom we have been
accustomed to look at without it—to make Men just where Iniquity has for
years been fashionable and familiar." The presumption that white prejudice was formidable yet conquerable underlay the first movement abolitionist enterprise.[58]

57. The assumption that slavery degraded its victims and made them poor candidates for virtuous freedom was shared by black antislavery activists. See, for example,
Johnson, *Oration on the Abolition of the Slave Trade*, 13; and Russel Parrott, *An Oration
on the Abolition of the Slave Trade; Delivered on the First of January, 1812, at the African
Church of St. Thomas* (Philadelphia, 1812), 9. In a speech before the Maryland House
of Delegates in 1789, William Pinkney argued that slavery made former bondspersons
especially suited for republican virtue. Hypothesizing that "he who best knows the value
of a blessing, is generally the most audacious in its preservation," Pinkney stated, "The
man that has felt the yoke of bondage must for ever prove the assertor of freedom." See
Pinkney, *Speech*, 13–14. Pinkney's position was not picked up by first movement abolitionists. On the argument for a black cultural and economic divide in early-nineteenth-
century Philadelphia, see Nash, *Forging Freedom*, 219–223.

58. PPAS, Series 2, reel 11, III (unnumbered loose correspondence), HSP.

CHAPTER 4

"A Well Grounded Hope"

Sweeping Away the Cobwebs of Prejudice

Soon after American independence had become inevitable, the famed political activist and philosopher Thomas Paine wrote an open letter to the French philosophe the abbé de Raynal explaining his interpretation of the American Revolution's meaning. Paine accorded international relevance to the Revolution, depicting it as an event that would spread enlightened philanthropy, social progress, and the extension of the rights of humanity throughout both America and Europe. As Paine surveyed the state of the Western world in 1782, he identified the "only remaining enemy" to his heady optimism as *"prejudice."* While "some passions and vices are but thinly scattered among mankind," prejudice, "that demon of society ... like the spider, makes every where its home." Whether "the mind be as naked as the walls of an empty and forsaken tenement, gloomy as a dungeon, or ornamented with the richest abilities of thinking ... still prejudice, if undisturbed, will fill it with cobwebs." The "spider of the mind," as Paine denoted it, prejudice represented a ubiquitous presence threatening the promise of human betterment and societal advancement.[1]

Fortunately, according to Paine, the ascendance of the American Revolution now presented a prime opportunity to overcome prejudice. Paine believed that "our stile and manner of thinking have undergone a revolution, more extraordinary than the political revolution of the country." Societies across the Atlantic world had experienced a pathbreaking enlightenment. "We see with other eyes; we hear with other ears; and think with other thoughts, than those we formerly used." Americans had been reborn, in

1. Thomas Paine, *A Letter Addressed to the Abbe Raynal, on the Affairs of North-America; in Which the Mistakes in the Abbe's Account of the Revolution in America Are Corrected and Cleared Up* (Philadelphia, 1782), 44–45. For an extended overview and analysis of Paine's letter, see Darrel Abel, "The Significance of the Letter to the Abbé Raynal in the Progress of Thomas Paine's Thought," *Pennsylvania Magazine of History and Biography*, LXVI (1942), 176–190.

Paine's estimation. "We can look back on our own prejudices, as if they had been the prejudices of other people." Recently "relieved from" prejudice's "shackles," Paine concluded that "every corner of the mind is swept of its cobwebs." To Paine, prejudice was composed of the unreasoned assumptions of unenlightened peoples, thrown into disrepute by the age of revolution.[2]

Though Paine, a nominee for membership to the Pennsylvania Abolition Society (PAS), did not directly refer to the prejudice held against people of African descent in his letter to Raynal, he might as well have. Paine's labeling of prejudice as at once a forbidding foe to social progress and at the same time the relic of a pre-enlightened era seamlessly captures the philosophy of first movement abolitionism. Predicated on an enlightened idealism that viewed white prejudice toward blacks as conquerable, the abolition societies and their black abolitionist partners nevertheless identified this prejudice as an imposing hurdle to emancipation. First movement abolitionists committed themselves to sweeping away the cobwebs of racial prejudice blocking the white public from perceiving black Americans' equal humanity and their capacity for freedom. For first movement abolitionists, the cultivation of black citizenship and the vanquishing of white prejudice were interwoven goals essential to ending slavery.

THIS LIGHT IS STILL INCREASING

Like Paine, abolitionists eyed prejudice as primed for destruction. Recovering the mindset of these activists during the post-Revolutionary and early national eras is essential to understanding why first movement abolitionists instituted an optimistic agenda for emancipation through African American incorporation and the defeat of white prejudice. Their reform vision was nourished by a host of factors that they believed pointed the way toward the progressive elimination of chattel slavery. The American Revolution—with its dictates of natural rights and universal human equality— appeared to place slavery on the ideological defensive in the years following the Revolutionary War. As interpreted by first movement abolitionists, the principles of the Revolution had made slavery a despised and indefensible practice. A belief that the American Revolution had initiated a wave of public opinion hostile to slavery spread throughout an Atlantic community of antislavery activists. A French abolitionist was convinced that the American Revolution "impressed upon the minds of most men a respect truly religious for the cause of liberty" and "an aversion, a horror for all

2. Paine, *Letter Addressed to the Abbe Raynal*, 45–46.

tyrannical proceedings, under whatever shape they are disguised, and whoever are the individuals that oppress." In this reading, the American Revolution had opened a spigot of antislavery sentiment that now gushed forth
and inundated both sides of the Atlantic world.[3]

The optimism of first movement abolitionists sprung not only from the
realm of ideology but also from tangible gains of the emancipatory cause.
By 1804, every state north of Maryland had either eliminated slavery immediately or set the institution on the road to ultimate extinction. At the
same time, various legislative initiatives in some of these states appeared
to clear the way for free black citizenship. Meanwhile, in the upper South
a wave of private manumissions seemed to signal a move away from the
slave-labor-centered tobacco economy. Between 1790 and 1810, the rate of
growth of the free black population in the United States outpaced that of
enslaved Americans, making the trend toward black freedom more noteworthy than the spread of chattel bondage. And these encouraging trends
were not limited to the American Republic. In Britain, a fledgling antislavery movement had produced a national petition campaign to abolish
the African slave trade and birthed international antislavery celebrities,
such as William Wilberforce and Thomas Clarkson. In 1794, the Revolutionary French government abolished slavery in all of France's colonies
and declared that "all men, without distinction of colour, domiciled in the
colonies, are French citizens," an event celebrated by American abolitionists as the beginning of "a memorable Epocha announced to an applauding
World." From the vantage point of hindsight, these developments fanned
chimerical confidence that slavery's infrastructure was crumbling. From
the perspective of abolitionists in locales such as Philadelphia or New York,
it was far from folly to assume human bondage, and the racial inequalities
that attended the institution, could be conquered.[4]

3. J. P. Brissot de Warville, *An Oration, upon the Necessity of Establishing at Paris,
a Society to Co-operate with Those of America and London, towards the Abolition of the
Trade and Slavery of the Negroes; Delivered the 19th of February, 1788, in a Society of
a Few Friends, Assembled at Paris, at the Request of the Committee of London*, trans.
Charles Crawford, in T. Clarkson, *An Essay on the Impolicy of the African Slave Trade* ...
(Philadelphia, 1788), 146–147.

4. David Brion Davis, *The Problem of Slavery in the Age of Revolution, 1770–1823*
(Ithaca, N.Y., 1975), 60; Robin Blackburn, *The Overthrow of Colonial Slavery, 1776–1848*
(New York, 1988), 225; Papers of the Pennsylvania Abolition Society (PPAS), Series 2,
reel XI, II, 79, Historical Society of Pennsylvania (HSP), Philadelphia. On voluntary
manumission in the upper South, see Eva Sheppard Wolf, *Race and Liberty in the New
Nation: Emancipation in Virginia from the Revolution to Nat Turner's Rebellion* (Baton
Rouge, La., 2006), 39–84; and Ira Berlin, *Many Thousands Gone: The First Two Cen-*

There also existed in the late eighteenth century a broad condemnation of the international slave trade as an inhumane relic of the barbaric past, the elimination of which many antislavery activists believed was the first step in the total abolition of slavery. Before the domestic slave trade mushroomed following the early-nineteenth-century cotton boom, American abolitionists assumed, as did their European counterparts, that ending the international slave trade would starve slavery of bondspersons and deny human bondage its subsistence. As the British West Indies experienced the stagnant growth of its enslaved population and economic decline following the American Revolution, and the most profitable slave colony in the Western Hemisphere, Saint Domingue, fell to pieces, slavery in the Atlantic world could be viewed as vulnerable. On the American side of the Atlantic, by 1790 several states had taken some form of legislative measure against the international slave trade. Even some eminent statesmen unaffiliated with antislavery predicted that the slave trade's end would lead eventually to the demise of institutional slavery. James Wilson interpreted the constitutional provision permitting the banning of the international slave trade after 1808 as "laying the foundation for banishing slavery out of this country." Wilson connected directly the slave trade's abolishment and slavery's termination.[5]

Immediately after the American nation's founding, it was slavery's defenders, not its opponents, who were on the defensive. The Virginia Revolutionary political vanguard, who for both ideological and economic reasons often spoke out resolutely against the African slave trade, isolated the

------

turies of Slavery in North America (Cambridge, Mass., 1998), 277–285. For the radical, though short-lived, ban on French colonial slavery and racialized citizenship, which resulted from the push of people of color and enslaved rebels on Saint Domingue, and a narrative of the events leading up to the French National Convention's 1794 decree abolishing slavery and making blacks of France's colonies citizens, see Jeremy D. Popkin, "The French Revolution's Other Island," in David Patrick Geggus and Norman Fiering, eds., *The World of the Haitian Revolution* (Bloomington, Ind., 2009), 199–222; and Robin Blackburn, *The American Crucible: Slavery, Emancipation, and Human Rights* (London, 2011), 182–204.

5. Speech of Mr. [James] Wilson, Dec. 3, 1787, in Jonathan Elliot, ed., *The Debates in the Several State Conventions on the Adoption of the Federal Constitution, as Recommended by the General Convention at Philadelphia, in 1787; Together with the Journal of the Federal Convention, Luther Martin's Letter, Yates's Minutes, Congressional Opinions, Virginia and Kentucky Resolutions of '98–'99, and Other Illustrations of the Constitution*, 4 vols., 2d ed. (Washington, D.C., 1854), II, 452. On the decline of the slave economy of the British West Indies and the larger case for abolitionist optimism connected to the African slave trade's seeming stagnation, see Davis, *The Problem of Slavery in the Age of Revolution*, 51–64.

lower southern states of Georgia and South Carolina with their refusal to unabashedly support slavery. Two years after the Federal Constitutional Convention, William Loughton Smith of South Carolina expressed the betrayal felt by lower southern politicians at the upper South's decision not to back an extension of the international slave trade. Smith called Virginia "our greatest enemy" and concluded that Georgia and South Carolina were alone in preserving the sanctity of slavery in the federal Republic. Smith also acknowledged that "our State is weak in the Union ... particu[larl]y that of holding Slavery ... the other States are all agst. us." Slavery's proponents unmistakably felt on the defensive in the early national era, brightening the outlook of abolitionists.[6]

Through a transatlantic exchange with their sister organizations in London and Paris, the American abolition societies crafted an optimistic viewpoint on the future fruits of their activism. That societies adverse to slavery had emerged across three Atlantic nations in a short period of time heartened first movement abolitionists. The fight to abolish slavery appeared, not parochial to any one nation or locale, but the product of an international campaign. Granville Sharp, president of the recently formed Society for Effecting the Abolition of the Slave Trade (SEAST) located in London, pronounced in 1788 that the society thought of its reform as "encompassing the whole globe" and would count its efforts complete only "when violence against the rights of humanity ceases everywhere." Jacques-Pierre

6. William Smith to Edward Rutledge, Aug. 10, 1789, in Charlene Bangs Bickford et al., eds., *Documentary History of the First Federal Congress of the United States of America, March 4, 1789–March 3, 1791*, XVI, *Correspondence; First Session: June–August 1789* (Baltimore, 2004), 1282–1283. During the Federal Constitutional Convention, as Georgia and South Carolina held steadfastly to securing the slave trade, Virginia and Maryland, states where plantations were overstocked with enslaved laborers, abandoned their southern neighbors on federal protection for the slave trade. A regional split was thus exposed between the upper and lower South that would resurface during the first congressional debates on slavery. New England and South Carolina brokered the eventual compromise on division over the slave trade at the Federal Convention. New England delegates agreed to support a twenty-year extension of the slave trade in exchange for procuring the South Carolinian delegates' votes that would give Congress a simple majority rather than a two-thirds plurality in passing commercial legislation. There was a clear ambivalence in the rhetorical denunciation of human bondage by much of Virginia's Revolutionary leadership and in their actual continuing commitment to the institution of slavery, a phenomenon the historian Joseph J. Ellis has dubbed the "Virginia straddle"; see Ellis, *Founding Brothers: The Revolutionary Generation* (New York, 2000), 113. The important point for the first abolition movement was that, between ideological discomfit with chattel bondage and the wave of manumissions in post-Revolutionary Virginia and Maryland, it seemed plausible that the upper South was turning away from slavery.

Brissot de Warville of Paris's antislavery society called on slavery's oppo-nents throughout the Atlantic world to "unite" with "a common consent to inform ... the government and the public" and "accustom our fellow citi-zens" to antislavery principles. Were activists to "make it [antislavery] their constant occupation," Brissot de Warville had little doubt that abolitionism would succeed. Across the Atlantic Ocean in 1791, Jonathan Edwards told the Connecticut Abolition Society that the "light" of antislavery had made remarkable strides. From New Hampshire to Virginia, France, and Britain, Edwards informed the society that "this light is still increasing, and in time will effect a total revolution." If only abolitionists continued to "remove the obstacles which intercept the rays of this light," Edwards foresaw slavery's ultimate dissolution.[7]

In their frequent correspondence, activists on both sides of the Atlantic gained a sense of antislavery and racially egalitarian progress. The Pennsyl-vania Abolition Society communicated to the Paris Society of the Friends of the Blacks in 1801 that it anticipated the end of the French Revolution would allow the "completion of the Grand design" of raceless citizenship foretold by the National Convention's 1794 extension of the rights of citi-zens to all free blacks in the French empire, a national achievement that the PAS similarly hoped to garner in the United States. The SEAST in-formed the PAS that it took "great pleasure" in hearing that "the public mind" is "daily" becoming more "enlightened" on slavery-related matters and expressed that "we cannot but believe that the dawn of that day is not far off, when skin shall no longer afford a handle for iniquity and a seat for prejudice." When the SEAST asked the New-York Manumission Society (NYMS) for an assessment of the progress of antislavery in New York, the manumission society replied that "a Liberality of sentiment be-gins to prevail, which will admit the Claim of Africans to a rank among rational Beings and to the natural Rights of Mankind." That "every part of the civilized world has shewn a disposition gradually to restore to the Afri-cans the equal rights of man" emboldened abolitionists and girded them for the fight ahead.[8]

7. J. R. Oldfield, *Transatlantic Abolitionism in the Age of Revolution: An Interna-tional History of Anti-Slavery, c. 1787–1820* (Cambridge, 2013), 20; Brissot, *Oration*, trans. Crawford, in Clarkson, *Essay on the Impolicy of the African Slave Trade*, 156–158; Jonathan Edwards, *The Injustice and Impolicy of the Slave Trade, and of the Slavery of the Africans: Illustrated in a Sermon Preached before the Connecticut Society for the Pro-motion of Freedom and for the Relief of Persons Unlawfully Holden in Bondage* ... ([New Haven, Conn.], 1791), 29–30.

8. PPAS, Series 2, reel 11, II, 1–2, 79, HSP; New-York Manumission Society

And it would be a long fight. Even though the abolition societies were confident in their activism, they had no illusions that their goals would be achieved overnight. The president of the New Jersey Abolition Society, William Griffith, took both domestic and international antislavery as a signal that "the public sentiment has been changed," emancipation allowing for blacks to become *"advanced* in the scale of intellectual and social existence." But Griffith also believed it could take up to a century to fully abolish slavery. The NYMS concurred. Soon after the society's founding, the standing committee wrote to its fellow members that, although "more Enlarged and liberal Principles" had taken hold on the topic of slavery, it would take "time" to "dispel the mist which Prejudice, self-Interest, and long Habit have raised." The standing committee suggested that "compleat Freedom, tho' considerably Remote, is still to be Expected." Gradualism was palatable to first movement abolitionists because they viewed society on a slow but steady march toward abolition and black uplift. Although they never forgot the potency of white prejudice, what separated first movement abolitionists from the gradualism associated with the later colonization movement was the former's unequivocal belief in the eradicable nature of these prejudices. Thus, after acknowledging white prejudice, the American Convention of Abolition Societies could, in the next breath, confidently assure abolitionists that their continued exertions toward the general education

---

(NYMS) Records, 1785–1849, XI, 95, New-York Historical Society (NYHS); *Federal Gazette and Philadelphia Evening Post,* Mar. 23, 1790, reprinted in *Maryland Journal* (Baltimore), Mar. 30, 1790, *New-York Packet,* Mar. 27, 1790, [2], and *Farmer's Journal* (Danbury, Conn.), Apr. 7, 1790. For the transatlantic networks of correspondence forged by abolition societies in the late eighteenth century, the individuals who sustained these networks, and the overlapping ideals of these activists, see Oldfield, *Transatlantic Abolitionism in the Age of Revolution,* 13–99. Though the NYMS, PAS, SEAST, and the Society of the Friends of the Blacks exchanged information, buoyed each other's spirits, and shared strategies, the goals of these respective societies were not identical. For example, the term *abolition,* while connoting the emancipation of enslaved people in the United States, in Britain and France referred exclusively to abolishing the slave trade. American abolition societies continuously coupled ending slavery and raising the status of people of color. The SEAST, while sharing the ideal of black uplift, focused almost wholly on banning British participation in the slave trade and stopping the importation of enslaved persons to the British West Indies. The Society of the Friends of the Blacks at first took its cue from the SEAST in homing in on the slave trade. But, as calls for nonracialized citizenship became a key element of the French Revolution, the Paris society shifted its attention to the status of free people of color in the French empire. The celebratory sense of international antislavery progress and the transatlantic exchange of ideas, information, and strategies began to weaken with the onset of war between France and Britain in 1793 and the growing politically partisan controversy over the French Revolution and its fallout in the United States.

of black Americans and the antislavery education of white Americans must ultimately "obtain a complete and universal triumph." The battle would be protracted, but it also would be won.[9]

Approaching this antislavery idealism from the perspective of antebellum America, at which time society increasingly polarized along racial lines and human bondage expanded exponentially, makes the words of first movement abolitionists regarding white prejudice and slavery's abolition sound quixotic. But, by contextualizing these abolitionists' views in the transatlantic enlightenment that swept post-Revolutionary America, their idealism begins to attain more than a glimmer of plausibility. Enlightenment thought was not uniformly antislavery. The focus of enlightenment thinkers on classifying and systematizing the natural world facilitated a pseudoscience of race that challenged single creation theory and concretized white ideas of black inferiority in the bodies of people of color. Some enlightenment philosophes also dismissed claims of inherent black equality, while others rejected the notion that ideas of natural equality could be practically applied to human societies without endangering order and stability. Yet viewing the enlightenment not as a singular movement with one set of ideas on topics like slavery or race, or as a unitary flow of concepts from Europe to America, opens a path to recognizing the first movement abolitionist vision of enlightenment antislavery reform. Enlightenment ideals brought into question centuries-old understandings of stratified relationships between kings and subjects, elites and commoners, and masters and slaves. In the eyes of many who subscribed to enlightenment philosophy, human society had been awakened from eons of superstition and ignorance and was now on a track of progress based on rational reflection and the recognition of the natural rights and elemental equality of men.[10]

9. William Griffith, *Address of the President of the New Jersey Society, for Promoting the Abolition of Slavery, to the General Meeting at Trenton, on Wednesday the 26th of September 1804* (Trenton, N.J., 1804), 5–7; NYMS Records, VI, 22, NYHS; *Minutes of the Proceedings of the Tenth American Convention for Promoting the Abolition of Slavery and Improving the Condition of the African Race* ... (Philadelphia, 1805), 35.

10. Caroline Winterer convincingly argues against the typical depiction of the enlightenment as a one-way flow of ideas from Europe to America and effectively profiles the many enlightenments that unfolded in early America. See Caroline Winterer, *American Enlightenments: Pursuing Happiness in the Age of Reason* (New Haven, Conn., 2016). On the relationship of the enlightenment to race, see Andrew S. Curran, *The Anatomy of Blackness: Science and Slavery in an Age of Enlightenment* (Baltimore, 2011); Silvia Sebastiani, *The Scottish Enlightenment: Race, Gender, and the Limits of Progress*, trans. Jeremy Carden (New York, 2013); Emmanuel Chukwudi Eze, ed., *Race*

Ascribing universality to human nature and a positivist belief in the power of societal progress, or the idea that reformers could improve the corporeal world by shaking off the mindset of an antiquated era, first movement abolitionist philosophy possessed all the hallmarks of this enlightenment idealism. The first abolition movement is an important incarnation of enlightenment thought in America and should be recognized as such. The stress of enlightenment ideas on the power of reason, natural rights, individual liberty, a disregard for the authority of tradition (that is, racial slavery and white prejudice), and the centrality of moral sense and empathy to human interaction were all trademark characteristics of first movement abolitionist ideology. First movement abolitionists depicted antislavery as a "light" illuminating truths formerly unrecognized. Their self-declared mission was to "dispel the clouds" of white prejudice toward blacks, which had formed during a pre-enlightened period. They were committed to reason and rational persuasion as a potent force that could eventually tear apart slavery and black degradation. In 1794, the American Convention sanguinely asserted that "the progressive and rapid influence of reason and religion, are in our favour." One poem aptly expressed the enlightenment-based confidence of many first movement abolitionists.

Foul fiends, depart! your pow'r is gone,
In slavery man no more shall dwell;
Behold the day of reason dawn,
And superstition's clouds dispel!

Could not the same enlightenment forces that had quashed British imperialism in America also break apart centuries' worth of unreflective white

---

and the Enlightenment: A Reader (Cambridge, Mass., 1997); Bruce Dain, *A Hideous Monster of the Mind: American Race Theory in the Early Republic* (Cambridge, Mass., 2002); and James Delbourgo, "The Newtonian Slave Body: Racial Enlightenment in the Atlantic World," *Atlantic Studies*, IX (2012), 185–207. For racial pseudoscience in antebellum America, which enlightenment thought helped to give rise to, see William Stanton, *The Leopard's Spots: Scientific Attitudes toward Race in America, 1815–59* (Chicago, 1960). Enlightenment thought could also be used for subtler proslavery ends. Planters throughout the Atlantic world adopted enlightenment-based ideas of the rationalization of labor and increased worker efficiency to boost workloads and shore up enslaved discipline on plantations. See Justin Roberts, *Slavery and the Enlightenment in the British Atlantic, 1750–1807* (Cambridge, 2013). For the overall ambiguity of enlightenment thought as it relates to slavery, see David Brion Davis, *The Problem of Slavery in Western Culture* (Ithaca, N.Y., 1966), 391–421. The enlightenment also applied to gender and women in ambivalent ways. See Sarah Knott and Barbara Taylor, ed., *Women, Gender, and the Enlightenment* (Basingstoke, U.K., 2005).

prejudices toward blacks? To the American Convention and the abolition societies of the early Republic, the answer to this question was, quite understandably from their frame of reference, a resounding yes.[11]

Black civic leaders of the urban mid-Atlantic joined with the abolition societies in expressing the same optimistic belief that slavery and prejudice were destined to fall. New York City's Methodist minister William Miller argued that the mere acknowledgement that blacks were "men" was powerful enough "to raise us from the foul abyss of indignity into which we have been plunged." In 1789, members of Philadelphia's Free African Society anticipated that "a happy day" was just over the horizon in which "every yoke" would be broken and the "oppressed" would "go free." They had "a well grounded hope" that "captivity shall cease, and buying and selling mankind have an end." George Lawrence of the New York African Society for Mutual Relief declared to an 1813 congregation of free blacks that "the time is fast approaching when the iron hand of oppression must cease to tyranize" African Americans. Lawrence assured his audience that soon "our tree of liberty shall reach the sun." This assurance of free black progress and its power to dissuade the white public from supporting racial slavery connected the abolition societies with free black community leaders in a shared commitment to the antislavery ideals of enlightenment optimism.[12]

11. *Minutes of the Proceedings of a Convention of Delegates from the Abolition Societies Established in Different Parts of the United States* ... (Philadelphia, 1794), 17, 19; *General Advertiser* (Philadelphia), June 27, 1794, [2]; *United States Chronicle* (Providence, R.I.), July 10, 1794, [4]. Caroline Winterer underscores an alternative relationship of American enlightenment thought to antislavery—one that called for the colonization of freedpeople rather than their incorporation. Yet this type of enlightened antislavery found form in individual writings and unrealized proposals, rather than in a coherent, organized campaign like that of first movement abolitionism (Winterer, *American Enlightenments*, 166–170). The literature on the enlightenment in America has recently witnessed a resurgence. See John M. Dixon, *The Enlightenment of Cadwallader Colden: Empire, Science, and Intellectual Culture in British New York* (Ithaca, N.Y., 2016); Dixon, "Henry F. May and the Revival of the American Enlightenment: Problems and Possibilities for Intellectual and Social History," *William and Mary Quarterly*, 3d Ser., LXXI (2014), 255–280; Nathalie Caron and Naomi Wolf, "American Enlightenments: Continuity and Renewal," *Journal of American History*, XCIX (2013), 1072–1091; and Darren Staloff, *Hamilton, Adams, Jefferson: The Politics of Enlightenment and the American Founding* (New York, 2005). For earlier interpretations, see Henry F. May, *The Enlightenment in America* (New York, 1976); Donald H. Meyer, *The Democratic Enlightenment* (New York, 1976); Henry Steele Commager, *The Empire of Reason: How Europe Imagined and America Realized the Enlightenment* (Garden City, N.Y., 1977); and Robert A. Ferguson, *The American Enlightenment, 1750–1820* (Cambridge, Mass., 1994).

12. William Miller, *A Sermon on the Abolition of the Slave Trade: Delivered in the African Church, New-York, on the First of January, 1810* (New York, 1810), 4; George

AN INVULNERABLE BULWARK AGAINST
THE SHAFTS OF MALICE

While first movement abolitionists firmly believed they could upend racial prejudice, they remained aware of its long-standing hold on the imaginations of white Americans. It is not surprising that Quaker activists, critical to so many elements of the first abolition movement, early enunciated the problem posed by prejudice to realizing emancipation. Having spoken with many slaveholders over several years, John Woolman knew perhaps better than any other white American the ways prejudice provided a prop for slavery's perpetuation. By the time Woolman published *Considerations on Keeping Negroes* in 1762 (a sequel to his *Some Considerations on the Keeping of Negroes,* released eight years earlier), he had toured many of the mid-Atlantic and southern states, sitting down with slaveholders and, through calm but firm antislavery arguments, engaging with them on their rationales for holding people in bondage (see Figure 10). These exchanges gave Woolman great insight into the underlying impediments to ending racial slavery. Foremost among these impediments, according to Woolman, was the negative associations that the great majority of white Americans attached to people of African descent. "Through the Force of long Custom," Woolman wrote, "the Idea of Slavery" had come to be intimately "connected with the Black Colour, and Liberty with the White." Thus, "many Black People, of honest Lives, and good Abilities" found themselves in bondage merely because of their ancestry.[13]

At the same time as Woolman rejected color as a legitimate tool of enslavement, he recognized the power prejudice held over many Americans in justifying racial slavery. Though "the Colour of a Man avails nothing, in Matters of Right and Equity," the long-established practice of enslaving persons of African descent had introduced "false Ideas" that had become "twisted into our Minds," and now only with "Difficulty" could they "get fairly disentangled." Woolman described the obstacles prejudice put in the way of black freedom in metaphorical terms:

Lawrence, *An Oration on the Abolition of the Slave Trade, Delivered on the First Day of January, 1813, in the African Methodist Church* (New York, 1813), 13, 15; "Epistolary Correspondence," circa September 1789, in W[ilia]m Douglass, *Annals of the First African Church, in the United States of America, Now Styled the African Episcopal Church of St. Thomas, Philadelphia* ... (Philadelphia, 1862), 29.

13. John Woolman, *Considerations on Keeping Negroes; Recommended to the Professors of Christianity, of Every Denomination; Part Second* (Philadelphia, 1762), 28–29. On Woolman's tours to visit slaveholding Friends, see *The Journal of John Woolman,* introduction by John G. Whittier (Boston, 1871), 78–158.

CONSIDERATIONS

ON KEEPING

NEGROES;

Recommended to the PROFESSORS of
CHRISTIANITY, of every *Denomination*.

PART SECOND.

By *JOHN WOOLMAN*.

*Ye shall not respect Persons in Judgment ; but you shall
hear the Small as well as the Great : You shall not be
afraid of the Face of Man ; for the Judgment is
GOD's.* Deut. i. 17.

PHILADELPHIA:

Printed by B. FRANKLIN, and D. HALL. 1762.

FIGURE 10. Title Page from John Woolman, *Considerations on Keeping Negroes;
Recommended to the Professors of Christianity, of Every Denomination;
Part Second* (Philadelphia, 1762). Courtesy, New York Public Library

A TRAVELLER, in cloudy Weather, misseth his Way, makes many Turns while he is lost; still forms in his Mind the Bearing and Situation of Places, and though the ideas are wrong, they fix as fast as if they were right. Finding how Things are, we see our Mistake; yet the Force of Reason ... do not soon remove those false Notions, so fastened upon us, but it will seem in the Imagination as if the annual Course of the Sun was altered; and though, by Recollection, we are assured it is not, yet those Ideas do not suddenly leave us.

The traveler, representing the American public, had long been falsely navigating the terrain of humanity. Blocked by the clouds of prejudice from seeing the true light of the basic equality of enslaved people, the institution of slavery had, in the minds of whites, turned into the only path for black-white relations. Woolman in 1762, and the first movement abolitionists who would follow in his wake, believed that the long since mapped-out landscape of slavery in America, and the correspondingly derogatory conceptions of people of African descent it promoted, could not be torn up overnight, even if this delineation had been proven wrongheaded.[14]

Other leading Quaker antislavery figures also singled out prejudice as both a shaky fortification protecting racial slavery and one that would not easily be scaled. The same year that Woolman's *Considerations on Keeping Negroes* appeared in print, Anthony Benezet expressed similar sentiments in a pamphlet opposing slavery and the slave trade. Enmeshed in a fight to end slaveholding among his fellow Quakers, Benezet nonetheless aimed his arguments at a broader reading public that he hoped to convert to the incipient cause of antislavery. Calling human bondage "contrary to the Dictates of Reason, and the common Feelings of Humanity," Benezet asked why racial slavery had become so entrenched in American society. Though founded on "Tyranny, Oppression and Cruelty," Benezet

---

14. Woolman, *Considerations on Keeping Negroes*, 29–30. Race as a pseudo-biological category of permanent and immutable distinctions between white and black did not solidify until the nineteenth century. But white prejudice toward people of African descent and ideas of difference dividing white from black were already in place by the time of Woolman's writings. See Miriam Eliav-Feldon, Benjamin Isaac, and Joseph Ziegler, eds., *The Origins of Racism in the West* (Cambridge, 2009); David M. Goldenberg, *The Curse of Ham: Race and Slavery in Early Judaism, Christianity, and Islam* (Princeton, N.J., 2005); Sharon Block, *Colonial Complexions: Race and Bodies in Eighteenth-Century America* (Philadelphia, 2018); James H. Sweet, "The Iberian Roots of American Racist Thought," *WMQ*, 3d Ser., LIV (1997), 143–166; and David Brion Davis, *Inhuman Bondage: The Rise and Fall of Slavery in the New World* (Oxford, 2006), 48–76.

believed that Americans had learned to accept uncritically the "iniquitous" practice of holding people as property. A century of the "Example and Use" of blacks serving as bondspersons had made racial slavery normative and "reconcile[d]" Americans to an inhuman custom that "to our unprejudiced Minds, would strike us with Amazement and Horror." Yet, as Benezet knew well, white American minds were not unprejudiced. The New Jersey Quaker David Cooper wrote in 1772 that it was the "power of prejudice" that kept Americans from admitting that enslaved people were entitled to "enjoy their natural rights as fully ... as the rest of mankind." Cooper sought to cut through the "fallacious reasonings and absurd sentiments" derived from the "habit and custom" of prejudice, which had made "familiar the degrading and ignominious distinctions" white Americans drew "between people with a black skin and ourselves." It was in trying to revolutionize white American attitudes toward slavery and black inequality that Quaker activists like Woolman, Benezet, and Cooper helped to set the agenda of first movement abolitionism.[15]

First movement abolitionists clearly identified white prejudice as one of the biggest obstacles in their quest for emancipation. Echoing Woolman, the abolition societies painted prejudice as a sort of mental fog, blocking the minds of many white Americans from deciphering the tyranny of racial slavery and the fundamental equality of persons of African descent. This "mist" clouding the judgment of white Americans resulted from the institution of slavery, the abolition societies concluded. The NYMS believed many whites associated the dehumanizing institution of bondage with the people subjected to its oppressive wrath. In a 1788 letter to the SEAST, the NYMS wrote that it was "from the abhorrence with which the human mind naturally contemplates slavery" that African Americans were "too often considered as a Race of Beings of inferior Rank." The American Conven-

15. [Anthony Benezet], *A Short Account of That Part of Africa, Inhabited by the Negroes; with Respect to the Fertility of the Country; the Good Disposition of Many of the Natives, and the Manner by Which the Slave Trade Is Carried on* ... (Philadelphia, 1762), 4; [David Cooper], *A Mite Cast into the Treasury; or, Observations on Slave-Keeping* (Philadelphia, 1772), iii; Cooper, *A Serious Address to the Rulers of America, on the Inconsistency of Their Conduct respecting Slavery: Forming a Contrast between the Encroachments of England on American Liberty, and, American Injustice in Tolerating Slavery* (Trenton, N.J., 1783), 5. On the "discovery of prejudice" by Quaker antislavery activists and Revolutionary American elite thinkers, see Winthrop D. Jordan, *White over Black: American Attitudes toward the Negro, 1550–1812* (Williamsburg, Va., and Chapel Hill, N.C., 1968), 274–281. I follow Jordan in his stress on the critical self-examination of white prejudice by American writers like Woolman as well as the broader currency this questioning of racial prejudice had among some late-eighteenth-century writers.

tion presumed that the humanity of persons of color had become buried under the weight of chattel bondage. "Many remain under the erroneous notion," the 1805 Convention lamented, "that the blacks are a class of being not merely inferior to, but absolutely a species different from the whites ... intended, by nature, only for the degradations and sufferings of slavery." Slavery had perverted white American conceptions of the nature of people of color. The PAS gestured to this daunting reality when it identified "much prejudice to be overcome and much error of opinion to be corrected, in regard to the moral qualities, and mental powers of the African race." First movement abolitionists warned that no effective blueprint for abolition could withstand this prejudice if white American perceptions of people of color persisted unchanged.[16]

To overcome white prejudice, free people of color would need to take center stage. Black abolitionists in New York City and Philadelphia, in conjunction with the abolition societies, assembled their strategy for targeting white prejudice from identical assumptions. Both groups focused much of their activism on the need to convince the white public that black Americans were capable of a virtuous, republican exercise of their freedom. As early as 1793, urban mid-Atlantic black leaders publicly cautioned their communities of color against being "lazy and idle" and warned free persons that "base pursuits, habits of idleness, and unguarded insolence" would "reduce us to misery ... and be a stumbling block" to those who "remain in bondage." Black abolitionists exhorted free African Americans to "walk worthy of our profession wherein we are called" and "free the mind from every trace of that ignominious state [slavery]" through "virtue and education," which would show beyond the shadow of a doubt that the emancipated were "not only capable of self-government, but also of becoming honourable citizens and useful members of society." The American Convention could not have agreed more, reminding free persons of color in the printed minutes of its 1805 meeting: "One great obstacle to [emancipation], it is in your power and it is eminently your duty to remove; the enemies of your liberty have loudly and constantly asserted that you are not qualified to enjoy it." Only through rejecting "idleness, gambling and dissipation" and embracing "industry," "morality," "education," "temperance,"

16. NYMS Records, VI, 96, NYHS; *Minutes of the Proceedings of the Tenth American Convention for Promoting the Abolition of Slavery* (1805), 35; PPAS, Series 1, reel 2, 155, HSP. For the abolition societies' depiction of prejudice as a "mist," see *Minutes of the Proceedings of the Eleventh American Convention for Promoting the Abolition of Slavery and Improving the Condition of the African Race ...* (Philadelphia, 1806), 17; NYMS Records, VI, 22, NYHS; and PPAS, Series 1, reel 1, II, 207, HSP.

and "virtue"—and in turn making themselves "good and useful citizens" of the Republic—did the abolition societies think free blacks could help emancipation win out.[17]

By founding free black schools, issuing addresses to persons of color to comport themselves virtuously, and publicizing instances of African American achievement, the abolition societies relied heavily on societal environmentalism. Black abolitionists likewise articulated a thoroughgoing adherence to societal environmentalism in their antislavery efforts. Soon after the federal capital moved to Philadelphia, the free black ministers Richard Allen and Absalom Jones told slaveholders, "If you would try the experiment of taking a few black children, and cultivate their minds with the same care ... as you would wish for your own children, you would find upon the trial, they were not inferior in mental endowments." In rejecting the claim that "Africans are inferior to white men in the structure both of body and mind," William Hamilton, the first president of the New York African Society for Mutual Relief, announced a year after the abolition of the slave trade that knowledge and "science has beg[u]n to bud with our race." Holding up examples of black literary accomplishment, including the antislavery orations of Peter Williams, Jr., and Henry Sipkins, Hamilton confidently proclaimed that "soon shall that contumelious assertion of the proud be proved false, to wit, that Africans do not possess minds as ingenious as other men." As people of color increasingly evidenced their inherent abilities, white prejudice would fall away.[18]

17. A[bsalom] J[ones and R[ichard] A[llen], *A Narrative of the Proceedings of the Black People, during the Late Awful Calamity in Philadelphia, in the Year 1793: And a Refutation of Some Censures, Thrown upon Them in Some Late Publications* (Philadelphia, 1794), 27; Henry Johnson, *An Oration on the Abolition of the Slave Trade, by Henry Johnson; with an Introductory Address, by Adam Carman; Delivered in the African Church in New-York, January 1, 1810* (New York, 1810), 14; Richard Allen, Eulogy of Warner Mifflin, in *Articles of Association of the African Methodist Episcopal Church, of the City of Philadelphia, in the Commonwealth of Pennsylvania* (Philadelphia, 1799), 19; Russell Parrott, *An Address, on the Abolition of the Slave-Trade, Delivered before the Different African Benevolent Societies, on the 1st of January, 1816* (Philadelphia, 1816), 10; Joseph Sidney, *An Oration, Commemorative of the Abolition of the Slave Trade in the United States; Delivered before the Wilberforce Philharmonic Association; in the City of New-York, on the Second of January, 1809* (New York, 1809), 15; *Minutes of the Proceedings of the Tenth American Convention for Promoting the Abolition of Slavery* (1805), 38; *Minutes of the Proceedings of the Eighth Convention of Delegates from the Abolition Societies Established in Different Parts of the United States ...* (Philadelphia, 1803), 13.

18. J[ones] and A[llen], *Narrative of the Proceedings of the Black People*, 24; William Hamilton, *An Address to the New York African Society, for Mutual Relief, Delivered in the Universalist Church, January 2, 1809* (New York, 1809), in Dorothy Porter, ed., *Early*

To fortify a public presence of virtuous citizenship for the reception of prejudiced whites, Richard Allen and Absalom Jones embarked on a mission to exemplify their community's republican rectitude. When a yellow fever epidemic gripped Philadelphia during the fall of 1793, Allen and Jones answered the call of Doctor Benjamin Rush, who, concluding that blacks were immune to the dreaded disease, asked that African Americans come to the aid of afflicted whites. The two black leaders gathered volunteers of color who served as nurses, gravediggers, and medical attendants for hundreds of infected whites. Unfortunately, not only were African Americans just as prone to contracting yellow fever as white Americans, but Mathew Carey, an Irish American printer and future supporter of the colonization movement, accused black nurses of taking advantage of the situation by charging exorbitant prices for their services and pilfering from white homes. In a popular pamphlet he printed after the fever had subsided, Carey did praise the conduct of certain African American volunteers, including Jones and Allen, but fingered "the vilest" of the city's blacks as guilty of heinous crimes.[19]

Allen and Jones told a different story. At first glance, it seems strange that these two men, whom Carey singled out for applause, would pen a tract opposing Carey's depiction of events. However, fearing that Carey's pamphlet would "prejudice the minds of the people in general against us" by portraying all blacks as dishonorable and vice-ridden, Allen and Jones felt "justice to our colour" called for the true story to be told. Although they acknowledged that a handful of blacks had probably acted injudi-

Negro Writing, 1760–1837 (Boston, 1971), 36. For further examples of black abolitionists' faith in societal environmentalism, see John Teasman, An Address Delivered in the African Episcopal Church, on the 25th March 1811, before the New York African Society for Mutual Relief; Being the First Anniversary of Its Incorporation (New York, 1811), 9–10; Johnson, Oration on the Abolition of the Slave Trade, 11–14; Adam Carman, An Oration Delivered at the Fourth Anniversary of the Abolition of the Slave Trade, in the Methodist Church, in Second-Street, New York, January 1, 1811 (New York, 1811), 19–20; and Lawrence, Oration on the Abolition of the Slave Trade, 11–12.

19. Mathew Carey, A Short Account of the Malignant Fever, Lately Prevalent in Philadelphia: With a Statement of the Proceedings That Took Pace on the Subject in Different Parts of the United States (Philadelphia, 1793), 77; J[ones] and A[llen], A Narrative of the Proceedings of the Black People, 12–13. Carey published pieces hostile to slavery and the slave trade in the periodicals he edited during the late eighteenth century. Yet he also showed an inclination to support black removal schemes as a solution to slavery, and by 1828 he came to fully support and advocate for the American Colonization Society. On Carey's antislavery and its grounding in colonizationist principles, see Beverly C. Tomek, Colonization and Its Discontents: Emancipation, Emigration, and Antislavery in Antebellum Pennsylvania (New York, 2011), 63–92.

ciously, the authors listed several examples of republican self-sacrifice by African American volunteers, such as Caesar Cranchal. When he offered to nurse sickly whites, Cranchal vowed to all he assisted, "'I will not take your money, I will not sell my life for money.'" Overall, "our services were the production of real sensibility," wrote Allen and Jones, and they assured the public that "we sought not fee nor reward." The authors closed their pamphlet by appealing to all free African Americans to keep in mind that "much depends upon us for the help of our colour." Because the "enemies of freedom plead" black intemperance "as a cause why we ought not to be free," Allen and Jones implored those not enslaved to "consider the obligations we lay under, to help forward the cause of freedom." These obligations included making tangible to the public the claims of abolitionists that black freedom could be as virtuous as white liberty.[20]

Allen and Jones had good reason to urge their fellow blacks to closely monitor their conduct in freedom. Like the abolition societies, African American abolitionists framed their activism in response to the proslavery argument that black inferiority justified racial enslavement. Slavery's apologists questioned the fitness of black people for freedom in a republic ostensibly based on universal liberty. Black activists shot back that persons of color were indeed capable of an ordered, virtuous liberty. One telling example of this discursive interplay can be found in a 1790 New York City newspaper debate. Writing in reference to antislavery petitions submitted to the first federal Congress, a proslavery author under the nom de plume "Rusticus" began a six-part set of essays by conceding that slavery contradicted the fundamental principles of a free and enlightened society. For Rusticus, however, the problem of slavery lay, not in its incompatibility with the American Republic, but with the impossibility of persons of color being anything other than slaves. "As plainly as I conceive, that the ox is born to plough my ground," Rusticus wrote, "the wool hairy negro by innate inferiorities ... is the slave of other nations." Rusticus mocked the idea of turning a "sheep-hairy African negroe" into "a spirited, noble, and generous American Freeman!" If enslaved blacks were set free into white society, the writer predicted they would stain the glory of a virtuous and prosperous America.[21]

A self-identified black writer, "Africanus," responded to Rusticus by aiming to debunk the idea of "*our* inferior nature." Fundamental human law,

20. J[ones] and A[llen], *A Narrative of the Proceedings of the Black People*, 4, 10, 12, 27.
21. *Gazette of the United States* (New York), Feb. 20, 1790, 360, Feb. 27, 1790, 367, Mar. 3, 1790, 372.

184]   "A WELL GROUNDED HOPE"

as expressed in the Bible, made clear that "God, who hath made the world, hath made of one blood all the nations of men that dwell on all the face of the earth." Turning to environmentalist explanations for black differences in appearance and civil attainments, Africanus refuted that "we are an inferior link in the great chain of creation." Using himself as an example of black citizenship, Africanus wrote that "the American and the African are one species" and that he was personally "equal to the duties of a spirited, noble, and generous American freeman." Proslavery allegations of the natural inferiority of all those of African descent mandated that black abolitionists publicly respond with an insistence on African American aptitude for civic incorporation.[22]

Well aware of proslavery assertions of black inferiority, abolitionists of color consistently highlighted the need for their compatriots to counter the indictments of slavery's defenders by putting on public display a virtuous black freedom. The former African Free School student Joseph Sidney pushed blacks to demonstrate "that *sobriety, honesty,* and *industry* are among the distinguishing traits in our characters." Were persons of color to "unceasingly" guide their actions by "pure and upright conduct" it would "effectually put to silence every cavil which may be offered against African emancipation, and must eventually convert our enemies into friends." Henry Johnson, a New York City freeholder, challenged the emancipated to "improve and prove ourselves worthy of all the privileges" of liberty. Through the adoption of the "habits of industry, frugality, and honesty," free persons could put themselves on "the sure road to happiness, respectability and prosperity." George Lawrence believed blacks should play their part in bringing about abolition by "abounding in good works, and causing our examples to shine forth as the sun at noon day." This course of action would "melt" the "callous hearts" of those who doubted emancipation "and render sinewless the arm of sore oppression." By becoming republicans of color, free blacks strove to "form an invulnerable bulwark against the shafts of malice," exploding the fallacious accusations of slavery's proponents and the white public prejudice upon which proslavery arguments rested.[23]

Even as they railed against those who discounted the ability of the emancipated to exercise their liberty responsibly, black abolitionists granted

22. Ibid., Mar. 3, 1790, 372.

23. Sidney, *Oration, Commemorative of the Abolition of the Slave Trade,* 15; Johnson, *Oration on the Abolition of the Slave Trade,* 14; Lawrence, *Oration on the Abolition of the Slave Trade,* 11; Peter Williams, Jr., *An Oration on the Abolition of the Slave Trade; Delivered in the African Church, in the City of New-York, January 1, 1808* (New York, 1808), 26.

that slavery made many bondspersons less than desirable candidates for membership in civil society. But the source of the problem was slavery, not race. One black activist commented that it was understandable for enslaved people, the mere "property of others," to disregard the "propriety of conduct, habits of industry, or precepts of morality." Slavery represented a "hopeless situation" in which the enslaved were "lost in a sense of wretchedness," their "natural strengths" going "uncultivated." Another African American orator observed that slavery "keeps down all the noble faculties of the soul, debases and corrupts human nature, and reduces man to be a mere instrument in the hand of his fellow-man." Russell Parrott, a Philadelphia free black printer and confidant of James Forten, remarked in 1812 that slavery "enervates the mind" and "corrodes the tender feelings of the heart," making it "insusceptible of those manly virtues." Henry Johnson explained that when "a person of colour is seen frequenting houses of infamy, and wasting his time in disgraceful pursuits" the skeptics of black freedom must remember that "he is the offspring of ignorance and misfortune ... a mind ... whose energies have been devoted to a third person's control." In the same vein as their white abolitionist allies, free black community leaders of the mid-Atlantic cast doubt on the ability of untutored formerly enslaved people for virtuous liberty. Yet, just as with the abolition societies, these black activists assured the white public that African American degradation stemmed solely from slavery, and not any intrinsic traits.[24]

The institutions of an emerging community would play a crucial role in elevating blacks degraded by slavery. Churches, mutual aid societies, and other associations acted as institutional strongholds for the rising generation within which free blacks promulgated a strategy of African American uplift to fight white prejudice. Free people of color set up their own churches. In Philadelphia, Richard Allen, Absalom Jones, and others were forced from their seats by white Methodists toward the end of the service one Sunday in 1792. Allen had long held the ambition to start an independent black church, and the seating controversy gave him and Jones the

---

24. Johnson, *Oration on the Abolition of the Slave Trade*, 11–13; Carman, *Oration Delivered at the Fourth Anniversary of the Abolition of the Slave Trade*, 19; Russel[l] Parrott, *An Oration on the Abolition of the Slave Trade; Delivered on the First of January, 1812, at the African Church of St. Thomas* (Philadelphia, 1812), 9. This concession about the potential unsuitability of formerly enslaved people for civil and civic membership was likewise made by white abolitionists, who also dismissed this critique of black liberty by holding to a societal environmentalist belief in the capacity of those who had been enslaved to transform into republican citizens.

support from African Americans that they needed. With the assistance of PAS member Benjamin Rush, whose unflagging assistance Allen thought "will never be forgotten among us," enough money was raised to construct an exclusively black house of worship by 1794, creating the St. Thomas African Episcopal Church of which Absalom Jones was chosen as pastor. That same year, Allen, a devout Methodist, founded the Bethel Church for black Methodists. In New York, black Methodists, including Peter Williams, William Hamilton, and William Miller, won recognition of a separate church in 1796 and in 1801 finished constructing the African Methodist Episcopal Zion Church. Twelve years later, Miller and Thomas Sipkins, Henry Sipkins's father, were among a number of black Methodists who splintered from Zion to establish the Asbury Methodist Episcopal Church. All four of these churches were key sites for African American community development throughout the early national period.[25]

To go along with churches, free blacks also established mutual aid societies that supplied much-needed support for a community of persons recently liberated from slavery. Two of the earliest and most extensive of the aid societies were the Free African Society of Philadelphia and the New York African Society for Mutual Relief. The Free African Society, founded in 1787, primarily by Richard Allen and Absalom Jones, and the New York African Society for Mutual Relief, formed in 1808 with charter members that included Peter Williams, Jr., Henry Sipkins, and William Hamilton, had benevolent and moral purposes: benevolent in that they created communal funds that members could draw from in times of distress and moral

25. Richard Allen, *The Life Experience and Gospel Labors of the Rt. Rev. Richard Allen; to Which Is Annexed, the Rise and Progress of the African Methodist Church in the United States of America; Containing a Narrative of the Yellow Fever in the Year of Our Lord 1793; with an Address to the People of Color in the United States* (Philadelphia, 1880), 16; Christopher Rush, *A Short Account of the Rise and Progress of the African M. E. Church in America* ... (1843; rpt. New York, 1866); Gary B. Nash, *Forging Freedom: The Formation of Philadelphia's Black Community, 1720–1840* (Cambridge, Mass., 1988), 110–121. Chroniclers of African American Christianity used to interpret the seating incident in Philadelphia as the catalyst for the independent black church movement there. It has now been shown, however, that the seating controversy took place five years after Allen and three years after Jones had first tried to raise funds for a freestanding black church. There is little doubt that the 1793 seating incident galvanized support among black Philadelphians for the black church movement. But it was their desire to create a house of worship that could express the views and address the concerns of the budding free black community of Philadelphia that originally convinced Allen and Jones of the need to establish an independent church. And it was the financial support of a handful of white Philadelphians that ultimately made the black church movement a successful one.

in that they demanded a strict code of behavior from their members. Additional mutual relief societies—the Friendly Society of the St. Thomas African Church (1796), the Wilberforce Philanthropic Association (1809), and the African Marine Fund (1810)—followed the model of the Free African Society and the New York African Society for Mutual Relief. Both mid-Atlantic black churches and mutual aid societies became central locales for disseminating to the larger free black population the ideals of republican living that community leaders believed persons of color should embody. The many black churches, relief societies, and educational outlets spreading throughout early national New York City and Philadelphia meant that "the thick fogs of ignorance" that had for so long shrouded African Americans were "gradually vanishing . . . dissipated by the superior radiance of increasing knowledge." Thousands of formerly enslaved people were "emerging from the depth of obscurity" to the echelons of enlightenment, making black activists certain that "we may anticipate a pleasing reform in the manners of many of our brethren." The present was encouraging. The future was bright.[26]

Having experienced the prejudice John Woolman poetically described in 1762 firsthand, free people of color needed no convincing of the blockades it put in the way of abolishing slavery and racial inequality. A societal environmentalist reform strategy that wedded the rise of virtuous republi-

26. Henry Sipkins, *Oration on the Abolition of the Slave Trade; Delivered in the African Church, in the City of New-York, January 2, 1809* (New York, 1809), 20; Carman, *Oration Delivered at the Fourth Anniversary of the Abolition of the Slave Trade,* 20; Johnson, *Oration on the Abolition of the Slave Trade,* 13; Douglass, *Annals of the First African Church,* 15–46; Winch, *Philadelphia's Black Elite: Activism, Accommodation, and the Struggle for Autonomy, 1787–1848* (Philadelphia, 1988), 5–7; Daniel Perlman, "Organizations of the Free Negro in New York City, 1800–1860," *Journal of Negro History,* LVI (1971), 181–184; *Constitution and Rules to Be Observed and Kept by the Friendly Society of St. Thomas's African Church, 1831; Philadelphia* (Philadelphia, 1797), in Porter, ed., *Early Negro Writing,* 28–32; *Constitution of the African Marine Fund, for the Relief of the Distressed Orphans, and Poor Members of This Fund* (New York, 1810), ibid., 42–44. In their rules, guidelines, and overall shape, the free black societies mirrored the plethora of white social improvement societies that were founded in this same period. The first president of the New York African Society for Mutual Relief cast that society as one of many being formed at that time when he noted that "the spirit of Liberty, improvement, and philanthropy pervades the people" of the United States and that "societies for the purpose of spreading useful knowledge, diffusing virtuous principles" were "sprouting up everywhere"; see William Hamilton, *An Address to the New York African Society, for Mutual Relief,* ibid., 39. For an analysis of the New York societies that place them in African rather than American cultural origins, see Craig Steven Wilder, *In the Company of Black Men: The African Influence on African American Culture in New York City* (New York, 2001).

cans of color with a withering white prejudice girded black abolitionists for the lengthy battle ahead. It also underscored that the newly liberated had to transform their former encumbered existence in slavery into virtuous, ennobled free lives to stamp out the immense level of prejudice that greeted black Americans in freedom.

TO EMPLOY THE PEN AND THE PRESS

Although a strict faithfulness by free blacks to newly independent America's standards for virtuous citizenship constituted an important front in the fight against white prejudice, first movement abolitionists held that this imperative alone could not eradicate slavery. Also needed was an antislavery enlightenment of the white public. First movement abolitionists endeavored to reform the environment in which white Americans formed judgments on the character of blacks. Premised on the same theory of societal environmentalism that abolitionists applied to African American citizenship, this antislavery enlightenment would make way for a society-wide acceptance of emancipation. To abolish slavery, first movement abolitionists believed that they needed to alter the way the white public thought about black people. In a letter to the PAS, William Pinkney, then an ardent young legislator who had delivered a speech in the Maryland House of Delegates supporting the easing of restrictions on private manumission, assessed that, for slavery to be abolished, the "public Mind" had to "be taught" the "rights" to which people of color "ought to be restored." The abolition societies sought to teach the white public just such a lesson.[27]

The American Convention became one important nexus in this drive to tackle white prejudice. The Convention's role in providing programmatic guidance and advice to its constituent societies equipped this body for the diffuse but essential mission of overturning white prejudice. Nestled alongside recurrent reminders to the abolition societies to address the educational development of free blacks, the American Convention inserted pleas to the societies to focus on alerting the white public both to the injustice of slavery and, as important, the underlying equality of African Americans. Those Americans who "acquiesce in the sophistry of the advocates" of slavery, the 1795 Convention declared, did so "merely from want of reflection" left over from an unenlightened era. "The force of reason, and the persuasion of eloquence" could "revive in the minds of our fellow citizens"

27. *Minutes of the Proceedings of the Tenth American Convention for Promoting the Abolition of Slavery* (1805), 35; PPAS, Series 2, reel 11, III (unnumbered loose correspondence), HSP.

the oppression of slavery. Antislavery tracts would play a pivotal role in "en-lighten[ing] the public mind" and "preparing" white Americans for "the re-ception of important truths," namely the sins of slavery and the humanity of enslaved and free blacks. Heeding the connection between white pub-lic enlightenment and slavery's abolition, the Delaware Abolition Society, in a report to the American Convention, asserted that "sound reasoning, must finally break down the mounds which the prejudices of education, and avarice have erected between Africans and humanity." Dogged efforts to expose white Americans to the unenlightened nature of their prejudices would eventually earn for people of color freedom and equal dignity.[28]

The American Convention's plan for combating white American preju-dices mirrored its reform program for formerly enslaved people. The Con-vention's urgent requests for the abolition societies to "prepare" and "im-press" the white "public mind" with the justness of black liberty matched its effort to "prepare" and "impress" the black American mind for the proper exercise of freedom. "The man whose mind is clouded by preju-dice," the Convention told the abolition societies, must "have truth fre-quently repeated, and presented" so that "his errors can be corrected, his prejudices subdued, and the noble feelings of philanthropy excited in his breast." In other words, the white public needed to be conditioned to see the wrongs of slavery and convinced of the virtue of people of color, just as former bondspersons had to be placed in the proper environment to cultivate their innate ability for citizenship. For first movement abolition-ists, these two environmental developments would work in tandem, allow-ing formerly enslaved people to gradually advance beyond slavery's fet-ters and white prejudices to be gradually quelled. Then "the light of truth" would "break through the dark gloom of oppression" and the "practice of the people" would "be conformable to their declaration — 'That all men are born equally free, and have an unalienable right to Liberty.'" The synergy between defeating prejudice and abolishing slavery was paramount to first movement abolitionist activism.[29]

28. *Minutes of the Proceedings of the Second Convention of Delegates from the Aboli-tion Societies Established in Different Parts of the United States* ... (Philadelphia, 1795), 26–31, esp. 28; *Minutes of the Proceedings of the Eighth Convention of Delegates from the Abolition Societies Established in Different Parts of the United States* ... (Philadel-phia, 1803), 32; *Minutes of the Proceedings of the Fourth Convention of Delegates from the Abolition Societies Established in Different Parts of the United States* ... (Philadel-phia, 1797), 26; *Minutes of the Proceedings of the Tenth American Convention for Pro-moting the Abolition of Slavery* (1805), 18, 28.

29. *Minutes of the Proceedings of the Twelfth American Convention for Promoting the Abolition of Slavery and Improving the Condition of the African Race* ... (Philadel-

Exactly who made up the white public to which the American Convention referred? First movement abolitionists never explicitly defined their target audience. But highlighting their focus on crafting an antislavery reading public provides some clarity. American Revolutionary and early national thought emphasized the need for an engaged and informed public to help steer the new Republic. From this emphasis came the outsized role of public opinion in shaping the course of the new nation. Public opinion, and who composed it, remained an amorphous concept in the years following American independence. But, for first movement abolitionists, shaping public opinion might yield tangible results. For instance, if voters could be convinced of slavery's injustice, then perhaps more state legislatures would abolish slavery, or those that already had would strengthen enforcement measures relating to gradual emancipation statutes. Additionally, if the reading public became more sensitive to the interests and humanity of people of African descent, then maybe slaveholders and dealers would think twice before trampling on the basic rights of black Americans— a practice the PAS and NYMS knew all too well through the reports of their acting and standing committees. Moreover, the shared sphere of early national print culture lent itself to the possibility of molding broad public hostility to slavery and racial prejudice. Low postage rates, improvements in transportation, and the skyrocketing growth of American periodicals facilitated the corporate circulation of news and public opinion. Thus, an antislavery tract published in rural Connecticut or urban Pennsylvania could be republished in several towns and cities across the Republic, taking a seemingly isolated piece and vastly expanding its potential effect at the very time that Americans were defining themselves as a nation.[30]

---

phia, 1809), 30; *Minutes of the Proceedings of the Fifth Convention of Delegates from the Abolition Societies Established in Different Parts of the United States* ... (Philadelphia, 1798), 20. The consonant language the American Convention used when referring to restructuring the thought and behavior of both black and white Americans reveals that the abolition societies' paternalism was not directed at people of color alone.

30. To give a sense of the colossal growth in printed reading material during the early years of the American Republic, the number of newspapers in circulation between 1780 and 1790 nearly tripled, from 38 to 106, and by 1820 861 newspapers were in print. See William A. Dill, *Growth of Newspapers in the United States: A Study of the Number of Newspapers, of the Number of Subscribers, and of Total Annual Output of the Periodical Press, from 1704 to 1925, with Comment on Coincident Social and Economic Conditions* (Lawrence, Kans., 1928), 11. On the central role of post offices in facilitating the spread of newspapers and periodicals in the early national era, see Richard B. Kielbowicz, "The Press, Post Office, and Flow of News in the Early Republic," *Journal of the Early Republic*, III (1983), 255–280. For the importance of public opinion in the politics of early national America and the role of print culture in directing it, from two very dif-

To uncouple the white public from its disparaging ideas about people of color and expunge racial prejudice from the new nation, therefore, first movement abolitionists turned to the world of print. As Richard Allen and Absalom Jones's pamphlet on black actions during Philadelphia's 1793 yellow fever crisis shows, black activists were aware of the importance of print in persuading the white public. The abolition societies, too, took the power of print culture seriously. The PAS credited antislavery essays of the Revolutionary era for the adoption of laws prohibiting the slave trade in several states and even for the gradual emancipation policy of Pennsylvania. By "excit[ing] the attention of the public" to the plight of enslaved people, the tracts had gained important allies for the cause of abolition. Concerned with the public's perception of its activities, the NYMS in 1792 stated that "a diffusion of the principles on which they act" was as important as the society's activism. From this emphasis on print came a concerted effort to shape the minds of the reading public in ways favorable to the first abolition movement. The American Convention's choice to publish its proceedings and distribute them for public consumption was itself an important foray into the antislavery print sphere. But the Convention wanted to systematize antislavery publishing. Informing the abolition societies that "it is our duty to employ the pen and the press" to "convince our countrymen of the injustice and impolicy of ... slavery," the Convention recommended the creation of antislavery publication committees. All four of the mid-Atlantic societies established committees to publish abolitionist literature.[31]

---

ferent historical perspectives, see Colleen A. Sheehan, "The Politics of Public Opinion: James Madison's 'Notes on Government,'" *WMQ*, 3d Ser., XLIX (1992), 609–627; Sheehan, "Madison and the French Enlightenment: The Authority of Public Opinion," *WMQ*, 3d Ser., LIX (2002), 925–956; and Seth Cotlar, *Tom Paine's America: The Rise and Fall of Transatlantic Radicalism in the Early Republic* (Charlottesville, Va., 2011), 161–188. For efforts by the abolition societies to influence public opinion, specifically the PAS, see Dee E. Andrews, "Reconsidering the First Emancipation: Evidence from the Pennsylvania Abolition Society Correspondence, 1785–1810," *Pennsylvania History*, LVIV, Special Supplemental Issue, *Empire, Society, and Labor: Essays in Honor of Richard S. Dunn* (Summer 1997), 230–249. Trish Loughran has convincingly argued that "there was no national print culture" before the technological and transportation improvements of antebellum America; see Loughran, *The Republic in Print: Print Culture in the Age of U.S. Nation Building, 1770–1870* (New York, 2007), 3. Yet, granting that historians should avoid claims of a Republic-wide print culture in the early national era, the widespread practice of newspaper editors' reprinting pieces from commensurate periodicals undeniably extended the reach of individual items of writing and gave them greater potential purchase.

31. PAS to London Society, Oct. 20, 1787, PPAS, Series 1, reel 1, I, HSP; NYMS Records, VI, 164, NYHS; *Minutes of the Proceedings of the Twelfth American Convention*

FIGURE 11. *Freeman's Journal* Masthead, May 26, 1790.
From *Early American Newspapers, Series 1*, an *Archive of Americana* collection,
published by Readex (Readex.com), a division of NewsBank, Inc., and in
cooperation with the American Antiquarian Society

To carry out this push to shape public opinion, the abolition societies drew on both its own members and allies in the print trade. A PAS membership list from 1789 reveals that more than 5 percent of those members who had joined the society following its reorganization in 1787 were printers. One of the most active of these printers, Joseph Cruikshank, had been publishing antislavery tracts for almost two decades, including one of Anthony Benezet's pamphlets. Another, Francis Bailey, edited the Philadelphia newspaper the *Freeman's Journal* (see Figure 11). The NYMS also counted printers among its numbers, such as the newspaper editor Phillip Freneau.[32]

Not only society members but also partnerships forged with printers sympathetic to antislavery extended the ability of the first abolition movement to reach the reading public. The one-time president of the NYMS, John Jay, served as a patron to Francis Childs, whose *Daily Advertiser* consistently carried antislavery news and opinion in the early 1790s. In Phila-

for Promoting the Abolition of Slavery (1809), 29–30; *Minutes of the Proceedings of the Tenth American Convention for Promoting the Abolition of Slavery* (1805), 35. For the Delaware Abolition Societies' antislavery print activities, see ibid., 18; and Monte A. Calvert, "The Abolition Society of Delaware, 1801–1807," *Delaware History*, X (1963), 303–304.

32. Gary B. Nash and Jean R. Soderlund, *Freedom by Degrees: Emancipation in Pennsylvania and Its Aftermath* (New York, 1991), 130; Philip S. Foner, *The Democratic-Republican Societies, 1790–1800: A Documentary Sourcebook of Constitutions, Declarations, Addresses, Resolutions, and Toasts* (Westport, Conn., 1976), 12. Cruikshank published Benezet's *Some Historical Account of Guinea, Its Situation, Produce, and General Disposition of Its Inhabitants; with an Inquiry into the Rise and Progress of the Slave-Trade, Its Nature and Lamentable Effects* ... in Philadelphia in 1771.

delphia, the PAS could count on the support of the printer Eleazar Oswald during this same period. A Revolutionary War veteran and staunch Antifederalist turned Democratic-Republican, Oswald extended his understanding of American rights and liberties to people of color in the pages of his *Independent Gazetteer*. Oswald's newspaper published some of the most strident abolitionist and racially progressive material of the early national era, much of which was probably sourced from or penned by PAS members and the society's advocates. Seth Cotlar has profiled Oswald's antiracist and antislavery publishing as part of what he depicts as the radical effort of a host of printers, thinkers, and writers to create a truly democratic Atlantic world in which political, social, and economic equality would not be limited to elites but would apply also to ordinary people, including persons of African descent. Beginning in the mid-1790s, Oswald, and the group of Democratic-Republican printers to which he belonged, pulled back from publishing this abolitionist, racially egalitarian material as partisan concerns (including the importance of southern slaveholders to the Democratic-Republican coalition) increasingly took precedence over antislavery. Yet, during the nation's dawning years, the abolition societies possessed ample conduits through which they could saturate the print sphere with writings reflective of their abolitionist philosophy.[33]

A sizable portion of the antislavery material that the abolition societies passed on to their printer associates had British and, to a lesser degree, French origins. By 1790, the growing antislavery movement in Britain had produced a flurry of antislavery publications, from Thomas Clarkson's renowned essays denouncing the slave trade to William Cowper's affecting antislavery poetry. London's SEAST along with Paris's Society of the Friends of the Blacks kept up an active correspondence with the PAS and NYMS and showered these two organizations with antislavery poems and essays. The leading American abolition societies responded by appointing committees to read over the writings and then submit them to various newspapers, magazines, and printers for republication. The PAS and NYMS also sent antislavery publications and news to their sister groups in Europe, especially those illustrating the equal talent of blacks. Consequently, early national antislavery print culture was a transatlantic creation

33. On Francis Childs, see Bickford, Kenneth R. Bowling, and Helen E. Veit, eds., *Documentary History of the First Federal Congress*, X, *Debates in the House of Representatives, First Session: April–May 1789* (Baltimore, 1992), xxxviii–xxxix. For the social and political beliefs underpinning Oswald and his fellow Democratic-Republican printers, examples of the antislavery literature they published, and these printers' turn away from first movement abolitionist values, see Cotlar, *Tom Paine's America*, 55–67.

forged from communication between American and European abolition societies.[34]

With a diverse array of antislavery writings and many channels through which to broadcast these materials, the abolition societies constructed a racially egalitarian idiom to combat white American prejudices. Based on equalitarian and natural rights principles and rooted in sentimental empathy for the enslaved, these antislavery writings championed the human rights of persons of color rather than the property rights of slaveholders. Hoping to push public opinion against slavery and the slave trade, racially egalitarian antislavery literature exhorted white Americans to dispense with their prejudices and begin to view enslaved people as equal human beings instead of chattel. This literature's roots lay deep within significant cultural changes taking place in the late eighteenth century. A new cult of sensibility arose from such ontological doctrines as John Locke's epistemological emphasis on sensationalism, Scottish enlightenment conceptions of the moral sense, and the centrality of sympathy to social formation. The man of feeling identified with the sufferings and pains of others as if they were his own. It became a sign of refinement to make sympathetic connections with society's sufferers. Hitched to the natural rights philosophy of universal equality, the cult of sensibility provided important opportunities for reformers. American abolitionists took advantage of this development by encouraging readers to empathize with enslaved blacks and oppose the institution of bondage.[35]

34. The London and Paris societies frequently sent antislavery writings to their organizational counterparts in the United States, particularly the PAS. See PPAS, Series 1, reel 1, I, 34–35, 39, 70, 133, 148, 174, 282, HSP; and NYMS Records, VI, 115–116, NYHS. For the circulation of antislavery printed matter among the American, British, and French abolition societies in the 1780s and 1790s, see Oldfield, *Transatlantic Abolitionism in the Age of Revolution*, 48–59.

35. Lynn Hunt, *Inventing Human Rights: A History* (New York, 2007). When discussing the "limitations" of late-eighteenth-century antislavery, Winthrop Jordan finds the "absence of any clear disjunction" between the human rights of the enslaved and the property rights of slaveholders by both antislavery activists and the greater early national American society. Much of the antislavery literature disseminated during this same period, however, contradicts this dichotomy and points to a subtler yet no less compelling challenge to the property rights of slaveholders. See Jordan, *White over Black*, 351. David N. Gellman also demonstrates the presence of racially egalitarian antislavery literature in the newspapers of the young Republic, focusing on the public debate over gradual emancipation in New York during the 1790s. See David N. Gellman, "Race, the Public Sphere, and Abolition in Late Eighteenth-Century New York," *JER*, XX (2000), 607–636; and Gellman, *Emancipating New York: The Politics of Slavery and Freedom, 1777–1827* (Baton Rouge, La., 2006), chap. 6. For the dynamic growth of a print sphere

Poems gave lyrical expression to antislavery literature. Antislavery poetry communicated indignation at the injustice of holding sentient fellow humans in chattel bondage. Poets often dramatized imagined scenes of slavery-induced horror as a way of hammering home slavery's brutality. "The African Slave's Soliloquy" depicted the plight of an enslaved man dragged from his native land and into bondage. Describing a scene in which his village is set on fire, his children burned to death, and his wife left disconsolate and alone, this bondsman found himself in abject servitude—"he groans with weighty woes oppresst, / What sad sensations rankle his breast." The enslaved man was haunted by nightmares wherein "I see my parents, hear my children cry, / And in the flaming cottage see them die." A poem titled "The Tender's Hold" took readers to the scene of a slave ship disembarking from the African coast and put its audience in the misery of this tragic moment. "Dragg'd by oppression's savage grasp, / From every dear connextion, / 'Midst putrid air, O! hear them gasp, / And mark their deep dejection." Other poems painted macabre portraits of enslaved life. "The Island Field Negro" indicted the barbaric cruelty of slaveholders.

> *One* with a gibbet wakes his negroe's fears,
> One to the wind-mill nails him by the ears;
> *One* keeps his slave in dismal dens unfed,
> One puts the wretch in pickle ere he's dead;
> *This*, to a tree suspends him by the thumbs,
> That, from his table grudges even the crumbs![36]

laden with sensibility and the important role this development played in Revolutionary and early national America, see Sarah Knott, "Sensibility and the American War for Independence," *American Historical Review,* CIX (2004), 19–40; Knott, *Sensibility and the American Revolution* (Williamsburg, Va., and Chapel Hill, N.C., 2009); Nicole Eustace, *Passion Is the Gale: Emotion, Power, and the Coming of the American Revolution* (Williamsburg, Va., and Chapel Hill, N.C., 2008); and Catherine O'Donnell Kaplan, *Men of Letters in the Early Republic: Cultivating Forums of Citizenship* (Williamsburg, Va., and Chapel Hill, N.C., 2008).

36. *Impartial Gazetteer, and Saturday Evening Post* (New York), June 14, 1788, [4]; *Weekly Museum* (New York), Nov. 2, 1793, [2]; *New-Jersey Journal, and Political Intelligencer* (Elizabethtown), Mar. 23, 1790; *Freeman's Journal; or, the North-American Intelligencer* (Philadelphia), Mar. 2, 1791. See also *New-York Packet,* Mar. 9, 1786. Publishing "The Island Field Negro," which depicted the horrors of West Indian slavery, can be viewed as safely avoiding direct censure of American slaveholders, or perhaps even working to soothe the consciences of whites in American slave societies by inviting them to draw favorable contrasts with their own treatment of people of African descent. Yet early national newspapers did not shy away from publishing pieces directly criticizing American slaveholders. In defending antislavery petitioners to the first federal Congress

After detailing the inhumanity of human bondage, antislavery poems often invited readers to make empathetic associations between themselves and the enslaved. "An Elegy on African Slavery" played on readers' sentiments by declaring: "O! ye whose gen'rous breasts, can, weeping, bend / O'er the pale victim of despair and pain, / Your tears with mine in feeling concert blend, / And mourn with me man's cruelty to man." One poem was based on the agony of an enslaved boy, who wept as he was separated from his good friend by sale. The author began the piece by asking rhetorically, "And can'st thou weep? Alas! poor Negro Boy, / And feel the warmth of hope and chill of fear; / Can *Separation* thus thy soul employ, / And draw from thee the sympathetic tear?" The next logical step after drawing attention to this child's feelings was to relate to the boy's emotional pain. "Full well I know the pangs you now endure; / And blush to think, that those of lighter dye / Unmov'd can view the miseries they procure." An "Address to the Heart, on the Subject of American Slavery" called on all those "whose hearts are attuned to sympathy" to "Awake!" and "let the miseries of others be your own." It may be hard for the contemporary reader to look past the intense sentimentality of this late-eighteenth-century literary genre. But the degree to which these poems presented enslaved people as fellow human beings, and not property or beasts of burden, as slavery's defenders wished the public to think of blacks, marked an important contribution to the abolition societies' goal of changing the public's view of African Americans.[37]

Antislavery poetry deliberately erased the color line to discredit the arguments of slavery's defenders and shake the white public's sense of racial differences. One of the most famous examples of this type of antislavery poetry was penned by the English author William Cowper and published

---

from a torrent of attacks by lower southern congressmen during the House of Representatives' debates over slavery in 1790, one author in New York's *Daily Advertiser* wrote: "Wherefore then, O ye! who live by sucking, as it were, the blood of your fellow creatures, who pamper your bodies, and riot in luxury at the expence of the liberty and happiness of men, equally susceptible of pain and pleasure with yourselves, dare ye glory in your shame, and brand with the most scurrilous epithets, every one, who promoted by humanity ventures to question your right to any property in the human species?" See *Daily Advertiser* (New York), Mar. 23, 1790, [2], Mar. 27, 1790, [quotation on 2], Mar. 30, 1790, [2].

37. *Philadelphia Repository and Weekly Register,* Oct. 31, 1801, 408; *Independent Gazetteer* (Philadelphia), Apr. 9, 1796, [4]; "Address to the Heart, on the Subject of American Slavery," *American Museum, or Repository of Ancient and Modern Fugitive Pieces, Prose and Poetical* (Philadelphia), I, no. 6 (June 1787), 538, 542; *New-York Packet,* Mar. 29, 1787, [4].

extensively in the American press. In "The Negro's Complaint," Cowper ridiculed the significance attached to skin color. "Fleecy locks, and black complexion, / Cannot forfeit nature's claim; / Skins may differ—but affection / Dwells in *black and white* the same." He ended the piece by having an enslaved African tell bondage's defenders to "Deem our nation brutes no longer, / Till some reason ye shall find / Worthier of regard, and stronger / Than the *colour of our* kind." While Cowper refuted skin color as a marker of human difference, additional poems affixed the humanity of white and black. "Reflections on the Slavery of the Negroes" said simply that a black person's "soul he has, immortal as our own; / And flesh and blood as rich as monarchs boast." His "birth and feelings, passions, powers, and wants, / Decline and death, to ours similar." A like-minded poem echoed these thoughts in asserting: "One common Father form'd each kindred frame, / One common will inspir'd the vital flame; / By the same laws, we breathe an equal air, / Fruits of one love, and objects of one care." If white and black shared the same inner core of being, then how could one person justly claim absolute ownership over another?[38]

Coming from black speakers, arguments for the inner equality of the races posed an even greater challenge to white prejudice. By endowing African Americans with eloquence, antislavery writers reversed the well-established literary black figure, whose pidgin dialect and woeful ignorance only reinforced claims of racial inferiority. In a rejoinder to the negative characterization of blacks in the popular play *The Padlock*, Mungo in the poem "Mungo Speaks" reveals his true virtue. "T'ank you, my Massas! have you laugh your fill?— / Then let me speak, nor take that freedom ill." When given the chance to speak, Mungo reminds his readers of the essential humanity that he shares with whites—"Alike our wants, our pleasures, and our pains"—and dismisses the demarcating lines of slavery, "Comes freedom then from colour? Blush with shame." Mungo concludes by calling on the "sons of Freedom!" to "equalise your laws; / Be all consistent—plead the Negro's cause." As with Mungo's impassioned plea for consistency, antislavery writers often gave black speakers a superior moral compass and had them chastise whites for their hypocrisies. "The Last Anniversary" imagined an enslaved person witnessing a Fourth of July celebration.

38. *Burlington Advertiser, or Agricultural and Political Intelligencer* (N.J.), Nov. 9, 1790, [3], reprinted in *Dunlap's American Daily Advertiser* (Philadelphia), Feb. 11, 1791, [2], and *Spooner's Vermont Journal* (Windsor), Nov. 12, 1792, [4]. See also *Time-Piece, and Literary Companion* (New York), June 16, 1797, 168; *Public Advertiser* (Philadelphia), Feb. 2, 1807, [2]; and *New-York Daily Gazette*, Aug. 14, 1789, 786.

Must *I* toil and groan, then, in slavery and pain
In sight of yon arbor of joy,
And hear freemen swell a melodious strain
And shout for the rights they destroy?
How joyous the wretch at the head of the throng,
How full of benevolence he?
And those who now raise a devotional song;
By those, ah! I ceas'd to be free.

Through a keen sense of the incongruity of a nation celebrating freedom while enslaving its fellow countrymen, the imagined bondsperson in this poem displayed a more discerning understanding of authentic republican virtue than those free whites who gathered annually to fete America's independence.[39]

There was no greater remonstrance of racial prejudice than when free black writers conveyed opposition to slavery. In 1789, "A Free Negro" launched a spirited invective aimed at slave traders and natural philosophers who attempted to dehumanize those of African descent. Freed as a youth and given the benefits of a literary education, the author had decided from an early age to advocate "the true principles, on which the liberties of mankind are founded." Hoping to advance the cause of slavery's

---

39. *Independent Journal; or, the General Advertiser* (New York), Mar. 8, 1788, [3], reprinted in *Albany Journal; or, the Montgomery, Washington and Columbia Intelligencer,* Mar. 17, 1788, [4]; *Farmer's Cabinet* (Amherst, N.H.), Aug. 11, 1807, [1]. See also "The Negroes' Prayer" from *Freeman's Journal; or, the North-American Intelligencer,* Feb. 16, 1791, [2], for a poem allegedly written by an enslaved man from Virginia eloquently speaking out against his bondage. David Gellman acknowledges the use of a black literary voice for racially egalitarian ends, viewing it as an attempt by antislavery writers to imagine blacks as eligible for citizenship. See Gellman, *Emancipating New York,* 115–127. Although Gellman's interpretation is persuasive, this racially egalitarian literary device more elementally sought to establish the intrinsic humanity and essential sameness of blacks and whites. This simple but powerful assertion was a crucial prerequisite for making the argument to the white public that African Americans were capable of citizenship. An imagined black voice deploying pidgin dialect was often used to disparage African Americans in the early national print sphere, but this was not always the case. For a remarkable exception, see the "Anecdote" of Sambo the Revolutionary War black soldier, first published in *Essex Journal and New-Hampshire Packet* (Newburyport, Mass.), Jan. 19, 1791, [4], and then widely reprinted as far south as Baltimore. For a rare example of a black voice employed to directly justify slavery, see *City Gazette and Daily Advertiser* (Charleston, S.C.), Feb. 9, 1795, [3]. The piece depicts an enslaved speaker who is leading a group of his fellow bondspersons giving thanks for their slavery. In part it reads, "Thy burdens yield, nor grief, nor pain, / Thy toils demand no tear." This was an obvious response to the antislavery harnessing of a fictive black voice that dramatized slavery's inhumanity.

abolition, he submitted his essay as a tool for assisting in the "deliverance" of his black brethren from bondage. Like many other antislavery authors and activists, this free black essayist believed that removing white prejudice was the mandatory initial step in eradicating slavery. As absurd as it sounded, blacks needed "to prove that we are men." The author believed that white prejudices were not simply barriers to black freedom; they were visceral forces weighing down black freemen. Slavery's apologists wrongly claimed that the "innate perverseness of our minds" and "nature" itself had "marked us out for slavery." But, "if treated like other men, and admitted to a participation of their rights," blacks, he assured the reading public, would be just as virtuous as whites. The writer's own literary skill attested to that very argument.[40]

Additional literary forms contrived by antislavery writers made direct appeals to readers to recognize the aptitude and intelligence of enslaved people. Bemoaning that the practice of bondage fettered the innate talents of enslaved blacks, these pieces asserted that African Americans would be every bit the equal of whites if only given the chance to cultivate their natural endowments. The obituary of Thomas Fuller, an enslaved Virginian who died at the age of eighty in the winter of 1790, illustrates this type of antislavery literary approach. Fuller's obituary pervaded the press, finding its way into newspapers in the upper South, mid-Atlantic, and northern regions. The obituary began by informing its readers that Fuller was a "prodigy." Possessing unmatchable mathematical skills, he could answer abstruse calculative inquiries "in less time than ninety-nine men in an hundred would take with their pens." Fuller was, the writer emphasized, a *"self-taught Arithmetician"* and an *"untutored Scholar"*; had he been given the same opportunities as his "fellow-men," not the "Royal Society of London, the Academy of Sciences at Paris, nor even *Newton* himself need have been ashamed to acknowledge him as a Brother in Science." After placing Fuller in the same sphere as the enlightenment's leading scientist, the author ruled "in favour of the genius, capacity and talents, of our ill-fated black

40. A Free Negro, "Letter on Slavery; by a Negro," *American Museum: or Repository of Ancient and Modern Fugitive Pieces, etc.; Prose and Poetical*, VI, no. 1 (July 1789), 77–80 (quotations on 78), reprinted in *Osborne's New-Hampshire Spy* (Portsmouth), Apr. 14, 1789, [1], and extracted in *New-York Journal, and Patriotic Register*, Sept. 11, 1790, [2]. The essay originated in England. Given the way writers often took on different guises in the pseudonymous press of the Atlantic world in this period, it is impossible to know whether the piece was written by someone of African descent. Yet, even if it was not penned by a person of color, unlike pieces that clearly were imaging a black voice this writer presented himself as a free black man. For a similar example, see the "Africanus" essays in *Gazette of the United States* (New York), Mar. 3, 6, 1790.

Brethren." It was the prejudices of a misguided white public, the obituary closed, as "ill-founded in fact, as they are inhuman in tendency!" that perpetuated slavery and prevented prodigies like Fuller from fully realizing their potential.[41]

One of the most acclaimed free blacks of early national America offered abolitionists a prime opportunity to further broadcast African American capability. In 1791, James Pemberton of the PAS wrote to the Baltimore printer William Goddard, asking him for copies of the free black surveyor and astronomer Benjamin Banneker's soon-to-be-published almanac. The prefatory note to the first edition of Banneker's almanac spelled out the ramifications of this work for American antislavery. Banneker's learning shone above "thousands of whites, liberally educated," who could not match this self-educated free black man in "intellectual acquirements and capacities." Alluding to the emerging theory of polygenesis, the opening to the almanac used the accomplishments of Banneker as evidence against those who believed blacks had an "origin different from the whites." As emancipation gave many more African Americans the chance to pursue education, cases similar to Banneker's would "multiply," and people of color could display their innate genius. Banneker's example was not the only one of an accomplished free black used by first movement abolitionists to strike at white prejudice. The American Convention and PAS member Benjamin Rush published the remarkable story of James Derham, a free black physi-

41. *Alexandria Advertiser* (Va.), Dec. 9, 1790. Thomas Fuller's obituary was one of the most widely circulated antislavery pieces in the early national era. See reprints in *Pennsylvania Mercury, and Universal Advertiser* (Philadelphia), Dec. 16, 1790 (alternative version), [1]; Dec. 21, 1790, [4] (quotations in the text are from this issue); *Columbian Centinel* (Boston), Dec. 29, 1790, 123; *Freeman's Journal; or, the North-American Intelligencer*, Dec. 22, 1790, [2–3]; *New-York Daily Gazette*, Dec. 22, 1790, 1218; *Independent Gazetteer, and Agricultural Repository* (Philadelphia), Dec. 25, 1790, [3]; *Thomas's Massachusetts Spy: Or, The Worcester Gazette*, Jan. 6, 1791, [2]; *Salem Gazette* (Mass.), Jan. 4, 1791, [3]; *Hampshire Gazette* (Northampton, Mass.), Jan. 12, 1791, [3]; *Connecticut Journal* (New Haven), Jan. 12, 1791, [4]; *Vermont Gazette* (Bennington), Jan. 17, 1791, [4]; *Western Star* (Stockbridge, Mass.), Jan. 18, 1791, [1]; and *United States Chronicle: Political, Commercial, and Historical* (Providence, R.I.), Mar. 17, 1791, [3]. Fuller was referred to as "Negro Tom" and "the African calculator" in an attempt, perhaps, to highlight that, although not of European descent, he had capacities in line with the most accomplished of whites. See *Pennsylvania Mercury* (Philadelphia), Dec. 30, 1790, [2–3], for an antislavery piece using the death of Fuller as a springboard to attack the slave trade and slavery. The antislavery obituary stemmed from Benjamin Rush's certificate of accomplishment for Fuller, first published by the PAS in local newspapers in 1789. See PPAS, Series 1, reel 1, I, 61, HSP.

cian of New Orleans. Born in slavery in Philadelphia, Derham served as a physician's assistant to his British surgeon master during the Revolutionary War before he was sold to another physician who eventually agreed to grant his freedom. Having heard of his talents, Rush approached Derham to give the young black doctor some medical pointers. Instead he found Derham "suggested many more to me," demonstrating that one's early life in slavery by no means foreclosed the faculties of human improvement.[42]

Antislavery essays constituted a straightforward but no less vigorous means by which to mobilize an antislavery public. The NYMS sponsored antislavery orations. Samuel Miller's and Elihu Smith's orations were both published in pamphlet form. The speakers dissected and then denounced arguments in favor of black bondage and told white Americans that the nascent nation's experiment in free government would never endure without slavery's abolition. Similar orations were delivered before and printed by the New Jersey, Delaware, Connecticut, and Maryland abolition societies.[43]

42. James M'Henry to Messrs. Goddard and Angell, Aug. 20, 1791, in Benjamin Banneker, *Benjamin Banneker's Pennsylvania, Delaware, Maryland, and Virginia Almanack and Ephemeris, for the Year of Our Lord, 1792* ... (Baltimore, [1792]). The preface was printed in *American Museum, or, Universal Magazine*, XII, no. 3 (September 1792), 185–187. Joseph Cruikshank, a PAS member and antislavery printer, sold copies of Banneker's almanac. See PPAS, Series 2, reel 11, I, 88–90, HSP, for Pemberton's letter to Goddard, Sept. 9, 1791. Rush's certificates of accomplishment for James Derham and Thomas Fuller were published in *Freeman's Journal*, Jan. 7, 1789, [3], and reprinted in *Thomas's Massachusettes Spy: Or, The Worcester Gazette*, Jan. 29, 1789, [1], *New-Hampshire Spy*, Feb. 3, 1789, [4], *Salem Mercury* (Mass.), Feb. 3, 1789, [4], and *Cumberland Gazette* (Portland, Me.), Feb. 12, 1789, [4]. The PAS sent these certificates of accomplishment to the London Society for the Abolition of the Slave Trade. See PPAS, Series 1, reel I, I, 61, 73–79, HSP.

43. NYMS, VI, 189–190, NYHS; Samuel Miller, *A Discourse, Delivered, April 12, 1797, at the Request of and before the New-York Society for Promoting the Manumission of Slaves, and Protecting Such of Them as Have Been or May Be Liberated* (New York, 1797); E. H. Smith, *A Discourse, Delivered April 11, 1798, at the Request of and before the New-York Society for Promoting the Manumission of Slaves, and Protecting Such of Them as Have Been or May Be Liberated* (New York, 1798); Griffith, *Address of the President; Mirror of the Times, and General Advertiser* (Wilmington, Del.), May 30, 1801; George Buchanan, *An Oration upon the Moral and Political Evil of Slavery: Delivered at a Public Meeting of the Maryland Society for Promoting the Abolition of Slavery, and the Relief of Free Negroes, and Others Unlawfully Held in Bondage; Baltimore, July 4th, 1791* (Baltimore, 1793); Zephaniah Swift, *An Oration on Domestic Slavery; Delivered at the North Meeting-House in Hartford, on the 12th Day of May, A.D. 1791; at the Meeting of the Connecticut Society for the Promotion of Freedom, and the Relief of Persons Unlawfully Holden in Bondage* (Hartford, Conn., 1791); Edwards, *The Injustice and Impolicy of the Slave Trade;* Theodore Dwight, *An Oration, Spoken before the Connecticut Society,*

Some of the antislavery addresses of the late eighteenth century could make seemingly startling challenges to what appeared to be ideological dogma. In 1789, PAS member and printer Joseph Cruikshank published William Pinkney's address to the Maryland Assembly. In his speech, Pinkney met the problem of prejudice facing antislavery activists by turning African American enslavement into an argument for black liberty. Were the nation's enslaved people emancipated, hypothesized Pinkney, they would be "bound by gratitude, as well as by interest, to seek the welfare of that country from which they have derived the restoration of their plundered rights." A formerly enslaved person who had "felt the yoke of bondage must for ever prove the assertor of freedom, if he is fairly admitted to the equal enjoyment of its benefits." Thus, enslaved people's bondage made them, as freedpersons, especially fit for republican liberty. Correspondingly, to eviscerate the white public's linkage between blackness and slavery, the American Convention published addresses urging white Americans to "use" their "reason and social affections for the purposes for which they were given." To the Convention these "purposes" were realizing that "nature has made no essential distinction in the human race, and that all the individuals of the great family of mankind have a common claim upon the general fund of natural bounties." With proper guidance, the public would come to realize the inequity of chattel bondage.[44]

The antislavery literature of first movement abolitionism aspired to sway white Americans into accepting that black Americans had a legitimate right to freedom. Through a myriad of formats and literary approaches, first movement abolitionists conducted a comprehensive enterprise to influence white public opinion. Whether making overtures to the sentimental empathy of readers and deriding the arbitrariness of racial distinctions through poetry or crafting reasoned, cerebral cases for the claims of people of color to liberty in essays, first movement abolitionist philosophy penetrated early national print culture. At the same time as they petitioned legislatures for antislavery measures and guarded the legal rights of free

---

for the Promotion of Freedom and the Relief of Persons Unlawfully Holden in Bondage; Convened in Hartford, on the 8th Day of May, A.D. 1794 (Hartford, Conn., 1794).

44. William Pinkney, Speech of William Pinkney, Esq. in the House of Delegates of Maryland, at Their Session in November, 1789 (Philadelphia, 1790), 13–14; Address of a Convention of Delegates from the Abolition Society, to the Citizens of the United States (New York, 1794), 5; Minutes of the Proceedings of a Convention of Delegates from the Abolition Societies (1794), 23; Minutes of the Proceedings of the Seventh Convention of Delegates from the Abolition Societies Established in Different Parts of the United States ... (Philadelphia, 1801), 37–38.

persons of color, abolitionists took up the more opaque challenge of revolutionizing white ideas about black people.

THE COMMENCEMENT OF THAT HAPPY ERA

Slave trade orations delivered from 1808 through 1815 by urban mid-Atlantic black leaders embody the ultimate expression of the first movement abolitionists' program for deposing white prejudice. The strategy of free blacks serving as agents in combatting whites' negative attitudes toward people of color, print as a vessel for disseminating the movement's messages to the public, and, most fundamentally, the optimistic outlook that committed abolitionists to their mission of shattering white prejudice—all came together in these addresses. Beginning in 1808, black churches in New York and Philadelphia annually marked the anniversary of the abolition of the international slave trade with speeches promoting the first movement abolitionist conviction that slavery and white prejudice could, indeed would, be overcome by the long but sure march of antislavery progress. This sense of momentum came in spite of setbacks. By the second decade of the nineteenth century, state-level emancipation had begun to stall, slaveholders dominated the federal government, and racial proscriptions hindering northern free black life were on the uptick. But in their speeches turned pamphlets, black activists of New York and Philadelphia projected a more expansive perspective. In tracing the long-term trajectory of black improvement and uplift, their narratives typified the persistent optimism so critical to first movement abolitionist activism.

Congress outlawed the international slave trade in 1808, following the British Parliament's lead in banning the traffic a year earlier. Antislavery activists on both sides of the Atlantic considered the legal cessation of the slave trade a monumental achievement that would lead irrevocably to the disintegration of institutional slavery. The ban garnered a bevy of communal gatherings held by black northerners in celebration of what they marked as an auspicious day for African American freedom. In New York and Philadelphia, African American activists delivered yearly orations that laid out a narrative of their enslavement and transition to freedom, fostered a free black identity, and proffered a formula for clinching the complete abolition of slavery. Subsequently printed for public consumption, the orations had two audiences: the black gatherers for whom the orators outlined a progressive history and whom they encouraged to continue making strides in freedom, and the greater reading public, who might take note of the eloquence and abilities of free people of color while perceiving the aptitude of black northerners to sculpt virtuous communities worthy of freedom. The slave trade orations were a uniquely African American "literary genre" and, as such, quickly attained a conventional quality.[45]

Nearly every address began by portraying the abolition of the international slave trade as the conspicuous harbinger of an ever-growing black freedom. Joseph Sidney thought the ban on the Atlantic slave trade a big "stride" in the direction of "the total abolition of slavery in America" and "a progress towards the consummation of our fondest hopes," which forecast that the antislavery movement would "finally triumph!" Adam Carman told his listeners to "rejoice at the event, and never forget the highly favorable and encouraging laws now provided for our welfare." George Lawrence delighted in his confidence that "this heaven born plant [the abolition of the slave trade] shall bring forth the full fruits of emancipation, and divulge that bright genius so long smothered in slavery." Henry Sipkins took the abolition of the slave trade as a sign that this example "will ere long become the unanimous voice of the world." Russell Parrott's effusive-

45. Dickson D. Bruce, Jr., *The Origins of African American Literature, 1680–1865* (Charlottesville, Va., 2001), 106–112 (quotation on 106). My analysis of the abolition of the slave trade orations is based on close readings of all thirteen published speeches delivered in New York and Philadelphia between 1808 and 1815. For extended scholarly coverage of the orations, see Leslie M. Alexander, *African or American? Black Identity and Political Activism in New York City, 1784–1861* (Urbana, Ill., 2008), 17–30; Mitch Kachun, *Festivals of Freedom: Memory and Meaning in African American Emancipation Celebrations, 1808–1915* (Amherst, Mass., 2003), 30–41; David Waldstreicher, *In the Midst of Perpetual Fetes: The Making of American Nationalism, 1776–1820* (Williamsburg, Va., and Chapel Hill, N.C., 1997), 328–330, 342–347; Manisha Sinha, "To 'Cast Just Obliquy' on Oppressors: Black Radicalism in the Age of Revolution," *WMQ*, 3d Ser., LXIV (2007), 149–160; and Sinha, *The Slave's Cause: A History of Abolition* (New Haven, Conn., 2016), 150–152. Alexander sees a split in the addresses between some black orators who advocated racial uplift and incorporation and others who encouraged African nationalism and emigration. Waldstreicher depicts the orations as "black nationalist celebrations" (328) but emphasizes how the orators used the tools of American nationalism for their own inventive nation-making ends. Bruce concludes that Christian providence was the major motif of the addresses. Kachun is interested in the orations mainly for the precedents they set in memory making and freedom festivals for later generations of black activists. Sinha argues that the orators sought to "construct a counternarrative of slavery and freedom to the dominant national story of freedom inaugurated by the American Revolution" (150) and calls the orations "oppositional in content" (152). The abolition of the slave trade orations criticized slavery and racial prejudice that endured in the new Republic. But, in contrast to Sinha, I view the orators as sketching a far more optimistic and progressive portrait in which the speakers emphasized the advancements of people of color and saw these gains as fitting into the larger societal trajectories of both the new United States and the larger Atlantic world. Free black Bostonians also held annual celebrations of the slave trade's abolition where white ministers, rather than African Americans, delivered the orations.

ness knew no national boundaries, couching the slave trade's cessation as the "commencement of that happy era, in which Freedom shall reign to the 'furthest verge of the green earth.'" The orators impressed on their fellow blacks the massive import of the slave trade's abolition and communicated to them the efficacious results it foretold.[46]

After this rosy introduction, the orators invariably narrated a history of African enslavement. They set in diametric opposition a history of European vice and greed-stricken depravity that brought about Atlantic slavery and a primordial African nobility and virtue that had fallen victim to rapacious slave traders. Before Europeans arrived, Africa had been filled with "simplicity, innocence, and contentment," its "blissful regions" and "innocent inhabitants" a product of the "beneficent hand of nature." Being "rich in the enjoyments of liberty and all the glory nature could afford," Africans made their continent a site of "Liberty, Peace and Equality." Then came the Europeans. The "harmless Africans" were "easy prey to European wiles." Initially realizing that Africans possessed rights and liberties "inherent in them," Europeans lost sight of the equal creation of all people and came to view black enslavement as "a matter of right." Slave traders instilled "a spirit of avarice, and love of luxury" in all those they came across, making the once "paradisaical garden" of the African continent "groan from its sea line to its center." The romanticized idea of Africa's Edenic serenity despoiled by calculating Europeans had been invented by white antislavery writers. White activists produced widely circulated tracts condemning the slave trade with which black activists were clearly familiar. And yet black orators would put their own twist on this well-established antislavery literary convention.[47]

46. Sidney, *Oration, Commemorative of the Abolition of the Slave Trade*, 4; Carman, *Oration Delivered at the Fourth Anniversary of the Abolition of the Slave Trade*, 6; Lawrence, *Oration on the Abolition of the Slave Trade*, 6; Henry Sipkins, "Introductory Address," in Williams, *Oration on the Abolition of the Slave Trade*, [10]; Parrott, *Oration on the Abolition of the Slave Trade* (1812), 4.

47. Williams, *Oration on the Abolition of the Slave Trade*, 12; Sipkins, *Oration on the Abolition of the Slave Trade*, 8, 9, 11; Hamilton, *Address to the New-York African Society, for Mutual Relief*, in Porter, ed., *Early Negro Writing*, 35; Lawrence, *Oration on the Abolition of the Slave Trade*, 7–8; Carman, *Oration Delivered on the Fourth Anniversary of the Abolition of the Slave Trade*, 10. For a penetrating look at the rhetorical and ideological links between white and black antislavery discourse in the Revolutionary and early national eras, see Bruce, *The Origins of African American Literature*, 39–143. William Miller and William Hamilton tweaked the portrait of primitive Edenic pre-European contact Africa by connecting Africa to ancient Egypt and insisting that Africans were among the "first learned nation." But they still portrayed European slavers as corrupting Africans and saw the end of the slave trade as rescuing Africa from the degrada-

From the corruption of Africa, black abolitionists asked their audiences to imagine the sheer terror and incommunicable sadness that the transformation from freedom to slavery must have stamped on its "wretched victims." The orators described parents and children, brothers and sisters being separated forever as they were "torn from their native land" and placed on slave-trading vessels. Next, the Middle Passage was colored by the "dejected countenances" of the enslaved and marked by their "streaming eyes" and "fettered limbs." The speakers envisaged the "piercing cries" and "pitiful moans" these poor men and women surely let forth. When they arrived in the Americas, their painful subjugation continued. Treated as mere "vendible article[s]" and "viewed and considered as commercial commodities," the enslaved fell into lives fit for "domestic beasts." Doomed to "the lash, extreme hunger, and incessant hard labour" of plantation life, enslaved people could look forward only to the "emancipating grave" as a final respite from their mortal torture. This deliberately visceral description of enslavement must have resonated particularly strongly with many on hand to celebrate the slave trade's abolition who knew personally the deprivations of chattel bondage. Though free, black activists wove the story of the enslaved into their own existence and empathized with the experiences of those relegated to slavery.[48]

The orators used this dire delineation of African enslavement as an elaborate setup to accentuate the impressive progress of black Americans. Where "sophistry, falsehood, cruelty, and tyranny" had held sway, now, "in these United States, reason, truth, humanity, and freedom, have finally obtained a glorious triumph." Where human bondage had gone on unchecked, now, with the abolition of the slave trade, "the sources of slavery" were "drying away" and the "condition" of African Americans "fast ameliorating." Since the "hydra from which issued all our sufferings, has received its death wound" slave trade oration speakers concluded that the time was close at hand when "the rich fruits of liberty shall be strewed in the paths of every African, or descendant." The northern states were "fast

———

tions brought on by the era of the transatlantic slave trade. See Miller, *A Sermon on the Abolition of the Slave Trade*, 4–5 (quotation on 4); and Hamilton, *An Oration on the Abolition of the Slave Trade, Delivered in the Episcopal Ashbury African Church, in Elizabeth-St., New York, January 2, 1815* (New York, 1815), in Porter, ed., *Early Negro Writing*, 392–399.

48. Hamilton, *Address to the New York African Society, for Mutual Relief,* in Porter, ed., *Early Negro Writing,* 35; Williams, *Oration on the Abolition of the Slave Trade,* 19; Carman, *Oration Delivered on the Fourth Anniversary of the Abolition of the Slave Trade,* 11–13; Johnson, *Oration on the Abolition of the Slave Trade,* 11.

conceding" black liberty, and the southern states "must comply." A Philadelphian orator reminded free persons of color that "our present situation,
contrasted with" what it was before the age of emancipation and the abolition of the slave trade, "presents a picture highly animating to the humane
mind" and averred that, "under the mild influence of the laws of Pennsylvania, *we* are rapidly advancing in every useful improvement." Making clear
that "very different are the days that we see, from those that our ancestors
did," black abolitionists tried to imbue the members of their communities
with a strong sense that the tide of history was on the side of the formerly
oppressed.[49]

For proof that white Americans would eventually come to discern that
all persons of color were eligible for freedom and civic equality, black abolitionists of the mid-Atlantic turned to white antislavery figures and their
abolitionist organizations. Slave trade orators often thanked a pantheon of
antislavery luminaries like Thomas Clarkson, William Wilberforce, John
Woolman, Anthony Benezet, and Benjamin Rush (to name but a few).
These men had "voluntarily stepped forward . . . to restore our natural
rights" and "dared to oppose the strong gales of popular prejudice." In con-
secrating themselves to "the vindication of our rights, and the improvement of our state," they had "laid the foundation of the happiness we now

49. Sidney, *Oration, Commemorative of the Abolition of the Slave Trade*, 5; Hamilton,
Address to the New York African Society, for Mutual Relief, in Porter, ed., *Early Negro
Writing*, 35; Miller, *Sermon on the Abolition of the Slave Trade*, 11; Lawrence, *Oration on
the Abolition of the Slave Trade*, 11–13; Parrott, *Oration on the Abolition of the Slave Trade*
(1812), 9. Whatever white American hypocrisy and failure to live up to Revolutionary republican ideals of liberty and equality that did exist was located in the southern states,
not the northern ones, according to the mid-Atlantic abolition of the slave trade orators.
See Sidney, *Oration, Commemorative of the Abolition of the Slave Trade*, 7. The optimism of this era's black abolitionists might have peaked with the War of 1812. Americans
viewed martial service as the paramount expression of republican devotion to country.
Free black activists saw the coming of war with Britain as a golden opportunity to put
before the white public their republican virtue. In the summer and fall of 1814, "A Citizen of Colour" wrote an open letter to the city's African Americans conveying that "our
patriotism is now put to the test." The writer thought that the war would demonstrate
black New Yorkers' zeal for "exert[ing] ourselves, whenever or wherever our services are
needed, for the protection of our beloved state" (*New-York Evening Post*, Aug. 20, 1814,
[3]). As he gathered black volunteers for the war effort, a Philadelphia African American activist informed whites, "You have secured to yourself a band of citizens . . . whose
bosoms are ready to be bared in your service, and whose blood will cheerfully flow in
your defence" (Russell Parrott, *An Oration on the Abolition of the Slave Trade; Delivered
on the First of January, 1814, at the African Church of St. Thomas* [Philadelphia, 1814],
13). Denied service in the militia, free black volunteers formed companies that built
trenches and fortified the defense of New York City and Philadelphia from British attack.

enjoy." There were also the abolition societies of New York and Pennsylvania, which, "attached to the principles of liberty and the rights of man," not only pushed for emancipation but established free black schools. By circulating antislavery literature, giving antislavery speeches, and petitioning legislatures, the societies were "calculated to awaken sentiments of compassion" for the enslaved. The emergence of organized abolitionism signified that the "day star" of black freedom had now dawned, "dispersing the dark clouds" that had covered African Americans in slavery.[50]

Despite celebrating the many advances of persons of color, the slave trade orators ended their speeches by confronting the one barrier that stood in the way of emancipation: white prejudice. Henry Sipkins was one of several orators who blamed the "strong imbibed opinion of our [black] inferiority" for still "shed[ding] on the mind[s]" of many white Americans "its wizard darkness." Nursed by those whites who "ungenerously denounce us vagrants, indolent and beastly rioters, mere nuisances in society," and buffeted by the "unmerited reproach" of "those perfidious men" who "brand us as an inferior species of human beings," white prejudice presented the "most insuperable difficulties" to finalizing the project of black freedom. Here was where free persons of color who took in these orations could make all the difference. If the newly emancipated would "cling closely to the paths of virtue and morality" and avail themselves of an education, they would "give an effectual blow" to slavery's defenders. Free blacks were standing on the grand stage of abolitionism and had it in their power to act as a powerful antidote to all those whites skeptical of emancipation's feasibility.[51]

50. Williams, *Oration on the Abolition of the Slave Trade*, 11–12, 21, 24; Lawrence, *Oration on the Abolition of the Slave Trade*, 5, 13; Hamilton, *An Address to the New York African Society, for Mutual Relief*, in Porter, ed., *Early Negro Writing*, 39. Characterizing white activists and abolition societies as prime enablers of African American liberty and black emancipation is one of the most pervasive themes in the abolition of the slave trade addresses. See Absalom Jones, *A Thanksgiving Sermon, Preached January 1, 1808, in St. Thomas's, or the African Episcopal, Church, Philadelphia: On Account of the Abolition of the African Slave Trade, on That Day, by the Congress of the United States* (Philadelphia, 1808), 18–19; Sipkins, *Oration on the Abolition of the Slave Trade*, 16–17; Parrott, *Oration on the Abolition of the African Slave Trade* (1812), 7; Parrott, *An Oration on the Abolition of the Slave Trade* (1814), 10; Sidney, *Oration on the Abolition of the Slave Trade*, 6–7, 15–16; Carman, *An Oration, Delivered on the Fourth Anniversary of the Abolition of the Slave Trade*, 19; and Johnson, *Oration on the Abolition of the Slave Trade*, 9.

51. Sipkins, *Oration on the Abolition of the Slave Trade*, 20, 21; Johnson, *Oration on the Abolition of the Slave Trade*, 11; Lawrence, *Oration on the Abolition of the Slave Trade*, 11; Carman, *Oration Delivered at the Fourth Anniversary of the Abolition of the Slave Trade*, 19; Parrott, *Address, on the Abolition of the Slave-Trade* (1816), 10. Although

The orations commemorating the abolition of the slave trade served many purposes. They celebrated an event that black and white abolitionists believed to be of lasting consequence to African American liberty, helped to construct and reinforce a history and identity for free black northerners, broadcast an articulate and competent black leadership class, and rendered an optimistic portrait of the movement to end slavery and racial prejudice. Just as critically, the orations' deliverers asked free black northerners to do their part to move forward the first abolition movement. Black abolitionists of early national New York and Philadelphia believed it was on the relentless strivings of the already emancipated to live up to their equal potential as republican citizens that the objective of shattering white prejudice and demolishing human bondage would either stand or fall.

First movement abolitionism aimed to annihilate American bondage through the simultaneous enlightenment of black and white Americans. While gradual abolition permitted formerly enslaved people to transform themselves into republican citizens, airing their aptitude for virtuous liberty, first movement abolitionists aimed to persuade skeptical white Americans to endorse black freedom and incorporation. In many ways, this was an audacious plan of reform. Undertaking to change the image of a people

---

these orations have sometimes been interpreted by historians as early enunciations of black nationalism, scrutinizing the abolition of the slave trade addresses shows us that African and American identity were not mutually exclusive for black New Yorkers and Philadelphians of the early national era. Black orators, in their creative usage of the traditional antislavery rhetoric of Africa's original virtue, characterized Africa as a site of black righteousness that persons of color needed to recapture as they made the switch from slavery to virtuous citizenship. Just as Africans found relief from the privations of the slave trade and were able to reembrace their pure, idyllic past—"the clouds which have hovered with destruction over Africa" giving way to "the most brilliant rays of future prosperity"—so, too, would black Americans—"emerging from the depths of forlorn slavery"—reconnect with their prior African glory and natural morality. Although the slave trade orators unambiguously identified with Africa and its people, this black antislavery discourse looked decidedly to the American Republic, not to Africa, as the final destination of the newly emancipated. In this way the slave trade orators were not proto-black nationalists. Nor at this juncture did they think relocating to Africa would answer the problem of American slavery. See Williams, *Oration on the Abolition of the Slave Trade*, 19; and Sipkins, *Oration on the Abolition of the Slave Trade*, 20. On the slave trade orations as expressions of a black nationalist identity, see Alexander, *African or American?* 17–30. For a succinct and trenchant critique of applying the framework of black nationalism to African American abolitionist activism in the early Republic and antebellum periods, see Patrick Rael, "Free Black Activism in the Antebellum North," *History Teacher*, XXXIX (2006), 215–253.

210]   "A WELL GROUNDED HOPE"

who for hundreds of years had been viewed by greater white society as little more than private property and convincing prejudiced white Americans that emancipated blacks could be anything more than depraved vassals upon gaining their freedom was no easy mission. A white public who had for centuries conjoined blackness with enslavement and linked people of color with vulgar, base, and benighted attributes would not easily take to being reshaped by the antislavery ideals of first movement abolitionists. The progressive philosophy of societal environmentalism and the winning of emancipation and antislavery laws, both at home and abroad, helped reassure first movement abolitionists that their hopes were reasonable. An integral indicator that their reform vision had merit also came from African Americans themselves. As a substantial free black populace emerged in post-Revolutionary New York and Philadelphia, black activists looked to form virtuous communities that could answer the public's doubts about abolition.

Ultimately, free black abolitionists and the abolition societies were too optimistic in thinking that creating virtuous communities of color and waging an intensive campaign to counter white prejudice could break apart American slavery. Penning antislavery tracts, planting abolitionist opinion in the nation's newspapers, and publishing slave trade orations could not put a dent in the economic imperatives that drove slavery's expansion and made slaveholding more monetarily alluring than ever before. Furthermore, for every virtuous free black displaying republican citizenship, many whites pointed to others among the emancipated who, they claimed, failed to live up to the benchmarks of civic propriety. As cities grew and industry developed, class distinctions became more visible among blacks. African American abolitionists and the abolition societies bemoaned that many whites dismissed free black accomplishments by condemning people of color among the growing population of poor urbanites. Facing a number of new challenges, first movement abolitionists would discover their antislavery optimism thrown into doubt. By the second decade of the nineteenth century it was the seeming staying power of white prejudice and the resilience of slavery that confronted antislavery activists of all stripes.

CHAPTER 5

"Unconquerable Prejudice" and "Alien Enemies"

The Roots and Rise of the American Colonization Society

When the New York pastor William McMurray took to his pulpit to preach against human bondage in the summer of 1825, he made what at first sounded like standard antislavery arguments. No matter a bondsperson's "complexion or his country," McMurray declared, the enslaved possessed "natural sensibilities" alike with all other people. Chastising the American Republic for contradicting its founding creed, the *"self-evident truth, that all men are born equal,"* he predicted that the abolition of slavery would place "the brightest gem in the crown of a nation's glory."[1]

McMurray's plan for effecting emancipation, however, departed greatly from that of first movement abolitionists. Gradual emancipation in the mid-Atlantic had been, according to McMurray, an utter failure. Free persons of color were "contemned and despised" because of the "indelible mark" of blackness. Relegated to "vice and poverty" by the "insuperable barrier to advancement" of white prejudice, emancipated blacks became "the pests of the neighbourhoods in which they reside," constituting serious threats to public safety. The permanency of black degradation made emancipation in the South, where a much larger population of people of color lived, a daunting and dangerous prospect. Fortunately, McMurray assured his listeners, there was a solution. The American Colonization Society (ACS) wisely advocated for black removal. Through the colonization of black Americans in Africa, not only would white Americans be able to "get rid of our black population" and thus make emancipation safe and palatable, but also those of African descent could reach a level of "equality" in

1. William McMurray, *A Sermon Preached in Behalf of the American Colonization Society, in the Reformed Dutch Church, in Market-Street, New York, July, 10, 1825* (New York, 1825), 13–14, 17.

their ancestral homeland that they could never achieve within the United States.[2]

McMurray's speech, sponsored by the ACS, represented a sweeping shift from the reform program of the first abolition movement. For first movement abolitionists, slavery created a corrupted societal environment that degraded blacks and blinded whites to the inherent equality of African Americans. The abolition societies and their black allies believed that, if persons of color could achieve virtuous citizenship through moral and educational uplift, white prejudice would be overcome and the barriers to African American equality and the justifications for human bondage would simultaneously shatter. According to colonzationists, however, the problem facing antislavery advocates was race, not slavery. As colonizationists saw it, an unalterable racial divide between white and black Americans created a fixed societal environment of black inferiority in which prejudice was unconquerable. The reality of an unchangeable white prejudice made freedom a mockery in the North and an impossibility in the South as long as African Americans remained within the nation's borders. Colonizationists turned their backs on the reformers who came before them by arguing that slavery could not be abolished through black incorporation. Unless those of African descent were removed from American society, colonizationists insisted, emancipation constituted a delusional hope.

THE PROVENANCE OF COLONIZATIONIST THOUGHT
In the fall of 1796, the Pennsylvania Abolition Society (PAS) learned of a detailed proposal by the jurist St. George Tucker for the gradual abolition of slavery in his state of Virginia that had been published in Philadelphia earlier that year by the printer Mathew Carey. Perhaps heartened that a prominent southerner had taken a very public stance in favor of emancipation, the PAS asked its Committee of Correspondence—a group of society members responsible for the distribution of antislavery literature—to consider printing additional copies of Tucker's pamphlet for wider circulation. But, at the PAS's next full meeting, the Committee of Correspondence, after having closely perused Tucker's plan, deemed the pamphlet not of a "nature" fit for promotion by the society. Why had the PAS rejected an opportunity to seemingly further its agenda—one based on the idea of antislavery progress and enlightenment? Answering this question reveals the pivotal distinctions between first movement abolitionist proponents of

2. Ibid., 18–19.

black incorporation and antislavery advocates of black removal. PAS members had rightly concluded that Tucker, in arguing that white prejudice was insurmountable and that free blacks must be prohibited from the rights of citizenship, possessed a version of African American freedom at diametrical odds with their own.[3]

Tucker's emancipation plan was a product of the tail end of a historical moment in the late-eighteenth-century upper South that generated a particular brand of antislavery. By the Revolutionary era, Maryland and Virginia had begun to move away from the cultivation of tobacco and increasingly focused on a mixed agricultural regime less conducive to enslaved labor. At the same time, Revolutionary rhetoric of liberty swept the American colonies, and thousands of the region's enslaved people brought about their own freedom, fleeing with the British army during the War of Independence. Meanwhile, some prominent white Revolutionaries from the upper South acknowledged the awkward ideological position of proclaiming universal liberty for all people while holding many in bondage. This antislavery potential yielded tangible results. The region's surplus of enslaved laborers made its political leaders amenable to anti–slave trade measures, and state legislatures enacted laws that limited or banned the importation of enslaved blacks into the region. The passage of voluntary manumission measures also allowed individual slaveholders to act on Revolutionary antislavery principles, economic self-interest, or both in freeing their bondspersons, with enslaved persons themselves often initiating this process by pressing for freedom. Between 1782, when Virginia enacted a voluntary manumission law, and 1806, when the law was effectively repealed, as many as ten thousand enslaved blacks gained their liberty, and free black communities sprouted up in the state. The Maryland state legislature allowed debate on a gradual emancipation bill in 1789 and permitted manumission by will beginning in 1790. Time would ultimately prove these developments specious. Beginning in the last decade of the eighteenth century, a conservative reaction set in, including laws prohibiting free blacks from entering upper southern states and mandating that people of color leave their states of residence upon being liberated. Additionally, the fledgling interstate slave trade gave new life to the region's slave market. Yet, from the 1770s through the 1790s, a handful of the upper South's Revolutionary gentry questioned slavery.[4]

3. Papers of the Pennsylvania Abolition Society (PPAS), Series 1, reel 1, I, 267–268, Historical Society of Pennsylvania (HSP), Philadelphia.

4. Ira Berlin, *Many Thousands Gone: The First Two Centuries of Slavery in North*

Within this late-eighteenth-century time frame, two of Virginia's political vanguard, Thomas Jefferson and St. George Tucker, one writing at the
beginning of this period and the other at its end, elucidated a vision of
black freedom and white prejudice that would serve as a seminal source for
the ACS's recipe of reform. But, despite fundamental differences between
first movement abolitionists and progenitors of colonizationist thought
like Jefferson and Tucker (discussed below), one must acknowledge certain
antislavery assumptions that they shared. The PAS might have considered
printing Tucker's pamphlet in the first place because it emerged from a
genre of writing in accordance with many aspects of prevailing antislavery
thought. Jefferson and Tucker identified a startling gap between Americans' avowed devotion to liberty and the pervasiveness of chattel bondage. In 1786, Jefferson, though he held many people in slavery, wrote that
he thought it "incomprehensible" that an American slaveholder could "inflict on his fellow men a bondage, one hour of which is fraught with more
misery than ages of that which he rose in rebellion to oppose." A decade
later, Tucker presented slavery as a problem in an American society remade
by the Revolution. A Bermuda-born slaveholder, Tucker nevertheless proclaimed the "incompatability of a state of slavery with the principles of our
government, and of that revolution upon which it is founded." He thought
it not a little bit hypocritical that, "whilst we were offering up vows at the
shrine of Liberty," Virginia's bondspersons were subject to "a *slavery,* ten
thousand times more cruel." Nor did Tucker view the problem of slavery as
one that could be simply noted as inconsistent with independent America's
founding values. The effort to end slavery was a "cause . . . in which all
hearts should be united, every nerve strained, and every power exerted."

America (Cambridge, Mass., 1998), 256–290; Cassandra Pybus, *Epic Journeys of Freedom: Runaway Slaves of the American Revolution and Their Global Quest for Liberty*
(Boston, 2006), 3–72; Eva Sheppard Wolf, *Race and Liberty in the New Nation: Emancipation in Virginia from the Revolution to Nat Turner's Rebellion* (Baton Rouge, La.,
2006), 39–84; Winthrop D. Jordan, *White over Black: American Attitudes toward the
Negro, 1550–1812* (Williamsburg, Va., and Chapel Hill, N.C., 1968), 346. Wolf argues that
the bulk of manumissions in post-Revolutionary and early national Virginia came from
motives unrelated to Revolutionary ideology, such as the "loyal behavior" of enslaved
people, and "reinforced rather than challenged" the institution of slavery (Wolf, *Race
and Liberty in the New Nation,* 44). For the barriers to abolitionism and the backlash
against manumission and growing black freedom in the upper South, see T. Stephen
Whitman, *Challenging Slavery in the Chesapeake: Black and White Resistance to
Human Bondage, 1775–1865* (Baltimore, 2007), 45–72; Ira Berlin, *Slaves without Masters: The Free Negro in the Antebellum South* (New York, 1974), 79–107; and Wolf, *Race
and Liberty in the New Nation,* 109–129.

To comport the new nation's principles with its actions, Americans had to commit themselves to solving the problem of slavery.[5]

Like the abolition societies, Tucker emphasized equality as the guiding ideal of post-Revolutionary America and blamed the unenlightened colonial past for perverting this principle through the practice of chattel bondage. He quoted the Virginia Declaration of Rights, "'That *all men* are by nature *equally free* and *independent,*'" adding italics to underscore the universality of these maxims. The artificial institution of slavery had worked to "degrade" people of color "below the rank of human beings, not only politically, but also physically and morally," accustoming white Virginians to such a noxious violation of the equality of men. The result was a "partial system of morality which confines rights and injuries, to particular complexions." Yet Tucker believed the time had come to "learn to regard them [people of African descent] as our fellow men, and equals." Tucker would go on to explain why he believed formerly enslaved people could not be incorporated as equal citizens into Virginian society. Still, he shared the belief of abolitionists that nature had endowed all with a baseline equality and that this fact demanded that human bondage be addressed.[6]

Although he would deny that people of color could raise their status in freedom, Jefferson, akin to abolitionists, recognized that the environment of slavery negatively affected whites and blacks who lived in slaveholding societies. Slaveholding, Jefferson wrote during the Revolutionary War, brought "the most unremitting despotism on the one part, and degrading submission on the other." Imbibing the evils of slavery from their earliest days, white Virginians had been "nursed, educated, and daily exercised in tyranny," leaving them to "trample on the rights of the other." Slaveholding whites had become "stamped" by slavery's "odious peculiarities" and had come to conceive of enslaved people "as legitimate subjects of property as their horses and cattle," even though "that degradation was very much the work of *themselves and their fathers.*" Jefferson is, for good

5. Thomas Jeffersson to Jean Nicolas Dimeunier, June 26, 1786, in Julian P. Boyd et al., eds., *The Papers of Thomas Jefferson*, X, *22 June to 31 December 1786* (Princeton, N.J., 1954), 63, in Ari Helo and Peter Onuf, "Jefferson, Morality, and the Problem of Slavery," *William and Mary Quarterly*, 3d Ser., LX (2003), 609; St. George Tucker, *A Dissertation on Slavery: With a Proposal for the Gradual Abolition of It, in the State of Virginia* (Philadelphia, 1796), 10–11, 30. For background on the life, family, and experiences of St. George Tucker leading up to his embrace of antislavery, see Phillip Hamilton, *The Making and Unmaking of a Revolutionary Family: The Tuckers of Virginia, 1752–1830* (Charlottesville, Va., 2008), 8–70.

6. Tucker, *Dissertation on Slavery*, 10, 30, 50–51.

reason, better known for dismissing the explanation of societal environmentalism for black inequality. But he had little doubt that the environment of slavery damaged the morals and behavior of all involved with the
institution. Both strict adherents of enlightenment philosophy, Tucker and
Jefferson lamented slavery as having taken root in an ignorant age, talked
up the ideal of natural equality, and recognized slaveholding as a deleterious practice discordant with enlightened social mores.[7]

If the writings of Jefferson and Tucker demonstrate how Revolutionary and enlightenment-based ideology informed antislavery throughout
early America, they also show how these same underlying values could
lead in very different directions when it came to developing specific plans
to deal with the problem of slavery. Analyzing Tucker's and Jefferson's
proposed solutions to slavery highlight the strategic gulf separating first
movement abolitionist ideals of black improvement and incorporation to
abolish American bondage, on the one hand, from concepts of racial exclusion and black removal as a means of ending slavery, on the other. In
his *Notes on the State of Virginia*, published in America in 1787, Jefferson
gave a notorious explanation for black inferiority. Jefferson's denigration of

7. Thomas Jefferson, *Notes on the State of Virginia*, ed. William Peden (Williamsburg, Va., and Chapel Hill, N.C., 1982), 162; Jefferson to Edward Coles, Aug. 25, 1814,
in Merrill D. Peterson, ed., *Thomas Jefferson; Writings: Autobiography; A Summary
View of the Rights of British America; Notes on the State of Virginia; Public Papers;
Addresses, Messages, and Replies; Miscellany; Letters* (New York, 1984), 1344, in Helo
and Onuf, "Jefferson, Morality, and the Problem of Slavery," *WMQ*, 3d Ser., LX (2003),
587. Jefferson possessed an idea of moral progress that depicted societal moral codes
as capable of being gradually refined and progressively improved. Yet this improvement
had to take place within particular civic communities. Progressive change, like the abolition of slavery, according to Jefferson, could happen only organically from the altered
attitudes of a broader enlightened public—a development in the case of white Virginian
ideas about slavery that he believed would take place glacially. This conception of moral
progress mirrored first movement abolitionist ideas of enlightened, progressive reform,
but, unlike with the abolition societies and their black partners, it contributed to Jefferson's inaction on taking public antislavery stands. Jefferson repeatedly argued that the
white Virginia public was not ready to contemplate emancipation even as Jefferson himself on several occasions declined to help influence this public in an antislavery direction. On the always ambivalent and often complex ways the Revolutionary- and early
national–era Virginia gentry addressed slavery, see Robert McColley, *Slavery and Jeffersonian Virginia* (Urbana, Ill., 1964); Duncan J. MacLeod, *Slavery, Race, and the American Revolution* (London, 1974); Wolf, *Race and Liberty in the New Nation;* Alan Taylor,
The Internal Enemy: Slavery and War in Virginia, 1772-1832 (New York, 2013); and
Melvin Patrick Ely, "Richard and Judith Randolph, St. George Tucker, George Wythe,
Syphax Brown, and Hercules White: Racial Equality and the Snares of Prejudice," in
Alfred F. Young, Gary B. Nash, and Ray Raphael, eds., *Revolutionary Founders: Rebels,
Radicals, and Reformers in the Making of the Nation* (New York, 2011), 323–336.

African Americans, however, was primarily a rationalization for abolition based on colonization, not the product of abstract racist musing. Jefferson registered his support for a bill of emancipation that he claimed to have co-authored but never presented to the state legislature. The bill would have freed all enslaved people born after the passage of the act gradually, males at twenty-one and females at eighteen, and provided the emancipated with agricultural and educational training that could equip them for life as free persons. Unlike the gradual abolition laws of the mid-Atlantic, however, the bill Jefferson referred to would have required the colonization of those liberated upon gaining their freedom, though to where they would be colonized he did not specify.[8]

Jefferson's rationalization for colonization was based on what he viewed as the immutable and irreducible differences between white and black persons. As historian Peter Onuf has delineated, Jefferson conceived of people of African descent as a distinct nation with a fundamentally different nature from that of white Americans. Viewed in this light, Jefferson's infamous disquisition on what he saw as the natural and perpetual inferiority of persons of African descent can be seen not only as one of the earliest American enunciations of an antiblack racial pseudoscience but also, more immediately, the product of a particular vision of antislavery. Jefferson was less concerned with defaming persons of color than he was determined to prove whites and blacks were unalterably separate sets of people. Referencing the version of emancipation held by the mid-Atlantic abolition societies, Jefferson asked rhetorically, "Why not retain and incorporate the blacks into the state?" While abolitionists argued that American rights and liberties should be extended "without distinction of colour," in Jefferson's estimation the "real distinctions which nature has made" rendered a plan of abolition joined with black incorporation as unthinkable as it was unfeasible.[9]

8. Jefferson, *Notes on the State of Virginia*, ed. Peden, 137–138. The bill titled "Concerning Slaves" did not include an emancipation clause, though Jefferson maintained that it was added in an amendment. Although it is unclear what role, if any, Jefferson played in drafting the bill, we do know that in his capacity as chairman of the committee to revise Virginia's laws he refused to put any abolitionist legislation before the state legislature. Ultimately, Jefferson's antislavery rhetoric does not match his public record or his private actions. See Paul Finkelman, *Slavery and the Founders: Race and Liberty in the Age of Jefferson* (Armonk, N.Y., 1996), 118–120, 153–156.

9. Jefferson, *Notes on the State of Virginia*, ed. Peden, 138–139; Charlene Bangs Bickford, Kenneth R. Bowling, and William Charles diGiacomantonio, *Documentary History of the First Federal Congress of the United States of America, March 4, 1789–March 3, 1791*, VIII, *Petition Histories and Nonlegislative Official Documents* (Baltimore, 1998),

And what were these "real distinctions"? First, Jefferson took note of what he saw as the "physical distinctions," including the "colour, figure, and hair" and the "disagreeable odour" of blacks, these features standing in an inferior position to those of their aesthetically preferable white counterparts. Jefferson described blacks as "dull" and "tasteless" with "reason much inferior" to whites. Although they had vivid powers of sensation—especially when it came to sexual pursuits—those of African descent lacked the higher powers of reflection. Even one of the few compliments Jefferson gave to African Americans was an insult in disguise. He conceded that blacks were "at least as brave, and more adventuresome" than whites but explained these traits as the result of "a want of forethought." To the master of Monticello, a veritable ocean of differences separated black from white and made evident the folly of efforts to allow for these two groups of people to live free and equal side by side.[10]

Jefferson countered societal environmentalist arguments that black inequality was the product of the condition of slavery rather than the character of the enslaved. He pointed to the artistic and philosophical accomplishments of enslaved Romans and attributed them to their being "of the race of whites." Meanwhile, at best freedom to enslaved blacks in America had produced the poet Phillis Wheatley, whose work Jefferson contemptuously dismissed as being "below the dignity of criticism." Jefferson rejected the most fundamental tenet of abolitionists when he insisted that persons of color be judged "on the same stage with the whites," ignoring their argument that bondage denied the enslaved entrance onto that very stage and created an artificial inequality that Jefferson saw as natural.[11]

A long-standing antagonism pitting black against white was central to Jefferson's advocacy for colonization. If nature had made blacks fundamentally different from whites, slavery had made them white Americans' natural enemies. The very same environment of slavery that Jeffer-

326. On Jefferson's conception of enslaved blacks as a distinct and separate nation within the American nation of free whites, see Peter S. Onuf, *Jefferson's Empire: The Language of American Nationhood* (Charlottesville, Va., 2000), 147–188. Jefferson's famous qualifying reservation of his theories of black inferiority in *Notes* as a "suspicion only" (143) are really beside the point if one views his long descriptions of natural black difference as primarily a means of justifying colonization based on black-white incompatibility, rather than solely as an exercise in pseudoscientific racial speculation.

10. Jefferson, *Notes on the State of Virginia*, ed. Peden, 138–139.

11. Ibid., 138–142. In one specific instance, Jefferson did seem to acknowledge the role of the social environment in explaining his allegations of black inferiority. The "disposition to theft" among persons of color, he wrote, had to be "ascribed to their situation, and not to any depravity of the moral sense" (142).

son blamed for turning white Virginians into tyrants transformed blacks "into enemies" of the state. He imagined that "ten thousand recollections, by the blacks, of the injuries they have sustained" in slavery meant that the formerly enslaved and whites could never inhabit the same republic. He feared that "a revolution of the wheel of fortune" could bring about the successful uprising of vengeful enslaved people upon the white populace, and he could only hope that emancipation would proceed from "the consent of the masters, rather than by their extirpation." Jefferson was haunted by the specter of race war. Slavery acted as a lid sealing the inevitable warring antagonism between white and black in any form of emancipation without black repatriation. Only colonization could relieve white society of slavery safely and at the same time "declare" persons of color "a free and independant people" in a colony, and perhaps eventually a nation, of their own. Jefferson's emphasis on the permanence of black degradation within greater white society and his stress on the incompatibility of white with black foreshadowed two of the basic principles of the ACS's ideology nearly three decades before the society's founding.[12]

St. George Tucker, in his plan for gradual abolition submitted to the Virginia legislature in 1796, stressed more than Jefferson the almighty power white prejudice played in precluding emancipation without black removal. Jefferson coupled claims of black inferiority with the "Deep rooted prejudices" of whites that he believed closed off any chance of abolition absent colonization. These prejudices embodied a logical outgrowth of the alleged racial differences Jefferson went to great pains to demonstrate. Yet, for Jefferson, the determining factor mandating colonization was the unshakable division between enslaved blacks and free whites. For Tucker, white prejudice, above any alleged difference in the natures of white and black people, blocked the incorporation of emancipated people of color into civil society.[13]

The dilemma of white prejudice confronting any plan of emancipation in Virginia, according to Tucker, was grounded in demographics. In a letter to the Massachusetts clergyman Jeremy Belknap, Tucker explained that antislavery advocates in Virginia faced an imposingly large black population. Tucker used census data, which included both enslaved and free blacks, to calculate that the ratio of black to white in Virginia was two persons of color for every three whites. But, considering the tidewater region alone, where both Tucker and the largest concentration of enslaved persons

12. Ibid., 138, 163.
13. Ibid., 138.

resided, blacks outnumbered whites. In a refrain that would be repeated by later advocates of colonization, Tucker argued that the model of emancipation in the northern states, where far fewer people of African descent lived, could not apply to large slave states like Virginia. Instead, Tucker saw in Virginia's predicament the specter of Saint Domingue. Tucker shared with Jefferson a belief in the antagonism of white and black Virginians and a fear of race war, gesturing to the "possibility that they [enslaved people] may one day be roused to an attempt to shake off their chains" and "generate a civil war" that would result in "the extermination of one party or the other." But, writing after revolution and war had engulfed Saint Domingue, Tucker could turn to a tangible example to illustrate these fears. He worried that the "calamities which have lately spread like a contagion through the West Indian Islands" might overtake Virginia. That the French National Convention had abolished slavery and given citizenship rights to people of color in one fell swoop provided a "solemn warning to us" of the consequences were the Old Dominion to institute a similar policy.[14]

Unlike Jefferson, Tucker equivocated on the question of whether people of African descent were naturally inferior to whites. But claims of inherent black inferiority were beside the point. For Tucker, the real barrier to emancipation in Virginia was the racial prejudice of the white public— a prejudice so strong that white Virginians would never countenance a large population of free and enfranchised people of color living among them. And on the topic of white prejudice Tucker departed as starkly from first movement abolitionists as Jefferson did on the inherent capacity of blacks for equal freedom. As Tucker saw it, racial prejudices had "taken such deep root in our [white Virginians'] minds" that it was "impossible to eradicate" them. According to Tucker, however much white prejudice contradicted the values of natural equality and the principles of the American Revolution, and putting aside the debatable assumptions about the nature of blacks upon which white prejudice rested, white Virginians could not accept the idea of a considerable number of free blacks as incorporated members of the body politic.[15]

14. St. George Tucker to Jeremy Belknap, June 29, 1795, in "Queries Relating to Slavery in Massachusetts," Massachusetts Historical Society, *Collections*, 5th Ser., III (Boston, 1877), 405–406, 408; Tucker, *Dissertation on Slavery*, 41.

15. Tucker, *Dissertation on Slavery*, 89. Tucker excerpted from Jefferson's *Notes* at length to substantiate that blacks and whites could never live together in a society free from slavery, and he included Jefferson's arguments for the innate inferiority of people of African descent. Yet Tucker also added a note stating that slaveholders themselves were far from unbiased judges of the inherent capacity of blacks and called the arguments of

Whereas first movement abolitionists talked of dispelling the mists of prejudice and tearing down the cobwebs that prejudice put in the minds of whites, Tucker wrote of "almost innate, prejudices" and advised against "an attempt to smother those prejudices which have been cherished for a period of almost two centuries." Tucker argued that manumitted blacks in Virginia were sentenced by the tribunal of public opinion to a life of "civil inferiority." Since blacks were degraded perhaps beyond repair by immovable prejudice, abolition would "turn loose a numerous, starving, and enraged banditti" on whites unless Virginians implemented an alternative emancipation plan to that of states such as Pennsylvania.[16]

Tucker did not believe it was realistic to mandate the colonization of all emancipated individuals. But rather than try to "obliterate those prejudices, which now form an obstacle" to free black incorporation, Tucker proposed to encourage them. He called for free persons of color to be legally stripped of all political, property, and judicial rights, entailing on them a kind of *"civil* slavery" that would, Tucker euphemistically added, "render it their inclination" to leave Virginia on their own accord. Tucker admitted that his proposal, walking a tightrope between voluntary and involuntary black removal, "favour[s] strongly of prejudice." He confessed that anyone who put forth an abolition plan had to either "encounter, or accommodate himself to prejudice." Tucker "preferred the latter" of these two choices. After all, asked Tucker, "if prejudices have taken such deep root in our minds, as to render it impossible to eradicate ... ought not so general an error, if it be one, to be respected?" Tucker did not foreclose the possibility that in "time" white prejudice might be overcome—though, from the perspective of first movement abolitionism, there is a deep irony that he held out hope for black incorporation only after civil and civic restrictions that reinforced racial prejudice were put on free blacks. At its core, Tucker's plan for emancipation was ultimately premised on accommodating rather than combating white prejudice.[17]

James Beattie, who attacked David Hume's claims of natural black inferiority, "powerful" (89). At the same time, Tucker did nod to assertions of natural difference between whites and blacks. See Tucker to Belknap, June 29, 1795, in "Queries Relating to Slavery in Massachusetts," MHS, *Colls.*, III (1877), 408; and Tucker, *Dissertation on Slavery*, 89, 91.

16. Tucker to Belknap, June 29, 1795, in "Queries Relating to Slavery in Massachusetts," MHS, *Colls.*, 5th Ser., III (1877), 406; Tucker, *Dissertation on Slavery*, 76, 88–90. Even as Tucker pointed to white prejudice as the biggest barrier to emancipation in Virginia, he also acknowledged the sanctity of property rights and insisted that "just compensation," by way of a very gradual abolition, had to be included in any viable emancipation plan (81).

17. Tucker, *Dissertation on Slavery*, 75–76, 88–96. Tucker found colonization demo-

Though different in approach, Jefferson's and Tucker's plans both proposed mandatory emancipation. Ferdinando Fairfax, a third Virginian
planter and cofounder of the ACS, drew up a voluntary gradual manumission plan in 1790. Fairfax couched large-scale voluntary manumission
as a middle ground between the natural rights to freedom arguments of
slavery's opponents and the natural rights to property arguments of the
institution's defenders. He thought that manumitted blacks had to be removed from Virginia because of prejudices that "operate so powerfully as to
be insurmountable." Persons of African descent formed a "separate interest" from whites that made their freedom dangerous without free black expatriation. In Fairfax's judgment, the establishment of a free black colony
in Africa would safeguard white Virginians from those liberated and entice
slaveholders to manumit their bondspersons. Looking to reconcile Revolutionary ideals that caused them to question slavery with their belief in the
menace of free black incorporation, Jefferson, Tucker, and Fairfax turned
to the removal of freedpersons as the answer.[18]

None of their plans came to fruition. Tucker's proposal for gradual abolition, purposefully sensitive to the concerns of slaveholding Virginians
and the white public, was roundly rejected by the state legislature, which
refused to even entertain the possibility of emancipation legislation. The
continuing economic relevance of chattel bondage in the upper South and
trepidation among whites over what to do with formerly enslaved people
doomed any concrete blueprints for ending slavery in post-Revolutionary

---

graphically impractical and prohibitively expensive, writing that "surely he [Jefferson]
could not have weighed the difficulties and expence of an attempt to colonize 300,000
persons." See Tucker to Belknap, June 29, 1795, in "Queries Relating to Slavery in Massachusetts," MHS, *Colls.*, 5th Ser., III (1877), 407. Colonization aside, other logistics in
Tucker's plan for emancipation were similar to the one Jefferson referred to in *Notes*,
with the notable exception that Tucker's proposal would have kept in slavery the first
generation of enslaved males born after the act's passage. See Tucker, *Dissertation on
Slavery*, 91–94.

18. Ferdinando Fairfax, "Plan for Liberating the Negroes within the United States,"
American Museum, or, Universal Magazine (Philadelphia), VIII, no. 6 (December 1790),
285–287. Along with Jefferson and Fairfax, James Madison also supported colonization
as the only potential means of instituting a viable abolition plan, explaining his support in terms that likewise singled out white prejudice as a major barrier to any form of
emancipation that did not include black removal. Madison wrote that "the prejudices of
the Whites ... proceeding principally from the difference of colour must be considered as
permanent and insuperable." See James Madison, "Memorandum on an African Colony
for Freed Slaves," [circa Oct. 20, 1789], in Charles F. Hobson et al., eds., *The Papers of
James Madison*, Congressional Series, XII, *2 March 1789–20 January 1790, with a Supplement, 24 October 1775–24 January 1789* (Charlottesville, Va., 1979), 437–438.

Virginia. Moreover, leading Virginian politicians were heavily invested in the institution. Though Tucker's reservations about slavery were sincere, just days after the Virginia legislature rejected his plan he arranged for the sale of one of his enslaved laborers and her two children, capturing his, and that of the handful of other Old Dominion planters who wrote against human bondage, ambivalent relationship to slavery.[19]

While propositions for black removal and emancipation inspired by the Revolutionary era fell far short of becoming law, by the early nineteenth century white Virginia's concern over the presence of free blacks reached new heights. In the summer of 1800, Gabriel, a literate enslaved artisan, recruited a host of other enslaved and free blacks in a plan to march on the state capital of Richmond. Gabriel was inspired by a mix of American Revolutionary ideology, the revolution in Saint Domingue, and the democratic ideals of Jeffersonian Republican working-class partisans. He wanted black and white laborers to unite against elite Federalist merchants. Yet Gabriel also made clear that his aim was to free both himself and his fellow bondsmen. That he intended to march his rebels under a banner reading "death or Liberty" told the mass of white Virginians all they needed to know. Although Gabriel's plot was delayed in late August by rain and was subsequently foiled, the uncovering of a planned massive slave revolt shook white Virginians.[20]

19. Taylor, *The Internal Enemy*, 107. Though most prominent Virginians who considered abolition plans supported some form of black removal, their version of antislavery was not the only one in the state. Robert Pleasants, a Quaker activist and founder of the Virginia Abolition Society, opposed colonization, calling instead for those blacks who would be gradually liberated to gain "all the previlidges of other Citizens" over time. Yet the political lobbying of the Virginia Abolition Society and Robert Pleasants was met with even more dismissal by the state legislature than Tucker's efforts. See Nicholas Perry Wood, "Considerations of Humanity and Expediency: The Slave Trades and African Colonization in the Early National Antislavery Movement" (Ph.D. diss., University of Virginia, 2013), 56–58 (quotation on 56).

20. On Gabriel's Rebellion, see Douglas R. Egerton, *Gabriel's Rebellion: The Virginia Slave Conspiracies of 1800 and 1802* (Chapel Hill, N.C., 1993); James Sidbury, *Ploughshares into Swords: Race, Rebellion, and Identity in Gabriel's Virginia, 1730–1810* (Cambridge, 1997); and Michael L. Nicholls, *Whispers of Rebellion: Narrating Gabriel's Conspiracy* (Charlottesville, Va., 2012). Historians have interpreted Gabriel's Rebellion quite differently. Egerton argues that Gabriel was driven by political motives, identified with artisanal republican values, and sought to upend the socioeconomic power of white merchants—viewing those whites in particular, and not all white Virginians, as the targets of his plot. Sidbury stresses the religious motivations of Gabriel and his co-conspirators. Unlike Egerton, Nicholls depicts Gabriel's plot, not as a political or ideological one that linked black and white artisans, but the result of enslaved and free blacks looking to strike at the institution of slavery. Regardless of how Gabriel's Rebel-

The events of the summer of 1800 brought renewed attention to discussions of emancipation. George Tucker, a younger cousin of St. George Tucker, submitted a letter to a member of Virginia's Assembly soon after the preemption of Gabriel's uprising. In contrast to his older cousin, and especially Thomas Jefferson, Tucker played up what he saw as the same basic nature of black and white Virginians. Tucker interpreted Gabriel's plot as having displayed that, in "this vast march of the mind," black Virginians, although "far behind us [free whites]," were "likely to advance much faster." Sounding like an abolitionist, Tucker wrote that the exposure of black Virginians to the ideals of "natural rights" and their proximity to urban centers of learned exchange "tend a thousand ways to enlighten and inform them," in turn sparking their "love of freedom," which was an "inborn sentiment" of all humankind.[21]

Yet, whereas abolitionists saw black progress as a reason to celebrate, Tucker greeted this same development with dread. The problem was that integrating formerly enslaved people, whom Tucker referred to as "such discordant materials," into free Virginian society represented an "impossibility." Even the improved civil state of people of color could not overcome a long history of slavery that turned whites and blacks—and here Tucker did echo Jefferson—into incorrigible enemies. In fact, integration only put blacks and whites on a collision course toward race war. Thus, Tucker urged the removal of emancipated blacks to rescue whites from the "eating sore" that was chattel bondage.[22]

Gabriel's plot along with a growing free black population in the state triggered the Virginia legislature to request that Governor James Monroe correspond with President Jefferson about establishing a colony where free blacks could be sent. When no colony was established, advocates for

___

lion is interpreted, for most white Virginians the plot only reinforced and underlined their assumption that blacks, enslaved or free, were enemies of white society.

21. *Letter to a Member of the General Assembly of Virginia, on the Subject of the Late Conspiracy of the Slaves; With a Proposal for Their Colonization* (Baltimore, 1801), 5–7 (quotations on 6, 7).

22. Ibid., 5, 14–16 (quotations on 5, 14). Interestingly, the younger Tucker rejected his older cousin's proposal for freeing the enslaved and stripping them of nearly all civic and civil rights without colonizing the liberated. George Tucker viewed such a policy as displaying "more honor to the heart than to the head." Because freed blacks would "never rest satisfied with any thing short of perfect equality," the only alternative to colonization was full citizenship rights for the liberated, a thought that nearly no white Virginian could contemplate, at least publicly. Therefore, Gabriel's plot made it even less likely that upper southerners would fashion a proposal for emancipation that did not include mandatory black removal.

black expatriation found another opening. They sought to amend Virginia's voluntary manumission law of 1782 to require the removal of manumitted blacks. Warning that "whoever emancipates a slave may be inflicting the deadliest injury upon his neighbor," proponents of free black removal successfully altered the manumission law in 1806 when the legislature decreed that those released from slavery had to leave the state within a year of being liberated. What may be labeled Virginia's nonemancipationist colonization policy set off a ripple effect throughout the upper South. Maryland and Kentucky countered Virginia's legislators in 1807 by passing acts banning the immigration of free persons of color, and North Carolina followed suit soon after. If any plan to gradually abolish slavery was far too divisive to enact, upper southern legislatures could pass laws that addressed an abiding concern of pro- and antislavery advocates alike in the region: the presence of free blacks. The preoccupation of many upper southern whites with the supposed danger free blacks posed to slave societies would exert important influence at the ACS's founding.[23]

Another critical contribution to the ideology of the ACS originated with the religious activism of the New England Congregationalist theologian Samuel Hopkins. During the Revolutionary period, Hopkins developed the theory of disinterested benevolence, which equated godliness with pursuing social morality on earth. Good Christians, to assure their election to heaven, needed to spread human happiness and improve the lives of those around them. To Hopkins, no human institution called for more reform than slavery. True Christianity, in Hopkins's eyes, was antagonistic to human bondage. Wherever Christianity was "fully and faithfully preached, and cordially received and obeyed," slavery could not survive. Here, "no one

23. John Henderson Russell, "The Free Negro in Virginia, 1619–1865" (Ph.D. diss., Johns Hopkins University, 1913), 65–72 (quotation on 67); Lacy K. Ford, *Deliver Us from Evil: The Slavery Question in the Old South* (Oxford, 2009), 59–65. Revealed not long after the discovery of Gabriel's plot, the uncovering in January 1802 of another insurrection of enslaved people, this one planned for Easter weekend of that year, helped to garner support for free black removal. For increasing white Virginian opposition to African American freedom and the state's growing focus on removing free blacks, see Wolf, *Race and Liberty in the New Nation*, 109–127. The North Carolina law against black immigration did not place an outright ban on the entrance of persons of color into the state. But the costly bonds it required of black immigrants acted as a prohibition to their entrance. The series of laws banning the immigration of free blacks sparked by the Virginia legislature in 1806 was more a continuation of anti-free black legislation than a new phenomenon. For the growing hostility of upper southern whites to free blacks in the late eighteenth and early nineteenth centuries, as embodied by a spate of legal codes and initiatives, see Berlin, *Slaves without Masters*, 91–99.

will forfeit his liberty ... and no man will make a slave of another." Viewing the gospel as an antislavery weapon in the hands of pious Christians, Hopkins espoused the Christianization of Africa as a redemptive measure by white Americans to atone for the sin of slavery. He wanted to send Christianized free persons of color to Africa, where they could spread the gospel and rescue Africans from "ignorance and barbarity." With the arrival of Christianity on African shores, the natives would turn away from the slave trade and therefore ultimately doom the institution of slavery. In this way, "good shall be brought out of all the evil" that slavery had entailed on human civilization.[24]

Hopkins tried for nearly two decades to realize his wish for the Christian missionary redemption of Africa. After taking the helm at the First Congregational Church in Newport, Rhode Island, in 1770, he identified two native-born enslaved Africans who were members of his church as worthy propagators of the gospel. Once the freedom of these two black parishioners was secured, Hopkins undertook a campaign to raise money for their education and subsequent transportation to Africa. In 1776, Hopkins and his fellow Congregationalist minister Ezra Stiles published a call for public donations for the mission, which now included two additional African-born blacks of Newport. In their plea to the public, Hopkins and Stiles looked to capitalize on fledgling American opposition to the slave trade by pitching the mission as a means of enabling subscribers to "bear testimony" against "the great inhumanity and cruelty of enslaving so many thousands of our fellow men." The mission would have the twin benefit of helping to realize the millennialist dream of Christianizing all of earth, especially those nations in Africa that "now worship false gods, and dwell in the habitations of cruelty, and the land of the shadow of death." Despite these appeals, as the swirl of the Revolutionary War sidelined his solicitations, Hopkins was not able to raise sufficient funds to carry out the mission.[25]

Undaunted, soon after American independence Hopkins renewed his efforts. But, when he did so, beginning in the mid-1780s, Hopkins tweaked his rationale for the mission. With emancipation policies having swept

24. Stanley K. Schultz, "The Making of a Reformer: The Reverend Samuel Hopkins as an Eighteenth-Century Abolitionist," American Philosophical Society, *Proceedings*, CXV, no. 5 (Oct. 15, 1971), 353; Samuel Hopkins, *A Discourse upon the Slave-Trade, and the Slavery of the Africans; Delivered in the Baptist Meeting-House at Providence, before the Providence Society for Abolishing the Slave-Trade, etc.; at Their Annual Meeting, on May 17, 1793* (Providence, R.I., 1793), 9, 19, 22.

25. Ezra Stiles and Samuel Hopkins, *To the Public* (Newport, R.I., 1776), 3.

New England, a new focus on the place of free blacks in northern society had taken hold of reformers. Hopkins tapped into this topic as a motivating factor in sending American blacks to Africa in a 1789 letter he wrote to the English antislavery reformer and co-organizer of the British Sierra Leone Colony in Africa, Granville Sharp. Hopkins explained to Sharp that blacks in New England were "unhappy" with whites' constantly "looking down upon them, and being disposed to treat them as underlings, and denying them the advantages of education and employment"; these factors acted to "depress their [blacks'] minds and prevent their obtaining a comfortable living." So the mission would not only Christianize Africa but also redeem the lives of black Americans.[26]

By 1793, when Hopkins gave a speech before the Providence Abolition Society asking for support, he had come to cite the problem of white prejudice as an impetus for his missionary venture more bluntly. Fifteen years earlier, Hopkins, in prototypical first movement abolitionist terms, had implied African American incorporation as the logical result of abolition— keeping distinct plans for black freedom and the emigration of people of color to Africa. But, in the wake of New England emancipation, Hopkins adjusted his emphasis. Although not calling for the stripping of black rights like St. George Tucker, Hopkins, in an appendix aimed specifically at the white public that he added after delivering his 1793 address, explained that removing to the land of their forefathers would allow people of African descent to "be raised to an acknowledged equality with the white people." Here Hopkins nodded to the ideological mores of equal liberty, still regnant in late-eighteenth-century America, but in a manner that placated the prejudices of many white New Englanders. Hopkins agreed with men like Jefferson and Tucker that white prejudice was invincible. "The whites," he explained, were "so habituated, by education and custom, to look upon and treat the blacks as an inferior class of beings" that persons of color "never can be raised to an equality" in the United States. But, whereas Revolutionary-era Virginian proponents of colonization presented black removal as a vehicle for protecting white Americans from eternally degraded African Americans, Hopkins stressed his scheme as a way to "com-

26. Samuel Hopkins to Granville Sharp, Jan. 15, 1789, in *The Works of Samuel Hopkins, D.D., First Pastor of the Church in Great Barrington, Mass., afterwards Pastor of the First Congregationalist Church in Newport, R.I.: With a Memoir of His Life and Character*, I (Boston, 1854), 140–141; Joseph A. Conforti, *Samuel Hopkins and the New Divinity Movement: Calvinism, the Congregational Ministry, and Reform in New England between the Great Awakenings* (Eugene, Ore., 1981), 148, 151.

pensate the blacks" for slavery by allowing them to achieve in Africa "all the liberty and rights to which they have a just claim" and accentuated his concern for the well-being of people of color.[27]

The abolition societies of New England balked at backing Hopkins's emigrationist project. Moses Brown of the Providence Abolition Society thought Hopkins's plan impractical and wanted to continue to focus his efforts on combating Rhode Islanders' participation in the slave trade. When Hopkins pitched his plan to the Providence Society in 1793, its members declined to lend him substantive support. Hopkins also sought the approval of the Connecticut Abolition Society—the most Congrega-tionalist- and least Quaker-aligned of the abolition societies—guessing that were it to endorse his efforts the PAS, New-York Manumission Society (NYMS), and Rhode Island Society "might fall in afterwards and join to carry it on." But Hopkins failed to receive the Connecticut Society's offi-cial sanction. Though Hopkins never realized his missionary-based emi-grationist goals, his hopes of Christianizing Africa and empowering freed blacks to experience the egalitarian promises of the Revolution denied them in America left a lasting impression on the northern reformers who took part in the ACS.[28]

In the post-Revolutionary and early national eras, a scattering of white Americans linked antislavery with black removal, sketched projects for the colonization of liberated blacks, or sought the repatriation of persons of African descent. These plans took a variety of forms. Jefferson, whose commitment to ending slavery appeared half-hearted and dubious, con-centrated on claims of the permanent inferiority of people of color and the unbridgeable disparities between whites and blacks to justify his coloni-

27. Hopkins, *Discourse upon the Slave-Trade, and the Slavery of the Africans*, 20, appendix. For Hopkins's 1776 usage of free black incorporation as an argument in favor of emancipation, see [Samuel Hopkins], *A Dialogue concerning the Slavery of the Afri-cans; Shewing It to Be the Duty and Interest of the American Colonies to Emancipate All Their African Slaves* ... (Norwich, Conn., 1776), 43–46. In *A Dialogue*, Hopkins empha-sized the negative environmentalist effects of slavery on enslaved persons and stressed the need to foster a more positive environment in freedom for liberated blacks.

28. Hopkins, *Discourse upon the Slave-Trade, and the Slavery of the Africans*, ap-pendix; Conforti, *Samuel Hopkins and the New Divinity Movement*, 148–153 (quota-tion on 153). Hopkins also met more overt shunning of his African missionary vision. Some New England Congregationalists of different theological persuasions from Hop-kins sneered at his efforts, such as the Boston minister who thought that "the Negroes had better continue in Paganism than adopt Mr. H[opkins's] scheme" (Franklin Bow-ditch Dexter, ed., *The Literary Diary of Ezra Stiles, D.D., LL.D., President of Yale College*, I, *January 1, 1769–March 13, 1776* [New York, 1901], 414 n. 6).

zationist plan. Tucker, a sincerer advocate of slavery's termination, found white prejudice to be an unbreakable barrier to emancipation without black removal. And Samuel Hopkins, whose desire for the improvement of people of color made him sound the most like first movement abolitionists, identified the Christianization of Africa and the abolition of the slave trade as two goals of his proposal. Whatever their differences, the linkage these thinkers made between black freedom and expatriation was anathema to the first abolition movement. But, in this period, while abolitionists cohered around an emancipationist agenda of black citizenship and the defeat of white prejudice, black removal and colonization remained the unrealized schemas of individuals rather than the guiding principles of a movement. Upon the formation of the ACS, that changed.

THE FOUNDING OF THE ACS

On December 21, 1816, a mix of clergy, planters, and politicians assembled at the Davis Hotel in Washington, D.C., to preside over the ACS's inaugural meeting. More than twenty individuals, all white men, attended. Having been formed in a southern locale and speaking to an issue that interested many leading figures of the upper South, the ACS's founding was dominated by southerners. Longtime Virginian proponent of black removal Ferdinando Fairfax, influential Old Dominion bishop William Meade, future president and Tennessean slaveholder Andrew Jackson, Maryland congressman Robert Wright, and Kentuckian Speaker of the House of Representatives Henry Clay were among the attendees. The southern origins of the ACS and the makeup of its early membership compared to the Quaker-influenced, northern-based abolition societies contributed to first movement abolitionists' suspicion of the organization. But, even in its early years, the ACS was not solely southern. When the ACS held elections for its officers at its second meeting in January 1817, five of the thirteen vice presidents appointed were from the mid-Atlantic and New England. The mission statement of the ACS's initial gathering, moreover, declared that the society was "desirous of aiding in the great cause of philanthropy, and of promoting the prosperity and happiness of our country" while encouraging efforts to "diffuse knowledge, civilization and the benign influence of christian religion" abroad and furthering "the rights of man." This was the sort of unifying language that both northerners and southerners could cheer.[29]

29. *Daily National Intelligencer* (Washington, D.C.), Dec. 31, 1816, [3]; *A View of Exertions Lately Made for the Purpose of Colonizing the Free People of Colour, in the United States, in Africa, or Elsewhere* (Washington, D.C., 1817), 10 (quotation), 13; Matthew

The ACS fused the guiding themes of earlier expressions of colonization but did so in ways that spoke to the sociopolitical climate of early-
nineteenth-century America. One imprint on the ACS came from the heirs
of Hopkins's doctrine of disinterested benevolence. By the end of the War
of 1812, a plethora of benevolent societies had surfaced throughout the
northern states. Peace societies, temperance societies, educational societies, among many other similar reform enterprises, were all products of
the evangelical Christian mission to promote the public good and morally
purify American society. With urban growth, this movement came to focus
on the increasing presence of impoverished and, these reformers thought,
immoral segments of the population.[30]

Free blacks, liberated from the chains of bondage but held down by
white prejudice from experiencing genuine freedom, represented especially acute threats to the order and stability of society, according to northern colonizationists. Though first movement abolitionists had assumed
that slavery impaired its victims, northern colonizationists made claims of
free black degradation a singular focus. They looked to systematically prove
the "degraded character" of free blacks, who they insisted filled jail cells,
crowded into urban poorhouses, and saturated city streets with drunkenness and criminal behavior. For these reformers, free blacks embodied the
larger societal evils that they had committed to combat. Therefore, when
northern evangelicals presented colonization as allowing white Americans
to be "cleared of" free blacks, they revised Hopkins's earlier concern for
black inequality. Colonization could not only save people of color from indefinite inferiority but rescue the white body politic from the alleged ills
of free blacks.[31]

Spooner, "'I Know This Scheme Is From God': Toward a Reconsideration of the Origins
of the American Colonization Society," *Slavery and Abolition*, XXXV (2014), 563; P. J.
Staudenraus, *The African Colonization Movement, 1816–1865* (New York, 1961), 27–28.

30. For an overview of the flowering of reform movements in the early Republic, see
Ronald G. Walters, *American Reformers, 1815–1860* (New York, 1978); Robert H. Abzug,
Cosmos Crumbling: American Reform and Religious Imagination (New York, 1994);
Steven Mintz, *Moralists and Modernizers: America's Pre-Civil War Reformers* (Balti-
more, 1995); and Paul Boyer, *Urban Masses and Moral Order in America, 1820–1920*
(Cambridge, Mass., 1978), 1–54.

31. Robert Finley to John P. Mumford, Feb. 14, 1816, in Isaac V. Brown, *Memoirs of
the Rev. Robert Finley, D.D. Late Pastor of the Presbyterian Congregation at Basking
Ridge New-Jersey, and President of Franklin College, Located at Athens, in the State of
Georgia; with Brief Sketches of Some of His Contemporaries, and Numerous Notes* (New
Brunswick, N.J., 1819), 77. For a representative depiction of northern free blacks by colo-
nizationists that drilled the argument of black societal depravity, see "Degraded Charac-

Despite its emphasis on black degradation, the northern reform wing of the ACS highlighted the liberating potential of colonization for black Americans and their African brethren. Robert Finley, a New Jersey Presbyterian minister and an architect of the ACS, elaborated his understanding of the blessings colonization could bestow on persons of color in the promotional pamphlet *Thoughts on the Colonization of Free Blacks*. The minister called for the "gradual separation of the black from the white population," writing that the benefits for those of African descent were "numerous and great." Asserting that people of color were "capable of improvement," Finley thought they need only be returned to Africa and their "minds will then expand and their natures rise." Much like Hopkins, Finley believed the introduction of Christian civilization would permit white Americans to repay the debt of enslavement and might even turn Africa into "a seat of liberal learning," making the African continent "civilized and christianized." Elias B. Caldwell, a well-connected Washington lawyer and enthusiastic advocate of evangelical reform, echoed Finley's sentiments at the ACS's first meeting. Colonization, Caldwell told the gathering, could allow African Americans to "enjoy equal rights and privileges with those around them" while bringing Christianity and civilization to Africa and "redeeming many millions" of currently heathen Africans.[32]

Both Finley and Caldwell believed colonization could stimulate emancipation by providing slaveholders with an external outlet for freedpeople. Southern founders of the ACS did not share this perspective. Whether they sought to strengthen slavery or simply rid the South of free blacks, these planter-politicians renounced the view that the ACS should encourage emancipation. Like Finley, the Virginia Federalist Charles Fenton Mercer helped to engineer the ACS's founding. Yet Mercer brought a very different perspective that remained unconnected to any form of antislavery. Discovering that the Virginia legislature had contemplated colonization in 1800, Mercer wanted to revive what had by 1816 become a moribund movement. Mercer had spent time in England and left there horrified at the prospect of a growing underclass in the United States that might mirror the lower classes of industrialized Great Britain. Although Mercer be-

ter of the Coloured Population," *African Repository and Colonial Journal*, II (July 1826), 152–154 (quotation on 152).

32. [Robert Finley], *Thoughts on the Colonization of Free Blacks* ([Washington, D.C., 1816]), 1, 5–7; Finley to Mumford, Feb. 14, 1816, in Brown, *Memoirs of the Rev. Robert Finley*, 77; *A View of Exertions Lately Made for the Purpose of Colonizing the Free People of Colour*, 6–7.

lieved impoverished whites could be reformed and educated, he feared that free persons of color were inassimilable because of the "everlasting mark" of black skin. He harkened back to Tucker's belief that free blacks would forever remain an "idle, worthless, ignorant and corrupt" population that threatened white society unless they could be removed. Yet Mercer was a product of Virginia's early-nineteenth-century emphasis on free black removal irrespective of abolition. Unlike Tucker, he thought black removal should have "nothing, whatever, to do with domestic slavery." Having come of age a generation after Thomas Jefferson and St. George Tucker, the quandary of how to address what many white Virginians saw as a conspicuous class of permanently degraded free blacks, not the problem of slavery, preoccupied Mercer.[33]

Slaveholding attendees at the ACS's initial proceedings aired their conviction that the society should leave abolition off the table. Henry Clay, chosen to chair the 1816 meeting, made sure to tell his audience that the ACS would not "deliberate on, or consider at all, any question of emancipation," adding that it was "no part of the object of this meeting to touch or agitate, in the slightest degree" the "delicate question" of slavery. Robert Wright of Maryland wanted his fellow ACS members to know that he held "the most delicate regard to the rights of property" and warned that the society must not "furnish the means of transporting out of the reach of the master his property." The eccentric Virginia congressman John Randolph announced that colonization would "tend to secure the property of every master in the United States over his slaves." Free blacks were notorious "promoters of mischief" who excited "discontent" among the enslaved and jeopardized the slave system, Randolph explained in a familiar planter refrain. Therefore, removing the freed would fasten the fetters of bondage ever more securely on the enslaved. Clay made the same point more obliquely when he extolled the ACS for aiming to "rid our own country of a useless and pernicious, if not a dangerous portion of its population." For prominent southern members of the ACS there existed no connection between colonization and emancipation. Black removal would address solely the problematic presence of free blacks.[34]

33. Charles Fenton Mercer, quoted in Douglas R. Egerton, "'Its Origin Is Not a Little Curious': A New Look at the American Colonization Society," *Journal of the Early Republic*, V (1985), 466–472 (quotations on 468, 469, 470). As he worked to reintroduce a colonization plan in the Virginia legislature, Mercer spoke about black removal with several Washington elites, including Elias Caldwell. Robert Finley might even have been introduced to the idea of colonization through Mercer's conversations with Caldwell.

34. *A View of Exertions Lately Made for the Purpose of Colonizing the Free Persons*

As they forged a national society, therefore, northern and southern ACS spokesmen articulated different goals. One connecting thread, however, stitched them together. They shared a belief in the incompatibility of free blacks with the body politic and the intractable barrier of white prejudice to black uplift within the United States. Robert Finley believed that colonization would result in the Republic's being "saved [from] many a pang" that the potential "intermixture" of the races and widespread black poverty would place on white Americans. A prejudice "too deep rooted to be eradicated" would hold down persons of color in America, hence the need to remove them to Africa. Elias Caldwell judged that white prejudice would continue to leave blacks in America depraved and "exclude them" from participation in society with the "soundest reason." Henry Clay dubbed persons of African descent victims of "unconquerable prejudice." If they remained in the United States, black people would continue "through all succeeding time, degraded and debased, aliens" in a country that was not theirs, Clay somberly explained. Robert G. Harper of Baltimore added his voice to the chorus when he wrote on behalf of the ACS that white attitudes "condemned" blacks "to a state of hopeless inferiority" and caused whites to associate all persons of color with slavery. It is no accident that colonizationists, finding common ground on the need to remove persons of African descent from the American Republic, named their group the American Society for Colonizing the Free People of Color and said nothing about abolishing slavery in the organization's constitution.[35]

Soon after the ACS's founding, auxiliary societies began to appear in the mid-Atlantic, showing at least some support among the reform communities there for colonization. Though they endeavored to colonize free blacks,

---

of Color, 5, 9–10. Although he did not share with northern ACS founders the idea that black removal might be used as a tool of abolition, Clay did mention the civilization of Africa as a benefit of colonization. Randolph's claims that colonization would strengthen slavery coincided with his belief that it would stimulate manumission by providing a safe haven for masters to dispose of freed blacks, who would otherwise threaten slave society. Therefore, encouraging manumission and bolstering slaveholding property rights were not contradictory for Randolph. For Randolph's nuanced views on slavery, see Nicholas Wood, "John Randolph of Roanoke and the Politics of Slavery in the Early Republic," *Virginia Magazine of History and Biography,* CXX (2012), 106–143.

35. [Finley], *Thoughts on the Colonization of Free Blacks,* 5; *A View of Exertions Lately Made for the Purpose of Colonizing the Free People of Colour,* 5–6; *The First Annual Report of the American Society for Colonizing the Free People of Color, of the United States; and the Proceedings of the Society at Their Annual Meeting in the City of Washington, on the First Day of January, 1818* (Washington, D.C., 1818), 18, 29–30, 38. For the Constitution of the ACS, see *A View of Exertions Lately Made for the Purpose of Colonizing the Free People of Colour,* 11.

these short-lived societies also made evident their belief that the activism of the ACS would lead eventually to the abolition of slavery. In Philadelphia, citizens gathered in the Pennsylvania State House during the summer of 1817 to form the Philadelphia Auxillary to the ACS. Those on hand at this meeting listened to an address by Elias Caldwell, who amended the ACS's founding documents when he maintained that emancipation was the ACS's intent. The colonization of free blacks would not only have the effect of "ameliorating the condition of the Slave" but also of tempering the "apprehensions of the master" and leading, "at no distant time," to "the utter extirpation of SLAVERY." In the fall of 1817, a group of New-Yorkers meeting in Manhattan founded the New-York Auxiliary Colonization Society. An address by the managers of the new society asserted that colonization would "render slavery impossible in the southern states." Despite the best efforts of the mid-Atlantic's earliest ACS backers, there is evidence that reformers in the region remained skeptical of the colonization movement's abolitionist intentions. Speaking for a bloc of attendees at the Philadelphia meeting who had walked out, a writer from a local newspaper cautioned that colonization "would be fatal to the gradual and final Abolition of Slavery." Another essayist in the same newspaper asked the "Southern Gentlemen" members of the ACS whether by removing free blacks they intended to "rivet" more strongly on enslaved people *the fetters of servitude.*" That the Philadelphia and New York auxiliaries vanished from the historical record within a year of their first appearance indicates a largely skeptical Philadelphia and New York antislavery community.[36]

The strategy of the ACS only reinforced this skepticism. Backed by a litany of federal politicians and national figures, the ACS viewed Congress as its close ally. The managers of the ACS communicated as much when they wrote to fellow member Henry Clay that the society's mission of establishing a colony of black Americans in Africa should be "patronized by the Government, so as to become essentially national in its means and its objects." Obtaining federal aid was at the top of the ACS's agenda. But, in a federal government dominated by southern slaveholders, getting federal support meant shearing the ACS of any abolitionist objectives. A little more

36. *Poulson's American Daily Advertiser* (Philadelphia), Aug. 8, 1817, [3], Aug. 9, 1817, [3], Aug. 12, 1817, [3]; *Commercial Advertiser* (New York), Dec. 9, 1817, [2]. For evidence that the mid-Atlantic auxiliaries officially called for the colonization of free people of color, and not abolition, see the New-York Auxiliary Colonization Society's constitution in *New-York Columbian,* Oct. 31, 1817, [2]. Broad dissemination of the speeches of Clay and Randolph at the ACS's initial meeting might have contributed to the organization's tepid reception in the mid-Atlantic.

than two years after the formation of the ACS, Charles Mercer, by now a member of Congress, proposed a bill that would become known as the Slave Trade Act of 1819. The act used the 1808 abolition of the slave trade as a rationale for the federal funding of an African colony. Mercer's bill gave President James Monroe, a fellow Virginian and colonization sympathizer, the power to "make such regulations and arrangements, as he may deem expedient, for the safekeeping, support, and removal" of blacks who had been transported into the United States in contravention of the 1808 international slave trade ban. Congress earmarked one hundred thousand dollars for Monroe to dispatch the navy to the West African coastline and use federal governmental authority to oversee the resettlement of persons of color freed by the prohibition on international slave trade imports. In close consultation with the ACS, Monroe would approve the purchase of land in Africa for a colony with the much broader purpose of repatriating the free black population writ large and paving the way for the founding of Liberia.[37]

The ACS repackaged late-eighteenth-century ideological precedents for colonization by revising these ideas to meet the agenda of its members, products of a different generation with overlapping but not identical concerns. Though influenced by northern reformers and clergy, the early years of the ACS took a decidedly upper southern orientation, as politicos like Charles Mercer focused exclusively on expatriating free persons of color and sought to leave the institution of slavery undisturbed. While

37. Henry Clay et al., "Letter from the Committee of the Colonization Society to the House of Representatives," Jan. 23, 1819, in *Report of Mr. Kennedy, of Maryland, from the Committee on Commerce of the House of Representatives of the United States: On the Memorial of the Friends of African Colonization* (Washington, D.C., 1843), 224; *The Debates and Proceedings in the Congress of the United States ... Fifteenth Congress—Second Session: Comprising the Period from November 16, 1818, to March 3, 1819, Inclusive ...* (Washington, D.C., 1855), 2545. For James Monroe's relationship to and support of colonization, see Daniel Preston, "James Monroe and the Practicalities of Emancipation and Colonization," in Beverly C. Tomek and Matthew J. Hetrick, eds., *New Directions in the Study of African American Recolonization* (Gainesville, Fla., 2017), 129–145. The Slave Trade Act did not lead directly to the founding of Liberia but did play an essential role in making the establishment of Liberia possible. See Eric Burin, "The Slave Trade Act of 1819: A New Look at Colonization and the Politics of Slavery," *American Nineteenth Century History*, XIII (2012), 1–14. On the inception of Liberia and its nineteenth-century history, see Tom W. Shick, *Behold the Promised Land: A History of Afro-American Settler Society in Nineteenth-Century Liberia* (Baltimore, 1980); Amos J. Beyan, *The American Colonization Society and the Creation of the Liberian State: A Historical Perspective, 1822–1900* (Lanham, Md., 1991); and Marie Tyler-McGraw, *An African Republic: Black and White Virginians in the Making of Liberia* (Chapel Hill, N.C., 2007).

Elias Caldwell vowed to reform-minded Philadelphians that the colonization movement would result in slavery's eventual destruction, the ACS had
become a viable organization by committing to the removal of free blacks,
not the abolition of slavery. But a cross-regional sense among the ACS's
founders that white prejudice was impregnable, and their unfavorable view
of the character of free blacks within the United States, would leave the
door open to the society's northern rise.

A MARKED LINE OF DISTINCTION

By the 1820s, white attitudes toward free blacks in the mid-Atlantic had
deteriorated in ways that made colonization a more attractive movement.
Two nearly simultaneous developments beginning as early as the turn of
the nineteenth century set the groundwork for a white public increasingly
hostile to free persons of color. First, the pace of African American migration to the urban centers of Philadelphia and New York soared. Between 1790 and 1820, the free black population in New York City expanded
nearly tenfold, while in Philadelphia it grew five times as large. This colossal growth stemmed especially from a migratory pattern driven mainly by
steady manumissions of enslaved southerners. Forced to leave Virginia
after being freed, denied a haven in surrounding states, and subject to
a host of racially restrictive legislation in the upper South, many of the
manumitted fled the land of their bondage and made the trip north. If the
upper South provided the push of migration, the thriving free black communities of Philadelphia and New York provided the pull. The impressive
presence of autonomous black churches, mutual aid societies, and a small
but successful African American middle class held out promise to liberated
people of color that their freedom could be meaningful.

Yet upon their arrival in the urban mid-Atlantic these migrants found
their opportunities limited. Many of them lacked knowledge of skilled
trades, were illiterate, and possessed a general unfamiliarity with urban
life. Already financially destitute from the deprivations of slavery, some
quickly became reliant on public support for survival. Others, desperate to
make ends meet, turned to petty theft. Although some formerly enslaved
southerners thrived in their new environment, those who did not unin-
tentionally fed already prevalent white doubts about the capacity of African Americans for responsible freedom. To compound matters, extensive
southern black immigration happened to coincide with burgeoning indus-
trialization and the resulting growing pains it brought to urban America.
Free blacks found themselves the scapegoat on two sides. Middle- and
upper-class whites wrongly fingered free persons of color as being wholly

responsible for mounting crime and poverty. Concurrently, the white working class, disempowered by the de-skilling of their professions and pitted against free blacks for wage work, targeted African Americans as an easy outlet for their frustrations.[38]

Alarm over the presence of free blacks manifested itself in legislative attempts to restrict black migration into mid-Atlantic states and clamp down on the rights of African Americans already there. In February 1813, Jacob Mitchell, a member of the Pennsylvania Assembly, presented a petition to the state legislature from inhabitants of Philadelphia soliciting the state government to restrict the residence of free blacks in the city. The memorial alleged that more than "4000 runaway negroes" walked the city streets and called on the legislature to register all black Philadelphians in order to keep out southern migrants of color. Complaining that all African Americans were public "nuisances," the petitioners requested that those who were found guilty of crimes be sold "for a term of years" upon their conviction. The memorial also asked for a special tax on free blacks to support poor persons of color who otherwise, the petitioners believed, would continue to swell the rolls of the public dole. A similar memorial from the mayor and alderman of Philadelphia arrived a month later. In response, Pennsylvania assemblymen drew up An Act to Prevent the Migration of People of Color into the City and County of Philadelphia. The bill passed the House but failed in the Senate of the state assembly. Undeterred, like-minded petitioners submitted similar remonstrances to the Pennsylvania legislature throughout the 1820s and 1830s. Though none of the various bills that resulted became law, they symbolized the enduring disdain a growing number of whites held for the state's black population. The petitioners' proposals were intended to link Pennsylvania with the upper South in excluding African Americans from state borders and imposing discriminatory policies on resident free blacks. These efforts demonstrate the receptiveness of a portion of the white public in the mid-Atlantic for black exclusion.[39]

38. Gary B. Nash, *Forging Freedom: The Formation of Philadelphia's Black Community, 1720–1840* (Cambridge, Mass., 1988), 173. African Americans of the urban mid-Atlantic were far more likely to commit petty offenses having to do with the need for economic survival than violent crime or assault. But the white public neglected to acknowledge the sociological, or environmental, reasons for black crime. For the often contentious and always complex relationship of the white working class to African Americans in the early Republic, see David R. Roediger, *The Wages of Whiteness: Race and the Making of the American Working Class* (London, 1991); and Eric Lott, *Love and Theft: Blackface Minstrelsy and the American Working Class* (New York, 1995).

39. *Journal of the Twenty Third House of Representatives of the Commonwealth of Pennsylvania; Commenced at Harrisburg, Tuesday, the First of December, in the Year*

Even as the current of white prejudice in the mid-Atlantic aimed its ire at the black population as a whole, a white northern popular culture of racial derision emerged that specifically belittled the African American middle class. Though a numerical minority compared with their less-affluent brethren, the northern free black middle class stood out as a highly visible bloc of socioeconomically successful individuals. Consisting of perhaps 20 to 30 percent of free black northerners, these men and women had achieved the hallmarks of republican respectability and virtuous citizenship. Abolitionists both applauded and helped to cultivate the northern black middle class, reading its emergence as in part owing to the fruits of their movement. But it was the very achievements of these free blacks that appeared to provoke the white public, thus exposing a serious weakness in the first movement abolitionist formula for fighting white prejudice.[40]

---

of Our Lord, One Thousand Eight Hundred and Twelve, and of the Commonwealth the Thirty Seventh (Harrisburg, Pa., 1812 [1813]), 417 (quotations), 481–482; *Journal of the Twenty Fourth House of Representatives of the Commonwealth of Pennsylvania; Commenced at Harrisburg, Tuesday the Seventh December, in the Year of Our Lord, One Thousand Eight Hundred Thirteen, and of the Commonwealth the Thirty Eighth* (Harrisburg, Pa., 1813 [1814]), 264, 448, 495, 498; Edward Raymond Turner, *The Negro in Pennsylvania: Slavery—Servitude—Freedom, 1639–1861* (Washington, D.C., 1911), 152; *Journal of the Thirtieth House of Representatives of the Commonwealth of Pennsylvania, Commenced at Harrisburg, Tuesday the Seventh of December, in the Year of Our Lord One Thousand Eight Hundred and Nineteen, and of the Commonwealth the Forty Fourth* (Harrisburg, Pa., 1819–1820), 341, 511; *Journal of the Forty Third House of Representatives of the Commonwealth of Pennsylvania, Commenced at Harrisburg, Tuesday, the Fourth of December, in the Year of Our Lord, One Thousand Eight Hundred and Thirty-Two, and of the Commonwealth the Fifty-Seventh,* I (Harrisburg, Pa., 1832–1833), 23, 87, 144. In Delaware and New Jersey, the legislature did enact laws restricting the immigration of African Americans and the movement of resident free blacks. In 1807 and 1811, as white Delawareans' hostility to black freedom grew, the legislature banned black migration to the state—punishable by imprisonment and possible reenslavement—and took away resident status from blacks who traveled outside Delaware for longer than six months. A New Jersey law of 1785 prohibited free blacks manumitted in other states from entering New Jersey and decreed that resident free persons of color could not "travel or remain" in any county other than the one in which they were emancipated without a certificate signed by two justices of the peace (William Paterson, ed., *The Laws of the State of New-Jersey; Revised and Published, under the Authority of the Legislature* [Newark, N.J., 1800], 313). In 1798, the New Jersey legislature permitted free blacks from out of state to enter New Jersey only with a certificate of freedom.

40. There is no singular definition of "middle class" in this period, but I have included those African Americans who were artisans, those who worked autonomously, and those who had professions generally considered of middling or higher status. My rough estimate of this group's share of the free black population refers to Philadelphia and New York City and is drawn from Nash, *Forging Freedom*, 148–152; Shane White, *Somewhat More Independent: The End of Slavery in New York City, 1770–1810* (Athens,

Many northern whites were apparently uncomfortable with and disapproving of the potential for black equality. Between 1816 and 1828, a series of broadsides mocked the annual celebrations of black Bostonians in recognition of the international slave trade's abolition. These festivities highlighted black liberty and displayed black respectability in what, by neutral accounts, appeared as orderly and solemn events. Black Bostonians infused these celebrations with a comparable set of rituals that marked other public civic ceremonies of this era, including processions, speeches, and toasts. Yet the "Bobalition" broadsides took pains to berate these processions, giving a pidgin dialect to its participants and casting the day's ceremonies as disorderly spectacles. The broadsides inverted the intended meaning of the commemorations (which also increasingly became targets of white animosity in analogous celebrations in Philadelphia and New York) as the depraved manifestations of a distinct, inferior people. Conspicuous displays of black citizenship and civic involvement had generated a vicious racist response.[41]

It should come as little surprise that it was in Philadelphia, which contained the largest community of middle-class blacks in the mid-Atlantic, that condescending caricatures of black respectability became especially prevalent. As early as 1819, an illustration parodying black freemasonry appeared in the city. The racially ridiculing cartoons of the illustrator Edward Clay turned the mockery of black gentility into a genre. Clay's *Life in Philadelphia*, which first appeared in 1828, was meant to satirize the social pretensions of urban life in the early Republic. Making African Americans the subjects of his lampooning pen, Clay derided black efforts at socioeconomic uplift through his burlesque etchings. One cartoon depicted a black man and woman dressed in lavish attire on an apparently warm day. The

---

Ga., 1991), 158–161. For the argument that free black middle-class achievement and conspicuousness drove white northern racial hostility and violence, see Emma Jones Lapsansky, "'Since They Got Those Separate Churches': Afro-Americans and Racism in Jacksonian Philadelphia," *American Quarterly*, XXXII (1980), 54–78.

41. For analyses of the Bobalition broadsides, see Joanne Pope Melish, *Disowning Slavery: Gradual Emancipation and "Race" in New England, 1780–1860* (Ithaca, N.Y., 1998), 171–183; and David Waldstreicher, *In the Midst of Perpetual Fetes: The Making of American Nationalism, 1776–1820* (Williamsburg, Va., and Chapel Hill, N.C., 1997), 336–342. For a positive account of the first free black commemoration of the abolition of the slave trade in Boston, see *Independent Chronicle* (Boston), July 18, 1808, [3]. For evidence of white hostility and mockery directed at the abolition of the slave trade commemorations of black New Yorkers, see Shane White, "'It Was a Proud Day': African Americans, Festivals, and Parades in the North, 1741–1834," *Journal of American History*, LXXXI (1994), 40–41.

man asks "Miss Chloe" how she is holding up in "dis hot weader," and Miss Chloe responds that the heat is making her "aspire too much." The pun, which scorned free blacks for aspiring to a respectable status, was lost on no one.[42]

Analogous prints parodied African American gentility. Calling on Miss Dina, a washerwoman (itself a message that persons of color were fit only for menial labor), a black man finds that she is not available but asks her friend to "pay my devours" to her. Two extravagantly robed blacks return from a ball in a third of Clay's cartoons. The female asks her escort, Mr. Lorenzo, if he enjoyed the dance, and Mr. Lorenzo responds that "pon de honour ob a gentleman" he found the ball "vastly indelicate" and "only fit for de common people!!" (see Figure 12). Persons of color could only embarrass themselves by trying to display the attributes of bourgeois America, Clay seemed to be saying.[43]

The *Life in Philadelphia* series also included caustic drawings of black respectability meant to communicate antipathy for the sheer presence of middle-class persons of color. In a print entitled *Dark Conversation*, set against a cloudy background, an aristocratically dressed black man, putatively referencing the weather, notes that it was a "Bery Black looking day" to a finely clothed African American couple. They respond it was in fact "Bery stormy," as "De Blacks flying about so make it Petickly Disagreable." Reflecting what must have been the sentiments of his audience, Clay interpreted genteel blacks in Philadelphia's public places as unwelcome figures hovering over the city like storm clouds that the white public preferred to simply go away.[44]

Other illustrations, not part of the *Life in Philadelphia* series, communicated parallel racial anxieties of working-class whites, many of whom rued the presence of black laborers. An engraving titled *The Results of Abolitionism!* imagined blacks inverting the racial hierarchy of work. A black foreman yells at two white workers to "Hurry up them bricks," while an African American bricklayer taunts the "white rascals" and commands them to bring him mortar. All of these racially divisive prints shared the as-

42. [Edward Williams Clay], *Life in Philadelphia*, Plate 4, *"How You Find Youself Dis Hot Weader Miss Chloe?"* (Philadelphia, [1830]), Library Company of Philadelphia.
43. [Edward Williams Clay], *Life in Philadelphia*, Plate 3, *"Is Miss Dinah at Home?"* (Philadelphia, 1828), [Clay], *Life in Philadelphia*, Plate 13, *How You Like de Waltz, Mr. Lorenzo?* (Philadelphia, 1829), Library Company of Philadelphia.
44. W[illiam] Summers, *Life in Philadelphia*, Plate 1, *Dark Conversation* (London, [circa 1833]), Library Company of Philadelphia. The artist William Summers redrew previous versions of Clay's cartoons for publication.

FIGURE 12. *Life in Philadelphia*, Plate 13, *How You Like de Waltz,*
Mr. Lorenzo? [By Edward Williams Clay]. Philadelphia, 1829.
Courtesy, the Library Company of Philadelphia

sumption that African Americans were unwanted and alien outsiders, conversely incapable of proper decorum and a threat to white dominion. The popular dissemination of white prejudice assaulted black respectability and projected hostility toward the existence of free persons of color in the American Republic.[45]

As white public enmity for northern free blacks grew, political discourse on the national and state levels both highlighted and heightened this increasingly bleak racial environment. In February 1819, James Tallmadge, a federal congressman from New York, ignited a yearlong national controversy over the future of slavery in the western territories by inserting into Missouri's bill for statehood an amendment to restrict "the further introduction of slavery" and institute gradual emancipation for those enslaved people already residing in the territory. Tallmadge's amendment set off a fiery and exhaustive debate over the constitutionality of federal congressional restriction of slavery.[46]

When Tallmadge offered his amendment, he was, in essence, attempting to export the gradual abolitionist policy of New York by grafting it onto Missouri, calling not only for a ban on the importation of enslaved persons but the emancipation of all children born into slavery in the soon-to-be state at the age of twenty-five. The abolition societies supported Tallmadge and wholeheartedly identified his call for the restriction and gradual end of slavery in Missouri with the emancipationist agitation they had long championed. The NYMS called a special meeting five days after Tallmadge's amendment was introduced to the House. It resolved that Tallmadge and his New York colleague John Taylor were to be lauded for seeking to forward a "cause of justice, of humanity, and of freedom." Tallmadge and Tay-

45. *The Results of Abolitionism!* (United States, [circa 1835]), Library Company of Philadelphia. For a sharp analysis of some of these racially charged prints, see Patrick Rael, *Black Identity and Black Protest in the Antebellum North* (Chapel Hill, N.C., 2002), 162–167.

46. *Debates and Proceedings in the Congress of the United States ... Fifteenth Congress — Second Session,* 1170. On the significance of the Missouri crisis and Compromise, see Robert Pierce Forbes, *The Missouri Compromise and Its Aftermath: Slavery and the Meaning of America* (Chapel Hill, N.C., 2007); Leonard L. Richards, *The Slave Power: The Free North and Southern Domination, 1780–1860* (Baton Rouge, La., 2000), 52–82; Matthew Mason, *Slavery and Politics in the Early American Republic* (Chapel Hill, N.C., 2006), 177–212; John Craig Hammond, *Slavery, Freedom, and Expansion in the Early American West* (Charlottesville, Va., 2007), 55–75; Padraig Riley, *Slavery and the Democratic Conscience: Political Life in Jeffersonian America* (Philadelphia, 2016), 208–252; Glover Moore, *The Missouri Controversy, 1819–1821* (1953; rpt. Gloucester, Mass., 1967); and Richard H. Brown, "The Missouri Crisis, Slavery, and the Politics of Jacksonianism," *South Atlantic Quarterly,* LXV (1966), 55–72.

lor responded that their antislavery aims shared with the NYMS "the same grand designs" and told the society "that the very humane and benevolent objects of your association, may ultimately receive their full accomplishment, is our constant desire and ardent prayer." The NYMS then printed a pamphlet with its resolutions and correspondence with Tallmadge and Taylor, making public their alliance. Two months later, the PAS associated Tallmadge's amendment with its own efforts as causes that would "ultimately prevail over Interest Prejudice Oppression and Power." The American Convention viewed the campaign to restrict and abolish slavery in Missouri reflective enough of its agenda to print one thousand copies of the antislavery speeches of high-profile slavery restrictionist congressmen. Debate over Tallmadge's amendment, therefore, served as a proxy for national commentary on the activism of first movement abolitionists.[47]

While northern congressional supporters of slavery's restriction evoked the principles of equality in the Declaration of Independence to support their case, antirestrictionist congressmen directly countered the Declaration's assertion of natural equality as an abstraction, inapplicable to the question of slavery. One of these congressmen was a former ally of the first abolitionist movement, William Pinkney. Thirty years earlier, Pinkney had condemned slaveholding southerners as hypocrites for using "liberty for our text, and actual oppression for our commentary." Now he flatly stated that the "self-evident truths announced in the Declaration of Independence are not truths at all, if taken literally." Instead they were "abstract aphorisms," and inequality was the natural reality of American society. Senator Louis McLane of Delaware agreed, concluding that the Declaration "had no reference to those persons who were at that time held in slavery." Rather than a statement at odds with human bondage, the Declaration did not apply to the institution of slavery. McLane also explicitly racialized the Declaration, arguing that the document symbolized an "act of open resistance on the part of the white freemen of the colonies" and was "never designed to assume or assert any principle whatsoever" relating to people of

47. *Speech of the Honorable James Tallmadge, Jr. of Duchess County, New-York, in the House of Representatives of the United States, on Slavery; to Which Is Added, the Proceedings of the Manumission Society of the City of New-York, and the Correspondence of Their Committee with Messrs. Tallmadge and Taylor* (New York, 1819), 19–20; PPAS, Series 1, reel 1, II, 305, HSP; *Minutes of the Seventeenth Session of the American Convention for Promoting the Abolition of Slavery, and Improving the Condition of the African Race; Convened at Philadelphia, on the Third Day of October, 1821* (Philadelphia, 1821), 24. For the role of abolitionists in the Missouri debates and their contributions to slavery restrictionists' congressional efforts and strategy, see Manisha Sinha, *The Slave's Cause: A History of Abolition* (New Haven, Conn., 2016), 186–188.

African descent. Temporal distance from the American Revolution helped slavery's congressional proponents wage a direct war on the Declaration's principles, so key to abolitionists, and argue unabashedly that they had originally been intended to apply to white Americans only.[48]

Antirestrictionists also exploited black inequality and white prejudice in the North to strike against restrictionists' use of the Declaration. Antirestrictionists referred to northern white prejudice and black civic inequality to accentuate the impracticality of applying egalitarian ideals to the topic of slavery. Kentucky senator Richard M. Johnson noted that "a universal prejudice" against persons of African descent withheld from them "the blessings of freedom" upon their emancipation. Johnson then asked congressmen from northern states that had abolished slavery point-blank, "If your humanity has conquered your prejudice ... where are your magistrates, your governors, your representatives, of the black population?" Although northern restrictionists "proclaimed them [blacks] equal," they did not follow through on making formerly enslaved people equal. Louis McLane challenged his colleagues to name a single state in which "the emancipated negro has been admitted to the enjoyment of equal rights

48. William Pinkney, *Speech of William Pinkney, Esq. in the House of Delegates of Maryland, at Their Session in November, 1789* (Philadelphia, 1790), 8; Henry Wheaton, *Some Account of the Life, Writings, and Speeches of William Pinkney* (New York, 1826), 595; *The Debates and Proceedings in the Congress of the United States ... Sixteenth Congress—First Session: Comprising the Period from December 6, 1819, to May 15, 1820, Inclusive ...* (Washington, D.C., 1855), 341, 296, 1154–1155. For the extensive use of and reference to the Declaration of Independence by both restrictionists and antirestrictionists during the Missouri debates, see Philip F. Detweiler, "Congressional Debate on Slavery and the Declaration of Independence, 1819–1821," *American Historical Review*, LXIII (1958), 598–616; and Sean Wilentz, "Jeffersonian Democracy and the Origins of Political Antislavery in the United States: The Missouri Crisis Revisited," *Journal of the Historical Society*, IV (2004), 375–401. Pinkney's extensive attack on the Declaration as a tool of antislavery came in a speech that was not recorded. Much of the record of what he said comes secondhand from other congressional speakers citing his arguments during the Missouri debates, though Pinkney did briefly reiterate his dissociation of the Declaration from antislavery in a later speech. When called out for previously being an advocate of emancipation, Pinkney claimed that he still favored the manumission rights of slaveholders. Nonetheless, over the course of his political career, Pinkney went from vociferously attacking slavery to meticulously defending the constitutionality of expanding human bondage. See Monroe Johnson, "William Pinkney, Legal Pedant," *American Bar Association Journal*, XXII (1936), 639–642. For additional examples of the antirestrictionist position that the Declaration did not apply to slavery and was not intended to include enslaved people, but rather embodied a practical document setting the course for independence, see *Debates and Proceedings in the Congress of the United States ... Sixteenth Congress—First Session*, 301, 1005, 1071, 1154.

with the white population." He announced that there were "none." In the Missouri debates, northern white prejudice and black inequality became damning evidence to counter a racially inclusive interpretation of Revolutionary principles that had underpinned abolitionist arguments since the nation's founding.[49]

The connection between first movement abolitionism and the Missouri crisis was only strengthened after the constitution Missourians sent to Congress prohibited free blacks from coming into the state. Citing the privileges and immunities clause of the Federal Constitution, restrictionists—who had seen their cause fall short with the compromise that allowed slavery unrestricted in Missouri—argued that Congress should reject Missouri's constitution because it violated the citizenship rights of free black Americans, rights for which the abolition societies and their black allies had long fought. Southern defenders of slavery responded by impugning their northern colleagues for waxing eloquent on the rights of black citizens while people of color in their home states languished in a category far below citizenship. Charles Pinkney of South Carolina incredulously asked northern restrictionists if they could "be serious" in threatening to hold up the admission of Missouri based on ideals of color-blind citizenship even as they held their own free black population in "contempt" and drew a "marked line of distinction ... between them and the whites" that left persons of color "so unlike a citizen, and so almost wholly without his privileges." Pinkney used northern black inequality to combat the arguments of his restrictionist foes.[50]

But antirestrictionists did not have to look merely to southerners for support. Arguably the most vociferous defense of the position that free

49. *Debates and Proceedings in the Congress of the United States ... Sixteenth Congress—First Session*, 357, 1155. For examples of antirestrictionist arguments that the Declaration was an inapplicable principle by which to guide social formation, see ibid., 350, 1384.

50. *The Debates and Proceedings in the Congress of the United States ... Sixteenth Congress—Second Session: Comprising the Period from November 13, 1820, to March 3, 1821, Inclusive* ... (Washington, D.C., 1855), 1135; Kettner, *The Development of American Citizenship*, 312–314; Forbes, *The Missouri Compromise and Its Aftermath*, 107–114. The Missouri debates did not center primarily on the applicability of the Declaration of Independence to slavery, ideas of race and black exclusion, or northern racism. Rather, I have focused on these themes because they reveal a sociopolitical landscape increasingly unfavorable to the ideals of first movement abolitionism. The congressional debates on the Missouri crisis in whole, extensive as they are exhausting to read, included a host of issues such as the federal government's jurisdiction over slavery, slavery's territorial expansion, the institution's constitutionality, slaveholder property rights, and the domestic slave trade, among many other topics.

blacks were not citizens, and that northerners needed to defer to their southern counterparts on the issue of slavery, came from a full-fledged apostate to first movement abolitionism: the Philadelphian Tench Coxe. The former secretary of the PAS had been reprimanded years earlier by the society's acting committee for arranging for the sale of enslaved Pennsylvanians out of state. Coxe had made amends and expressed similar ideological convictions to those of the PAS as late as 1809. But, with a series of essays published in the staunchly Jeffersonian Republican *Democratic Press* in the winter of 1820, Coxe outed himself as an unapologetic defender of southern slave interests. By the time Coxe wrote these essays, he was a fervent adherent of the Democratic-Republicans, a party whose coalition in the North had come increasingly to respect and defend the slaveholding rights of their southern counterparts based on a cross-sectional acceptance of slavery in the South. Once a subscriber to race-free citizenship, Coxe now presented people of color as "uncivilized or wild men, without our [white Americans'] moral sense." Black Americans had *"not yet evinced ... to be capable of genuine modern civilization"* and had not shown themselves "capable of being that free, moral and responsible agent, which a citizen must be." There was no need to worry about the status of a people incapable of exercising the rights of free persons.[51]

To prove that Congress should respect the constitution of Missouri, Coxe knew that he had to go beyond laying out the theoretical inferiority of black Americans. Congruent with Congressional antirestrictionists, Coxe argued that black Americans were never considered part of the "social compacts" made by the Revolutionary generation. But he did more than that. In an attack against the merits of the first abolition movement, Coxe linked the supposedly degraded state of northern black freedom with the alleged failures of gradual emancipation. A multitude of black civic exclusions and

51. *Democratic Press* (Philadelphia), Nov. 25, 1820, [2]; Gary Nash, "Race and Citizenship in the Early Republic," in Richard Newman and James Mueller, eds., *Antislavery and Abolition in Philadelphia: Emancipation and the Long Struggle for Racial Justice in the City of Brotherly Love* (Baton Rouge, La., 2011), 95–96, 105. Coxe maintained the inviolability of slaveholding property rights and underlined the economic ties between North and South that slavery fostered. For an in-depth and sensitive treatment of how northern Democratic-Republicans struggled with and came to support a race-based understanding of democracy that championed equality but abetted slavery, see Riley, *Slavery and the Democratic Conscience*. The timing of Coxe's essays, published as Congress was debating the Missouri constitution and its prohibition of free black entrance into the territory, and his focus on proving that blacks never were considered, and could never become, citizens was clearly aimed at supporting the antirestrictionist position in Congress.

civil inequalities, which characterized "even humane Pennsylvania," should cause "the friends of humanity" to reassess their reformism. The "'freedom' and 'equality' of the African people in the middle, northern and eastern states constitute yet but an *abstract proposition*—a *half truth*—a *practical sophism.*" Gradual emancipation only conferred *"paper enfranchisements,"* not true liberty, to its recipients. Here Coxe was telling abolitionists, and other northerners who might have felt galvanized by the Missouri crisis to rally around the cause of antislavery, that their efforts were a waste of energy. The problem of slavery might one day be solved by a form of black removal, but in the meantime white northerners needed to respect the rights of slaveholders and divest themselves of any foolhardy notions of the citizenship rights of blacks.[52]

Within a year of the publication of Coxe's racially virulent essays, nearly all of New York's free black men lost their literal paper enfranchisement. During the New York state Constitutional Convention of 1821, people of color were stripped of their political citizenship. Free blacks in New York City asserted a dynamic presence in the early national political sphere. But when New York's Bucktail Republicans, a state faction of the national Democratic-Republican party, determined that persons of color voted

52. *Democratic Press*, Nov. 25, 1820, [2], Dec. 22, 1820, [2]. Coxe published a total of thirteen essays in this series under the title "Considerations respecting the Helots of the United States, African and Indian, Native and Alien, and Their Descendants of the Whole and Mixed Blood." As Gary Nash points out, Coxe's use of the term "helot," a repressed group in ancient Sparta who occupied a status between slavery and freedom, was a clear reference to the former PAS secretary's view of the condition and rightful place of black Americans (Nash, "Race and Citizenship in the Early Republic," in Newman and Mueller, eds., *Antislavery and Abolition*, 104). Although Coxe presented a thorough and strident defense of the antirestricitonist position, his arguments did not reflect the average northern voter. The Missouri crisis stirred white northern support for restricting slavery, eliciting numerous public meetings expressing hostility to slavery and its expansion. It was exactly this popular expression of northern antislavery sentiment that Coxe was trying to push back against. And that he did so by relying on arguments of permanent black inequality and questioning the efficacy of northern emancipation both reflected the racial hostilities facing free blacks in cities like Philadelphia and foreshadowed the arguments of later northern colonizationists who would contend that gradual emancipation without black removal had been a complete failure. Coxe's colonization proposal would remove free blacks to the American West, not Africa, though his interest in an actual plan for black removal can be characterized as cursory at best. In a later series of essays, Coxe abandoned his support for colonization and instead advocated for the diffusion of slavery, a position taken by many upper southern slaveholders that conveniently supported their economic interests in selling bondspersons west in the mushrooming domestic slave trade. See Jacob E. Cooke, *Tench Coxe and the Early Republic* (Chapel Hill, N.C., 1978), 515–516.

overwhelmingly for their Federalist foes, African American voting rights were exposed to the whims of party politics.[53]

Black disfranchisement in New York was primarily the product of political partisanship. Still, in justifying their actions, advocates of black disenfranchisement painted black New Yorkers as apolitical, degraded dependents who lacked the rationality and mores necessary to take part in the emergent democratic political system. Convention delegate Jonathan Ross labeled African Americans "a peculiar people, incapable, in my judgment, of exercising that privilege [suffrage] with any sort of discretion, prudence, or independence." Free persons of color had no "just conceptions of civil liberty" and were "consequently indifferent to its preservation." Preying on white New Yorkers' fears of black immigration, Ross worried that continuing black suffrage "would serve to invite that kind of population to this state," the prospect of which he "most sincerely deplore[d]." Ross concluded that the convention should recognize emancipation but keep free blacks as distinct dependents, outside the reach of ballot boxes.[54]

Samuel Young, a Bucktail from western New York, reiterated many of Ross's arguments, but he also used white prejudice to defend black disenfranchisement. Confidently asserting African American inferiority, Young stated: "The minds of the blacks are not competent to vote. They are too much degraded to estimate the value, or exercise with fidelity and discretion that important right." Although Young conceded that black improvement might someday necessitate their inclusion in the body politic, he judged that the current inferior condition of free blacks in New York compelled the convention to "withhold that privilege which they will inevitably abuse." Proffering an unabashedly racialized understanding of political citizenship, Young announced that "public sentiment" opposed black

53. On black disfranchisement in New York, see Dixon Ryan Fox, "The Negro Vote in Old New York," *Political Science Quarterly*, XXXII (1917), 252–275; Christopher Malone, *Between Freedom and Bondage: Race, Party, and Voting Rights in the Antebellum North* (New York, 2008), 23–55; Nathaniel H. Carter, William L. Stone, and Marcus T. C. Gould, eds., *Reports of the Proceedings and Debates of the Covention of 1821 . . .*, in David N. Gellman and David Quigley, eds., *Jim Crow New York: A Documentary History of Race and Citizenship, 1777–1877* (New York, 2003), 90–200; Paul J. Polgar, "Whenever They Judge It Expedient: The Politics of Partisanship and Free Black Voting Rights in Early National New York," *American Nineteenth Century History*, XII (2011), 1–23; and Sarah L. H. Gronnigsater, "'Expressly Recognized by Our Election Laws': Certificates of Freedom and the Multiple Fates of Black Citizenship in the Early Republic," *WMQ*, 3d Ser., LXXV (2018), 465–506.

54. Carter, Stone, and Gould, eds., *Reports*, in Gellman and Quigley, *Jim Crow New York*, 107–108.

enfranchisement. "This distinction of colour is well understood. It is unnecessary to disguise it, and we ought to shape our constitution so as to
meet the public sentiment." Like his Bucktail colleague Ross, Young recommended continuing the process of emancipation but walling off free
blacks from political rights.[55]

One of the most influential Bucktails, Peter R. Livingston, vocalized his
support for disfranchising black voters. Agreeing with Young that black
New Yorkers were "not competent to vote," Livingston added that African Americans also lacked the "intelligence" and "purity of principle" to
vote. Livingston counseled his fellow delegates that free black voters were
"dangerous" to New York's "political institutions" and added that keeping
them enfranchised would be like placing "a weapon into their hands to
destroy" the state. Intimating that they could be made tools in the hands
of ambitious politicians, Livingston sardonically averred that, when black
voters "approach the ballot boxes, they are too ignorant to know whether
their vote is given to elevate another to office, or hang themselves upon
the gallows." Opponents of black voting rights, though they failed to insert
the qualifying word "white" in a clause redefining male suffrage, successfully imposed a $250 freehold for black voters, effectively disfranchising
the overwhelming majority of the state's African American population.[56]

First movement abolitionists had centered much of their campaign on
cultivating a public culture inimical to white prejudice. From publishing
essays, poems, and other printed material that engendered empathetic connections between whites and blacks to producing and displaying virtuous
black citizenship for public reception, the abolition societies and their African American allies believed that racial prejudice would ultimately wither.
But, by the 1820s, the northern public sphere had taken a chastening turn
against first movement abolitionist doctrine. Caricatures disparaging free
black life and brutally satirizing African American gentility saturated the
northern press. Many whites recoiled at ballooning black migration into
mid-Atlantic cities. Black voters had their suffrage rights stolen in the very
mid-Atlantic state where they had been the most politically active. And
politicians used this worsening racial climate to defend slavery's spread,

55. Ibid., 122–125.
56. Ibid., 136. With fierce opposition from New York's Democrats, the state's Constitution was not revised to incorporate equal black male voting rights until 1874. NYMS
member and American Convention delegate Peter Jay was one of the most vocal proponents of maintaining black voting rights at the 1821 New York Convention. Yet there is
no record of the NYMS's taking official action to protest or petition against the de facto
disfranchisement of black New Yorkers.

mock northern emancipation, and deride the idea that American Revolutionary principles of liberty and equality applied to people of color.

INSUPERABLE OBSTACLES

Into this milieu of ascending white prejudice and diminishing black rights stepped the ACS. Until the mid-1820s, colonizationists had focused on garnering federal funding to send black Americans to the organization's colony, Liberia. Differing from other reform organizations of the period that looked to local organizing and voluntary contributions of time and money, the ACS viewed itself as a beneficent arm of the federal government. For this strategy to work, the ACS required the active support of prominent Americans with national name recognition who would give the organization the legitimacy it needed for direct federal support. While auxiliary societies might form to provide fundraising campaigns or bring additional endorsements from public figures, the ACS did not see these state and local outfits as centrally important elements of its program. The problem for the managers of the ACS was that the federal government would not cooperate. Especially after the Missouri crisis, southern legislators—so influential in congressional decision making—became increasingly wary of any organization that could in any way be interpreted as interfering with their peculiar institution, even taking into account the ACS's professions that the society would leave chattel bondage in the South untouched.[57]

Mostly frustrated in their lobbying of Congress, the ACS took a new tact with the appointment of Ralph Gurley as secretary of the society in 1825. Gurley wanted to refashion the ACS into a voluntary organization. Gurley envisioned the ACS as a national movement, but in very different ways than its founders. The ACS's Washington headquarters would still serve as "a central spring," but its "pulsations should send life and vigour into" the auxillary societies that Gurley sought to establish throughout the country. Gurley hoped to create a network of auxiliary societies capable of raising funds for the transportation of persons of color to Liberia, effec-

57. Staudenraus, *The African Colonization Movement*, 69–75; Eric Burin, *Slavery and the Peculiar Solution: A History of the American Colonization Society* (Gainesville, Fla., 2005), 15; Nicholas P. Wood, "The Missouri Crisis and the 'Changed Object' of the American Colonization Society," in Tomek and Hetrick, eds., *New Directions in the Study of African American Recolonization*, 146–165. Despite the ACS's frustrations on the federal level, David Ericson has substantiated narrow but enduring national governmental support for the ACS for decades after 1819, specifically to fund the resettlement in Liberia of Africans seized by the American navy in its efforts to suppress the African slave trade. See David F. Ericson, "The American Colonization Society's Not-So-Private Colonization Project," ibid., 111–128.

tively making up for the dearth of federal money the ACS received. At the same time, these auxiliaries would impart a reformist zeal to their parent organization. To drum up enthusiasm for colonization, Gurley spread the ACS's message far and wide. He established the nationally circulated journal, *African Repository*, and engaged with traveling agents who could visit local communities to encourage the formation of auxiliary organizations.[58]

A Connecticut-born Presbyterian, Gurley was imbued with the evangelical reform doctrines that had inspired the northern wing of the ACS at its founding. Gurley spoke passionately of the need to redeem Africa, Christianize pagan Africans, and relieve free black Americans from their miserable inequality. He also made clear that the ACS sought the "gradual abolition of slavery," though by "voluntary dissolution" and with the approbation of white southerners. If Gurley designed to put the ACS's ideological rationale more in line with northern social reformers than with southern politicians, he also wanted to appeal to the "moral principle" and "moral feelings" of white Americans instead of the motives of "interest or expediency" that had dictated the ACS's reform strategy since 1816. For Gurley, a key part of this overture to "moral principle" meant explaining that colonizationists aimed to rescue the "notoriously ignorant, degraded and miserable, mentally diseased, broken-spirited" persons of color of the northern cities by sending them to Africa. The deteriorating state of race relations in the North certainly made this message more powerful.[59]

One of Gurley's prime targets were social reformers of the mid-Atlantic. With a large free black population and a long history of involvement in causes associated with African American uplift, the region seemed amenable to Gurley's plans. In fact, it was. Between 1823 and 1829, auxiliary societies to the ACS were founded in Philadelphia, New York, Princeton, New Jersey, and Wilmington, Delaware. These auxiliaries revived the interpretation of black removal to Africa that emphasized the emancipatory possibilities of the movement. They argued that colonization would relieve free blacks from the surrounding environment of white prejudice and the white public from enduring black degradation. They also insisted that colonization would usher in abolition in the South by giving slaveholders a dis-

58. Speech of Mister Gurley, in "Annual Meeting of the Colonization Society," in *African Repository and Colonial Journal*, I, no. 1 (March 1825), 18; Staudenraus, *The African Colonization Movement*, 97–100, 117.

59. Resolution of Mr. Gurley, Feb. 19, 1825, in "Annual Meeting of the Colonization Society," *African Repository and Colonial Journal*, I, no. I (March 1825) 17; ibid., I, no. 2 (April 1825), 34, 37; ibid., I, no. 3 (May 1825), 68.

tant land where they could send freedpeople. Though the message of these "benevolent" or "humanitarian" colonizationists was not new, mid-Atlantic colonization societies gave organizational sanction to an ideology of reform adverse to nearly every principle of the first abolition movement.[60]

For mid-Atlantic colonizationists, the immutability of white prejudice stood as the primary supposition of their reform program. To Lucius Elmer of the New Jersey Colonization Society (NJCS), the "former origin" of freedpersons and the color of their skin "impose[d] an impassible barrier" to black integration. Stacey Potts, also of the NJCS, avowed that a wall between white and black as "fixed and changeless as the shade of colour by which" those of African descent were "distinguished" made colonization a necessity. A member of the New-York State Colonization Society (NYSCS), arguing that the "separation of the blacks from the whites" was essential, exclaimed that "laws may declare a black man to be free; but they cannot make him white." Speaking on behalf of the Pennsylvania Colonization Society (PCS), John H. Kennedy seconded this line of thought when he concluded that "prejudices" put "insuperable obstacles" in the way of black freedom "where no legal disabilities exist." First movement abolitionists had based their reform on the idea that white prejudice was fluid and capable of being overturned. Mid-Atlantic colonizationists believed white prejudice was an indestructible force. They naturalized the boundaries between black and white in ways that separated them little from the justifications Thomas Jefferson had given for black removal.[61]

60. The Wilmington Union Colonization Society was founded in 1823, the New Jersey Colonization Society in 1824, the Pennsylvania Colonization Society in 1827, and the New-York State Colonization Society in 1829. For background on northern "benevolent" and "humanitarian" colonizationists, see George M. Fredrickson, *The Black Image in the White Mind: The Debate on Afro-American Character and Destiny, 1817–1914* (Middletown, Conn., 1971), 6–27; Beverly C. Tomek, *Colonization and Its Discontents: Emancipation, Emigration, and Antislavery in Antebellum Pennsylvania* (New York, 2011); Nicholas Guyatt, "'The Outskirts of Our Happiness': Race and the Lure of Colonization in the Early Republic," *JAH*, XCV (2009), 986–1011; and Hugh Davis, "Northern Colonizationists and Free Blacks, 1823–1837: A Case Study of Leonard Bacon," *JER*, XVII (1997), 651–675. On the Pennsylvania Colonization Society, see Tomek, *Colonization and Its Discontents*, 43–62, 93–131. For the New Jersey Colonization Society, see James J. Gigantino II, *The Ragged Road to Abolition: Slavery and Freedom in New Jersey, 1775–1865* (Philadelphia, 2015), 175–189.

61. *Proceedings of the First Annual Meeting of the New Jersey Colonization Society; Held at Princeton, July 11, 1825; with Extracts From the Report, etc.* ([Princeton, N.J., 1825]), 13; *Proceedings of the Third Annual Meeting of the New Jersey Colonization Society, Held at Princeton, N.J. August 15, 1827; to Which Is Added the Report of the Board of Managers, etc. etc.* (Princeton, N.J., 1827), 23; *African Colonization: Proceedings of*

That free persons of color were blocked by white prejudice from improving their condition created a degenerate class of depraved vassals, according to mid-Atlantic colonizationists. The emancipated had nothing at stake in a society in which they lived but were not a part. Speaking before the 1829 meeting of the NYSCS, Eliphalet Nott called free blacks an "outcast and isolated race," who were "shunned" and "despised" by the white community. Filling jail cells as "convicts" and staffing menial positions, persons of color were denied "all the incentives to exertion" that created virtue in whites. Another New York colonizationist thought white prejudice made American blacks "depressed to the dust" and left them "a race of beings but little elevated above the brutal creation." Joseph Ingersoll of the PCS testified that the denial of "political equality" and "social rights" to free blacks meant that they were "colonized in the heart of the land of their birth." To Ingersoll, white "habit" and "prejudice" had "totally excluded" African Americans from improvement in the United States. Augustus Taylor tagged those of African descent "a degraded population," whose state "cannot be bettered so long as they remain among us." In their hurry to paint a grim portrait of African American life, these colonizationists ignored the communities of republicans of color that both free black activists of New York and Philadelphia and the abolition societies had worked hard to foster.[62]

the New-York State Colonization Society, on Its Second Anniversary; Together with an Address to the Public, from the Managers Thereof (Albany, N.Y., 1831) 5; John H. Kennedy, *Sympathy, Its Foundation and Legitimate Exercise Considered, in Special Relation to Africa: A Discourse Delivered on the Fourth of July 1828, in the Sixth Presbyterian Church, Philadelphia* (Philadelphia, [1828]), 4. For other examples of mid-Atlantic colonizationists expressing a belief in the impregnable nature of white prejudice, see William T. Hamilton, *A Word for the African: A Sermon, for the Benefit of the American Colonization Society, Delivered in the Second Presbyterian Church, Newark, July 24, 1825* (Newark, N.J., 1825), 23; *African Colonization: Proceedings of the New-York State Colonization Society, on Its First Anniversary; Together with an Address to the Public, from the Managers Thereof* (Albany, N.Y., 1830), 20; and *Extracts from an Article in the North American Review for January, 1824; on the Subject of the American Colonization Society* (Princeton, N.J., 1824), 7.

62. *African Colonization: Proceedings, of the Formation of the New-York State Colonization Society; Together with an Address to the Public, from the Managers Thereof* (Albany, N.Y., 1829), 8; Nathaniel S. Prime, *The Year of Jubilee; but Not to Africans: A Discourse, Delivered July 4th, 1825, Being the 49th Anniversary of American Independence* (Salem, N.Y., 1825), 16; Joseph R. Ingersoll, *Address of Joseph R. Ingersoll at the Annual Meeting of the Pennsylvania Colonization Society, October 25, 1838* (Philadelphia, 1838), 10; *Proceedings of the First Annual Meeting of the New Jersey Colonization Society,* 27. On the mid-Atlantic auxiliaries' emphasis on free black degradation, see also *Proceedings of the New-York State Colonization Society, on Its Second Anniversary,* 26; and *Proceedings of a Meeting Held at Princeton, New-Jersey, July 14, 1824, to Form a*

Mid-Atlantic colonizationists were convinced that intractable white prejudice and eternal black degradation made emancipation absent black removal highly malignant to the white body politic. In an about-face from his earlier optimism, Samuel Miller, a former member of the NYMS, told a gathering of colonization supporters in New Jersey that, because persons of color "will be *treated*" and *"feel* as inferiors," their "degraded *character*" would make them "a constant source of annoyance, or corruption" and a "danger to the whites." They "could never," Miller instructed his audience, "be trusted as faithful citizens." The vice president of the NJCS, James Green, characterized free blacks as "this enormous mass of revolting wretchedness" who embodied a "deadly pollution" that would infect "the whole with a moral and political pestilence" were they not swept out of the Republic. The NYSCS resolved in 1829 that emancipated blacks consisted of "alien enemies." Colonization, the society intoned, would "remove" the "alarming evil" of "a distinct, a degraded, and a wretched race" resident among white Americans. If first movement abolitionists believed formerly enslaved people could become virtuous citizens, mid-Atlantic colonizationists thought such visionary ideas only imperiled the societies into which blacks were liberated.[63]

Notwithstanding their pessimistic take on the condition of African Americans, mid-Atlantic colonizationists did profess their commitment to black uplift. But, even in an area of seeming agreement between first movement abolitionists and the ACS auxiliaries, these two groups could not have been farther apart. For mid-Atlantic colonziationists, it was only outside the United States that people of color could raise their status (see Figure 13). In a July 4 address dedicated to gaining supporters for colonization in New York, the Reverend Nathaniel S. Prime affirmed that free black removal to Africa would save a people who had "previously groaned under the chains of bitter servitude" by granting them "the blessings of freedom and self-government." A Pennsylvania colonizationist verified

---

Society in the State of New-Jersey, to Cooperate with the American Colonization Society (Princeton, N.J., 1824), 17.

63. Samuel Miller, *A Sermon, Preached at New-Ark, October 22d, 1823, before the Synod of New-Jersey, for the Benefit of the African School, under the Care of the Synod* (Trenton, N.J., 1823); 13–14; *Proceedings of a Meeting Held at Princeton, New-Jersey, July 14, 1824,* 15; *Proceedings, of the Formation of the New-York State Colonization Society* (1829), 18. For additional instances of this rationale for colonization, see *Proceedings of the Third Annual Meeting of the New Jersey Colonization Society,* 14–15; and Nathaniel Bouton, *Christian Patriotism: An Address Delivered at Concord, July the Fourth, 1825* (Concord, N.H., 1825), 19–20.

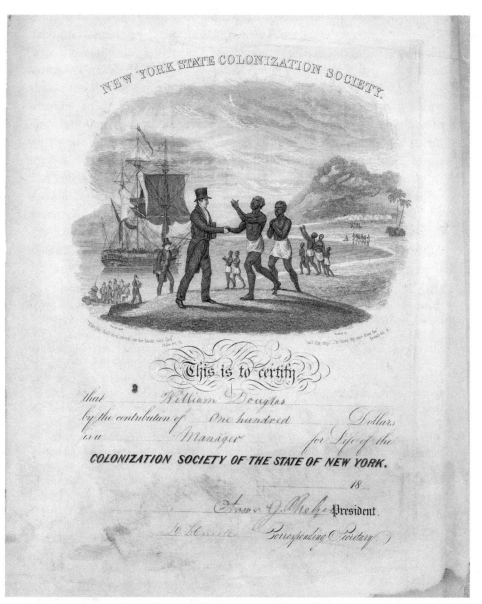

FIGURE 13. New York State Colonization Society Certificate of Membership.
In this illustration, grateful Africans gleefully greet colonizationists who are eager
to spread Christianity and "civilization" to the African continent. This imagined scene
reinforced the ACS's message that it was in Africa, not the American Republic,
where black progress and uplift would unfold—serving as a notable
contrast to the PAS's seal. Courtesy, Scripophilly.com

that in their "father-land," Africa, free blacks could enjoy "unrestrained liberty and perfect equality." The reform-minded New Jersey politician Theodore Frelinghuysen told the NJCS in 1824 that "no finger of scorn" existed to "extinguish" in free blacks "every hope of elevation" in Africa as it did in America. On the African continent, formerly enslaved people would find "manly independence" and shake off the stifling environment of white prejudice. NYSCS member Harmanus Bleeker pronounced that the ACS sought "real freedom" for African Americans in a land where they could "hold up their heads, and feel and act as freemen." Thus, colonization would permit those of African descent to improve themselves and actualize their freedom. But antithetically to first movement abolitionists, who based their entire reform program on the claim that people of African descent were equally entitled to the rights of American citizenship, mid-Atlantic colonizationists swore that black uplift would take place outside the United States and not within it.[64]

64. Prime, *The Year of Jubilee; but Not to Africans*, 18; J. R. Tyson, *A Discourse before the Young Men's Colonization Society of Pennsylvania, Delivered October 24, 1834, in St. Paul's Church, Philadelphia; with a Notice of the Proceedings of the Society, and of Their First Expedition of Coloured Emigrants to Found a Colony at Bassa Cove* (Philadelphia, 1834), 19; Theodore Frelinghuysen, *An Oration: Delivered at Princeton, New Jersey, Nov. 16, 1824; before the New Jersey Colonization Society* (Princeton, N.J., 1824), 11; *Proceedings of the New-York State Colonization Society, on Its Second Anniversary*, 12. An insistence on black uplift in Africa was widespread among northern colonizationists. See *Proceedings of the First Annual Meeting of the New Jersey Colonization Society*, 22–23; Miller, *Sermon, Preached at New-Ark*, 15; and Bouton, *Christian Patriotism*, 16. For the paradoxical thinking of those colonizationists who stressed black removal as an opportunity for African Americans to realize the promises of liberty and equality enshrined in the Declaration—the ideology of which, according to Nicholas Guyatt, formed the basis for the later doctrine of "separate but equal"—see Guyatt, *Bind Us Apart: How Enlightened Americans Invented Racial Segregation* (New York, 2016); and Guyatt, "'The Outskirts of Our Happiness,'" *JAH*, XCV (2009), 986–1011. George Fredrickson notes the many positive characterizations of the innate abilities of black Americans made by northern colonizationists and the efforts of some of these reformers to push back against pseudoscientific biological claims of racial difference (Fredrickson, *The Black Image in the White Mind*, 12–15). But, in their own rhetoric, northern colonizationists played up free black degradation to such a degree that they blurred the line between sociological explanations for African American inequality and permanent, innate ones. When humanitarian colonizationists called black degradation in the United States "inevitable and incurable," they came as close as they possibly could to an argument for permanent, inherent inferiority without explicitly claiming that black inferiority was innate. See "An Address to the Public, by the Managers of the Colonization Society of Connecticut," *African Repository, and Colonial Journal*, IV, no. 4 (June 1828), 118; Fredrickson, *The Black Image in the White Mind*, 17. According to northern colonizationists, as long as

Recognizing the divergence between their movement and the type of antislavery reform that had previously reigned in the region, mid-Atlantic colonizationists discounted the achievements of the first abolition movement. In Pennsylvania, colonizationists cast "doubt" on the outcome of the PAS's efforts. Though the PAS meant well, the benefits of their activism were little. Abolitionists' campaign to protect the rights of blacks had only attracted fugitives from slavery to the state. In turn, the PAS's stubborn insistence on aiding these alleged fugitives enraged southern slaveholders and made abolition much more unlikely than it would have otherwise been. For those whose liberty the PAS had fought to obtain, the only result was a nominal freedom. Though they had spent years attempting to prove the equal capacity of African Americans for freedom, the "moral inferiority of the black man in Pennsylvania" was "irresistible," in the eyes of colonization's boosters. It was high time, colonizationists concluded, that reformers embrace the "more hopeful expectations of success" that the ACS offered antislavery advocates.[65]

Colonizationists panned the undertaking of first movement abolitionists to incorporate free blacks into white society. Theodore Frelinghuysen complained that in New York and Pennsylvania, "after all the toils of benevolence," the activism of the NYMS and PAS had resulted only in a "separate, degraded, scorned, and humbled people" with "a line of demarcation" between black and white "drawn deep and broad; and durable as time." James Green denounced the abolition societies' program of emancipation for "entail[ing] upon us [white New Jerseyeans] ... an evil too intolerable to be borne." Gradual emancipation without black removal had released from bondage "worthless and idle negroes" who spent their time in "drunkenness, and quarrels, and riots." Green alerted white New Jerseyans that they would suffer in "ten-fold degree" the evils of free persons of color among them when the emancipation law, held up by the abolition societies as a victory for humanity, was complete. By presenting abolitionist activism as an unmitigated failure, mid-Atlantic colonizationists worked to turn public opinion against the reformers who had preceded them.[66]

-----

free people of color remained in the American Republic, black inferiority remained a de facto hereditary reality.

65. Tyson, *Discourse before the Young Men's Colonization Society of Pennsylvania*, 8–15; Kennedy, *Sympathy, Its Foundation and Legitimate Exercise Considered*, 7–8.

66. Frelinghuysen, *Oration*, 9; *Proceedings of a Meeting Held at Princeton, New-Jersey, July 14, 1824 to Form a Society*, 19–21. See also *Proceedings of the Third Annual Meeting of the New Jersey Colonization Society*, 18.

For all their differences, one goal linked mid-Atlantic colonizationists and the abolition societies: the abolition of slavery in the South. As often as they claimed black removal would carry with it genuine freedom for free persons of color, the region's ACS auxiliaries contended that colonization offered the sole path to the emancipation of enslaved southerners. Addressing the PCS, Francis Scott Key said that it was "well known" that colonization held out "the only mode in which the friends of Abolition could hope for much success." In the South, where public opinion and legislative enactment militated against freeing the enslaved without their consequent removal, colonization would tear down "a great obstacle" to black freedom and "directly" strengthen the "cause of Abolition," maintained Key. The PCS's board of managers, in the society's first report, wrote that they had every "reason to believe" colonization would "facilitate manumissions" and end up "hastening the entire extirpation of slavery." Eliphalet Nott informed a gathering of New York colonizationists that there were "owners of thousands of slaves ... impatient to emancipate them" if only arrangements could be made for their removal to Africa. Peter Vroom similarly made clear to the NJCS that the expatriation of persons of color would have the effect of "opening the way to a gradual—though general abolition of slavery." The mid-Atlantic colonization society auxiliaries consistently projected the ultimate demise of human bondage as the result of black removal, though they were often careful to add that slavery's end would come voluntarily on the part of southern masters.[67]

The ideology and rhetoric of the mid-Atlantic colonization societies signaled a striking departure from the reform agenda of first movement abolitionists. Whereas the first abolition movement had viewed white ideas of black inferiority as formidable but defeatable, mid-Atlantic coloniza-

67. *Report of the Board of Managers of the Pennsylvania Colonization Society, with an Appendix* (Philadelphia, 1830), 3–4; *The First Report of the Board of Managers, of the Pennsylvania Colonization Society; Read at the Annual Meeting Held April 9th, 1827; with an Appendix* (Philadelphia, 1827), 8; *Proceedings, of the Formation of the New-York State Colonization Society*, 21; *Proceedings of the First Annual Meeting of the New Jersey Colonization Society*, 24. See Kennedy, *Sympathy, Its Foundation and Legitimate Exercise Considered*, 9–10; *The Fourteenth Annual Report of the American Society for Colonizing the Free People of Colour of the United States; with an Appendix* (Washington, D.C., 1831), xii; *Proceedings of the New-York State Colonization Society, on Its First Anniversary*, 7, 10–11; and *Proceedings of the First Annual Meeting of the New Jersey Colonization Society*, 9. For the PCS's commitment to the manumission of enslaved southerners, see Eric Burin, "Rethinking Northern White Support for the African Colonization Movement: The Pennsylvania Colonization Society as an Agent of Emancipation," *Pennsylvania Magazine of History and Biography*, CXXVII (2003), 197–229.

tionists saw only impassable mountains of racial prejudice. The abolition societies and their black partners championed African American civic development and incorporation, but the PCS, NYSCS, and NJCS diagnosed people of color within the nation's borders as permanently damned to degradation. Yet the emancipatory prospect of black removal would transform some first movement abolitionists, still struggling to spread their antislavery formula southward, into colonizationists. For instance, it might have been the idea that colonization could aid abolition in the South that caused thirty-one PAS members to help found the PCS or join the ACS. As advocates of colonization and black removal spread their reformist message, first movement abolitionists would have to respond.[68]

By the time William McMurray made his pitch for the ACS in the summer of 1825, the antislavery reform scene had been remade from the period of the first abolition movement's campaign for statutory emancipation in the mid-Atlantic. Escalating racial divisions in the urban North, a popular culture of white hostility to black freedom, the disfranchisement of black voters in states such as New York, growing sectional divisions over slavery and its spread, and the failure of the first abolition movement to realize its promise of equal rights regardless of race—all resulted in pessimism among many reformers about the prospect of overturning white prejudice. Colonization, once the isolated expressions of small numbers of individuals, now encompassed an extensive movement and offered to a great number of white reformers the only viable solution to both the presence of slavery and the future of free black Americans. That it had become more realistic for many white reformers to envisage the removal of free blacks from the United States than to imagine the removal of racial prejudice suggests a drastically altered antislavery landscape from the 1780s.[69]

Beset by social, economic, cultural, and political trends that moved against their reform program, first movement abolitionists were hardpressed to maintain the earlier optimism of figures like Thomas Paine, who believed prejudice would soon fall away with the advancement of human reason and the ongoing social progress of an enlightened America.

---

68. Tomek, *Colonization and Its Discontents*, 61.

69. In addition to having their suffrage rights severely limited in New York, African Americans were disfranchised in New Jersey in 1807, Connecticut in 1818, Rhode Island in 1822, and Pennsylvania in 1838, along with several other southern and midwestern states between 1800 and 1830.

A speech written by a trustee of the NYMS's African Free School, Reuben Leggett, for delivery by a student at graduation day in 1819 typifies the increasingly dim outlook of a segment of the first movement abolitionist coalition. Leggett had the young black man, James Fields, ask his audience: "Why should I strive hard, and acquire all the constituents of man, If the prevailing genius of the land admits as such, but in an inferior degree. . . . No one will employ me. . . . No one will have me in his office. . . . Drudgery and servitude then are my prospects." At times, words written by black northerners themselves sounded no less gloomy. Peter Williams, Jr., in a notable change from his confidence about eventual racial equality years earlier, deplored in 1830 that "the freedom to which we have attained is defective" and that "the rights of men are decided by the colour of their skin." The piercing question of whether their reform agenda still applied to the problem of slavery would increasingly consume both the abolition societies and their fellow black abolitionists.[70]

70. Anna Mae Duane, *Suffering Childhood in Early America: Violence, Race, and the Making of the Child Victim* (Athens, Ga., 2010), 169–170; Peter Williams, Jr., Address at St. Philip's Protestant Episcopal Church, July 4, 1830, in Philip S. Foner and Robert James Branham, eds., *Lift Every Voice: African American Oratory, 1787–1900* (Tuscaloosa, Ala., 1998), 116.

CHAPTER 6

A Prudent Alternative or
a Dangerous Diversion?

First Movement Abolitionists Respond to Colonization

On August 10, 1817, a large gathering of Philadelphia's black citizens convened to explain to the public their views of colonization. Six months earlier,
in a more hastily called meeting only weeks after the American Colonization Society (ACS) formed, thousands of African Americans had met in
Richard Allen's church to denounce the colonization movement. Now black
Philadelphians sought to lay out to the white public their "feelings and apprehensions." Those assembled gave many reasons for opposing what they
called "the plan of colonizing." In removing "a portion of our brethren, who
are now held in slavery in the south," the ACS would cut "the cords, which
now connect them with us." The African colony, inhabited by those unpre-
pared "for their new situation," would become the "abode of every vice and
the home of every misery." Serving their own interests, slaveholders would
select whom to free and remove to Africa, choosing "only those ... dangerous to keep among them." Colonization would not only strengthen slavery
but break up families, thus replicating "the heart-rending agonies which
were endured by our forefathers when they were dragged into bondage"
and leaving those removed from the United States to "roam childless, wid-
owed, and alone, over the burning plains of Guinea." Free black Philadelphians had "no wish to separate from our present homes." They made clear
that they considered themselves citizens of the American Republic.[1]

While they explained why colonization was such a detrimental and
wrong-headed idea, black Philadelphians made sure to let the public know
why the version of northern emancipation and abolitionism that they be-

1. *Minutes of the Proceedings of a Special Meeting of the Fifteenth American Convention for Promoting the Abolition of Slavery, and Improving the Condition of the African Race ...* (Philadelphia, 1818), ii–iii.

lieved the ACS fundamentally challenged mattered. Two days before the August 10 meeting, a contingent of Philadelphia's whites met to back colonization and form an auxiliary society to the ACS. In response, Philadelphia's people of color, contesting this incursion of the ACS into their city, underlined what they saw as the benefits of northern emancipation. And they did so in first movement abolitionist terms. Freedom had given the formerly enslaved "opportunities for instruction and improvement" and "fitted for their liberty" those of African descent—a take on northern black freedom that could have come just as well from the pen of a member of the Pennsylvania Abolition Society (PAS). Along with the abolition societies, Philadelphia's blacks believed that "the gradual, but certain march of the cause of abolition" was "progressing" and that colonization only impeded the route to total emancipation. To disavow colonization, black Philadelphians asserted their faith in the first abolition movement's reform program.[2]

The abolition societies heard this disavowal loud and clear. When the American Convention's president, Richard Peters of the PAS, asked the prominent free black Philadelphian James Forten, for whom he had previously provided legal counsel, to map out for the abolition societies his community's opinions on the ACS, the sailmaker readily submitted the resolutions of the August 10 meeting. The views of Philadelphia's free blacks helped support the American Convention's dismissal of the ACS in the winter of 1818. The Convention committee assigned to weigh in on the ACS specifically cited the antipathy of many people of color for colonization and included the August 1817 statement of black Philadelphians in its printed minutes. Putting black Americans on an equal plane with their white counterparts as incorporated members of the same nation, the Convention called black opponents of colonization "our fellow men, who are natives of our common country, [and who] acknowledge an alliance and affection for no other." Like black Philadelphians, the Convention believed

2. Ibid., ii. The Philadelphia Society, Auxiliary to the American Society, for Colonizing the Free People of Colour of the ACS was formed on August 8, 1817, following a meeting of white Philadelphians at the State House. See *Poulson's American Daily Advertiser* (Philadelphia), August 8, 1817, [3]. The historical record does not indicate that the society lasted very long, and its demise may in part be attributed to black Philadelphians' issuing such a strident, public repudiation of colonization. Free black Philadelphians met for a third time in 1819 to censure African colonization in reaction to support among some free blacks for the ACS. See *Niles' Weekly Register* (Baltimore), Nov. 27, 1819, [201]. It does not seem that New York's black community was initially as steadfast or vocal in their opposition to the ACS, although that would change by the late 1820s and early 1830s.

the ACS's colonization plan would arrest "the slow but certain progress of those principles" that first movement abolitionists fought for and that were leading to "universal emancipation." Together, urban mid-Atlantic blacks and the American Convention had taken a stand against the ACS by proclaiming quintessentially first abolition movement ideals and rhetoric.[3]

Even as the abolition societies and their black allies expressed key tenets of first movement abolitionism, an array of dispiriting developments challenged their credo and forced them to continuously engage with colonization. Quickening northern white racism, abiding black inequality, and the endurance and dispersion of chattel slavery in the United States all tested the commitment of first movement abolitionists to their long-standing reform program. The response of abolitionists, black and white, to this changed environment was complex and multifaceted. Colonization's emergence as a potential tool for slavery's eradication drove a wedge between competing factions at the American Convention. As the focus of antislavery reform moved south, where support among abolition societies for black removal was stronger than in the mid-Atlantic, vanguard abolitionist organizations like the PAS and the New-York Manumission Society (NYMS) were forced to question whether their formula for black liberation applied. What ensued was a long and divisive debate that fractured the abolition societies and signaled the rising influence of colonization among white reformers as an answer to ending slavery.

Some prominent black reformers of the mid-Atlantic would support emigration ventures to Africa and Haiti. But, with their claims to American citizenship under direct threat from the ideology of the ACS, people of color more readily distinguished colonization from emancipation. Black ideas of emigration, which emphasized Christianizing and improving Africa and imagined Haiti as an escape hatch for some people of color from white American prejudice, could at times sound similar to colonization. Yet black support for emigration abroad and the desire of northern people of color to fight for freedom and equality at home were not mutually exclusive, as they were for most members and supporters of the ACS. Rarely did mid-Atlantic blacks marry emigration plans to strategies for abolishing slavery, as did some colonization supporters and American Convention members. People of color and the abolition societies of the mid-Atlantic had jointly discredited the ACS soon after its founding. But, by the beginning of the 1830s, it was black activists who had become the foremost

3. *Minutes of the Proceedings of a Special Meeting of the Fifteenth American Convention for Promoting the Abolition of Slavery* (1818), 50, 53.

champions of first movement abolitionist values, advancing the cause of combating slavery by overturning white prejudice and improving the condition of African Americans within the United States.

NORTHERN BLACK CONCEPTIONS OF COLONIZATION AND EMIGRATION

From entertaining emigration plans to rejecting the ACS, northern free blacks' intricate approach to questions of the place and future of people of African descent in America during the early nineteenth century is essential to understanding how abolitionists responded to the colonization movement. People of color devised plans for emigrating to Africa from the Republic's earliest years. The first groups of blacks in America to explore African emigration lived in New England. Boston's African Lodge of Free Masons and Newport's African Union Society (AUS)—both of which most likely included several individuals born in Africa—looked to improve the condition of their members and those they considered their brethren in Africa.[4]

Though these organizations, especially the AUS, wanted to establish African settlements independent of white control, their rationale for

---

4. The free black Bostonian and activist Prince Hall led the founding of the African Lodge of Freemasons. The Lodge received recognition by the Grand Lodge of England in 1784 (and was given the name African Lodge No. 459) after Hall and other free people of color were refused the right to organize an officially sanctioned lodge by the white St. John's Lodge of Boston. Hall was subsequently named grandmaster of the African Lodge, which rejected white American exclusion and closely identified with Africa even as it expressed ideals of morality and respectability consonant with traditional Masonic, and by extension republican, values. African lodges subsequently formed in several New England and mid-Atlantic states during the early Republic, and a separate branch of American freemasonry, referred to as Prince Hall Freemasonry, was born. On Prince Hall and black American freemasonry, see Peter P. Hinks and Stephen Kantrowitz, eds., *All Men Free and Brethren: Essays on the History of African American Freemasonry* (Ithaca, N.Y., 2013); James Sidbury, *Becoming African in America: Race and Nation in the Early Black Atlantic* (Oxford, 2007), 73–77; and Kantrowitz, "'Intended for the Better Government of Man': The Political History of African American Freemasonry in the Era of Emancipation," *Journal of American History*, XCVI (2010), 1001–1026. The AUS was founded by Newport blacks as a mutual relief and benevolent society in the same mold as comparable societies founded in late-eighteenth- and early-nineteenth-century Philadelphia and New York—such as the Free African Society of Philadelphia and the New York African Society for Mutual Relief. Although the AUS had similar rules and strictures to the mid-Atlantic societies, unlike its counterparts it advocated the emigration of at least a portion of free black Americans to Africa. On the AUS, see William H. Robinson, ed., *The Proceedings of the Free African Union Society and the African Benevolent Society, Newport, Rhode Island, 1780–1824* (Providence, R.I., 1976).

leaving the United States echoed a prominent white promoter of black emigration from the same region and period, New England Congregationalist Samuel Hopkins. Analogous to Hopkins, both members of the African
Lodge and the AUS accepted the permanency of white prejudice, argued
that only outside the United States would people of color gain the rights of
free persons, and framed the emigration of black Americans to Africa as a
way to bring Christianity to a pagan people. A 1787 petition by the African
Lodge to the Massachusetts General Court requesting financial aid for the
petitioners to relocate to Africa began by specifying the "very disagreeable
and disadvantageous circumstances" facing free blacks in Massachusetts.
The African Lodge believed these deleterious conditions were permanent,
predicting that they "must attend us, so long as we and our children live
in America." But in Africa "we shall live among our equals, and be more
comfortable and happy." The pious blacks belonging to the African Lodge
also pledged to form a church before emigrating and wrote to the General
Court that they would serve as an "inlightening and civilizing" influence
on heathen Africa. The AUS pictured emigration to Africa similarly. The
group wanted to bring Christian light to the "heathenish darkness and barbarity" of the African continent and noted sorrowfully the "many disadvan-
tages and evils which are likely to continue on us and our children, while
we and they live in" the United States.[5]

But, when AUS members attempted to join forces with what they thought
was a like-minded organization in the mid-Atlantic, their overtures were
rebuked. The Free African Society of Philadelphia (FAS)—a mutual relief
and free black improvement organization—had been founded by Richard
Allen and Absalom Jones in 1787 and maintained connections to Quaker
reformers and the PAS, as revealed in Chapter 3. In the summer of 1789,
by which time the PAS and black Philadelphians had already begun to
form an alliance based on preparing free persons of color for virtuous citizenship, the FAS received a letter from the AUS asking for solidarity in
the goal of "returning to Africa." Designating themselves "strangers and
outcasts in a strange land," members of the AUS referred to Africa, not
the United States, as "their own country." Emigration abroad would bring
people of color to a continent where they could be "more happy" and away
from a land where "thousands of our brethren" suffered under the "abject

5. Sidney Kaplan and Emma Nogrady Kaplan, *The Black Presence in the Era of the
American Revolution*, rev. ed. (Amherst, Mass., 1989), 206–209; W[illia]m Douglass,
*Annals of the First African Church, in the United States of America, Now Styled the Afri-
can Episcopal Church of St. Thomas, Philadelphia* ... (Philadelphia, 1862), 26.

state of slavery" while improving Africa through the migrants' Christian influence.[6]

With burgeoning allegiances to the reform program of abolition societies like the PAS, emigration did not appear a solution to slavery and racial inequality for many free blacks of the urban mid-Atlantic. The FAS replied to the AUS that, although it wished its members "the arm of divine protection," the society had "little to communicate" on the topic of African emigration. Instead, the FAS acknowledged the obstacles in the way of free black uplift but expressed a cautious optimism regarding the prospects of black freedom and equality in the United States. Most likely alluding to the PAS, the FAS wrote that "persons who are sacrificing their own time, ease and property" on behalf of Philadelphia's blacks denoted that the prophecy of human freedom "is fulfilling daily for us" and that moving outside the bounds of the United States was therefore unnecessary. In a letter to the African Lodge around the same time as its reply to the AUS, the FAS counseled Boston's blacks that they should maintain morally strict habits and warned that contrary behavior "enables our enemies to declare that we are not fit for freedom." This was classic first abolitionist movement advice.[7]

The emigrationist plans of the African Lodge and the AUS never materialized. Black American ideas of emigration, however, were revived and advanced further than before through the efforts of one man, Paul Cuffe. Born free in 1759 off the coast of Massachusetts on Cuttyhunk Island, Cuffe shared a generational and geographical perspective with the African Lodge and AUS. Yet Cuffe's vision of emigration brought new emphases. Cuffe enjoyed financial wealth as a New England merchant. With little formal education and humble beginnings, Cuffe had defied the odds. But his economic

6. Douglass, *Annals of the First African Church*, 26–27.

7. Ibid., 28–29, 32. Although the FAS clearly rejected the emigrationist overtures of the AUS in 1789, there is evidence that some black Philadelphians did, at least for a time, entertain the possibility of partial free black emigration to Africa. A petition addressed to the federal Congress, probably penned at some point during the 1790s and signed by a number of Philadelphian persons of color, asked for national legislators to help facilitate the establishment of an African colony similar to British-sponsored Sierra Leone. This hypothetical colony would act as an "Assalem for such as may meline [incline] who are free, to resort" to emigration to Africa, particularly those "at a loss for a livelihood." Even as this document demonstrates pro-emigrationist sentiment among blacks in Philadelphia in the early national period, the petition was never submitted to Congress. See Richard S. Newman, Roy E. Finkenbine, and Douglass Mooney, "Philadelphia Emigrationist Petition, circa 1792: An Introduction," *William and Mary Quarterly*, 3d Ser., LXIV (2007), 161–166 (quotations on 165). Although the exact date of the petition is unclear, it is safe to assume that it was written at some point during the residency of the federal Congress in Philadelphia, from December 1790 to May 1800.

success did not cause Cuffe to ignore the plight of his oppressed brethren. Although he supported black improvement in America, being the son of a native African gave Cuffe a great interest in and attachment to the continent of Africa. Cuffe's membership in the Society of Friends allowed him access to the transatlantic antislavery network of Quaker activists. It was this network that provided Cuffe with an opportunity to make good on his desire to lift up the land of his ancestors. In the summer of 1808, Friend James Pemberton, the vice president of the PAS, brought Cuffe's attention to the African Institution of London. Dedicated to "civilizing" and Christianizing Africa, the African Institution was looking for persons of color to help introduce Western forms of industry and agriculture to the English-controlled African colony of Sierra Leone. With an invitation from the governor of Sierra Leone, Cuffe set sail for Africa in December 1810.[8]

Cuffe's trip kicked off his lifelong mission to improve both the African continent and people of African descent. By the improvement of Africa and Africans, Cuffe meant several things. First, he wanted to offer Africans an alternative to the slave trade. Cuffe shared the nearly universal belief among both black and white antislavery activists that the slave trade had ruined the once proud people of Africa. By bringing non-slavery-related commerce to Africa, Cuffe planned to offer his black brethren deliverance from the sin of slave trading. But overcoming the depredations of slavery was not the only thing Cuffe hoped to give to Africans. Cuffe envisioned the spread of Christianity and American civilization to Africa as well. After all, Cuffe was the product of a republican society that believed commerce, Christianity, and American civilization were all interlocked. Third, and key to his plan, Cuffe sought to recruit black Americans willing to travel

8. James Pemberton to Paul Cuffe, June 8, 1808, in Rosalind Cobb Wiggins, [ed.], *Captain Paul Cuffe's Logs and Letters, 1808–1817: A Black Quaker's 'Voice from within the Veil'* (Washington, D.C., 1996), 77–78. Boston's African Lodge never received assistance from the Massachusetts state government and was not able to secure the funds necessary to establish an African settlement. The AUS's short-lived sister society, the Providence African Society, did manage to send a local black man named McKenzie (who was also a member of Prince Hall's Boston African Lodge) on an exploratory trip to Africa. As a result, the governor of Sierra Leone, Zachary Macaulay, agreed to accept the settlement of up to twelve black families who would be sent by the Providence Society. Yet the agreement hinged on each of the families getting letters in support of their moral character from several sources, including Samuel Hopkins. Hopkins refused to endorse the plans of the Providence Society, and the deal with Macaulay subsequently fell through. See Floyd J. Miller, *The Search for a Black Nationality: Black Emigration and Colonization, 1787–1863* (Urbana, Ill., 1975), 15–20. It was Cuffe who first made black emigration a full-fledged movement. On Cuffe's early life, see Miller, *The Search for a Black Nationality*, 22–24; and Sidbury, *Becoming African in America*, 145–146.

to Africa and transmit the values he wanted the natives to adopt. Cuffe hoped that by persuading some republicans of color to make a "Temporary residence" in Africa he could introduce "industry s[o]briety and frugality amongst the nations of that country." Ultimately, Cuffe sought for black Americans to forge commercial partnerships with Africans. It was in this partnership that Cuffe beheld the grandest effects of his plan. By making Africa "a Nation to be ... Numbered among the historians nations of the World," Cuffe would create a transatlantic network of industrious, pious, and respectable blacks. These virtuous blacks would then raise the status of the entire race by proving that all persons of African descent were equal to "the white Brother." This African / African American commercial plan based on black republican virtue is what made Cuffe's vision unique.[9]

Cuffe's initial interpretation of emigration provides a stark contrast with that of the ACS's later racially reactive colonization program, premised on black exclusion from the American Republic. Like some northern founders of the ACS, Cuffe sought the uplift and Christianization of Africans. Yet he grounded his understanding of emigration in a positive vision of the joint improvement of people of color in United States and Africa. Whereas the ACS would go on to push for total and permanent black migration and saw emancipation as dependent on black removal, at this juncture Cuffe sought partial and temporary African American emigration and did not couch his plan as a solution to the problem of slavery.

To gain financial support for his proposal and win converts to his cause, Cuffe toured cities with large free black communities. Unsurprisingly given the outlines of his plan, the mariner found a receptive audience among black activists of the mid-Atlantic—including Peter Williams, Jr., of New York and James Forten and Russell Parrott of Philadelphia. Forten, Philadelphia's thriving free black sailmaker, found great appeal in the commercial possibilities of Cuffe's plan. Though he had no intention of moving to Africa himself, Forten and his fellow black businessmen could brighten the prospects of their African brethren while extending their business interests.

Perhaps more profoundly than commercial considerations, Cuffe's goal of the regeneration of Africa resonated with black abolitionists of the mid-Atlantic. In their orations on the abolition of the slave trade, New York's and Philadelphia's free black community leaders anticipated the simultaneous uplift of Africans and African Americans as the precursor of a new

---

9. Miller, *The Search for a Black Nationality*, 25–30; Cuffe to William Allen, Mar. 22, 1811, 119, "The Memorial Petition," June 16, 1813, 252–253, and Cuffe to Cato Sawyer, Feb. 17, 1814, 271, all in Wiggins, [ed.], *Cuffe's Logs and Letters*.

era free of black degradation. As he extolled the egalitarian prospects of blacks in America, Williams correspondingly espied the imminent arrival of a "glorious day" when the "clouds which have hovered with destruction over the land of Africa" would give way to "the most brilliant rays of future prosperity." Cuffe's program must have appeared to the likes of Williams, Parrott, and Forten as the embodiment of their hopes for black improvement on both sides of the Atlantic. With the loyalty of prominent men of color secured, Cuffe initiated the establishment of African Institutions in Philadelphia and New York. Meant to open a correspondence with similar organizations in London and Sierra Leone, the African Institutions of the mid-Atlantic also scoured New York and Philadelphia for potential colonists and raised money for Cuffe's trips to Africa.[10]

But in 1816 Cuffe abruptly altered his program. Whereas he had once imagined the impermanent and small-scale emigration of free blacks from northern cities, he now advocated the permanent and wholesale settlement of manumitted blacks of the South. Cuffe wrote to Samuel Mills, soon to be cofounder of the ACS, in August 1816 about his changed idea of who would travel to Africa. Sharing the rhetoric of those members of the ACS who claimed African colonization would encourage emancipation, Cuffe explained that "it appears many" southern slaveholders were "willing to manimit their Slaves if Thay could Do it on Safe Ground." The "safe ground" Cuffe referred to was the removal of southern freedpersons. Cuffe had learned that white southerners were "much alarmed on account of the Africans rising." He thought that the creation of both an African and American colony that could receive the formerly enslaved upon their manumission might "prevent all Insurrection and bloodshed" currently feared by southern slaveholders. In subsequent letters to his supporters, Cuffe reiterated this entirely different idea, which now sounded a lot like black removal as envisioned by colonizationists.[11]

10. Peter Williams, Jr., *An Oration on the Abolition of the Slave Trade; Delivered in the African Church, in the City of New-York, January 1, 1808* (New York, 1808), 19; Julie Winch, *Philadelphia's Black Elite: Activism, Accommodation, and the Struggle for Autonomy, 1787–1848* (Philadelphia, 1988), 32–33. For similar rhetoric to that of Williams on the glowing future of Africa in the wake of the abolition of the international slave trade, see Lawrence, *An Oration on the Abolition of the Slave Trade,* 6; and William Miller, *A Sermon on the Abolition of the Slave Trade: Delivered in the African Church, New-York, on the First of January, 1810* (New York, 1810), 4–5. Blacks in Baltimore founded an African Institution in addition to those in New York and Philadelphia. Despite their efforts, the African Institutions could find very few potential emigrants willing to relocate to Sierra Leone.

11. Cuffe to Samuel J. Mills, Aug. 6, 1816, in Wiggins, [ed.], *Cuffe's Logs and Letters,*

What prompted Cuffe to transform his plan? The answer most likely lies in Cuffe's realization by 1816 that repackaging his emigrationist program could give new life to his dreams of rejuvenating Africa. Cuffe's trip to Africa in 1810 had met with some success. He had encountered a group of Africans eager to stimulate mercantile development and founded with them the Friendly Society of Sierra Leone, which was to nurture the commercial ambitions of the colony. Cuffe even got the British government to officially recognize his right to trade with Sierra Leone. But Cuffe happened to return to the United States just as the War of 1812 threatened his plans. Though he met with President James Madison and petitioned Congress, hostilities between England and the American Republic negated any chance that Cuffe might win federal recognition of trade between the United States and Sierra Leone. Undaunted, Cuffe set sail again for Sierra Leone in December 1815, this time with thirty-eight black American colonists. This trip, however, came at great economic cost as instability in Sierra Leone and assistance to the African American migrants exacted a heavy toll on Cuffe's finances. When Robert Finley and Samuel Mills contacted the black mariner about their own expectations for African colonization, Cuffe had open ears. The knowledge that Washington's political elites approved a colonization scheme involving Africa, irrespective of this scheme's philosophical departure from his own emigrationist attempts, must have given Cuffe hope that his faltering efforts might finally bring recognition and support from the federal government.[12]

At first, free black activists seemed open to supporting Cuffe despite his new conception of African American emigration. One explanation is their

---

432–433. On Cuffe's similar language in subsequent letters to his white colonizationist correspondents. See, for example, Cuffe to Samuel C. Aiken, Aug. 7, 1816, ibid., 434–435. Miller, *The Search for a Black Nationality*, 44–47, argues that the major change in Cuffe's understanding of black emigration was his new stress on how the colonization of Africa would benefit African Americans instead of Africans. Although Miller interprets Cuffe's original conception of colonization as bettering exclusively Africans, Cuffe's earlier visions did aim at raising up those of African descent generally, even if he mainly focused on Africans in Africa.

12. Miller, *The Search for a Black Nationality*, 27–47. Finley was careful to present only the emancipatory side of white colonizationist ideology, writing to Cuffe that an African colony would allow black Americans to "rise to their proper level" (Robert Finley to Cuffe, Dec. 5, 1816, Paul Cuffe Papers, New Bedford Free Public Library, Mass., quoted ibid., 45). There is no evidence that Cuffe endorsed the view of Finley that colonization could free the urban North of allegedly degraded blacks. Cuffe makes only veiled allusions to the permanent colonization of free people of color in his correspondence, referring mainly to the removal of manumitted black southerners. See Cuffe to Finley, Jan. 8, 1817, in Wiggins, [ed.], *Cuffe's Logs and Letters*, 492.

admiration for the man. When Cuffe died in the summer of 1817 he was mourned by Peter Williams, Jr., who delivered a eulogy for his friend in the African Methodist Episcopal Zion Church. Williams wanted his audience to appreciate that Cuffe had emerged from "poverty, ignorance and obscurity" to "wealth, to influence, to respectability." The memory of Cuffe, "a man who was truly great," Williams thought "should be placed in our bosoms" for "public imitation and esteem." Williams used this image of Cuffe to caution the crowd not to "hastily condemn a measure to which every fibre of his heart clung." Now that black emigration was becoming associated with the ACS, the reverend asked his parishioners to "suspend our judgments" of colonization until it was clear in what direction the movement was headed. The close friendships Cuffe crafted with free black leaders of the mid-Atlantic stopped them from censuring an idea that, though certainly different from Cuffe's original plan, shared overtones with the version of black emigration that men like Williams had actively supported before the founding of the ACS.[13]

Black activists seriously pondered an alliance with antislavery forces in the ACS for another, more grim reason. By 1816, black abolitionist optimism about racial uplift in America had lost momentum. Growing white northern hostility to the presence of persons of African descent, and enduring free black social and political inequality in cities like Philadelphia and New York, tested the progressive outlook of the urban mid-Atlantic's leading men of color. James Forten expressed his exasperation with the Pennsylvania Assembly's 1813 Act to Prevent the Migration of People of Color into the City and County of Philadelphia (see Figure 14). Having achieved economic success and republican respectability through biracial partnerships, Forten must have felt especially stung by how the proposed law depicted people of color as unwanted aliens and assumed black Philadelphians were worthy of no more than a second-class status. By compelling all African Americans to carry certificates of freedom and threatening with jail and reenslavement those who did not, Forten predicted that the legislation would "swallow our rights, as fellow creatures; our privileges, as citizens; and our liberties, as men!" He lamented that it was pointless for free blacks to cultivate institutions and organizations to "correct their morals and to render them not only honest but useful members to society." If the state's legislators gave their consent to the bill, all persons of color,

13. Peter Williams, Jr., *A Discourse, Delivered on the Death of Capt. Paul Cuffe, before the New-York African Institution, in the African Methodist Episcopal Zion Church, October 21, 1817 ...* (New York, 1817), 4–5, 16.

FIGURE 14. *James Forten*. 1818. Leon Gardiner Collection of American Negro Historical Society Records. Courtesy, Historical Society of Pennsylvania

no matter their social or economic standing, would be treated with blithe contempt.[14]

What the bill portended for black Pennsylvanians' future was bad enough, but equally troubling to Forten was the era of progress and promise it threatened to leave behind. The American nation had been founded on the ideal of equality, and the Revolutionary generation had realized that these words applied to "the white Man and the African," according to Forten. That Pennsylvania's political leaders had recognized color-blind rights was evident, Forten argued, from the ninth article of the 1790 state constitution stating that "all men are born equally free and independent, and have certain inherent and indefeasible rights." For years, Pennsylvania had applied "the same laws" to its black residents "in our rights and privileges" and refused to "particularize white and black." But now Pennsylvania's legislators proposed to lower the status of free blacks "below the brute" and leave virtuous people of color, "as good citizens as any men can be," fated to "feel the lash of oppression." Although Forten must have breathed a sigh of relief when the bill was not adopted, its drafting signaled troubling signs about the road ahead for free blacks in the state.[15]

By the time of the ACS's inaugural meeting in December 1816, black abolitionists found the ground they stood their activism on shifting. If the triumph of gradual emancipation, the abolition of the international slave trade, and the forward progression of many formerly enslaved people had symbolized the early national era, now the spread of slavery southwestward, a ripening white racial animus, and the resilience of chattel bondage seemed just as, if not more, noteworthy. With biting rhetoric in tow, Russell Parrott's 1816 abolition of the slave trade speech highlighted the hardships confronting black Americans more than any other address before it. Mourning the "injustice of retaining in ignominious servitude a class of fellow creatures" who were "of course worthy a better fate ... in a land, professedly the chosen retreat of liberty," Parrott asked openly, "What is our standing" and "What improvement do we derive" in "this enlightened confederacy"? He rued the sorrowful fact that the lives of far too many persons of color traveled "from infancy to manhood" on "one dark tract allotted to his proscribed feet, unillumed by hope." Parrott encouraged blacks to continue fighting prejudice by leading lives of virtue. Yet his lamentations capture the growing frustrations of free black activists.[16]

14. [James Forten], *Letters from a Man of Colour, on a Late Bill before the Senate of Pennsylvania* ([Philadelphia, 1813]), [1], 8, 11.

15. Ibid., 1, 3, 4, 6, 8, 11.

16. Russell Parrott, *An Address, on the Abolition of the Slave-Trade, Delivered be-*

Not only the spread of slavery and the threat of racially inimical laws but also the compromised socioeconomic condition of free black northerners increasingly bothered community leaders. In an 1815 address intended to celebrate the fifth anniversary of the New-York African Society for Mutual Relief's incorporation by the state government, Peter Vogelsang instead sardonically noted, "It is our unhappy lot to be so circumstanced, that we are overwhelmed with joy at the most common act of justice in our favour." Even as he grudgingly acknowledged that the condition of free blacks was "growing better slowly," more noteworthy to Vogelsang was the "unreasonable prejudice" used to deny people of color the training and employment needed to improve their social standing. Whites expected blacks to "'make bread of stones,'" and racial exclusion left untapped black ingenuity to rot in the "'bosom of disgrace and misery, where there is no recompence or reward—no hope of relief.'" At the beginning of the nineteenth century, many of Philadelphia's and New York's free black community leaders had beamed at African American progress and forecast the defeat of white prejudice. Now Vogelsang asked, "How long shall prejudice continue [as] a way-mark for the finger of derision to point at?" He wondered aloud whether God had intended "us [as] hewers of wood and drawers of water? Forbid it, O father of mercies, forbid it." His disappointment was palpable.[17]

Hopes for black American freedom and equality that had motivated the FAS to spurn African emigration two and a half decades earlier now appeared to some prominent mid-Atlantic men of color as the relic of a naive and overly optimistic period. On the heels of the ACS's formation, Robert Finley seized the opportunity that this pessimism seemed to give to white colonizationists by securing a meeting with several free black leaders of Philadelphia. James Forten, Richard Allen, and Absalom Jones were among those in attendance in early winter 1817 when the New Jersey minister made his case for the ACS. According to Finley's friend and biographer Isaac Brown, Allen, Forten, Jones, and the others entered the meeting "strongly prejudiced against" colonization. But after spending almost an hour being reassured by Finley of the benevolent intentions of the ACS and the efficacious results of its colonization plan, "they declared themselves fully satisfied ... that the thing [colonization] in itself was desirable for

fore the Different African Benevolent Societies, on the 1st of January, 1816 (Philadelphia, 1816), 4–5.

17. An Address Delivered before the New-York African Society for Mutual Relief, in the African Zion Church, 23d March, 1815; Being the Fifth Anniversary of Their Incorporation (New York, 1815), 11–16 (quotations on 11, 13, 14, 16).

them." Allen supposedly "spoke with warmth on some oppressions which they [people of color] suffer from the whites, and spoke warmly in favour of colonization in Africa." Of course, that the only detailed report of this meeting is from a friend of Finley's and a supporter of the ACS means that Brown's account should carry with it a rather large caveat. But a letter that Forten wrote to Cuffe in the same month as the Finley meeting sounded rhetorical notes congruent with colonizationist assumptions. Forten concluded that people of African descent "will never become a people untell they com[e] out from amongst the white people." One of black Philadelphia's most prominent members appeared willing to consider supporting colonization.[18]

Interestingly, the meeting with Finley took place after black Philadelphians issued an unambiguous repudiation of the ACS. But it was not the vanguard of the African American community that led the charge. Soon after the new year 1817, some three thousand of Philadelphia's persons of color gathered in Richard Allen's Mother Bethel Church to announce their judgment of the ACS. They left no question where they stood. "WHEREAS our ancestors (not of choice) were the first cultivators of the wilds of America," the meeting resolved that "we their descendants feel ourselves entitled to participate in the blessings of her luxuriant soil, which their blood and sweat manured." Free black Philadelphians reprobated the ACS for promoting African American exclusion, calling such a stance "in direct violation of those principles, which have been the boast of the republick." The people of color present at Mother Bethel were disturbed most by the ACS's emphasis on alleged black degradation. They disclaimed the "unmerited stigma attempted to be cast upon the reputation" of free persons of color. Instead of identifying with the pan-African identity promulgated by Cuffe and his followers, the crowd at Bethel looked to the enslaved of the South when they called southern bondspersons "our brethren" from whom they would "never" willingly "separate." If the black leadership class had not yet given up on working with white colonizationists, the larger community left no door open to an alliance with the ACS.[19]

18. Isaac V. Brown, [ed.], *Memoirs of the Rev. Robert Finley, D.D. Late Pastor of the Presbyterian Congregation at Basking Ridge New-Jersey, and President of Franklin College, Located at Athens, in the State of Georgia; with Brief Sketches of Some of His Contemporaries, and Numerous Notes* (New Brunswick, N.J., 1819), 101–102; Julie Winch, *A Gentleman of Color: The Life of James Forten* (Oxford, 2003), 191. Evidence that Absalom Jones was present at the meeting with Finley comes from James Forten to Cuffe, Jan. 25, 1817, in Wiggins, [ed.], *Captain Cuffe's Logs and Letters,* 502.

19. *Poulson's American Daily Advertiser,* Aug. 12, 1817, [3]. The Mother Bethel

276]   A PRUDENT ALTERNATIVE OR A DANGEROUS DIVERSION?

Though they joined their brethren in publicly denouncing the ACS, in private Philadelphia's black leaders expressed more ambivalence toward colonization. In addition to the aforementioned meeting with the ACS's Robert Finley, James Forten questioned the resolute rejection of colonization by the great majority of black Philadelphians. Forten chaired the hearing at Mother Bethel and, together with Russell Parrott, signed his name to the anti-ACS resolutions. Yet, in a letter to Cuffe penned not long after the gathering at Mother Bethel, Forten intimated that Philadelphia's blacks were thinking hyperbolically in believing that "all the free people would be compelled to" leave the United States and that the ACS simply peddled the desires of "the slave holders" who sought "to get rid of them [free blacks] to make their property more secure." But because "not one sole" among the meeting's attendees had been in favor of colonization, Forten had chosen to "remain silent." That he put his name to the resolutions critical of the ACS means Forten must have held reservations about the organization. Still, that Robert Finley had gained a meeting with Forten and other eminent free blacks indicates the willingness of some African American abolitionists to hear out the ACS.[20]

The apparently different reactions to the founding of the ACS by African American reformers like James Forten and the larger free black community of Philadelphia requires explanation. Forten might have illuminated why persons of color of his standing were open to learning more about the ACS when he purportedly told Finley that educational and economic uplift ironically made prominent free blacks feel "their degradation more acutely" and that "the more wealthy and the better informed any of them became, the more wretched they were made." Prominent black activists in Philadelphia and New York had been expressing grievances with America's racial climate around this time. Many of these men were worried that the American nation had moved away from Revolutionary mores of equality and were disheartened that the values of slavery's defenders appeared to be winning out. At the local level, they were dismayed that it seemed many more doors to black uplift and societal incorporation were closing than opening.[21]

---

meeting's resolutions were reprinted from New York to Virginia, including *National Advocate* (New York), Aug. 14, 1817, [2]; *Western Monitor* (Lexington, Ky.), Aug. 30, 1817, [2]; *American Watchman* (Wilmington, Del.), Sept. 20, 1817, [4]; and *Genius of Liberty* (Leesburg, Va.), Oct. 7, 1817, [1]. For the meeting with Finley, see Winch, *A Gentleman of Color,* 192–193.

20. Forten to Cuffe, Jan. 25, 1817, in Wiggins, [ed.], *Cuffe's Logs and Letters,* 502.
21. Brown, [ed.], *Memoirs of the Rev. Robert Finley,* 101. It is not known what Forten

Less-prominent persons of color arguably brought another perspective, one that tied them more fundamentally to the everyday activism of the PAS. In the acting committee's dogged work to enforce and expand statutory emancipation, illegally enslaved and other persons of color whose freedom was vulnerable gained agency by teaming up with PAS members to assert their fundamental rights. The PAS also maintained several committees meant to boost liberated blacks in the transition from slavery to freedom, including the society's committee of Guardians, which helped to secure employment for free blacks and served as a resource should employers abuse labor contracts. To many of Philadelphia's people of color in the early nineteenth century, large numbers of whom had migrated from slave societies of the upper South or Caribbean, the aid that the PAS offered must have provided a marked contrast with their enslaved past. Certainly, they faced rampant inequality and white hostility to their presence. But the assistance of white allies in the PAS had also given these men and women very tangible gains and hopes for continued progress in the United States. The continuing resolve of nearly all free black northerners to oppose colonization in Africa, in tandem with the wider broadcasting of the ACS's racially exclusionary views, also must have played a large role in persuading the black vanguard to reassess their position. Whatever the causes, from the issuance of the second denunciation of colonization by Philadelphian blacks in August 1817 Forten adopted obstinate opposition to the ACS.[22]

―――
actually said at the Finley meeting, as the words quoted in this paragraph come from the secondhand claims of Finley's biographer. Backers of the ACS, who were angling for black support for the organization, were hardly neutral observers in the debate within the African American community over colonization. But, taken together with Forten's remarks to Cuffe and his alarm at the growth of white prejudice in Philadelphia, it is plausible that Forten did in fact tell Finley something close to what he was quoted as saying.

22. The deaths of Cuffe and Finley in the fall of 1817 severed the main connection free black leaders of the mid-Atlantic had with African colonization and helped push them toward opposing the ACS. The publication in Philadelphia newspapers of an imagined dialogue between William Penn, Absalom Jones, and Cuffe (the latter two were recently deceased), who were acting as mouthpieces for the ACS in an effort to win black endorsement of the society, might have left a negative impression of the organization for black activists like Forten. See *Union United States Gazette and True American for the Country* (Philadelphia), June 6, 10, 1818, cited in Winch, *A Gentleman of Color*, 198; and Brown, [ed.], *Memoirs of the Rev. Robert Finley*, 313–345. Not all free persons of color opposed the ACS. A good portion of black support for the ACS came from southern slave states. Daniel Coker and Lott Carey, both of Virginia, are examples of prominent free blacks who were won over by the ACS and moved to Liberia to help establish

Although they overwhelmingly opposed the ACS, northern persons of color did not abandon support for all forms of emigration. The excitement over the potential of African American migration to Haiti highlights that certain emigration schemes could win the affection of large numbers of people of color in the mid-Atlantic. Haiti held obvious allure for free blacks of New York and Philadelphia. A nation of autonomous people of color who had broken the shackles of slavery and set up a republic of their own, Haiti embodied many of the qualities northern black activists had spent decades trying to prove to the white public that African Americans possessed. Capacity for self-government, virtuous citizenship, and self-sustaining independence, each of these attributes of republican ideology Haitians appeared to enjoy. Ardor for Haiti epitomized the enduring aspirations among free blacks for uplift and equality. While mid-Atlantic African American reformers continued to yearn for and work toward black incorporation, Haiti provided an insurance policy for those persons of color unable to improve their condition within an increasingly racially divisive America. Yet Haitian emigration did not serve for black northerners, as African colonization did for the ACS and its auxiliaries, as a solution to the problem of slavery or an acceptance of permanent black inequality in the United States.[23]

---

the colony. See Miller, *The Search for a Black Nationality*, 55–74; and John Saillant, ed., "Circular Addressed to the Colored Brethren and Friends in America: An Unpublished Essay by Lott Cary, Sent from Liberia to Virginia, 1827," *Virginia Magazine of History and Biography*, CIV (1996), 481–504. In response to African American opposition to the ACS, black emigrants to Liberia painted a rosy picture of their lives in Africa and depicted those who chose to stay in the United States as foolhardy. One circular written by African American Liberians claimed that upon landing in Africa "the burthen is gone," and "we certainly feel ourselves, for the first time, in a state to improve." The Liberians had only "pity" for African Americans, who knew but "the empty name of liberty" and wrongly remained "in a country that is not yours" under "the delusion which makes you hope for ampler privileges." See "Address of the Colonists to the Free People of Colour in the U.S.," in *Report of the Board of Managers of the Pennsylvania Colonization Society, with an Appendix* (Philadelphia, 1830), 24–25.

23. On northern black support for African American emigration to Haiti, see Sara Fanning, *Caribbean Crossing: African Americans and the Haitian Emigration Movement* (New York, 2015), 3. Fanning argues that prominent free black proponents of Haitian emigration, like Peter Williams, Jr., supported the idea of Haiti as a solution to the quandary of southern enslavement, the island nation acting as an outlet for freed persons of color, whose resettlement outside the United States would supposedly make southern U.S. emancipation possible. Yet there is little evidence supporting this claim. Fanning points to the statement by Williams that "the happiness of millions of the present and future generations, depends upon your prosperity." But Williams just as likely meant by this line that, if successful, the emigrants would prove the ability of

Haitian emigration piqued northern free black interest as early as 1818. Not until 1824, however, did a viable movement to migrate to the island nation surface. That year Loring Dewey, an agent of the ACS stationed in New York City, contacted the president of Haiti, Jean-Pierre Boyer, about the possibility of sending free persons of color to the independent black nation. Dewey was frustrated with black opposition to African colonization and hoped to win free black support for emigration to Haiti. Boyer, believing incorrectly that Dewey was writing for the ACS and not on his own initiative, welcomed what he thought was a prime opportunity for Haiti to gain official recognition by the United States government and receive American blacks who aspired to elevate their status. To attract potential migrants, Boyer offered generous terms to those who moved to Haiti. Migrants who agreed to work uncultivated areas would have their transportation paid for, get three acres of land free of charge, and be provided with provisions. Meanwhile, all migrants would be considered full citizens upon stepping foot on Haitian soil. Boyer sent an emissary, the charming Jonathas Granville, to free black communities in New York and Philadelphia to communicate his liberal offer. African American leaders responded enthusiastically by founding emigration societies and seeking to enlist support for Haitian emigration among their fellow persons of color.[24]

The Haitian government's offer came at exactly the time when race relations in the early-nineteenth-century North began to reach a nadir. Black

---

people of African descent to be virtuous free persons, thus making a stronger case for African American citizenship, rather than implying that manumitted blacks would be transported to Haiti en masse. See *Address of the Board of Managers of the Haytian Emigration Society of Coloured People, to the Emigrants Intending to Sail to the Island of Hayti, in the Brig De Witt Clinton* (New York, 1824), 7.

24. Winch, *A Gentleman of Color*, 209–214; Leslie M. Alexander, *African or American? Black Identity and Political Activism in New York City, 1784–1861* (Urbana, Ill., 2008), 40–42. For details on Boyer's offer, see "Jean Pierre Boyer, President of Hayti, to Mr. Loring D. Dewey, General Agent of the Society for African Colonization, at New-York," Apr. 30, 1824, in *Correspondence Relative to the Emigration to Hayti, of the Free People of Colour, in the United States; Together with the Instructions to the Agent Sent out by President Boyer* (New York, 1824), 8–10. New York's Haytian Emigration Society of Coloured People was founded during the first campaign for free black migration to Haiti in 1818. Black Philadelphians also supported Haitian emigration. Richard Allen played an especially central role in the campaign there to recruit emigrants to the island, serving as the leader of the Philadelphia Emigration Society. See Richard S. Newman, *Freedom's Prophet: Bishop Richard Allen, the AME Church, and the Black Founding Fathers* (New York, 2008), 247–258. See *Information for the Free People of Colour Who are Inclined to Emigrate to Hayti* (Philadelphia, 1825) for an example of the pro-Haitian literature produced by African Americans in Philadelphia.

supporters of Haitian emigration, who had always maintained great pride in the only independent free black nation, mixed a cheerless recognition of white prejudice with an optimistic sense of Haiti's liberating potential. New York's Haytian Emigration Society of Coloured People, led by Peter Williams, Jr., told migrants set to embark that they were going to "remove beyond the influence of the prejudices which oppose the civil, intellectual, and moral advancement of men of colour in the United States" to a place where "a dark complexion will be no disadvantage" and persons of color could "become independent and honourable . . . respectable and happy." It may be tempting to see overtones of the ACS in the words of Williams, and, indeed, the parallels are striking. But the Haitian emigration societies did not encourage total black removal or correlate their support for partial emigration with the abolition of slavery. Even though somewhere between six thousand and thirteen thousand African Americans made the exodus to Haiti, the realities of life there did not meet their expectations. Finding economic opportunities limited and falling victim to a black Haitian prejudice they hardly could have anticipated, most of the migrants came back to the United States disappointed. Although black Americans would continue to view Haiti as proof that people of African descent were capable of a sovereign liberty, the Haitian migration experiment ended only a few years after it had begun.[25]

Though mid-Atlantic blacks are rightly remembered for unequivocally renouncing the ACS, the ways they assessed their relationship to the American Republic are more nuanced. When slaveholder founders of the ACS alleged widespread black degradation and insisted that colonization would leave slavery untouched, the mass of black Philadelphians did not hesitate to denounce a scheme they saw as a threat to both their own well-being and that of their enslaved brethren. Paul Cuffe's African emigrationist program, his late-in-life alliance with northern colonizationists, and the worsening racial climate of the urban North complicated the initial reaction of some prominent black activists to the ACS. Moreover, ascending white prejudice and black exclusion in the North, along with pride in the first black republic, nudged some African American Philadelphians and

---

25. *Address of the Board of Managers of the Haytian Emigration Society of Coloured People*, 3. Language barriers and religious differences helped divide Haitians and black American emigrants. Many of Haiti's elite looked down on African Americans who came to the island, believing the emigrants were not sufficiently wealthy or educated and viewing them as intrusive outsiders. The Haitian government's promises to black Americans of economic prosperity and equal participation in the political process turned out to be untrue as well.

New Yorkers toward emigrating to Haiti. Pivotally, however, mid-Atlantic black communities did not view emigration as a panacea to institutional slavery or as a mechanism of abolition. For these communities, long accustomed to abolitionist agitation based on black incorporation, freedom and equality were battles to be waged on American, not foreign, shores.

AN UNAVOIDABLE TOPIC

If black abolitionists struck a balance between asserting their right and desire to live in the United States as free citizens and exploring emigration, the abolition societies would grapple intensely over the relevance of colonization to their reformism. The emergence of colonization onto the agenda of the abolition societies was indicative of a shift in the locus of antislavery reform from the mid-Atlantic to the South and Southwest. Thirty years after first movement abolitionists began their campaign for black freedom, their antislavery activism had borne much fruit. The successful lobbying for gradual abolition and the appeal of New York City and Philadelphia as safe harbors for freed blacks from the rural mid-Atlantic and upper South (an appeal to which the abolition societies contributed) had revolutionized the status of the region's African Americans. Whereas in 1790 60 percent of the mid-Atlantic's black population had been enslaved, by 1820 seven in ten persons of color were either free or on the path to eventual liberation. Yet, while abolitionists continued to guard the rights of those scheduled to be emancipated and looked to improve the socioeconomic standing of free black communities, they increasingly found that the basic liberty of African Americans was under attack. For, at the same time that slavery was shrinking in the mid-Atlantic, it was expanding in the South. The cotton boom, along with the steady admission of new slave states to the union, caused an insatiable appetite for slave labor in the southern states. With the price of bondspersons on the rise (increasing by approximately 40 percent between 1804 and 1820), many slave dealers made the trip north in search of additional enslaved laborers.[26]

26. In 1790, there were 45,210 enslaved and 17,874 free blacks in the mid-Atlantic, and in 1820 there were 71,934 free blacks and 17,856 enslaved people in the region. Putting aside Delaware, where no statutory abolition was passed, the proportion of free blacks in New York, New Jersey, and Pennsylvania in 1820 was even higher at 75 percent. See the University of Virginia Historical Census Browser, University of Virginia, Geospatial and Statistical Data Center, accessed Sept. 24, 2010, http://fisher.lib.virginia.edu/collections/stats/histcensus/index.html (site discontinued). On slave prices, see Samuel H. Williamson and Louis P. Cain, "Measuring Slavery in 2016 Dollars," MeasuringWorth, 2018, www.measuringworth.com/slavery.php. Slave prices varied widely depending on a host of factors, including the age, sex, skills, and so forth of the indi-

Slavery in the South made the kidnapping of free blacks in the mid-Atlantic a major concern for the abolition societies. The problem of kidnapping was especially endemic in states that bordered the upper South. In 1816, the Delaware Abolition Society reported to the American Convention that kidnappers had "invaded the dwelling of the freeman," sending many of the state's free blacks into "exile and slavery." Delaware's abolitionists blamed the growth of southern slavery for inflicting the "poison" of re-enslavement on their borders and producing "a numerous and loathsome brood of dealers in human flesh." The PAS agonized that many of Pennsylvania's free persons of color were "torn from their homes and relatives" by kidnappers and "forced to a great distance from the means of proving and defending their rights." Because southern states presumed black persons to be enslaved unless proven otherwise, aiding kidnapped free blacks was difficult. The PAS correctly noted that these "outrages upon personal freedom in the free states" derived from "the continuance of slavery in others." The widening dilemma of kidnapping by the mid-1810s tied the legitimacy of the abolitionist cause in the mid-Atlantic to fighting slavery in the South.[27]

---

vidual enslaved person. Yet the monetary prices paid for bondspersons clearly increased greatly in response to the rapid rise of the cotton economy and the spread of slavery. For the slave-based economy of the cotton South and its relationship to the valuations and prices of enslaved people, see Robert William Fogel and Stanley L. Engerman, *Time on the Cross: The Economics of American Negro Slavery* (Boston, 1974). For a rich account of the valuation of enslaved people during their life cycles and the perspectives of people of color held in bondage on being appraised, see Daina Ramey Berry, *The Price for Their Pound of Flesh: The Value of the Enslaved, from Womb to Grave, in the Building of a Nation* (Boston, 2017). Studies charting the growth of slavery in the South in the early nineteenth century include Adam Rothman, *Slave Country: American Expansion and the Origins of the Deep South* (Cambridge, Mass., 2007); John Craig Hammond, *Slavery, Freedom, and Expansion in the Early American West* (Charlottesville, Va., 2007); and Michael Tadman, *Speculators and Slaves: Masters, Traders, and Slaves in the Old South* (Madison, Wis., 1989).

27. *Minutes of the Proceedings of the Fourteenth American Convention for Promoting the Abolition of Slavery, and Improving the Condition of the African Race ...* (Philadelphia, 1816), 18; *Minutes of the Seventeenth Session of the American Convention for Promoting the Abolition of Slavery, and Improving the Condition of the African Race ...* (Philadelphia, 1821), 13–14. Kidnapping had been endemic in the mid-Atlantic long before slavery's expansion in the South. Yet the growth of southern slavery, along with the proliferation of free blacks in the mid-Atlantic and the surfacing of a widespread slave-dealing network, made kidnapping in the mid-Atlantic a larger problem than it was previously. The abolition societies deplored the dilemma of kidnapping and its connection to slavery in the South. See *Minutes of the Proceedings of the Fourteenth American Convention for Promoting the Abolition of Slavery* (1816), 23–24; *Minutes of the Proceedings of the Fifteenth American Convention for Promoting the Abolition of Slavery, and Improving the Condition of the African Race ...* (Philadelphia, 1817), 24;

Not just the protection of free blacks from reenslavement but the ambition to turn their reform agenda into a national initiative brought the abolition societies into a head-on encounter with the colonization movement. Reformers had started the American Convention of Abolition Societies in 1794 with the goal of attracting the participation of antislavery organizations from all parts of the new nation. Although reformers from mid-Atlantic societies dominated the Convention in its early years, societies from Maryland and Virginia had also sent delegates to Convention meetings through the 1790s, encouraging abolitionists from Pennsylvania and New York to believe that first movement abolitionism would not remain a northern phenomenon alone.

Soon after upper southern societies were founded, however, skeptical legislatures and a wary slaveholding public constrained the work of abolitionists. In Maryland, the House of Delegates considered the Baltimore-based abolition society inimical to the public good and the rights of the state's whites. A member of the Virginia Abolition Society reported that many Virginians conceived of organized abolitionism as "dangerous to the well-being of society." Slaveholders in Maryland and Virginia reified their ill will with damaging laws. The legislatures of these two states passed statutes that deterred freedom suits by putting enormous financial burdens on abolitionist plaintiffs and ensuring juries friendly to slaveholding defendants. In turn, this legislation compromised the ability of activists to secure liberty for illegally enslaved people of color—a primary enterprise of first abolition movement reform. By 1801, as white Virginians were still roiled by Gabriel's plot, the president of the abolition society headquartered in Richmond wrote to the American Convention of "a melancholy crisis" and "gloomy prospects with which we are on all sides surrounded." Organized abolitionism in the upper South was on the verge of being eliminated. An upper southern society would not be represented again at the American Convention until 1823.[28]

Minutes of the Eighteenth Session of the American Convention for Promoting the Abolition of Slavery, and Improving the Condition of the African Race ... (Philadelphia, 1823), 11–12; and PPAS, Series 1, reel 2, 47–48, HSP.

28. Ira Berlin, *Slaves without Masters: The Free Negro in the Antebellum South* (New York, 1974), 81–83 (quotation on 81); *Minutes of the Proceedings of the Seventh Convention of Delegates from the Abolition Societies Established in Different Parts of the United States* ... (Philadelphia, 1801), 22. Laws hostile to the abolition societies in Virginia and Maryland were bluntly aimed at eradicating abolitionism in the upper South. Maryland made those who brought freedom suits responsible for paying the costs of slaveholding defendants, in addition to the usual charges assessed to enslaved plaintiffs. In Virginia, the state legislature called for hearings judging the merits of freedom

Despite the disappearance of abolitionist-affiliated societies in the upper South, the American Convention continued to nurse expectations of rehabilitating abolitionism in the region. With total abolition assured in New York in 1817, the Convention spent much of the 1820s trying to encourage the formation of abolition societies in the South, with the intention of bringing southern antislavery back under its organizational umbrella. In 1821, the NYMS wrote to the Convention that it was "very desirable to us to see" activists "in the South and West becoming zealous advocates" of abolition. The NYMS thought the Convention should "encourage our distant brethren," whose "minds and hearts" they believed "in unison with our own," to establish societies for battling human bondage.[29]

The upper southern abolition societies of the 1790s and early 1800s had shared the reform agenda of their northern counterparts. Made up principally, though not completely, of like-minded Quaker activists, the southern societies formed free black schools, guarded the rights of persons of color, and lodged suits on behalf of illicitly enslaved individuals. They also drew from the same well of first movement abolitionist tropes, referencing the goal of "obviating popular prejudices" through enlightening both white and black minds. Yet, when upper southern abolition societies reemerged in the 1820s, mid-Atlantic Convention members would discover that, for antislavery activists below the Mason-Dixon line, black freedom in the South now depended on at least partial African American removal.[30]

As southern slaveholders began to contact the mid-Atlantic abolition societies about wanting to free their bondspersons, the stage was set for the American Convention to wrestle with the question of colonization. At the 1816 Convention, the PAS presented a bundle of letters from southern

---

suits before cases could go to trial, allowed plaintiffs court-appointed lawyers only, and issued a fine of one hundred dollars for the party responsible for bringing any case that did not result in a judgment of freedom for those held as bondspersons. Despite these draconian laws, and the increasingly malevolent approach of both the state and the public to upper southern abolition societies, the governor of Virginia, James Wood, served as vice president of the Virginia Abolition Society during his term in office (1796–1799) and later became the society's president. This remarkable fact shows that not all prominent political figures were either opposed to abolitionist efforts or too cautious to take a public stand in favor of antislavery activism.

29. *Minutes of the Seventeenth Session of the American Convention for Promoting the Abolition of Slavery* (1821), 7.

30. *Minutes of the Proceedings of the Tenth American Convention for Promoting the Abolition of Slavery and Improving the Condition of the African Race* ... (Philadelphia, 1805), 28.

and southwestern slaveholders professing their eagerness for manumission but fretting that they had been blocked from action unless they agreed to banish those whom they freed. One recently deceased Virginian slaveholder, Samuel Guest, gave freedom to three hundred enslaved people in his will. Yet state law required the relocation of the liberated. Cases such as this one convinced the Convention that something more than piecemeal solutions was necessary to address this "peculiarly trying situation" and facilitate southern manumissions. The Convention's delegates decided to petition Congress. The petition stated that "the progress of individual sentiment" among some slaveholders had brought about considerable opportunities for the liberation of southern bondspersons, whose freedom was often blocked by "the difficulty of finding an asylum" for those proposed to be manumitted. As a consequence, the Convention asked Congress to look into putting aside a portion of western territory "for the colonization of legally emancipated blacks." The petition proposed federally sanctioned colonization only for manumitted southern blacks, not for all persons of color in the United States.[31]

At this same meeting, the Convention considered transatlantic options for the repatriation of blacks from the upper South who, without leaving states such as Virginia, might not otherwise gain their freedom. In a clear reference to the quandary of upper southern manumission, the Convention assessed "that many people of colour" in the South "remain in bondage from difficulties in the minds of their owners as to their future disposition, and from the laws of many of the states prohibiting their residence therein after receiving their liberty." The delegates resolved to strike up a correspondence with the African Institution, which had already partnered with Paul Cuffe. A British reform group founded following Parliament's ban on the African slave trade, the African Institution sought to develop the colony of Sierra Leone as a destination for formerly enslaved individuals and a

31. *Minutes of the Proceedings of the Fourteenth American Convention for Promoting the Abolition of Slavery* (1816), 26–28, 32. Though the petition did not propose an ACS-style colonization plan, it did include the statement that a colony could "prevent the injury of the mixture of too large a proportion of such persons [manumitted blacks] amongst the white people." Perhaps owing to the founding of the ACS only months after this petition was drafted, the Convention did not use such racially divisive rhetoric again until the late 1820s, when southern antislavery societies began to assert more influence over the Convention's proceedings. See ibid., 37, for additional evidence of pragmatic support for colonization designed to aid southern manumissions and geared toward solving specific cases in which southern slaveholders wanted to manumit enslaved people but were prohibited from doing so without removing them from the state.

model for European ideals of Christian civilization and slave trade–free commerce on the Continent.[32]

In both its petition to Congress and its resolution to open communication with the African Institution, the Convention was reacting, not to white prejudice or alleged black degradation, but to specific instances in which the prospective freedom of bondspersons could not be obtained without their being removed from the state in which they were enslaved. Colonization had thus emerged on the Convention's agenda without its delegates feeling the need to respond to a competing reform movement or defend the merits of fighting slavery through black incorporation. The growing problem of free black kidnapping, the realization of statutory emancipation in the North, and the hope of rekindling organized abolitionism and facilitating manumission in the upper South had brought the Convention to ponder colonization. Its engagement with this topic had only begun.

THE STALWARTS VERSUS THE PRAGMATISTS

The founding of the ACS at the end of 1816 complicated the American Convention's handling of colonization and inaugurated a broader debate over strategy and tactics that would consume the abolition societies for years. At the 1817 Convention, now that a national organization supporting black removal had formed, a committee appointed to weigh in on colonization issued a cautious rebuke of the ACS program. The committee confirmed that "colonization appears to occupy the minds of a great multitude of our fellow citizens" and acknowledged the "large portion of talent and virtue" that seemed to make up the ACS. Communicating its skepticism over the motives of the ACS, however, the committee expressed the "unqualified wish" that colonization go unsupported "without an immutable pledge from the slaveholding states of a just and wise system of gradual emancipation." The Convention further insisted that "gradual and total emancipation of all persons of colour, and their literary and moral education, should precede their colonization." This latter statement amounted to an indirect rejection of ACS ideology, since the organization believed emancipation unattainable without the prior removal of free blacks and denied that African Americans could improve their condition in the United States. What is more, emancipation and black uplift, according to first movement abolitionist philosophy, would make colonization unnecessary by proving to white Americans that persons of color were capable of a virtuous freedom

32. *Minutes of the Proceedings of the Fourteenth American Convention for Promoting the Abolition of Slavery* (1816), 33.

and turning back the torrent of white prejudice on which the ACS based its reform.[33]

One year after its first statement on the colonization movement, the Convention's criticism of the ACS was not so measured. The 1818 Convention selected a committee to examine closely this prominent organization. The committee, headed by NYMS member Peter A. Jay, responded by issuing a decisive indictment of the ACS. Identifying the ACS as the brainchild of slaveholders, the committee's report excerpted statements from southern members of the organization arguing that colonization had nothing to do with emancipation and that the ACS would make slavery a stronger institution. The committee thought the ACS looked to remove from the Republic free blacks in order to "eternize the bondage" of the enslaved. Jay and his fellow committee members imagined colonizationists inflicting on free blacks every means of tyranny possible so that persons of color would be "driven to adopt, as a refuge from suffering and oppression, transportation to a grave in Africa." Although the 1817 Convention had left open the possibility that the ACS could conceivably support emancipation, the Jay report castigated the ACS for being run by hard-hearted slaveholders conspiring to bolster rather than abolish human bondage.[34]

The Jay report found it equally offensive to the cause of abolitionism that the ACS denied Africans in America were Americans. Expressing the committee's sensitivity to free black northern views of colonization, the report referenced the black community of Philadelphia's rebuff of the ACS and insisted that people of color had as much a right to inhabit the United States as white Americans, people of color rightly "consider[ing] themselves as well the children of" the American Republic "as we do ourselves." Once white Americans gave back North America to the indigenous peoples who had first lived on the land that became the United States, the ACS might expect persons of color to return to Africa, the committee caustically added. The Jay report made more than moral arguments, also shooting down the ACS for the "impracticability" of its plan. The exorbitant

33. *Minutes of the Proceedings of the Fifteenth American Convention for Promoting the Abolition of Slavery* (1817), 30–31. The Convention was guarded in its first public statement on the ACS both because the organization's stances were not totally clear yet and because first movement abolitionists were likely gratified to see the problem of slavery drawing the attention of such politically prominent Americans—the very types of figures whose support the abolition societies had always sought. The 1817 Convention assigned a committee to encourage the formation of more abolition societies, perhaps as an early effort to counter the ACS. See ibid., 27.

34. *Minutes of the Proceedings of a Special Meeting of the Fifteenth American Convention for Promoting the Abolition of Slavery* (1818), 47–49, 53–54.

cost of transportation and the previous failure of other African colonization ventures made the ACS's program of reform bankrupt on all fronts. In
sum, to the Jay committee the ideas of the ACS appeared to "portend ... to
the cause for which our Societies have been associated, every thing which
its friends and advocates ought to dread," and it was an organization the
American Convention had to oppose. The Convention voted unanimously
in favor of the report and prepared an address to its constituent societies
instructing them to "act in concert" in denying the ACS their support.[35]

The Jay report's adoption signified the enduringly negative view of the
ACS held by first movement abolitionist stalwarts. Wary of the ideology and
rhetoric of the ACS, these activists remained wedded to the well-established,
inclusive vision of abolitionism that worked toward black incorporation
and the elimination of white prejudice. Thomas Shipley of the PAS and
Peter A. Jay of the NYMS were both exemplary of those in the Convention
who rejected colonization outright. Shipley, born in 1784, the same year
the PAS was formed, became one of the society's most integral members
soon after he joined in 1817. Shipley immersed himself in the caseload of
the PAS's acting committee. By fighting for the fundamental liberty of black
Philadelphians, Shipley quickly developed empathy for black claims to the
rights of free citizens under Pennsylvania law. He was "scarcely ever absent
from the side" of Philadelphia's people of color, according to an author of
a memoir on Shipley, taking up the acting committee's caseload with an
"energy and zeal" that outmatched most abolitionists.[36]

Shipley also stood up for free black incorporation. Around the time he
became an abolition society member, for instance, the PAS assigned Shipley the task of traveling to the Pennsylvania capitol to lobby state legislators against approving bills banning black in-migration. In 1823, Shipley
served on a PAS committee formed to present a memorial to the Pennsylvania legislature that answered a letter from Maryland legislators to their
Pennsylvania peers. The letter suggested that the Pennsylvania Assembly

35. Ibid., 47–54, 60–68 (quotations on 50, 53, and 65). The 1818 Convention address
to the abolition societies made a thorough case against the ACS, closely echoing the Jay
report. See ibid., 65–68.

36. Isaac Parrish, *Brief Memoirs of Thomas Shipley and Edwin P. Atlee, Read before
the Pennsylvania Society for Promoting the Abolition of Slavery, etc.; Tenth Month, 1837*
(Philadelphia, 1838), 8, 11. Richard S. Newman likewise uses the term "stalwart" when
describing reformers who clung to first movement abolitionist principles, but for very
different purposes. Newman identifies "stalwarts" as those in the PAS who stuck dog-
matically to what he characterizes as conservative activist strategies in the face of calls
for more "radical" tactics. See Newman, *The Transformation of American Abolitionism:
Fighting Slavery in the Early Republic* (Chapel Hill, N.C., 2002), 54–55.

bar black migration to the Quaker state; Maryland's politicians alleged that unimpeded migration was enticing enslaved people from the upper South to run away. The PAS memorial stated that "no distinction of color is recognized in our [Pennsylvania's] code" and reminded Pennsylvania lawmakers that, legally, blacks in their state were "placed on an equal footing with others; if industrious, and honest, they prosper and are protected." Strengthening ties with Maryland, the memorial concluded, should not come at the price of sundering the "inherent rights" of persons of African descent. Consistently enmeshed in activism seeking to secure and guard the basic freedom and rights of people of color must have made Shipley, a frequent delegate to the Convention, hesitant to support an organization that insisted these same people had no future in the United States.[37]

Peter A. Jay, the son of John Jay (a charter member of the NYMS), embodied the NYMS's founding principle that those of African descent should "share, equally with us, in that civil and religious Liberty with which an indulgent Providence has blessed these States." Like his father, the younger Jay served at one time as the president of the NYMS. In 1821, he spearheaded the defense of black suffrage rights at the New York Constitutional Convention, passionately inquiring: "Why, sir, are these men to be excluded from rights which they possess in common with their countrymen? ... Why are they, who were born as free as ourselves, natives of the same country, and deriving from nature and our political institutions, the same rights and privileges which we have, now to be deprived of all those rights, and doomed to remain forever as aliens among us?" Jay spoke out against the view that blacks were permanently sentenced to inferiority, arguing that such a claim contradicted enlightenment precepts and forestalled black potential. This same allegiance to equal rights for blacks inspired Jay to condemn the ACS when he chaired the 1818 American Convention committee asked to look into colonization.[38]

---

37. Newman, *The Transformation of American Abolitionism*, 43; PPAS, Series 1, reel 1, II, 391, HSP. Newman dates an undated letter written by Shipley disclosing his lobbying efforts at the Pennsylvania state capitol on behalf of the PAS to 1814. Yet Shipley's biographer writes that Shipley did not join the PAS until 1817. Thus, either the PAS sent Shipley to represent it before he joined the society, which, considering Shipley's Quaker roots and the PAS's close ties to the Society of Friends, is possible, or the Shipley letter to which Newman refers was penned later than 1814.

38. New-York Manumission Society (NYMS) Records, 1785–1849, I, 4, New-York Historical Society (NYHS); David N. Gellman and David Quigley, *Jim Crow New York: A Documentary History of Race and Citizenship, 1777–1877* (New York, 2003), 183. For more on Peter A. Jay, see John Jay, *Memorials of Peter A. Jay: Compiled for His Descendants* ([Arnheim], Holland, 1929).

Adherents to the traditional formula for emancipation in the mid-Atlantic powered the Convention's resistance to colonization by delivering consistent reminders of their movement's original values. At the same meeting where the Convention would go on to impugn the ACS in 1818, its annual address to the abolition societies reasserted the organization's founding program. While the defense of slavery rested on the claim that "the African race is of an order of beings inferior to our own," the Convention was certain that gradual emancipation laws and black education would show the "fallacy" of white prejudice. As the Convention continued to discuss the topic of colonization eleven years later, stalwarts swore there was "a secret fire enkindled in the public bosom" that abolitionists could draw on to break down "Prejudices imbibed in youth and strengthened by age." The Convention address of 1821 informed the abolition societies that "nothing but perseverance" by the abolitionists could account for the "great change in the public opinion" that had brought about emancipation in the North. The stalwarts "confidently hope[d]" their activism would produce "a similar change in the South." The Convention also broadcast its enduring commitment to first movement abolitionism by continuing to deliver addresses to free blacks. The Convention persistently told persons of color that through lives of "virtue and sobriety" they would bring liberty to "thousands of your colour" by illustrating that those of African descent were equal to whites. Stick staunchly to the tried-and-true values of first movement abolitionism, the stalwarts were convinced, and the forces of emancipation would one day prove irresistible.[39]

Despite the resoluteness of stalwarts, colonization would long remain a viable topic of debate at the Convention. Beginning in 1819, a group of delegates promoting the partial emigration of manumitted blacks pushed the American Convention to confront whether a form of antislavery best described as pragmatic colonization could buttress abolitionism. A com-

39. *Minutes of the Proceedings of a Special Meeting of the Fifteenth American Convention for Promoting the Abolition of Slavery* (1818), 47, 63; *Minutes of the Twenty-First Biennial American Convention for Promoting the Abolition of Slavery, and Improving the Condition of the African Race* ... (Philadelphia, 1829), 21; *Minutes of the Seventeenth Session of the American Convention for Promoting the Abolition of Slavery* (1821), 56. For other times when stalwarts gave voice to their movement's traditional reform formula, see *Minutes of an Adjourned Session of the American Convention for Promoting the Abolition of Slavery, and Improving the Condition of the African Race* ... (Baltimore, 1826), 18; *Minutes of the Twentieth Session of the American Convention for Promoting the Abolition of Slavery, and Improving the Condition of the African Race* ... (Baltimore, 1827), 21–22; and *Minutes of the Eighteenth Session of the American Convention for Promoting the Abolition of Slavery* (1823), 40–41.

mittee at the 1819 Convention drafted a detailed proposal for a western colony of formerly enslaved people. With much lower costs for the relocation of the liberated and the relative proximity of the colony for potential migrants, the committee thought they had found a sensible alternative to African colonization. The committee's report carefully avoided association with the ACS by announcing that "any plan of colonization" with "even a remote tendency to rivet the unhallowed fetters of the slave, this Convention must withhold its concurrence." Still, the committee believed it had discovered the "benevolent aspect" of colonization. The committee presented its proposal as a practical plan that could act as an "incentive to individual emancipation" in the South. Yet, after submitting its report, the committee declined to offer resolutions urging the plan's adoption and advised the Convention to hold off on considering the proposal until more information could be gathered. The committee's proposal of a western colony for liberated blacks reveals that some abolition society members were willing to explore a partial colonization plan if it would contribute to their emancipatory aims.[40]

Pragmatic colonizationists conceived of partial black emigration as a tool of emancipation designed to abolish slavery in the South. Although on this point they agreed with some members of the mid-Atlantic ACS auxiliaries, unlike the ACS pragmatic colonizationists did not call for the removal of northern free blacks. Their pragmatic version of colonization was to be limited to persons of color in the southern states who could not otherwise be freed because of public opinion and legislative statutes. Though they at times turned to ideological arguments to justify their plans, such as the indomitability of white prejudice or the unbreachable division between white and black, these assertions did not form the major rationale for their support of colonization. A commitment to the incorporation of free people of color, on the one hand, and the necessity of the partial removal of southern blacks freed from slavery, on the other, could go together without contradiction for many pragmatic colonizationists.[41]

40. *Minutes of the Sixteenth American Convention for Promoting the Abolition of Slavery, and Improving the Condition of the African Race* ... (Philadelphia, 1819), 50–56 (quotations on 54).

41. I label *colonizationists* those American Convention members in favor of partial black emigration from the southern states because they repeatedly used the term "colonization" when describing their own proposals. See *Minutes of the Proceedings of the Fifteenth American Convention for Promoting the Abolition of Slavery* (1817), 13; *Minutes of the Proceedings of a Special Meeting of the Fifteenth American Convention for Promoting the Abolition of Slavery* (1818), 18; *Minutes of the Eighteenth Session of the American Convention for Promoting the Abolition of Slavery* (1823), 23; *Minutes of an*

Thomas Earle and Benjamin Lundy were two leading champions of pragmatic colonization at the American Convention, and they were emblematic of this unique approach to abolitionist reform. Earle of the PAS was a renegade Democratic politician who continued to be involved with antislavery while his party became more and more proslavery. A renegade member, too, of the PAS, Earle made partial colonization proposals to the American Convention time and again, even as the PAS consistently rejected them. As if to underscore the line pragmatic colonizationists drew between the colonization of manumitted blacks in the South and the rights of free people of color in the North, Earle led the defense of black voters from disfranchisement at the Pennsylvania Constitutional Convention of 1838. He was among those who argued that "withholding the basic right of citizenship from an entire class of people for no other reason than color was both immoral and unjust." Earle not only spoke abstractly in defense of black citizenship, he worked actively in support of it. During the 1830s, Earle became James Forten's primary legal counsel and, according to Forten's biographer, considered the African American sailmaker "his good

---

Adjourned Session of the American Convention for Promoting the Abolition of Slavery (1826), 37; and *Minutes of the Twenty-First Biennial American Convention for Promoting the Abolition of Slavery* (1829), 31, 34. Pragmatic colonizationists also used the terms "removal" and "emigration" interchangeably. By the use of the term *pragmatic colonizationists,* I do not intend to make equivalent the activism of its supporters, who unabashedly pushed for slavery's abolition, and adherents of the American Colonization Society, many of whom did not seek to end chattel bondage. That some Convention delegates viewed the terms "colonization" and "abolition" as synonymous is apparent from an 1829 Convention report in which a leading proponent of pragmatic colonization stated, "The public mind in the greater portion of our country appears more favourable to colonization than to any other proposed means of emancipation" (ibid., 32). Pragmatic colonizationists shared activist perspectives in common with a group of Pennsylvanian reformers Beverly C. Tomek has dubbed "humanitarian colonizationists," who were involved with the Pennsylvania Colonization Society. These humanitarian colonizationists "were convinced that slaveholders were trapped in a system they genuinely wanted out of" and thought that a black colony would allow for large-scale southern manumission; they also believed that "a successful colony would showcase black potential and convince all whites that slavery was wrong." See Tomek, *Colonization and Its Discontents: Emancipation, Emigration, and Antislavery in Antebellum Pennsylvania* (New York, 2011), 100. But there are also noteworthy differences between pragmatic colonizationists and humanitarian colonizationists. The latter group, unlike the former, focused on the impregnable nature of white prejudice and often spoke derogatorily of free blacks in justifying colonization, both characteristics that resulted from their alliance with the ACS, unlike some pragmatic colonizationists who partnered with the American Convention. Just as important a difference, the two leading pragmatic colonizationists—Thomas Earle and Benjamin Lundy—had ties to, and promoted the activism of, northern black reformers, while humanitarian colonizationsts lacked these same connections.

friend as well as his client." Earle had an unquestionable loyalty to the civil rights of free black Americans while believing that partial colonization of people of color in states with large enslaved populations would spur emancipation.[42]

Benjamin Lundy, another steadfast supporter of pragmatic colonization at the American Convention, was an itinerant antislavery activist and newspaper editor (see Figure 15). Probably the most irrepressible abolitionist figure of the 1820s, Lundy also personified the perspective of pragmatic colonizationists. Raised a devout Quaker in New Jersey, Lundy dedicated himself to abolitionism after witnessing the brutality of slavery up close when he moved in 1809 to Wheeling, Virginia. Sitting on the banks of the Ohio River, Wheeling acted as a key site in the interstate slave trade, as bondspersons were forced onto flat-bottomed boats on their way to sale in the proliferating cotton plantations of the South and Southwest. As he watched slave coffles pass through the town's streets, Lundy was acutely affected. "My heart was deeply grieved at the gross abomination; I heard the wail of the captive; I felt his pang of distress; and the iron entered my soul." Not unlike John Woolman, the New Jersey Quaker turned antislavery activist of an earlier generation, Lundy had experienced a conversion to the cause of abolition.[43]

Lundy's initial antislavery statements mirrored those of his fellow

42. Edward Price, "The Black Voting Rights Issue in Pennsylvania, 1780–1900," *Pennsylvania Magazine of History and Biography*, C (1976), 361; Winch, *A Gentleman of Color*, 301. For a biographical account of Earle, see Edwin B. Bronner, *Thomas Earle as a Reformer* (Philadelphia, 1948). Earle was berated by his fellow Pennsylvania Democrats for stridently speaking in defense of equal suffrage rights for blacks. For Earle's role in arguing against black disfranchisement at the Pennsylvania 1837–1838 state convention, see Price, "The Black Voting Rights Issue in Pennsylvania," *PMHB*, C (1976), 356–373; and Nicholas Wood, "'A Sacrifice on the Altar of Slavery': Doughface Politics and Black Disfranchisement in Pennsylvania, 1837–1838," *Journal of the Early Republic*, XXXI (2011), 96–97, 104. Though I have chosen to refer to them as pragmatic colonizationists in emphasizing the perspective and plans they brought to the American Convention, Lundy and Earle could justly be labeled emigrationists too—both supported Haitian emigration and had close ties with free black northerners and African American abolitionists. It should also be noted that Lundy and Earle undoubtedly sought slavery's abolition.

43. [Thomas Earle and Benjamin Lundy], *The Life, Travels, and Opinions of Benjamin Lundy; Including His Journeys to Texas and Mexico* ... (Philadelphia, 1847), 15. Other sources on Lundy's life and activism include Merton L. Dillon, *Benjamin Lundy and the Struggle for Negro Freedom* (Urbana, Ill., 1966); Jane H. Pease and William H. Pease, *Bound with Them in Chains: A Biographical History of the Antislavery Movement* (Westport, Conn., 1972), 90–114; and Manisha Sinha, *The Slave's Cause: A History of Abolition* (New Haven, Conn., 2016), 177–182.

FIGURE 15. *Benjamin Lundy.* Circa 1820. Portraits of Benjamin Lundy. ALO7938.
Courtesy of the Ohio History Connection

Quaker activists and reflected the ethics of first movement abolitionism. Now resident in the Quaker town of Saint Clairsville, Ohio, in 1816 Lundy founded the Union Humane Society. The society's constitution listed the Golden Rule, the natural equality of all, and the idea that skin color should not determine status as its operating ideals. In a refrain that could have come directly from the PAS or NYMS, the Union Humane Society stated that it wanted to "restore" to "our fellow men, the rights and priviliges of which they are deprived." The Union Humane Society's goals—including ending white prejudice, gaining "civil rights" for people of color, and making free blacks "useful members of civil and religious society"—were also fully in line with the aims of the mid-Atlantic abolition societies. Furthermore, Lundy laced his rhetoric with expressions of antislavery progress proto-typical of first movement abolitionists. He marveled that, although the African slave trade once had open proponents, no respectable statesmen of the early nineteenth century dared to defend the traffic, showing that the "the march of the mind is rapid." Lundy confidently declared that "THE ADVOCATES OF LIBERTY ARE SURE OF THEIR MARK" and knew that if they only would continue to "steadily pursue their object" the cause of abolition could not lose. Lundy's activist philosophy was cut from the same cloth as the mid-Atlantic abolition societies.[44]

In spite of his philosophical accordance with first movement abolitionism, Lundy would become a recurring proponent of colonization schemes. Why? First, whereas many of the leading first movement abolitionists lived in Philadelphia and New York, Lundy spent most of his activist years in southern slaveholding states. This geographical reality made Lundy more attuned to the mindset of white southerners who, as evidenced by the Revolutionary-era writings of Thomas Jefferson and St. George Tucker, overwhelmingly demanded that some form of black removal attend any plan of abolition. Soon after establishing his abolitionist newspaper the *Genius of Universal Emancipation* in 1821, Lundy moved to Greenville, Tennessee. Though he would relocate several more times, Lundy resided in slaveholding societies for nearly the entirety of his antislavery career. In tune with his peripatetic nature, Lundy's approach to abolitionism exuded flexibility and adaptation to on-the-ground realities. As Lundy's biographer has put it: "Any method that would weaken the system and at the same time free individual slaves won approval from him. To him the goal

44. *Constitution of the Union Humane Society* ([Saint Clairsville, Ohio, 1816]), [1–2]; [Benjamin Lundy], "John Randolph," *Genius of Universal Emancipation*, II, no. 1 (July 1822), 3–4 (quotations on 4).

[emancipation] seemed all important, the method less so." And as far as Lundy was concerned, in the upper South the goal of abolition would have to include the method of colonization.[45]

Lundy's pragmatic support for colonization balanced positions that to this point in the history of American antislavery had been occupied by disparate camps. He acknowledged the durability of white prejudice and played to white southern fears of race war even as he promoted free black rights and citizenship. Lundy argued that the prejudices of white southerners toward black freedom erected an "almost insurmountable barrier to the progress of emancipation." From youth to maturity for white southerners, derogatory ideas of persons of African descent had become "interwoven with our system of thinking and acting" so that it was only "with extreme difficulty that" white prejudice "can be overcome." Lundy, too, cautioned of looming racial violence were white southerners to leave the problem of slavery unaddressed. He cited the predictions of Jefferson and cautioned that "the awful period of retribution approaches." Yet, if such arguments put him in the ideological company of colonizationists, Lundy also believed that people of color were entitled to the rights of free members of the American body politic. He denied that any person, "no matter what may be his appearance," could "be compelled to quit his native land ... without a violation of the principle of justice" and called "the country in which a man is born ... his rightful home." Lundy backed these words with concrete proposals. Along with the "gradual though *certain* Emancipation of their slaves," he wanted upper southern legislatures to repeal laws that forced freed blacks out of their home states upon gaining their liberty, and he called for lawmakers to give black southerners the basic rights of free persons.[46]

Lundy advocated the partial colonization of southern persons of color to achieve emancipation in the region. As the proportion of black to white southerners was reduced, white prejudice and fears of black violence would give way. "I have no idea that *ever* they [emancipated blacks] will *all* be colonized, or that it will be necessary that they should be," insisted Lundy.

45. Dillon, *Benjamin Lundy and the Struggle for Negro Freedom*, 29. After leaving Greenville, Lundy moved to Baltimore. Following years of publishing his newspaper there, Lundy relocated to Washington, D.C. Lundy did spend the last few years of his life in the North, residing in Philadelphia and then Lowell, Illinois, from 1836 to 1839.

46. [Benjamin Lundy], "Abolition of Slavery; No. I," *Genius of Universal Emancipation*, I, no. 3 (September 1821), 33; [Lundy], "Emigration to Hayti.—No. I," ibid., IV, no. 1 (October 1824), 2–5 (quotations on 3, 4); [Lundy], "Emigration to Hayti.—No. II," ibid., IV, no 2 (November 1824), 17–22 (quotation on 19).

Interested in colonization no "further than it will subserve the cause of emancipation," Lundy assured readers of the *Genius of Universal Emancipation* that partial colonization would encourage nonslaveholding whites to push their legislators to pass gradual emancipation statutes. Additionally, a viable colony of freed blacks (in locations Lundy advocated, including Haiti, Mexico, and Texas) would encourage "many extensive" slaveholders, who had "not only expressed a willingness, but a desire, to liberate" their bondspersons if arrangements could be made for them to be "sent out of the country," to voluntarily give up slavery. Lundy further demonstrated his pragmatic support for colonization by publishing pieces in his newspaper promoting emancipation through black removal from the South and devoting space to African American denunciations of the ACS.[47]

Lundy pointed to his sole aim of the *"the total abolition of slavery in the United States"* to distinguish his advocacy of pragmatic colonization from the reform of the ACS and its affiliates. Because the ACS had done nothing substantial to "unite the work of *Emancipation"* with colonization "as a means of to do away the system of slavery" and "extend to slaves that justice" the nation owed them, it provided "not the least hope" of abolishing the peculiar institution. Lundy's relationship with the ACS and its boosters was multidimensional. He did not view the organization as a direct vehicle for abolition. Nor did he look to the society for a solution to righting the wrongs of slavery. Lundy did believe, however, that the ACS helped to "indirectly" aid the abolitionist cause by helping to raise the condition of those blacks colonized under its auspices and by generating public discussion

47. *Philanthropist,* Dec. 12, 1817, 110–111 (quotations on 111); [Lundy], "Emigration to Hayti.—No. 1," *Genius of Universal Emancipation,* IV, no. 1 (October 1824), 2–5 (quotations on 5). For Lundy's publication of black denunciations of the ACS and his support for *Freedom's Journal,* the black-run newspaper that thoroughly rejected the ACS, see Investigator, "From Freedom's Journal: Colonization Society," *Genius of Universal Emancipation; or American Anti-Slavery Journal, and Register of News,* New [3d] Ser., I, no. 15 (Oct. 14, 1827), 119; and "Freedom's Journal," *Genius of Universal Emancipation,* [2d Ser.], II, no. 23 (Apr. 14, 1827), 182. Lundy proposed multiple plans of emancipation over his career as an antislavery publicist and activist that differed in detail and emphasized shifting approaches. But his overall commitment to the partial colonization of enslaved persons freed by prospective emancipation statutes or individual slaveholders remained consistent. Lundy viewed Haiti as a key destination for manumitted upper southern blacks in his advocacy of partial black colonization as a necessary precursor to abolishing American slavery. Lundy was one of the most enthusiastic supporters of Haitian emigration, and he continued to advocate for African American migration to Haiti as a vehicle for abolition into the early 1830s, long after other reformers, both white and black, had abandoned supporting African American migration to the first black republic in any form.

of slavery—which would tend over time to prove to white Americans the institution's injustices. Yet Lundy could also be unsparing in his criticism of the ACS. He labeled its "direct efforts" at black removal as being unable to "avail any thing worthy of the notice of this nation." Exasperated by the support of white Marylanders for colonization without any connected attempt at emancipation, Lundy wrote in 1826 that he was "sick of the continual clack about the removal of the *free people* of color. It will never, of itself, do a pin's worth of good." That the ACS contained *"rank advocates of slavery"* in their number clinched Lundy's skepticism of the organization's motives.[48]

First movement abolitionist stalwarts and pragmatic colonizationists engaged in a tactical tug-of-war at the American Convention throughout the 1820s. As the mid-Atlantic societies continued to supply nearly all the American Convention's delegates, its next few meetings after ratifying the 1818 Jay report included a pattern of rejecting plans of colonization and affirming the traditional first movement abolitionist program. In 1821, a committee on "the subject of colonization" once again repudiated it, calling on antislavery reformers to focus on abolishing slavery "in our land." In its address to the abolition societies, the Convention now hoped that the question of colonization had been "definitively decided," as "a colony, either in Africa or in our own country, would be incompatible with the principles of our government, and with the temporal and spiritual interests of the blacks." But upper southern societies would not let the Convention close the book on colonization. In 1823, the newly formed Manumission Society of Tennessee gently asked the Convention "whether it would not be proper, provided any thing be done towards colonizing the Blacks." Unmoved, the Convention refused to address the matter.[49]

48. [Lundy], "Emigration to Hayti.—No. IV," *Genius of Universal Emancipation*, IV, no. 5 (February 1825), 69; [Lundy], "Colonization Society," ibid., III, no. 11 (March 1824), 132; [Lundy], "Colonization Society," *Genius of Universal Emancipation, and Baltimore Courier*, [2d Ser.], I, no. 15 (Dec. 10, 1825), 117; Lundy's editorial note attached to A Citizen, "For the Genius of Universal Emancipation," ibid., [2d Ser.], I, no. 10 (Jan. 7, 1826), 149.

49. *Minutes of the Seventeenth Session of the American Convention for Promoting the Abolition of Slavery* (1821), 43–45, 57; *Minutes of the Eighteenth Session of the American Convention for Promoting the Abolition of Slavery* (1823), 18, 26. In 1821, the Convention did devise a plan for the emancipation of enslaved southerners without colonization. Slaveholding states would pass gradual abolition legislation and repeal antiblack laws. Southern slaveholders would be required to educate the children of their bondspersons, and the manumitted would stay on the land of their former owners after receiving their freedom. The freed could earn small wages and be encouraged in sobriety and hard work, which would bring more profit to planters (under the assump-

State and national developments in the early 1820s might have acted to focus the attention of the Convention on establishing the rights of free blacks in the United States rather than trying to secure these rights for persons of color outside the American Republic's borders. In February 1821, Congress approved the admission of Missouri as a slave state by tacitly allowing its constitution to ban the entrance of free blacks. Eight months later, the New York Constitutional Convention all but stripped free black men of their suffrage rights. Also in 1821, Washington, D.C.'s municipal government severely restricted the liberty of free people of color in the nation's capital, a "very oppressive" action the NYMS believed "of vital importance to our character as a nation." Taken together, the American Convention considered these laws a "disgusting subject." Their assessment was only furthered in 1822 when South Carolina's legislature passed the first of many Negro Seamen Acts confining to prison all black mariners while their ships were in Charleston ports—acts that the PAS rightly feared would serve as a cover for the kidnapping and selling as slaves northern African American seamen from states like Pennsylvania. But, instead of the escalating imperilment of free black rights tilting the Convention toward softening its stance on colonization, stalwarts doubled down in their fidelity to the first movement abolitionist playbook. The 1821 Convention appointed a committee for "securing to free persons of colour, throughout the union, the enjoyment of their natural and social rights, by procuring judicial decisions thereon, or endeavouring to obtain a repeal or a modification of the laws hostile thereto." The long-winded name of this committee nevertheless communicated a clear message: the Convention would continue to agitate for the rights of free people of color as American citizens.[50]

---

tion that free labor was more profitable than slave labor) and uplift the emancipated. "And thus the interest of the master, and the melioration of the condition of the slave, would be gradually and reciprocally advanced in the progress of this experiment." The plan, however, never received the approval of the PAS and was soon abandoned. See *Minutes of the Seventeenth Session of the American Convention for Promoting the Abolition of Slavery* (1821), 50–55; and Robert Duane Sayre, "The Evolution of Early American Abolitionism: The American Convention for Promoting the Abolition of Slavery and Improving the Condition of the African Race, 1794–1837" (Ph.D. diss., Ohio State University, 1987), 258–263.

50. PPAS, Series 1, reel 13 (unnumbered loose correspondence), July 19, 1821, HSP; *Minutes of the Seventeenth Session of the American Convention for Promoting the Abolition of Slavery* (1821), 22; PPAS, Series 1, reel 1, II, 395–397, HSP. The 1821 Convention turned down western colonization in a paternalistic manner by arguing that the allegedly degraded sociopolitical state of many blacks would make the colony a failure and rob free persons of color of improvement through education and moral uplift within the United States. Even when the Convention broached the topic of the emigration of

In spite of repeated opposition, by 1825 pragmatic colonizationists had renewed their push to get the Convention to adopt a colonization plan. One reason for colonization's reemergence was the presence of colonization advocates such as Thomas Earle of the PAS and, to a lesser extent, the NYMS's William Stone—a newspaper editor who published pieces favorable to colonization and emancipation and attended the 1826 Convention. These men thrust colonization onto the Convention's agenda at the very same time that the ACS was making inroads in mid-Atlantic reform communities. During the last half of the 1820s, four ACS auxiliary societies were founded in the mid-Atlantic region. To Earle and Stone, colonization was fast becoming the new reality of antislavery activism, and the Convention needed to adapt or lose all relevancy.[51]

The second half of the 1820s also brought more southern involvement in the Convention, with delegates from upper southern societies present at every remaining meeting of the decade—and often in large numbers. The growing contingent of upper southern societies resulted in large part from the activism of Benjamin Lundy. Lundy spent much of his life trying to convert southerners to abolitionism and brought with him to the American Convention a vast knowledge of the southern antislavery perspective. He wanted the Convention to adjust itself to what he saw as the reality that the freedom of enslaved people in the South would require their partial removal from the region. Lundy's mission to plant a viable abolitionist movement in the South helped generate, by his count, more than one hundred abolition societies during the 1820s. Though these societies were small

---

willing free blacks to Haiti, the committee appointed for this purpose issued a report interpreting the possibility of Haitian migration through a first movement abolitionist lens. The committee lauded Haiti. Its independent republic could be "looked to as an example for refuting prejudices against the Blacks." See *Minutes of the Eighteenth Session of the American Convention for Promoting the Abolition of Slavery* (1823), 31.

51. Attending only one American Convention meeting, Stone appears to have been only a fleeting participant in its activities. Perhaps frustrated by the Convention's rejection of black removal, by the 1830s Stone had broken off his alliance with the abolition societies and was serving as a manager of the New-York State Colonization Society— distinguishing him from pragmatic colonizationists like Earle and Lundy. By 1834, Stone actively opposed the American Anti-Slavery Society and the rising immediate abolition movement, even approving of riots against its supporters. See Bertram Wyatt-Brown, *Lewis Tappan and the Evangelical War against Slavery* (Baton Rouge, La., 1969), 118. For Stone's involvement in the ACS, see Eli Seifman, "The United Colonization Societies of New-York and Pennsylvania and the Establishment of the African Colony of Bassa Cove," *Pennsylvania History*, XXXV (1968), 23–44; and *The Eighteenth Annual Report of the American Society for Colonizing the Free People of Color of the United States ...* (Washington, D.C., 1835), 5.

and for the most part short-lived, they nonetheless heartened many mid-Atlantic abolitionists who were hopeful that their existence boded well for southern antislavery. Enthusiasm for southern abolitionism even enabled Lundy to move the Convention, which had never met outside Philadelphia, to his home city of Baltimore for sessions held in 1826 and 1828. Washington, D.C., hosted the 1829 meeting.[52]

As opponents of colonization at the Convention would soon be reminded, however, the advocates of emancipation in the South were committed to black removal. In public statements intended for local consumption, the upper southern societies appropriated language that had long characterized the discourse of antislavery advocates in the region. The Anti-Slavery Society of Maryland told a public meeting of Baltimoreans that colonization would "secure us from rebellion, massacre and blood." In Virginia, the Loudoun Manumission and Emigration Society thought that "the difficulty and inconvenience which would arise from the incorporation" of freed blacks beckoned their resettlement outside the state. A "difference in colour, and the debasing influence of slavery" meant that white southerners could only be "relieved" of slavery by the removal of formerly enslaved persons.[53]

But, apprehensive of the mid-Atlantic abolition societies' long-standing opposition to colonization based on arguments that appealed to white antislavery southerners, the upper southern societies recalibrated their rhetoric to highlight the more practical claims that abolition was not feasible in the South without the expulsion of persons of color. In its 1829 address to the Convention, the Benevolent Society of Alexandria for Ameliorating and Improving the Condition of the People of Colour spoke directly to colonization's opponents when it wrote that abolition would be "much retarded in this country, by any opposition (however well intended)" to black removal. It was an undeniable fact, the address added, that southern masters were "not willing that the slaves shall be liberated to remain among us." The Washington City Abolition Society argued that a viable colonization plan would allow abolitionists to see whether the many southern slaveholders who claimed they would free their bondspersons upon their

52. Sayre, "The Evolution of Early American Abolitionism," 263–270, 295. For the enthusiasm of mid-Atlantic abolitionists for the participation of southern antislavery societies at the Convention, see PPAS, Series 1, reel II, 47–48, HSP.

53. "Address, from the Anti-Slavery Society of Maryland, to the Citizens of the State," *Genius of Universal Emancipation and Baltimore Courier*, [2d Ser.], I, no. 2 (Sept. 5, 1825), 12; "Of the Manumission and Emigration Society of Loudoun, to the Public," ibid., [2d Ser.], I, no. 11 (Nov. 5, 1825), 85.

subsequent removal were "in earnest." The Anti-Slavery Society of Maryland took this tack one step farther. It assured the Convention that opponents of emancipation in the upper South relied on the position that "it will be extremely impolitic to emancipate the slaves, upon any other condition than that of their removal." Yet with a viable colonization plan the "ground, upon which" slavery's defenders protected chattel bondage would itself be "removed, and they must comply." If the removal of freedpersons might silence slavery's defenders, whose arguments first movement abolitionists had for decades sought to defeat, then how could the Convention completely shut out the possibility of adopting a plan of colonization?[54]

With the 1826 meeting of the Convention in Baltimore, and armed with the testimony of southern antislavery societies, colonization's proponents felt the time was right for laying out a plan of their own. The NYMS's William Stone and the Anti-Slavery Society of Maryland member William Kesley put before the Convention a proposal that linked colonization with emancipation. It called for the "gradual, but certain, extinguishment of slavery, and the transportation of the whole coloured population, now held in bondage" to Africa or Haiti through federal funding. Displaying the influence of southern societies (and perhaps the ACS and its auxiliaries) on the Convention, the 1826 colonization proposal included the statement that it sought to "rid the country … of a population, whose continuance among us is so unnatural, and whose rapid multiplication is so alarming." This language likely reflected the perspective of its sponsors—Stone, who would go on to break ties with the Convention and join the New-York State Colonization Society, and Kesley, who as a member of the Maryland society was well-versed in upper southern colonization rhetoric. Yet, in an attempt to appeal to the Convention's perennial regard for black rights, the proposal also called on Congress to ban the separation of enslaved families, recognize enslaved marriages, and require masters to teach enslaved people to read. Even with these sweeteners, and the Convention's southern location, the colonization element of the plan did not even go up for a vote.[55]

The Convention proved more amenable to proposals that explicitly favored volitional African American emigration and emphasized black

54. *Minutes of the Twentieth Session of the American Convention for Promoting the Abolition of Slavery* (1827), 56; *Minutes of the Twenty-First Biennial American Convention for Promoting the Abolition of Slavery* (1829), 63; *Minutes of an Adjourned Session of the American Convention for Promoting the Abolition of Slavery* (1826), 30.

55. *Minutes of an Adjourned Session of the American Convention for Promoting the Abolition of Slavery* (1826), 5–8 (quotations on 6), 42; Sayre, "The Evolution of Early American Abolitionism," 205–208.

agency. In 1825, Thomas Earle looked to have the Convention adopt his resolution that its delegates endorse Senator Rufus King's initiative in the U.S. Congress, which would use proceeds from the sale of public lands to purchase enslaved persons and remove them to foreign countries, but countries, Earle added, "as they may choose for their residence." The 1825 Convention did not vote on Earle's resolution. At the 1826 meeting, however, following the rejection of Stone and Kesley's colonization plan, the Convention's delegates took up Earle's proposal and amended it to read that the "removal" of southern blacks would be "voluntary"—a much weaker statement from the perspective of colonizationists that still only gained the contested approval of the Convention by a 12–7 vote and probably carried the day only because delegates from upper southern societies outnumbered those from the old guard mid-Atlantic institutions for the first time in the Convention's history. A year later, with the Convention back in Philadelphia and mid-Atlantic delegates once again in the majority, Earle's effort to follow up the adoption of his resolution with a petition to Congress in support of it was "indefinitely postponed" on a motion by a fellow PAS member.[56]

Despite the continuing resistance of the mid-Atlantic abolition societies to colonization of any kind (outside dissenting members Thomas Earle and William Stone), the American Convention gave Haitian emigration a warmer reception. Both black activists and pragmatic colonizationists brought the topic of Haitian emigration to the Convention's agenda. In 1818, James Forten, along with the black New England educator and emigration proponent Prince Saunders, appeared before the American Convention. Saunders delivered an address calling the Convention's attention to Haiti. The Convention responded that it supported the goal of "render[ing] that island a safe asylum for such free people of colour in the United States and elsewhere, as may choose to emigrate to it." Benjamin Lundy, a devoted supporter of Haitian emigration, frequently used his newspaper to promote black American migration to the island and had

56. *Minutes of the Nineteenth Session of the American Convention for Promoting the Abolition of Slavery, and Improving the Condition of the African Race ...* (Philadelphia, 1825), 16; *Minutes of an Adjourned Session of the American Convention for Promoting the Abolition of Slavery* (1826), 42. Sayre suggests that Earle's amended resolution, even as a watered-down version of colonization, probably would not have been approved had the Convention been meeting in Philadelphia and not Baltimore. Delegates from upper southern societies outnumbered those from the PAS, NYMS, and the Delaware Abolition Society at the 1826 Convention by a count of eleven to nine. Of the mid-Atlantic societies' delegates, only Earle and Stone voted in favor of Earle's resolution. See Sayre, "The Evolution of Early American Abolitionism," 208–209.

Haiti in mind as a destination for freedpeople when he began to attend Convention meetings in the early 1820s. In 1823, a committee chaired by Thomas Earle reported that it was "gratifying to find the progress of Haytians, such as every day diminishes the number of their contemners and enemies" while contributing to "the number of those who are convinced of the moral and intellectual capabilities of the Blacks." The Convention as a body never took concrete steps to endorse Haitian emigration or to advocate for the mass migration of free or manumitted blacks to the island nation. But its delegates did speak very positively of the Haitian republic and did not reject the idea of Haitian emigration as they did African colonization.[57]

Thwarted repeatedly, pragmatic colonzationists undertook one final effort to pitch their program for emancipation in a manner the Convention would support. At the 1829 meeting, convened in Washington, D.C., Thomas Earle headed up a committee tasked with investigating what sort of abolition plan would work most effectively. Earle expressed frustration that "but small progress has, of late years, been made in the work of Emancipation." In a not-so-veiled swipe at the stalwarts, Earle questioned whether the version of abolition that might "be abstractedly the best" (the traditional formula of black uplift and incorporation) had any chance of being "generally adopted." Colonization's opponents, according to Earle, failed to take into account the much larger ratio of blacks to whites in the South. This racial demography inhibited white southerners from seriously entertaining any plans of emancipation, Earle thought. But if the "partial emigration" of persons of color in the South could reduce the proportion of black to white, not only would the freedom of thousands be secured but also for those remaining an emancipation along the lines implemented by

57. *Minutes of the Proceedings of the Fifteenth American Convention for Promoting the Abolition of Slavery* (1818), 55; Prince Saunders, *Memoir Presented to the American Convention for Promoting the Abolition of Slavery, and Improving the Condition of the African Race, December 11th, 1818* ... (Philadelphia, 1818); *Minutes of the Eighteenth Session of the American Convention for Promoting the Abolition of Slavery* (1823), 30. The 1819 and 1821 Conventions appointed committees that continued to explore Haitian emigration. In 1825, the PAS, in its address to the Convention, declared that it supported, rhetorically if not materially, "such of our coloured fellow citizens" who may voluntarily decide to resettle in Haiti at the same time as it dismissed the idea of Haitian emigration and African colonization as strategies of abolition. See *Minutes of the Nineteenth Session of the American Convention for Promoting the Abolition of Slavery* (1825), 13. The NYMS actively supported Haitian emigration, playing a role in the establishment of the Society for Promoting the Emigration of Free Persons of Colour to Hayti and looking to assist black American migrants to Haiti. See Sinha, *The Slave's Cause*, 170.

the mid-Atlantic states might become possible. Though Earle's plan could not have been more conciliatory to colonization's foes, the Convention decided to continue the committee without bringing its report to a vote, effectively silencing pragmatic colonizationists once and for all.[58]

The PAS acted as the motivating force behind the Convention's opposition to colonization. The oldest antislavery organization in the world stood unconvinced that connecting colonization with emancipation represented anything more than a radically wrong turn from first movement abolitionist precepts, notwithstanding the pragmatic colonizationist perspective of one of its own, Thomas Earle. In 1819, the PAS wrote urgently to the Convention about the need for abolitionists to withhold their support from the ACS. The PAS believed that emancipation in the mid-Atlantic had demonstrated that the formerly enslaved could be kept "in our country without hazard to our tranquillity." Freedom had brought "the elevation" of many ex-bondspersons whose "character" and "feelings" reflected those of virtuous free people. Whereas the ACS accepted white prejudice, the PAS proclaimed that abolitionists must "make no compromise with the prejudices of slavery, or with the slavery of prejudice." It was, not colonization, but "the principle of immutable justice!" that had to fire the activism of abolitionists, exclaimed the PAS.[59]

As late as 1832, the PAS was still hammering away at colonizationist ideology, reasoning to Convention delegates that "too great a reliance upon Colonization" had "tended to retard the progress of emancipation." Colonizationists only "stigmatized" free blacks "as a burden and nuisance" and cast "unjust imputations" on a people with the "same right to remain upon the soil of their nativity as ourselves." To the PAS, "the great barrier to

58. *Minutes of the Twenty-First Biennial American Convention for Promoting the Abolition of Slavery* (1829), 12, 28–35; Sayre, "The Evolution of Early American Abolitionism," 222–224.

59. *Minutes of the Sixteenth American Convention for Promoting the Abolition of Slavery* (1819), 9. The NYMS consistently reaffirmed first movement abolitionist values as well. See *Minutes of the Eighteenth Session of the American Convention for Promoting the Abolition of Slavery* (1823), 7; *Minutes of the Nineteenth Session of the American Convention for Promoting the Abolition of Slavery* (1825), 7–8; *Minutes of the Adjourned Session of the Twentieth Biennial American Convention for Promoting the Abolition of Slavery, and Improving the Condition of the African Race . . .* (Philadelphia, 1828), 36–40; and *Minutes of the Twenty-First Biennial American Convention for Promoting the Abolition of Slavery* (1829), 52. Unlike the PAS, by the late 1820s the NYMS had also come to advocate for pragmatic colonization, seen in both Michael Stone's role in the 1826 Convention proposal for colonization and the NYMS's addresses to the Convention of 1826 and 1829, which suggested the removal of freed blacks.

emancipation" still lay in slaying white prejudice, not in conforming to it. The society proudly identified first movement abolitionists as among "the few who still stand forth as standard bearers in the Cause of Liberty and Equality." And they made sure it would stay that way. With consistently high representation at the Convention, and stalwarts like Thomas Shipley among the society's delegation, the PAS oversaw the repeated defeat of colonization proposals. In the frequent contests between pragmatic colonizationists and first abolition movement stalwarts to determine the Convention's emancipationist course, it was the latter group that won out.[60]

But what did this victory mean? Stalwarts of first movement abolitionism beheld colonization as a highly dubious form of antislavery. That colonization became associated with the ACS at approximately the same time as the Convention began to confront the possibility of black removal irreparably compromised colonization as a form of emancipation in the eyes of stalwarts. With direct connections to southern slaveholders, and an ideology of reform premised on couching white prejudice as indomitable and free blacks as hopelessly degraded, stalwarts simply could not stomach any Convention-sponsored proposal associated with the ACS, however seemingly practical these plans appeared and irrespective of whatever ways their advocates had modified their proposals to distinguish them from the larger, national colonization movement. Yet, as principled as this stand might have been, it also marginalized the Convention—putting stalwarts at odds with the upper southern societies whose participation they craved but whose version of emancipation they could not abide—and regionalized its reach—alienating an upper southern region that did not share the vision of abolitionism that had been applied to the mid-Atlantic. By 1830, colonization had come to dominate white antislavery reform. Sticking staunchly to first movement abolitionist tactics thus appeared retrograde in a reform

60. PPAS, Series 1, reel 2, 23, 155–156, HSP. For additional instances of the PAS's abjuring colonization, see *Minutes of the Nineteenth Session of the American Convention for Promoting the Abolition of Slavery* (1825), 12; *Minutes of the Twenty-First Biennial American Convention for Promoting the Abolition of Slavery* (1829), 54; and PPAS, Series 1, reel II, 62, HSP. The PAS's own fight for black rights in Pennsylvania, from petitioning against discriminatory laws to their activities in unsuccessfully guarding against black disfranchisement in the state, informed the society's view that abolition and black citizenship were of a piece. See PPAS, Series 1, reel 1, 181–184, 393–398, reel 2, 157–161, 295, 300–305, 313–314, 326, HSP; *To the People of Color in the State of Pennsylvania* (Philadelphia, 1838); and *The Present State and Condition of the Free People of Color, of the City of Philadelphia and Adjoining Districts, as Exhibited by the Report of a Committee of the Pennsylvania Society for Promoting the Abolition of Slavery, etc. . . .* (Philadelphia, 1838).

environment remade by the ACS. For the American Convention's stalwarts, defeating pragmatic colonizationists had turned out to be a strategically pyrrhic victory.

TO PLEAD OUR OWN CAUSE, NOT A NEW ONE

While the American Convention splintered over colonization, mid-Atlantic black activists launched a public campaign to combat the ACS's reform doctrine, a campaign grounded in first movement abolitionist values. The impetus for New York's and Philadelphia's people of color publicly championing free black incorporation and the defeat of white prejudice came as an acute response to the ACS's surge in their home region. Before 1825, free blacks of the urban mid-Atlantic could identify the ACS as primarily the product of southern slaveholders who wished to strengthen slavery by removing free people of color from the United States. No doubt the ACS posed a threat, but it was mostly an external one whose members' inimical motives could be easily exposed. That all changed when Ralph Gurley took over as secretary of the ACS and tried to remake colonization into a voluntary movement based on benevolent rather than expedient motives. With Gurley's establishment of the colonizationist periodical the *African Repository* in 1825 and the founding of several mid-Atlantic auxiliary societies between 1823 and 1829, the ACS no longer constituted an extraneous danger. Now the ACS was targeting, and converting, seemingly genuine opponents of slavery. Yet not only did mid-Atlantic advocates of the ACS link emancipation with black removal to Africa, they also based much of their case for colonization on disparaging free blacks and playing up the perpetuity of white prejudice. As the American Convention divided over the issue of black removal and found its reform program drowned out by the ACS's appeal, free black activists stepped up to answer the ACS's foray into antislavery reform circles. And they did so with a familiar formula for fighting slavery.

This interplay between the efforts of the ACS to win over northern reformers and the reassertion of first abolition movement mores by black community leaders can be gleaned from two incidents, one in Philadelphia and the other in New York. In the December 1826 issue of the *African Repository*, Ralph Gurley published a memorial by a group of free blacks in Baltimore favoring colonization as a way of rebutting the "alleged indisposition of the free people of colour to emigrate." The memorial, apparently ghostwritten by a white colonizationist, depicted the "difference of colour" and white prejudice as leaving persons of African descent a "distinct caste" destined for "irremediable" failure in America. But in Liberia the memorialists and their brethren could enjoy "equal rights and respectability" while removal to Africa would "accelerate the liberation" of enslaved blacks. In February 1827, many of Philadelphia's persons of color gathered again in Richard Allen's Bethel Church to take on the ACS, this time explicitly answering the memorial appearing in the *African Repository*. They used the concept of republicans of color to argue that white prejudice could be beaten and slavery ended in the United States without colonization. The meeting resolved that "by an industrious, prudent, honest, and peacable course of life" persons of color could win "the respect of the community" and evince the "gradual but certain termination of those prejudices which still exist against us." In archetypical first abolition movement fashion, the gathering concluded that the defeat of white prejudice would "remove the strongest plea of the slave holder" and "aid in the liberation of our now enslaved brethren," making emancipation possible.[61]

New York's free blacks applied similar tactics as Philadelphia's persons of color in responding to colonizationists' swelling public voice. A group of black New Yorkers held a meeting called as a rejoinder to an address issued by the Colonization Society of the City of New York—an organization distinct from the New-York State Colonization Society but with a similar outlook. The address, delivered by the society's president, William Duer, and published in a local newspaper, urged white New Yorkers to support the ACS, dubbed African Americans "a distinct and inferior race," and called colonization "the most efficient, safe and practical measure for the abolition of slavery." The gathering of black New Yorkers spurred by Duer's public remarks was co-led by Phillip Bell, a former student of the NYMS's African Free School. Bell and his fellow persons of color blamed colonizationists for perpetuating "unjust and derogatory" ideas about black Americans and encouraging whites to wrongly believe that free blacks were "a growing evil, immoral, and destitute of religious principles." In its own address to the citizens of New York, a committee of three tried to set the record straight. The address "absolutely den[ied]" the assumption that "our condition cannot be improved here because there exists an unconquerable prejudice in the whites towards us." Instead of spending their energies stoking discrimination, colonizationists should acknowledge the "respect-

61. "Memorial of the Free People of Colour," and William Cornish et al., "A Memorial from the Free People of Colour to the Citizens of Baltimore," *African Repository, and Colonial Journal*, II, no. 10 (December 1826) 293, 295–297; [Lundy], "African Colonization," *Genius of Universal Emancipation*, [2d Ser.], II, no. 18 (Feb. 24, 1827), 141; Paul Goodman, *Of One Blood: Abolitionism and the Origins of Racial Equality* (Berkeley, Calif., 1998), 25.

able part of our people" and pursue the "improvement of our moral and political condition in the country of our birth." The address concluded optimistically with the resolve that "the time must come when the declaration of independence will be felt in the heart as well as uttered from the mouth." Only by fighting white prejudice and uplifting free blacks did these black New Yorkers believe slavery and racial inequality would one day end.[62]

African Americans' promulgation of first movement abolitionist reform methods gained an important medium when the black newspaper *Freedom's Journal* began publication in March 1827. The idea for *Freedom's Journal*, the first newspaper operated by African Americans in the United States, came from a bloc of New York's leading black activists—among them, Peter Williams, Jr., and William Hamilton. These men were looking for a more concerted response to colonizationist rhetoric and ideology in the northern public sphere and to the ACS's popularity among antislavery whites. The newspaper's backers selected Samuel Cornish as head editor (see Figure 16). Born a freeman in Delaware in 1795, Cornish migrated to Philadelphia in 1815 and became close friends with the black Presbyterian minister of that city, Jeremiah Gloucester. Serving as an educator, Cornish was in Philadelphia when local blacks denounced the ACS twice in 1817. In 1819, Cornish was ordained a Presbyterian minister. In the early 1820s, he moved to New York, where he sought to evangelize and uplift the city's destitute blacks. By 1824, Cornish had founded the First Colored Presbyterian Church of New York. At once painfully aware of the inequalities faced by free black Americans and an adherent of the belief that black education, morality, and virtue could dispatch white prejudice, Cornish possessed a first movement abolitionist mindset. He would go on to serve as an agent of the NYMS's African Free Schools and tried to enforce a strict code of sober and industrious behavior among his fellow blacks. Cornish was joined in his editorial post by John Russwurm, a Jamaican-born and college-educated activist who, through his experiences teaching black chil-

62. *New-York Commercial Advertiser*, Jan. 8, 1831, [2]; "An Address to the Citizens of New-York," in W[illia]m Lloyd Garrison, *Thoughts on African Colonization: Or an Impartial Exhibition of the Doctrines, Principles, and Purpose of the American Colonization Society; Together with the Resolutions, Addresses, and Remonstrances of the Free People of Color* (Boston, 1832), part II, 13–14, 14–17 (quotation on 13, 14). William Duer served as Columbia University's president at the same time as he was the president of the Colonization Society of the City of New York, adding authority to his appeal to the white public to support the ACS. Phillip Bell, born free in 1808, became deeply entrenched in black abolitionist circles in New York and would go on to serve as an editor on black activist newspapers, including the *Weekly Advocate* and the *Colored American*. On the life and activism of Phillip Bell, see Alexander, *African or American?* 206.

REV.^D SAMUEL CORNISH

Pastor of the First African Presbyterian Church in the City of N. York.

FIGURE 16. *Rev'd Samuel Cornish, Pastor of the First Presbyterian Church in the City of N. York.* By J. Paradise and F. Kearny. Courtesy, New York Public Library

dren, had only recently been familiarized with the depths of northern black inequality. Both Cornish and Russwurm wanted to improve the condition of free blacks and simultaneously viewed black uplift as a key weapon in the fight to abolish slavery.[63]

A black-run newspaper dedicated to uplifting the status of free persons of color and toppling slavery provided an innovation in the history of American abolitionism. The founding of *Freedom's Journal's* represented the maturation of a growing network of northern free black community leaders who directed churches, benevolent societies, and mutual relief organizations. These leaders, from the fiery abolitionist pamphleteer David Walker in Boston to first movement abolitionist veterans Richard Allen and James Forten in Philadelphia and Peter Williams, Jr., in New York, lent monetary support to *Freedom's Journal,* acted as agents for the periodical, or had their writings and speeches published in it. Along with other African American reformers, they also distributed the newspaper among several black northern communities and some sympathetic whites—the total number of subscribers reaching as many as 1,350. In its first issue, *Freedom's Journal* announced that the time had come for black Americans "to plead our own cause," as "Too long have others spoken for us" and "Too long" had white Americans "been deceived by misrepresentations." It was in counteracting these distortions that the writers who filled the pages of *Freedom's Journal* would channel their authorial labors.[64]

It is no accident that *Freedom's Journal* was founded just as the press in northern cities like New York and Philadelphia abounded with the discourse of the ACS. Like the American Convention, the mid-Atlantic's ACS auxiliaries published their proceedings and printed addresses from their members and allies, including the first movement abolitionist turned colonizationist Samuel Miller. Under the direction of Ralph Gurley, the ACS's *African Repository* circulated widely, pitching the antislavery nature of

63. David E. Swift, *Black Prophets of Justice: Activist Clergy before the Civil War* (Baton Rouge, La., 1989), 20–27. For additional background on Cornish's life, see Pease and Pease, *Bound with Them in Chains,* 140–161. For John Russwurm, see Sandra Sandiford Young, "John Brown Russwurm's Dilemma: Citizenship or Emigration?" in Timothy Patrick McCarthy and John Stauffer, eds., *Prophets of Protest: Reconsidering the History of American Abolitionism* (New York, 2006), 90–113.

64. Peter P. Hinks, *To Awaken My Afflicted Brethren: David Walker and the Problem of Antebellum Slave Resistance* (University Park, Pa., 1997), 102; Swift, *Black Prophets of Justice,* 39; Winch, *A Gentleman of Color,* 204; *Freedom's Journal* (New York), Mar. 16, 1827, 1. *Freedom's Journal* gained financial support from black leaders in Philadelphia such as James Forten. Advertisements in the paper's pages indicate that it relied on a black middle class that aspired to socioeconomic betterment.

colonization while frequently maligning free black northerners. Some northern ministers and reformers, too, used public occasions, such as the Fourth of July, to advocate colonization as a national good. Until the mid-1820s, the dominant antislavery voices in the mid-Atlantic—the PAS and NYMS—had been preaching the promise of black incorporation and the mission of overturning white prejudice. But now claims of unconquerable white prejudice and permanent black inferiority were coming from northern reformers, and not exclusively from slavery's defenders.[65]

Alarmed by this turn of events, northern black community leaders felt more compelled than ever to publicly challenge beliefs they viewed as antithetical to African American freedom. No longer did it appear adequate to overcome white prejudice by individual free blacks becoming republicans of color. Now activists like Samuel Cornish sought to broaden the construction of virtuous communities of free blacks. They would project a highly public voice for refuting derogatory ideas of African American freedom—a voice coming from blacks themselves. A periodical focused wholly on these ideals, and under the purview of black leadership, made *Freedom's Journal* a powerfully original contribution to abolitionism in America.[66]

65. The New Jersey Colonization Society, New-York State Colonization Society, Pennsylvania Colonization Society, and the Colonization Society of the City of New York all routinely published proceedings from their meetings or speeches before their societies for public consumption. In an early issue of the *African Repository*, Gurley named the "gradual abolition of slavery" an explicit aim of the colonization movement. Then, in the next issue, Gurley pronounced free blacks "notoriously ignorant, degraded and miserable, mentally diseased, broken spirited." See "Colonization Society," and "Extract from the Report of the Committee for the Mitigation and Gradual Abolition of Slavery throughout the British Dominions," *African Repository, and Colonial Journal*, I, no. 2 (April 1825), 39, 62; and "Colonization Society," *African Repository, and Colonial Journal*, I, no. 3 (May 1825), 68. For examples of public speeches given in support of the ACS and its auxiliaries during gatherings recognizing the Fourth of July, see Nathaniel S. Prime, *The Year of Jubilee; but Not to Africans: A Discourse, Delivered July 4th, 1825, Being the 49th Anniversary of American Independence* (Salem, N.Y., 1825); William B. O. Peabody, *An Address, Delivered at Springfield, before the Hampden Colonization Society, July 4th, 1828* (Springfield, Mass., 1828); and Wilbur Fisk, *Substance of an Address Delivered before the Middletown Colonization Society, at Their Annual Meeting, July 4, 1835* (Middletown, Conn., 1835).

66. The only book-length treatment of *Freedom's Journal* is Jacqueline Bacon, *Freedom's Journal: The First African-American Newspaper* (Lanham, Md., 2007). See also Timothy Patrick McCarthy, "'To Plead Our Own Cause': Black Print Culture and the Origins of American Abolitionism," in McCarthy and Stauffer, eds., *Prophets of Protest*, 115–133; Dickson D. Bruce, Jr., *The Origins of African American Literature, 1680–1865* (Charlottesville, Va., 2001), 163–174; Goodman, *Of One Blood*, 24–27; and David Brion Davis, *The Problem of Slavery in the Age of Emancipation* (New York, 2014), 179–183.

Interpreting *Freedom's Journal* as the harbinger of a new era in American abolitionism, however, is misleading. If the means of delivering the message was novel, the cause that *Freedom's Journal* pled was one that first movement abolitionists, black and white, had promoted together for many years. Cornish and Russwurm put forth their objectives in the first issue of *Freedom's Journal*. The newspaper would aim to "arrest the progress of prejudice" and be "devoted to the improvement of our brethren." Because many whites pounced on the "least trifle, which tends to the discredit of *any* person of colour" and "denounce[d] our whole body," *Freedom's Journal* would take on "the task of admonishing our brethren" to act with proper dignity in freedom even as the paper would ensure—by "lay[ing] our case before the publick"—that "our virtues" no longer "passed by unnoticed." In other words, *Freedom's Journal* would act as a bullhorn amplifying the values of republican citizenship among African Americans and broadcasting the many achievements of northern free blacks.[67]

Freedom's Journal was the brainchild of black abolitionists whose brand of activism had long been associated with first movement abolitionism— some of the periodical's founders and supporters had helped to construct the first abolition movement. Therefore, it is not surprising that the newspaper pressed free blacks to use their own lives to knock down white prejudice. With counsel that could have just as easily come from the NYMS or PAS, *Freedom's Journal* instructed persons of color that "propriety of conduct, never was more essential to any people than to us." Since whites made "no distinction" between "the virtuous and the vicious," the indiscretions of one member of the black community was used to disparage all African Americans. *Freedom's Journal* warned that free blacks must "do nothing which shall have the least tendency to excite these prejudices; but rather to strive as much as we can, to allay them." Like members of the abolition societies, Cornish and Russwurm at times chastised free blacks. The editors opined that, without their readers' efforts at reforming the "loose and depraved habits of many" free persons of color, these men and women would remain "ignorant, poor, and contemptible" while, just as importantly, sul-

67. *Freedom's Journal*, Mar. 16, 1827, 1. For depictions of *Freedom's Journal* as a break from a previous era of American abolitionism and with different conceptions of activism, see Newman, *The Transformation of American Abolitionism*, 11–13; Patrick Rael, *Black Identity and Black Protest in the Antebellum North* (Chapel Hill, N.C., 2002), 215; Goodman, *Of One Blood*, 24–25; McCarthy, "'To Plead Our Own Cause,'" in McCarthy and Stauffer, eds., *Prophets of Protest*, 115–117; and Ira Berlin, *The Long Emancipation: The Demise of Slavery in the United States* (Cambridge, Mass., 2015), 119–120.

lying the reputation of virtuous blacks. Moreover, the newspaper's prescription for mollifying white prejudice was identical to traditional first movement abolitionist advice. By acting with "INDUSTRY, PRUDENCE, and ECONOMY," keeping "a strict obedience to all the precepts of the gospel," and making sure "never to neglect any of the means of education," persons of color could do "battle against prejudices of longstanding." Bent on displaying the virtuousness of African Americans, black abolitionists now stressed the values of republicans of color more urgently than before.[68]

As much as *Freedom's Journal* tried to guide the conduct of free blacks to counterpoise white prejudice, it spilled much ink answering the ACS's racially exclusionary rhetoric. The newspaper confronted ACS avowals of permanent black inequality and the impossibility of emancipation without black expatriation by presenting African American uplift and mid-Atlantic abolitionism as unstoppable forces destined to advance throughout the nation. The editors and its correspondents shrewdly realized that the reform agenda of colonizationists rested on a bleak view of the state of free blacks and the progress of northern emancipation. *Freedom's Journal* answered with a hearty optimism characteristic of first movement abolitionism. In a series of essays taking on the ACS, an essayist under the pseudonym "Clarkson" wrote that, although "the monster prejudice" had underpinned human bondage for generations, the "march of correct sentiment" was "beginning to dispel the dark clouds" of slavery and black inequality. Contradicting colonizationists' claims that African Americans were a depraved people, Clarkson looked around and saw "thousands" of once enslaved and now free people who were "aspiring after character, property and distinction" and "rising from the depths of degradation ... to an honourable station in society." Clarkson wrote that, despite the allegations of colonizationsts that emancipation in the South could not happen absent black removal, the "moral influence which has emancipated the slaves of Pennsylvania

68. *Freedom's Journal*, Mar. 23, 1827, 6–7, Apr. 6, 1827, 14, Apr. 25, 1828, 26, July 13, 1827, 71, July 27, 1827, 78. The activist values set forth by *Freedom's Journal* were not necessarily shared by all free blacks in New York. A debate over the propriety of holding parades in 1827 to celebrate the total abolition of slavery in New York split the black community. *Freedom's Journal* opposed the planned parades, accusing these celebrations of contradicting the chaste, sober behavior that the newspapers, along with the NYMS, wanted to inculcate in the free black community, while other black New Yorkers embraced the opportunity of publicly honoring African American freedom. See Leslie M. Harris, *In the Shadow of Slavery: African Americans in New York City, 1626–1863* (Chicago, 2003), 122–128. During the 1830s, some black activists would reject the uplift formula altogether and argue instead for a more bellicose confrontation with white prejudice.

and New-York" would "free those of the Carolinas and Georgia." Not even the PAS could have issued a statement with such buoyant expectations.[69]

In constructing an alternative narrative of black liberty to that of colonizationists, *Freedom's Journal* explicitly tied its conception of antislavery reform to the abolition societies. The newspaper lauded the PAS and NYMS for netting results not "anticipated by the most sanguine friends of religion and humanity." In four decades of activism, the abolition societies had secured legislative emancipation, stimulated free black improvement, and seen to it that persons of color would enjoy "civil and political rights." *Freedom's Journal* also singled out the American Convention, contending that, since the abolition societies had come together into one body, "our condition has been gradually improving—our privileges have been extended—and in many cases, prejudice itself has had to give place to the dictates of reason." The newspaper used the first movement coalition of the abolition societies and free blacks to put colonizationists on the defensive. If colonizationists admitted that gradual abolition and black incorporation had given birth to persons of color with wealth, character, and respectability, they would have to acknowledge that prejudice was beatable and their advocacy of black removal was "the *very strong holds of slavery and oppression.*" For *Freedom's Journal*, and the rising tide of black abolitionism that the newspaper augured, rejecting colonization meant affirming first movement abolitionist principles.[70]

69. *Freedom's Journal*, Sept. 28, 1827, 115. For a comparably optimistic editorial, see ibid., June 8, 1827, 30. *Freedom's Journal* at times explicitly responded to the writings and speeches of the ACS and its northern auxiliaries, including a series of editorials published in retort to the speech of the New Jersey colonizationist William Hamilton in favor of the ACS. See ibid., Mar. 30, 1827, [9], and Apr. 13, 1827, [17]. In publicly countering the entreaties of genuinely antislavery whites who aligned themselves with the ACS (individuals who posed a particularly grave threat to the cause of abolitionism, according to *Freedom's Journal)* the newspaper incurred the wrath of some prominent northern reformers. One of these was a former member of the NYMS who had since come to support colonization, Samuel Miller. Miller submitted a statement to the *New York Observer* announcing that he was "entirely dissatisfied with the spirit and apparent tendency of" *Freedom's Journal* and affirmed that he remained committed to "the great cause of the improvement and final emancipation of the children of Africa throughout our country." Cornish and Russwurm reprinted Miller's statement, along with one of their own, unapologetically explaining that "if we have arraigned the motives" of the ACS and its supporters "we have done nothing more than we have a right to do" and informed Miller, a Presbyterian minister, that he was evidently "better acquainted with Ecclesiastical History and Church Government, than with politics or *colonization.*" See *Freedom's Journal*, Sept. 21, 1827, 110.

70. *Freedom's Journal*, Apr. 13, 1827, 19, Nov. 9, 1827, 138, Dec. 19, 1828, 296. For a sampling of other editorials from the *Freedom's Journal* lambasting African coloniza-

Northern free blacks felt the sting of colonization's rise to reform prominence more personally than stalwarts at the American Convention. Whereas the PAS viewed the colonization movement as an abrogation of their abolitionist reform formula, mid-Atlantic black activists saw the ACS as not only that but also a slander on their very lives. Whereas many pragmatic colonizationists at the Convention could separate their advocacy of the partial colonization of freedpeople in the upper South and their support for black American citizenship, northern abolitionists of color found the ACS's rhetoric too menacing to make such a distinction. And, whereas the American Convention fissured over black removal and diminished its ability to speak as an undivided body, mid-Atlantic abolitionists of color formed a united front to fight colonization in all forms. With a first movement abolitionist vernacular, they denounced the ACS in unequivocal, public, and eloquent ways.

By the close of the 1820s, first movement abolitionists discovered that the walls of slavery and prejudice would not fall as quickly or as completely as those of monarchy and absolutism. Prejudice's resilience was undeniable, and more white reformers were beginning to accept its presence as a permanent reality. The founding of the ACS in 1816 exemplified this shift, offering a new strategy for organized antislavery. In response, several members of the abolition societies switched their allegiance to the colonization movement. One of these reformers, James Milnor, while a member of the PAS, had regularly attended meetings of the American Convention. Milnor had served on an array of American Convention committees, including those that drafted addresses to free blacks promoting their virtuous

<hr>

tion, see ibid., May 18, 1827, 38, July 27, 1827, [73], Aug. 24, 1827, 94, Sept. 7, 1827, 102, Oct. 5, 1827, 117–118, Nov. 16, 1827, 141–142, and Nov. 30, 1827, 150. *Freedom's Journal* often excerpted the proceedings of the American Convention and reported on white and black abolitionists working together. White abolitionist organizations, including the PAS and the American Convention, reciprocated by subscribing to the paper. In 1827, the PAS lauded the establishment of *Freedom's Journal*, calling it a publication of "intrinsic merit" and "extensive usefulness," while telling the American Convention that the newspaper merited "our warmest support." See *Minutes of the Twentieth Session of the American Convention for Promoting the Abolition of Slavery* (1827), 38. *Freedom's Journal* ceased publication in March 1829, once John Russwurm, who had taken over head editorial duties from Cornish six months after the inaugural issue, shocked the periodical's subscribers by retracting his opposition to the ACS and accepting an official position in Liberia. Cornish then founded the newspaper the *Rights of All*, which was intended to serve as the successor to *Freedom's Journal* but lasted less than a year.

citizenship, and was elected president of the Convention in 1816. But the final Convention before the ACS's founding was also Milnor's last. In 1826, Milnor, now living in New York, reappeared in the historical record as a firm proponent of colonization. In a speech delivered in favor of the ACS, Milnor asserted his antislavery authority as someone who had labored for years in the "interests" of "that unhappy race." Even as he recognized the achievements of many individual free blacks, Minor now believed people of color were doomed to a "degradation for which there seems no remedy" as long as they resided in the American Republic. That colonization could appeal to a once firm adherent to first movement abolitionism demonstrates the allure of black removal for many genuine antislavery reformers of the 1820s. For those activists who remained affiliated with the American Convention, colonization proved an equally unavoidable topic. When the ACS forced the issue of colonization onto the American Convention's docket, it divided the abolition societies and its members between those who began to view colonization as the only means to achieve the total abolition of slavery and others who refused to accept black removal as anything but a betrayal of everything for which their movement had fought.[71]

Though they dissociated abolitionism from emigration and colonization, black activists in the urban mid-Atlantic also explored alternatives to the reform agenda of a movement with which they had long been affiliated. That men like James Forten and Richard Allen were briefly willing to hear out the pleas of the ACS and that others like Peter Williams, Jr., expressed enthusiasm for Haitian emigration illustrate that abolitionists of color, too, imagined additional routes to black uplift. Yet, as first movement abolitionist tenets increasingly gave way under the weight of colonization's growing attractiveness to white reformers, it was African American activists who would serve most prominently as the torchbearers for the pre-ACS antislavery agenda of defeating white prejudice and incorporating free blacks as citizens.

71. James Milnor, *Plea for the American Colonization Society: A Sermon, Preached in St. George's Church, New-York, on Sunday, July 9, 1826* (New York, 1826), 14–15. Beverly Tomek has identified thirty-one individuals who left the PAS to become members of the ACS or Pennsylvania Colonization Society, or donated to help pay for the removal of blacks to Liberia. See Tomek, *Colonization and Its Discontents*, 61.

A Movement Forgotten

With the publication of his widely read *Thoughts on African Coloniza-tion* in 1832, William Lloyd Garrison redefined what it meant to be an abolitionist. Garrison deemed colonization a sinful cause, and he wanted to make his fellow citizens aware of just how damaging he believed the American Colonization Society (ACS) had been to antislavery in America. One of Garrison's leading complaints about colonization was the gradual approach to emancipation taken by its proponents. Gradualism, according to Garrison, passively deferred to the rights of slaveholders, left unchal-lenged white prejudice, and ultimately perpetuated slavery by refusing to combat the immorality of holding fellow human beings as chattel. Instead of a mechanism of abolition, Garrison concluded that calls for the gradual end of slavery were "calculated to perpetuate the thraldom of our species." His answer to gradualism was immediate abolition, which demanded that slaveholders instantly confront the problem of slavery and free enslaved blacks. Garrison declared that the boundaries between gradualists and immediatists could not be clearer. In one corner stood the advocates of "'Immediate Abolition,'" who sought "'Equal Rights'" for African Americans and exclaimed "'No Expatriation.'" Opposite them were the friends of "'African Colonization,'" who counseled "'Gradual Abo-lition,'" insisted on "'No Equaltiy'" for persons of color, and worked for the "'Expulsion of the Blacks.'" In his attempt to draw a sharp dis-tinction between immediate abolitionists and colonizationist advocates of gradualism, Garrison constructed a dichotomy of antislavery activism that submerged the racially progressive roots of first movement abolitionism.[1]

1. W[illia]m Lloyd Garrison, *Thoughts on African Colonization: Or an Impartial Exhibition of the Doctrines, Principles, and Purposes of the American Colonization So-ciety; Together with the Resolutions, Addresses, and Remonstrances of the Free People of Color* (Boston, 1832), part I, 80, 147. Garrison was not the first activist to make a thorough call for immediate abolition; he was preceded in 1824 by the British Quaker reformer Elizabeth Heyrick. Heyrick's demand for, as the title of her pamphlet put it, *Immediate, Not Gradual Abolition* ... (London, [1824]), was animated by a combination of sources, including her belief in "the supremacy of individual conscience over social

Garrison's sketch of American antislavery concealed the original meaning of gradualism as understood by first movement abolitionists. He could, perhaps, be excused for his error. Garrison began his journalistic career as a partisan New England Federalist who identified with northern evangelical political causes, one of which included colonization. Then, in the spring of 1828, Garrison met Benjamin Lundy during Lundy's tour of Boston and was persuaded to make antislavery the sole focus of his editorial energies. Not only did Garrison hail from a northern reformist political milieu that saw colonization as essential to the gradual abolition of slavery, but the man who most inspired him to become an abolitionist, Lundy, was a proponent of gradual emancipation and a pragmatic colonizationist—viewing at least the partial repatriation of black Americans as necessary for any viable emancipation plan. Garrison would never join the ACS or agitate for its agenda. But it made sense for him to connect colonization with gradual abolition during his initial phase of antislavery activism.[2]

By the time *Thoughts on African Colonization* appeared in print, colonizationists had become the most visible champions of gradual emancipa-

---

and political institutions," her involvement in the boycott movement of West Indian sugar and other products grown by enslaved people, and her "passionate defense of slave resistance." See Manisha Sinha, *The Slave's Cause: A History of Abolition* (New Haven, Conn., 2016), 197 (quotation); and David Brion Davis, "The Emergence of Immediatism in British and American Antislavery Thought," *Mississippi Valley Historical Review*, XLIX (1962), 220.

2. Henry Mayer, *All on Fire: William Lloyd Garrison and the Abolition of Slavery* (New York, 1998), 51–56; Paul Goodman, *Of One Blood: Abolitionism and the Origins of Racial Equality* (Berkeley, Calif., 1998), 37. Garrison joined Lundy in running the *Genius of Universal Emancipation,* taking over editorial duties from September 1829 to January 1830, while Lundy went on one of his many antislavery conversion tours. During the period Garrison temporarily served as head editor of the periodical, he made perhaps his first public endorsement of immediate abolition. Yet Garrison's break from support for colonization was not complete. Although he called the antislavery program of the ACS "dilatory and uncertain" and colonization "as a remedy" to the abomination of American slavery "altogether inadequate," he still believed colonization should receive encouragement "as an auxiliary" to abolitionism—sounding very much like his mentor, Benjamin Lundy. Thus, Garrison's full break with colonization, however tepidly he had spoken in favor of it, was itself gradual. See W[illia]m Lloyd Garrison, "To the Public," *Genius of Universal Emancipation,* IV, no. 1 (Sept. 2, 1829), 5. Garrison also at this juncture supported the emigration of free blacks to Haiti, a cause that happened to be strongly advocated by Lundy as well. Lundy and Garrison split amicably, and Lundy did not greet the rise of immediatism with hostility. In fact, Lundy argued that no substantive ideology or tactics separated abolitionism of the 1830s from forms of abolitionism that had preceded it. See Merton L. Dillon, *Benjamin Lundy and the Struggle for Negro Freedom* (Urbana, Ill., 1966), 145–155.

tion. Antislavery reformers within the colonization movement had vocalized their intention to gradually abolish slavery through black removal
since the ACS's founding. But, when immediate abolitionists began renouncing the ACS in the early 1830s, northern colonizationists only grew
louder in their defense of gradual emancipation. Francis Scott Key, in 1830,
told the Pennsylvania Colonization Society that "a slave suddenly emancipated" did little good for either society or freedpersons. Calling "such emancipation ... at least questionable," Key believed that gradual emancipation
and the colonization of the liberated to Africa was the only answer to ending slavery in America. Another colonizationist was more direct. Dismissing the "new fangled notion of *immediate and total abolition*"in 1834, J. R.
Tyson castigated the "turbulent invective and acrimonious clamour" that
immediatists directed against "the ancient and recognised principles of
gradual emancipation." Mid-Atlantic auxiliaries to the ACS had censured
the abolition societies for coupling black freedom and African American
citizenship, an alleged error they believed at the heart of gradual northern emancipation writ large. With the rise of immediatism, several northern colonizationists now began to champion their own ideal of gradualism
more explicitly than before—one with black removal rather than incorporation at its core. In sum, the onset of immediate abolitionism touched off
a war of words between immediatists and colonizationists that masked the
vision of reform set out by gradual abolition's original advocates.[3]

As colonizationists and immediatists reproached one another, the first
abolition movement was falling apart. The reform philosophy of first movement abolitionists was based on the assumption of an ever-evolving antislavery progress: the securing of gradual emancipation statutes by state
legislatures, the cessation of the international slave trade, the extension of
equal rights to free blacks, the social, political, and economic uplift of African Americans, and the elimination of white prejudice. But, by the third
decade of the nineteenth century, the tide of antislavery progress seemed
undeniably to be regressing. Gradual abolition had been accomplished only
regionally, and the liberty of black people freed by these laws was threatened by the pandemic of kidnapping. Rather than withering, slavery had
spread to new states that entered the union, only augmenting the political
power of slaveholders. The international slave trade continued clandestinely

3. *Report of the Board of Managers of the Pennsylvania Colonization Society, with
an Appendix* (Philadelphia, 1830), 3; J. R. Tyson, *A Discourse before the Young Men's
Colonization Society of Pennsylvania, Delivered October 24, 1834, in St. Paul's Church,
Philadelphia* ... (Philadelphia, 1834), 41, 46.

at the same time as a domestic slave trade made the lives of the enslaved even more unbearable and the rights of free blacks even more insecure.[4]

On the state and local levels in the mid-Atlantic, where first movement abolitionism's pulse had always beat loudest, there appeared equally discouraging developments. White prejudice, which had looked to be on the defensive in the 1780s and 1790s, seemed on the upswing in the 1820s and 1830s. A popular culture of white prejudice demeaned black freedom. Racially discriminative labor practices barred many free persons of color from improving their socioeconomic condition. And the state legislatures of New York and Pennsylvania took from nearly all black Americans their voting rights in 1821 and 1838, respectively. First movement abolitionists continued to express optimism in the face of these deflating developments, yet it became increasingly difficult to make such a case persuasively. The gradual abolitionism of these reformers took another hit as the focus of antislavery shifted to the South, where the formula applied to mid-Atlantic states appeared to most reformers as unfeasible. Though stalwarts stymied pragmatic colonizationists at the American Convention, they could not change the fact that the only version of antislavery white southerners seemed willing to accept was colonization. And, by the time of Andrew Jackson's election to the presidency, even colonization was fast becoming an untenable position in an increasingly unapologetic proslavery South.[5]

4. On the domestic slave trade, see Walter Johnson, *Soul by Soul: Life Inside the Antebellum Slave Market* (Cambridge, Mass., 1999); Steven Deyle, *Carry Me Back: The Domestic Slave Trade in American Life* (New York, 2005); and Michael Tadman, *Speculators and Slaves: Masters, Traders, and Slaves in the Old South* (Madison, Wis., 1989). On the expansion of American slavery, see Edward D. Baptist, *The Half Has Never Been Told: Slavery and the Making of American Capitalism* (New York, 2014); Adam Rothman, *Slave Country: American Expansion and the Origins of the Deep South* (Cambridge, Mass., 2007); and John Craig Hammond, *Slavery, Freedom, and Expansion in the Early American West* (Charlottesville, Va., 2007). On kidnapping, see Carol Wilson, *Freedom at Risk: The Kidnapping of Free Blacks in America, 1780–1865* (Lexington, Ky., 1994); David Fiske, *Solomon Northup's Kindred: The Kidnapping of Free Citizens before the Civil War* (Santa Barbara, Calif., 2016); and Graham Russell Gao Hodges, *David Ruggles: A Radical Black Abolitionist and the Underground Railroad in New York City* (Chapel Hill, N.C., 2010).

5. For the worsening racial climate in the nineteenth-century North, see James Brewer Stewart, "The Emergence of Racial Modernity and the Rise of the White North, 1790–1840," *Journal of the Early Republic*, XVIII (1998), 181–217; Stewart, "Modernizing 'Difference': The Political Meanings of Color in the Free States, 1776–1840," *JER*, XIX (1999), 691–712; Bruce Dain, *A Hideous Monster of the Mind: American Race Theory in the Early Republic* (Cambridge, Mass., 2002); and David R. Roediger, *The Wages of Whiteness: Race and the Making of the American Working Class* (New York,

Colonization's pessimistic outlook matched the state of race relations and antislavery trends in the nation at large by the time immediate abolitionists arrived on the scene. Within this adverse environment for American antislavery, Garrison's famous introduction to his newspaper the *Liberator* reads as desperate as it does radical. Garrison told "southern oppressors ... northern apologists," and "all the enemies of the persecuted blacks" to "tremble" at the founding of his periodical and its call for immediate abolition. But Garrison justified the "severity" of his rhetoric in an analogy that revealed his perspective of a nation overrun by proslavery principles. "Tell a man whose house is on fire, to give a moderate alarm; tell him to moderately rescue his wife from the hands of the ravisher; tell the mother to gradually extricate her babe from the fire into which it has fallen." Rather than advancing, the cause of abolitionism had become consumed by slavery's growing strength. With the ACS pushing for the removal of persons of color as a solution to slavery and immediatists abandoning gradualist strategies, first movement abolitionists found themselves out of touch with the national conversation over slavery, race, and reform.[6]

Gradual abolitionism as first envisioned by societies like the Pennsylvania Abolition Society (PAS) and the New-York Manumission Society (NYMS) had been effectively sidelined from mainstream antislavery reform when the American Convention met for a final time in 1838. But the abolition societies pressed on with their activism. The PAS especially endured in asserting black rights and trying to secure the future of African Americans in the Republic. The PAS had helped fend off for years the recurring efforts of some Pennsylvania legislators to circumscribe the rights of black Pennsylvanians. At the state Constitutional Convention of 1837–1838, black suffrage rights were hanging in the balance. A proposal to disenfranchise African Americans was before the Convention when the PAS decided to take action. To answer the "violent and bitter prejudice against

---

1991). On the emergence of a more united and confident proslavery South in which colonization appeared as a threat, see Lacy K. Ford, *Deliver Us from This Evil: The Slavery Question in the Old South* (Oxford, 2009).

6. *Liberator*, Jan. 1, 1831, [1]. Some abolition society members joined the immediatist movement. For example, high-ranking PAS members Thomas Shipley, Edward P. Atlee, Evan Lewis, Isaac Barton, and Joseph Parker all announced their allegiance to immediate abolitionists while remaining supportive of the PAS. Shipley even led the formation of the Philadelphia Antislavery Society, an auxiliary of the immediatists' flagship organization, the American Antislavery Society. See Robert Duane Sayre, "The Evolution of Early American Abolitionism: The American Convention for Promoting the Abolition of Slavery and Improving the Condition of the African Race, 1794–1837" (Ph.D. diss., Ohio State University, 1987), 307–309.

the free people of color," the PAS planned to conduct a census reflecting the true condition of Philadelphia's black community. The census could "meet the enemies of the Coloured Man with irresistible argument" and stave off disfranchisement, the PAS thought. In a subsequent pamphlet publishing its findings, the PAS acknowledged the impressive level of free black wealth, success, and virtue in the city and explained African American inequality purely as a result of the stifling environment of prejudice. Here was a lasting tribute to the societal environmentalism of the first abolition movement. Fittingly enough for the tenor of the times, this appeal went unheeded. The same constitution that James Pemberton had so lauded as a beacon of black citizenship nearly forty years earlier now defined the right of suffrage as belonging to "every white freeman" over twenty-one, officially designating citizenship in racially exclusive terms.[7]

But not all was lost. As the influence of the American Convention and its constituent abolition societies on antislavery reform waned, black abolitionists who promoted first movement values systematically organized their activism. To solidify the abolitionist message of such outlets as *Freedom's Journal*, which ceased publication in 1829, African American activists founded a convention of black reformers in 1831. Showing that they had not completely abandoned the emigration of some persons of color as a response to white prejudice, abolitionists of color officially convened the first black convention to investigate the prospect of emigrating to Canada.[8]

7. Papers of the Pennsylvania Abolition Society (PPAS), Series 1, reel 2, 302–305, Historical Society of Pennsylvania (HSP), Philadelphia; *The Present State and Condition of the Free People of Color, of the City of Philadelphia and Adjoining Districts, as Exhibited by the Report of a Committee of the Pennsylvania Society for Promoting the Abolition of Slavery* ... (Philadelphia, 1838). As in New York, partisan politics played a large role in black Pennsylvanians' losing suffrage rights at the Pennsylvania Convention of 1837–1838. State Democrats wanted to placate southern Democrats uneasy about the security of their property rights in people in reaction to the vitriolic rhetoric of immediate abolitionists who condemned southern slaveholders. See Nicholas Wood, "'A Sacrifice on the Altar of Slavery': Doughface Politics and Black Disfranchisement in Pennsylvania, 1837–1838," *JER*, XXXI (2011), 75–106. The PAS recognized as much when they stated that the Convention displayed "a humble subserviency to the southern policy"; see PPAS, Series 1, reel 2, 326, HSP.

8. *Minutes and Proceedings of the First Annual Convention of the People of Colour, Held by Adjournments in the City of Philadelphia, from the Sixth to the Eleventh of June, Inclusive, 1831* (Philadelphia, 1831), 4, 12–13. Although *Freedom's Journal* was an important bridge to antebellum abolitionism, its editors never explicitly advocated the immediate abolition of slavery—though at least one editorial in the newspaper did. See Jacqueline Bacon, *Freedom's Journal: The First African-American Newspaper* (Lanham, Md., 2007), 234–235.

Although they supported black Americans who elected to move to Canada, the members of the Convention of the People of Colour (which included first movement black abolitionists such as William Miller, Henry Sipkins, and William Hamilton) focused on the improvement of those of African descent within the United States. One address explained that it was "to remove these prejudices dependent on the accidental diversities of colour" that they had met. Lambasting the ACS for "pursuing the direct road to perpetuate slavery," the Convention of the People of Colour implored black Americans to stay "devoted to our instruction and elevation" by remaining anchored to the mores of republicans of color. The third annual convention wrote that it "recognize[d] the idea, that intelligence, industry, economy, and moral worth, in connexion with the purifying power of heaven-born truth, are sufficient alone, to prostrate, this *iron hearted monster*" of slavery and prejudice. The black convention movement shared an ideological affinity with the American Convention and issued addresses that mirrored it in outlook and style. William Lloyd Garrison, who attended the first black convention and drew his inspiration from black activists, helped found an immediate abolition movement that unmistakably echoed the maxims of first movement abolitionists of the post-Revolutionary and early national past.[9]

What are Americans to make of the legacy of the nation's first abolition movement? It is hard to classify the activism of first movement abolitionists as a success if one were to measure by the movement's own lofty goals. Slavery was not totally abolished, racial equality remained elusive, and white prejudice lived on. Still, the first abolition movement accomplished much. Though they did not directly end slavery in America, the abolition societies and their illegally enslaved and free black allies played a pivotal part in achieving emancipatory statutes and then enforcing and expanding these laws to put human bondage on the road to extinction in the North. This activism not only brought liberty to hundreds of enslaved people but, in the long run, set a free North and slave South on a collision course that

9. *Minutes and Proceedings of the First Annual Convention of the People of Colour* (1831), 14–15; *Minutes and Proceedings of the Third Annual Convention, for the Improvement of the Free People of Colour in These United States, Held by Adjournments in the City of Philadelphia, from the 3d to the 13th of June Inclusive, 1833* (New York, 1833), 18–19. The Convention met through 1864. For the history of the black convention movement, see Patrick Rael, *Black Identity and Black Protest in the Antebellum North* (Chapel Hill, N.C., 2002). Revealing how influential black opposition to the ACS had been in his own break with colonization, Garrison excerpted dozens of black protest documents in *Thoughts on African Colonization*.

would eventually bring the complete abolition of slavery. Although they came up short in achieving equality for people of color, the first movement abolitionist program of black uplift and its commitment to African American rights and incorporation helped nurture a generation of reformers who would continue this racially redemptive quest. If they could not vanquish white prejudice, first movement abolitionists understood that eradicating the inequities of slavery required more than ending the institution of human bondage alone. Just as important, completing abolition meant reinventing the society that made slavery a viable institution in the first place, a lesson well taken in the post–Civil War South. Yet the most enduring legacy of America's first abolition movement was its abiding faith that a world free from black oppression and inequality was possible. It was this audacity to imagine such a society that inspired not only first movement abolitionists but also later exponents of racial justice—from immediate abolitionists in the antebellum period, to Radical Republicans during Reconstruction, to Civil Rights activists of the twentieth century.

ACKNOWLEDGMENTS

Every historical monograph is the product of years of work. But the years I spent working on this piece of scholarship are especially numerous. Tracing this project's long lineage over the near decade and a half journey that has culminated in this book reminds me how many people and institutions have been crucial to its production.

It all started in January 2005, as I began study in an MA program in history at George Mason University. It was a matter of serendipity that I happened upon the First Federal Congress Project, whose head editor, Charlene Bickford, was teaching a class on historical editing. As an assistant researcher at the project, I discovered a wealth of antislavery newspaper pieces that piqued my interest in the first abolition movement. I was never one to bore easily, and my interest has yet to wane. What's more, Charlene and the other editors, Ken Bowling, Chuck DiGiacomantonio, and Helen Veit, provided me with a deep appreciation for early American history. Also timely, during my first semester at George Mason I took Robert Hawkes's course on American slavery to freedom. His teaching opened my eyes to a topic that I knew embarrassingly little about, and the readings he assigned made me want to learn so much more. In composing my thesis on the debates over slavery and race during the first federal Congress, I was fortunate to have Lois Horton, a leading scholar of African American history, as my adviser. Her encouragement while overseeing my first long-form writing project made me believe I could become a historian of abolitionism. Along with Lois, Rosemarie Zagarri, whose scholarship on women and citizenship in the early Republic set a model for my analysis of race and citizenship in this same period, asked penetrating questions and made thoughtful critiques that helped me later to expand the project.

Soon after I enrolled in a Ph.D. program at the CUNY Graduate Center, I sought Jim Oakes as my adviser. It turned out to be a prudent decision. Jim encouraged me to ask big questions, make bold arguments, and write forcefully. At times his best advice could come when I least expected it. After finishing an essay on black disfranchisement in early national New York, I went to see Jim with the plan of embarking on a dissertation charting the racial origins of Jacksonian democracy. Jim, who was never one to impose his ideas on me, gently suggested that I consider reinterpreting the meaning of gradual emancipation instead. In retrospect this advice was foundational, steering me back toward early abolitionism. Jonathan Sassi likewise engaged with my work throughout my time at the Graduate Center, and his expertise on American antislavery aided me greatly. Other members of my dissertation committee, including Greg Downs and Chris Brown, got me thinking about how to start the transformation from dissertation to book. As I began the dissertation in earnest, the Early American Republic Seminar — a group of fellow early Americanists at the Graduate Center who met frequently to read one another's scholarship and that included John Blanton, David Gary, David Houpt, Cambridge Ridley Lynch, Joe Murphy, Glen Olson, Roy Rogers, Nora Slominsky, and Alisa Wade, among others — helped me stave off isolation and motivated me to write.

A postdoctoral fellowship at the Omohundro Institute of Early American History and Culture (OIEAHC) gave me the time, space, and resources to turn this book into a much better one than it would have otherwise been. At the roundtable that kicked off the first of several phases of revisions under the OIEAHC's aegis, Carolyn Eastman, Melvin Ely, Paul Mapp, Hannah Rosen, and Eric Slauter nudged me toward thinking more expansively about my book's agenda. It was at this roundtable that Michael Meranze first offered me comprehensive observations on the manuscript's strengths and weaknesses and gave conceptually astute suggestions—a favor he repeated during the last round of revisions and from which this book has benefited immensely. The OIEAHC's director, Karin Wulf, made sure I had all the support I needed and checked in with me frequently, while giving me valuable intellectual and professional counsel. Other members of the OIEAHC's community during my residence there, especially Allison Bigelow, Kathy Burdette, Ryan Kashanipour, Josh Piker, Brett Rushforth, Beverly Smith, and Kaylan Stevenson—helped make my time in Williamsburg both productive and memorable.

Fredrika Teute believed in this project and saw something big in it. I remember first encountering her in the audience of a panel in which I was presenting. She pushed me on a key argument of my paper, and I answered with the defensive brashness that only a graduate student could muster. When I later applied for the OIEAHC fellowship, I figured our interaction had doomed my chances. As it turned out, I was wrong. Though she retired before this project finished, her detailed comments on my dissertation, and our many long conversations, left a lasting impression on this book.

Nadine Zimmerli is the type of editor every author wishes they could have but almost no one ever gets. In the multistage process of revising that is the OIEAHC's hallmark, she grappled with my arguments, pushed me to sharpen my narrative, and subjected each paragraph to intensive scrutiny. That she did it all without alienating the author is a testament to her unflagging support and abiding friendship.

Though the OIEAHC is well known for the rigorous copyediting and source checking of its monographs, the care and attention Virginia Montijo Chew brought to the process exceeded my expectations and has made the text sleeker and the footnotes pristine. During the last round of outside review, Manisha Sinha's meticulous and trenchant reading of the manuscript challenged me in all the right ways and spurred me to clarify, highlight, and further explain several pivotal arguments. And Catherine Kelly's intervention resulted in a book cover with which I could not be more satisfied.

That departments as collegial and nurturing as the Arch Dalrymple III Department of History exist defies every rule of academia. Colleagues with whom I genuinely enjoy interacting have given me a sense of belonging and community at the University of Mississippi. From sharing tales of childrearing, to exchanging culinary tips, to discussing the trials of teaching, writing, and publishing, each one of the members of the faculty has helped make my professional life an enjoyable one. Those with whom I had particularly enlightening exchanges on first book writing, or who helped me in other ways to complete this project, include Mikaëla Adams, Jesse Cromwell, Charles Eagles, Darren Grem, Zack Kagan Guthrie, April Holm, Frances Kneupper, Marc Lerner, Becky Marchiel, Jarod Roll, Sheila Skemp, Susan Stearns, Annie Twitty, Jessie Wilkerson, and Noell Wilson.

The universe of every historian reaches far beyond institutional affiliation. At conferences, workshops, and seminars—through both formal comments given to me on essays that became incorporated into the book and more informal remarks and conversations—many fellow scholars helped me to refine my arguments, track down new sources, and rethink the history I sought to recover. Yesenia Barragan, Rick Bell, Holly Brewer, Corey Brooks, Matt Clavin, Andrew Diemer, Anthony DiLorenzo, Jim Downs, Max Edelson, Erika Edwards, Sarah Gronningsater, Nick Guyatt, Craig Hammond, Eric Herschthal, John Garrison Marks, Peter Onuf, Ed Pompeian, Nick Popper, Fabricio Prado, Patrick Rael, Paddy Riley, Carrol Smith-Rosenberg, John Saillant, Samantha Seeley, Billy Smith, Terri Snyder, David Spanagel, Matt Spooner, Whitney Stewart, Alan Taylor, Beverly Tomek, and David Waldstreicher make up an inclusive, but not exhaustive, list of these individuals. Matt Mason and Jim Gigantino offered me shrewd feedback on chapter drafts from the monograph. A few people merit special mention here. Nic Wood and I met just as we embarked on our respective dissertations. As a result of our many discussions and the research and writing we have shared, my own interpretation of American abolitionism has become more nuanced and complete. Scott Heerman's willingness to contend with and pick apart my analytical claims has been matched only by his formidable wit and giving spirit. Scott also read the manuscript at an important time in its development and gave me superb ideas on how to reorganize parts of it. David Gellman engaged closely with this project at both ends of its long arc. He reviewed an article that launched the book and then read and provided comments on the manuscript in its entirety. His scholarship on emancipation in New York served as a benchmark for my reinterpretation of first movement abolitionism.

Without the support of several repositories and academic institutions, I would not have been able to complete this project. Staff at the New-York Historical Society, the New York Public Library, the Schomburg Center for Research in Black Culture, the Historical Society of Pennsylvania, the Library Company of Philadelphia, the New Jersey Historical Society, and the Delaware Historical Society steered me toward applicable sources and dug up an assortment of documents and collections. Grants and fellowships, including those from the Gilder Lehrman Institute of American History, the Historical Society of Pennsylvania, the New-York Historical Society, the Library Company of Philadelphia, the CUNY Graduate Center, the Omohundro Institute of Early American History and Culture, and the University of Mississippi endowed me with funds to complete the many stages of research and writing. Earlier versions of portions of this book appeared as "Race and Belonging in the New American Nation: The Republican Roots of Black Abolitionism," in Whitney Nell Stewart and John Garrison Marks, eds., *Race and Nation in the Age of Emancipations* (Athens, Ga., 2018), 143–163; "'To Raise Them to an Equal Participation': Early National Abolitionism, Gradual Emancipation, and the Promise of African American Citizenship," *Journal of the Early Republic*, XXXI (2011), 229–258; "'Whenever They Judge It Expedient': The Politics of Partisanship and Free Black Voting Rights in Early National New York," *American Nineteenth Century History*, XII (2011), 1–23, https://www.tandfonline.com/doi/abs/10.1080/14664658.2011.559746.

My extended family—David, David Stephen, and Joanne Condon; Martin and Terry Stoger; Gloria, Danny, Tiffany, and Gabriela Guinn; Isabela and Nathan Coffman—have kept me grounded, and their support has come in myriad forms over the years.

There are five people to whom this book is dedicated. For as long as I can remember, my parents have given me their unqualified backing in everything I have pursued and influenced me in countless ways. Their careers as research scientists instilled in me an appreciation for the world of academia and helped steer me toward finding a vocation. Hearing stories during childhood of my father's experiences as a Holocaust survivor primed me to examine the malignant history of prejudice and challenges to it. My mother read more iterations of this project than anyone, offering thoughts and asking questions that often rivaled experts in the field. It would take multiple lifetimes to pay back all that my parents have done for me, and while this book does not come close to covering that debt, it is a testament to their enduring support.

I met Valerie soon after I started graduate school. Of all the good fortune I have been graced with, the chance encounter that brought us together is by far my most fortuitous moment. Her words of encouragement and incisive advice have, at critical junctures during the marathon that is researching and writing a history monograph, buoyed me. Witnessing the dedication she brings to her craft of new media art has inspired me to not just complete a book but become a better historian. Far more elementally, she is my best friend, my unparalleled confidant, and the person whose love anchors me. As the completion of this project causes me to reflect on all that we have built, I eagerly anticipate whatever the next chapter of our lives together might bring.

My daughters, Arlene and Josephine, have enriched my life beyond measure. Though they undoubtedly slowed the revision process, I cannot imagine a happier excuse for the delay. For someone who spends much of his waking hours engrossed in the written word, it is liberating to write that there are simply no words to convey the inestimable love they spark in me each day.

INDEX

Abbot, Benjamin, 65

Abolition, first movement: and interracial activism, 3–4, 10, 14, 75–76, 78,
82–91, 121, 140, 142, 157–165, 265–266,
277, 315, 324; defined, 4, 20; and gradualism, 4, 189, 209, 281, 290, 308, 319,
321–322; centrality of people of color to,
5; as racially progressive, 5, 8, 318; optimistic views of, 19, 23, 60–63, 65, 69,
76, 81, 167–175, 203–210, 259, 266, 309,
314, 321; commitment of, to free black
citizenship, 110–116, 124–125, 142–158,
164–165, 167, 212, 229, 238, 249, 254, 256,
265, 320; and societal environmentalism,
129–142, 156, 162, 164–165, 181, 187–188,
210, 212, 218, 323; and campaign to defeat white prejudice, 153, 167, 180–210,
221, 229, 238, 249, 264, 284, 288, 290,
305–306, 309, 312, 317, 320; and shared
Atlantic ideals and strategies, 170–171,
193–194; as distinct from European abolitionism, 172n; as an enlightenment
project, 173–175; and the Missouri crisis,
243, 245–247; adherents of, turned colonizationists, 254, 259, 311, 316–317; ideals
of, asserted in response to the colonization movement, 262–263, 298–299, 307–
309, 314–315; free black activists as the
torchbearers of, 263–264, 316–317, 324;
withering optimism among black advocates of, 271–276; stalwarts of, 288–290,
299, 304–307, 316, 321; and pragmatic
colonizationists, 291–307, 316, 318, 321;
legacy of, 324–325

Abolition, gradual, 4, 40, 54, 95, 209, 242,
322; and colonization, 7–8, 172, 217, 234,
251, 257, 286, 296–297, 302, 318–320;
and black incorporation, 156, 171–173,
315, 320. See also Emancipation, gradual

Abolitionism (British), 20, 168; and antislavery publishing, 193, 196–197

Abolitionism (French), 167; and 1794 abolition decree, 70, 168, 220; and black citizenship, 168, 171, 220

Abolitionism, immediate, 8–10, 15, 318, 320,
322, 324–325

Abolition of the slave trade orations, 181,
203–209; and the corruption of Africa,
205; and the tyranny of slavers, 205; and
the Middle Passage, 206; and free black
progress, 206–207, 268–269; and the
abolition societies, 208; and white prejudice, 208–209, 273; and the uplift of
Africa, 269

Abolition societies: paternalism of, 9, 13,
63, 90, 140, 151, 161–163, 190n; as conservative organizations, 9, 63, 117; and social
control, 9, 162; emergence of, 52–55;
membership in, 56–57, 61, 160; and elitism, 62–63, 85, 157. See also American
Convention of Abolition Societies

Account of the Regular Gradation in Man
(White), 127

Act for Preventing Suppressing and Punishing the Conspiracy and Insurrection of
Negroes and Other Slaves, An, 29

Act relative to Slaves and Servants, An, 110

Act to Prevent the Migration of People of
Color into the City and County of Philadelphia, 237, 271

Addison, Joseph, 136

Address to the Public (Pennsylvania Abolition Society), 133

Africa, 39–42, 153; as Edenic, 205; as a site
for black American freedom and equality,
211–212, 228, 231, 254, 256, 265; as a site
for a black American colony, 222, 231,
261, 265–266, 269–270, 287–288, 298,
302, 320; Christianization of, 226–229,
231, 251, 263, 265–268, 286

African Free School, 54, 67, 134, 141, 156,
184, 308–309; visits of, to homes of black